IGNAZ SEIPEL

IGNAZ SEIPEL. PHOTOGRAPH BY TRUDE FLEISCHMANN

Ignaz Seipel

CHRISTIAN STATESMAN
IN A TIME OF CRISIS

By Klemens von Klemperer

PRINCETON UNIVERSITY PRESS
PRINCETON, NEW JERSEY
1972

To Betty, Cathy, Jamie

Contents

Contents

Contents

Illustrations

Preface

THIS book might best be called a topical biography. I was led to write it by my interest both in Seipel as a personage and in the problems, theoretical as well as practical, which confronted him. It is with these interests in mind that I have delimited the scope of my work: I have tried to enter into the spiritual and religious secrets of Seipel's life, a topic for the theologian rather than for the historian, only inasmuch as they are necessary for an understanding of the political theorist and statesman. Moreover, I have paid little attention to the internal affairs of the Christian Socialist party, chiefly because most of the relevant party archives were missing.

One has to be able to live with one's subject for a good time while a book is being researched and written. Seipel's personality, emerging impressively from the mediocrity of his immediate political environment, has certainly been a continuous challenge to me. I have approached the problems of his statesmanship, I believe, without political prejudice, but admittedly with undiminishing fascination. Having charted, then, a rather difficult course in approaching my subject both biographically and topically, as well as with political detachment and scholarly involvement, I hope to give a vivid account of Seipel as a Christian statesman in a time of crisis.

Clearly this work, which deals essentially with the period between the two world wars, is not unrelated to my interest in Weimar Germany. While my focus on Austria is designed to call attention to the enormous, at the time unique, domestic and foreign problems which this small country faced after the dissolution of the great multinational Empire and after its loss of iden-

Preface

tity, it will also, I hope, add to the understanding of problems common to both "improvised" democracies, the German as well as the Austrian one.

Whoever works on a politically sensitive subject is likely to encounter some more or less understandable measure of distrust on the part of those who possess the pertinent information or documents. However, in my search for these I have invariably met with courtesy and encouragement. I shall not easily forget my second interview with the late Dr. Friedrich Funder, the grand old man of Catholic journalism and master of the Herold Verlag; the questionnaire which I submitted to him irritated him, prompting him to say: "Such questions only a Social Democrat would ask." However, when I explained that as a historian I could leave no question unasked, he not only settled down to a long interview, but also turned over to me the key to the archive, the Richard Schmitz Archive, over which he had control. And I do not believe that Dr. Funder would think of me as a traitor to his cause because I got some of my materials in the Socialist Karl Marx-Institut.

I am indebted to many people and institutions. The very architectural elegance of the Österreichisches Staatsarchiv on the Minoritenplatz in Vienna has given me a sense of the grandeur as well as the intricacies of European diplomacy; the former Generaldirektor Dr. Gebhard Rath and the present one, Professor Hanns-Leo Mikoletzky, have been generous in making their treasures available to me. Among the archivists I should like to mention in particular Herr Anton Nemeth, always helpful and resourceful. While working on the German Foreign Office documents I was guided by the late Dr. Johannes Ullrich, and while reading the films in the National Archives by Mr. Robert Wolfe. In Vienna and Salzburg, the Church has been as generous to me as the state; Sister Dr. Henriette Peters very kindly opened to me the documents of the Archive of the Archdiocese of Vienna, namely the archive of Archbishop Piffl and the private papers of Seipel, which had been transferred there recently from the

xiv

Order of the Servants of the Sacred Heart of Jesus. Dr. Hans Spatzenegger kindly put his work on Seipel in Salzburg at my disposal and also provided me with welcome copies of documents from the Archive of the Archdiocese of Salzburg. If in connection with the hospitality which I enjoyed in the house of the Herold Verlag I referred to Dr. Funder, I ought also mention his successor Dr. Willy Lorenz, who turned over to me whole collections of Seipel letters, and Frau Dr. Trude Schmitz, who I believe had some say in my obtaining access to her late father's archive. The family of the late Professor August Maria Knoll has been exceedingly kind in making their valuable Seipeliana available to me, as has the late Ambassador Lothar Wimmer. Professor Fritz Fellner has been so good as to put the unpublished parts of Josef Redlich's diary at my disposal. In the kingdom of scholars, though, Dr. Friedrich Rennhofer should be the sovereign, for while himself working on Ignaz Seipel he has generously shared his precious materials with me.

I owe thanks to the librarians of many libraries in Austria and in the United States. What would I have done without the reference librarians at Smith College in Northampton and Mrs. Agnes Petersen's ever helpful references from the Hoover Institution in Stanford, California, without Herr Bilinski's *Professorenzimmer* in the University of Vienna and Miss Irmtraut Jörg's materials from the Vienna Nationalbibliothek?

Of all those whom I have all too often and insistently engaged in discussions on Seipel I must beg forgiveness. My colleagues in Vienna, Professors Friedrich Engel-Janosi, Ludwig Jedlicka, Reinhold Lorenz, Heinrich Lutz, Gerald Stourzh, Adam Wandruszka, and Erika Weinzierl, may rest assured that they have helped me with their keen interest in my work as well as with their knowledge of my field. In this connection I should like to mention particularly those who have granted me special interviews: Dr. Wilhelm Czerny (from whom I learned a good deal about the ways of Austrian parliamentarianism), the late Dr. Funder, Professor Walter Goldinger, the late Professor August

Preface

Maria Knoll, Miss Marga Lammasch, Dr. Willy Lorenz, Dr. Ernst Mosing, Frau Dr. Alma Motzko, the late Prelate Dr. Karl Rudolf, Dr. Friedrich Schreyvogel (how vividly he enacted Seipel before me!), Dr. Raphael Spann, Dr. Anton Julius Walter, the late Ambassador Lothar Wimmer (and the unforgettable afternoons with him out in Purkersdorf), and the late Ernst Karl Winter.

For more than financial aid I am indebted to the Guggenheim Foundation, to the Fulbright Commission of the Department of State and to Smith College. They provided me with the means and time to work and also to travel repeatedly to Austria, and thus to recreate, insofar as is possible, the life and work of Ignaz Seipel out of the fullness of his environment.

I would finally like to register my gratitude to Miss Elizabeth S. Duvall for her editorial help, to Mrs. Hilda McArthur for presiding over the production of the typescript, to Miss Sandra Brazaitis for typing the bibliography, and to my editor, Mrs. Martyn Hitchcock, for her kindly vigilance over the manuscript. As always, I owe more thanks than I can put into words to my wife Betty.

Northampton, Mass.
September 1970

IGNAZ SEIPEL

WANDERING BETWEEN TWO WORLDS, ONE DEAD,
THE OTHER POWERLESS TO BE BORN.

Matthew Arnold, *Stanzas from the Grande Chartreuse*

Introduction

THE PLACE of Ignaz Seipel (1876-1932) in the history both of Austria and of Europe has so far been an uncertain one. Churchman, scholar, minister in the last imperial cabinet of Austria-Hungary, Chancellor and Foreign Minister of the first Austrian Republic and leader of its conservative party, the Christian Socialists, he began his remarkable career under the old Monarchy and pursued it into the turbulent period of decline, defeat, revolution, retrenchment, and almost continuous civil war which would at last lead the little country to espouse fascism by surrendering to its expatriate son, Adolf Hitler. General treatises on twentieth-century Europe usually make only brief reference to Seipel—though never without a marked note of awe. The Austria he represented was a distinctly small power between the two world wars, and while historians tend to agree that he was the one towering political personality in that small Alpine republic, they also tend to assume that the course of events, being determined by the affairs of the big powers, bypassed this statesman, whatever his skills. Historians have paid particular attention to Germany's role in shaping events in Central Europe.[1] The road to catastrophe seemed to lead clearly from the Wilhelmian quest for world power through the failure of the Weimar Republic to the sway of the Thousand-Year Reich which, lasting little longer

[1] For the purposes of this discussion I have adopted the terminology of Oscar Halecki in *Borderlands of Western Civilization* (New York, 1952), pp. 3ff. and 430ff.; he distinguishes between "West Central Europe" or Germany, and "East Central Europe" or the area, including Austria, which is ethnically multinational, historically without definite units, and geographically without permanent boundaries.

than twelve years, left behind a landscape of ruin and confusion. Germany has, for understandable reasons, become the type of twentieth-century political hubris, set a precedent for the failure of parliamentary democracy, and provided a model for fascism and totalitarian rule in Central Europe.

Seipel's world was, it is true, once removed from the centers where the *Grosse Politik* of the European powers was decisively shaped. In the old Monarchy, Robert Musil's "Kakania," clocks and trains ran more slowly than those in the rest of Europe. There one felt that one could leave the express train that raced through the heart of Europe, "get into an ordinary train on an ordinary railway line," and perhaps even "travel back home."[2] Austria existed on the margins of European industrial development. Only a fraction of its possessions, the Austrian hereditary lands and Bohemia, was part of the inner zone of Europe that was heavily industrialized during the nineteenth century; the rest belonged to the outer zone in which an agricultural pattern had prevailed. Both geographically and psychologically, as a shrewd observer remarked, Austria-Hungary was the European state closest to the "preeconomic East."[3] Somewhere through the Monarchy there ran a line, which Metternich had exactly and half-facetiously located along the Viennese *Landstrasse*, marking the outer limits of European civilization with all its achievements and comforts: east of this line streets ceased to be paved, people were tough but poor—hardened by suffering rather than work— and less deferent than western Europeans to the majesty of time.

Still other factors made the Monarchy marginal. Not the least of these was the attitude of the Austrian Church toward the industrial and scientific world: without being altogether negative, it was usually suspicious. Meanwhile, the special character of Habsburg rule and the cultural and ethnic peculiarities of East Central Europe had prevented the development there of true nation-states. Moreover, in contrast to governments in Western

[2] *The Man Without Qualities* (New York, 1953), p. 31.
[3] Henry Wickham Steed, *The Hapsburg Monarchy*, 4th ed. (London, 1919), p. 141.

4

Europe, Austrian government was constitutional only in name, and parliamentary institutions as well as traditions were shaky.

But it is worth noting at this point that it is precisely this marginal world, with its persisting contrasts and tensions between tradition and modernity, agriculture and industrialization, universalism and nationalism, religion and secularism, that in our century has deeply affected the fortunes of Europe as a whole. Both world wars had their origins in the unsettled political conditions of East Central Europe. Between the two wars the New Europe heralded by Woodrow Wilson and the Wilsonians did not come into being. While parliamentary democracy was formally introduced into the newly established states after 1918, none of them—with the possible exception of Czechoslovakia—had the tradition, the balanced social structure, or the economic stability necessary to make this form of government really effective.[4] In the twenties and thirties East Central Europe therefore became a sort of workshop for authoritarian rule. The call went out for nonpartisan government instead of parliamentarianism, for corporatism, for strong and heroic leaders, for dictatorship, for fascism. The eastward march of democracy in modern Europe stopped, for the time being at least, with the failure both of the Weimar Republic and of democratic government in East Central Europe. By studying any part of East Central Europe between the wars one can, then, see the problems of Weimar Germany in the broader perspective of the hazards and strains that democracy underwent in Central Europe as a whole.

There was another respect in which the Wilsonians' New Europe fell short of their hopes. No fitting substitute was devised for the supranational rule of the Habsburgs. The federalization of East Central Europe, projected during the war by Thomas G. Masaryk, remained a plan on paper. Wilson's gospel of self-determination, which had seemed compelling during the latter half

---

[4] For the disproportion between constitutional form and reality in East Central Europe between the two wars see Werner Conze, "Die Strukturkrise des östlichen Mitteleuropas vor und nach 1919," *Vierteljahrshefte für Zeitgeschichte*, i (October 1953), 319-38.

of the war, was not able to regenerate a multinational area in which various ethnic groups were intricately entangled. The newly created "nation-states" were in effect miniature multinational empires with considerable and insufficiently protected minorities. Fragmentation, together with rampant irredentisms, became the order of the day. The eastward march of the nation-state, like that of democracy, came to a halt in East Central Europe. The nation-state was not suited, it seemed, to the objective realities of the area. While it was sentimental and futile to wish the old Monarchy back into existence after 1918, it was certainly appropriate to search, in theory or in political practice, for some sort of federalism that would replace the vanished imperial structure. If East Central Europe as it emerged from the Paris Treaties was not to become a "depression area," and thus a tool of the great powers, it needed some imaginative pulling together. While the leaders of the Succession States saw this problem more and more clearly from the early twenties on, the realities of European diplomacy finally prevailed over plans for an organic reconstruction of East Central Europe. But though East Central Europe hardly took an active part in the affairs of Europe between the wars, it contributed centrally to the pathology of Europe that led to the Second World War.

One more consideration of a very general nature is pertinent to this study of Seipel. In 1918 the defeated states had to face, earlier than did the victorious nations, the fact of the decisive impact that the fratricidal war had had on the position of Europe in world affairs. By now we are all used to the ideas expressed in such phrases as Spengler's "decline of the West," Toynbee's "dwarfing of Europe," and Holborn's "political collapse of Europe." Just after the first war, however, the victorious powers could still cherish the illusion of victory, while Germany and Austria looked defeat straight in the eyes. Austria in particular was the first nation to undergo the process of contraction, of dwindling, later suffered by the great powers and even by Europe as a whole. And this process was especially poignant in Austria because there it was accompanied—even more than it was in Germany or, I would argue, in Russia—by a loss of national identity. The palaces and mansions of Vienna still evoked the splendors of monarchy and aristocracy, but they stood empty. The old army had been dissolved, and much of the large bureaucracy that had served the Empire was now superfluous. Banks and businesses had lost the hinterlands that had served them as commercial territories. The streets of the capital were now filled with shabby, hungry people, with war profiteers, and, starting in the late twenties, with tourists who came to view Vienna's obsolete grandeur as if the city were a museum. Its people were embittered, oppressed by the contrast between past greatness and present failure, and without hope for the future. Would those "inhabitants of the Carolingian Ostmark and heirs of the conquerors of the Turks," as Seipel once called the Austrians, ever be able to settle down and "cultivate their own little garden?"[5] Would the populace put up with degradation or, at best, mediocrity? There was no doubt that life in Vienna during the years following 1918 was poor and petty, with the "lower strata of Alpine feeble-mindedness"[6] setting the political tone. But what about the Austrians' memories, dreams, and aspirations? Would they not sooner or later call for a new, and now utterly utopian, greatness, for a great leader to free them from their misery? Clearly, while Austria's troubles came on early and distressingly, they turned out to be by no means unique. Insignificant and degrading as life was in Austria after the first war, it resembled that in Weimar Germany in many ways, and presaged many of the problems which other European countries were later to experience, one after another, upon losing their empires—England, then Holland and France.[7]

The problems that Seipel faced have had, then, a perennial

---

[5] Ignaz Seipel, letter to Dr. W. Bauer, in Paul Sweet, "Seipel's Views on Anschluss in 1928: An Unpublished Exchange of Letters," *Journal of Modern History*, XIX (December 1947), 323.

[6] Erich Heller, *The Disinherited Mind* (New York, 1959), p. 245.

[7] On this subject see the stimulating book by John Mander, *Great Britain or Little England?* (London, 1963), esp. sec. 15.

significance. Meanwhile he himself has become one of the most controversial figures among Central European statesmen of the twentieth century. This eagle-nosed, erect, ascetic, priestly, and impenetrable man had the "appearance of a Roman emperor" and has been called, with slight exaggeration, "Europe's most distinguished priest."[8] He overawed his friends and was deeply distrusted by his foes. To some he was a saintly character; to others he was the sinister Machiavellian, the man on horseback, or even the fascist. The poor people in their petitions to the Chancellor addressed him variously as "Your Holiness," "Cardinal," "Your Eminence, the Federal President," attributing to him honors and titles which he never in fact held.[9] Others, less reverent, sang in the streets of Vienna, to the tune of an old popular song:

> And on the gas lantern
> And on the gas lantern
> We shall hang the big lords.
> Yes, yes, the big lords,
> On the gas lantern.
>
> And who will be the first?
> And who will be the first?
> The first will Herr von Seipel be.
> Yes, yes, will Seipel be,
> He will Herr Seipel be![10]

---

[8] Richard Coudenhove-Kalergi, *Kampf um Europa* (Zurich, 1949), pp. 100f.

[9] Folder "Anschriften, die erheiterten," Seipel Archive.

[10] Leopold Kunschak, *Österreich 1918-1934* (Vienna, 1934), p. 80.

> Und an die Gaslatern,
> und an die Gaslatern
> da hängen wir die hohen Herrn.
> Ja, ja, die hohen Herrn,
> an eine Gaslatern!

8

"The Flying Prelate." Courtesy of Österreichische Nationalbibliothek, Vienna

Introduction

One of many contemporary political cartoons, called "The Flying Prelate," showed Seipel as an enormous bat, propelled by a swastika, casting darkness over the roofs of Vienna.[11]

While the literature on Seipel has so far, with only a few exceptions, fallen into two neat categories, hagiography and demonology, present-day Austrian historians have been reluctant to deal with the historical, human Seipel lest they conjure up a disturbing and still divisive ghost. This neglect of the historical Seipel has had the effect of highlighting the distorted figure of the embattled titan, of perpetuating the image, or images, of an almost legendary personage either more saintly or fiercer than was really probable. But now that over a third of a century has passed since Seipel's death—and also since that of the first Austrian Republic—the time has come for the historian to claim him, to extricate him from the prejudice and passion of friend and foe alike. Only in this way can the history of the first Austrian Republic be saved from the oblivion to which, compared with the history of the Weimar Germany, it has been consigned all too long. Only thus can this history be incorporated into the broader context of a comparative study of Central Europe between the wars and allow future generations of statesmen to benefit, perhaps, from its melancholy lesson.

But the story of Seipel's public career has a long and important prologue. His prepolitical career took up three-quarters of his life (1876-1918)—his early maturity as well as his formative years. It was during his young manhood, when he was entering the priesthood and becoming a scholar, when nothing as yet pointed toward a political career, that he developed the "grand

---

Wer wird der erste sein?
Wer wird der erste sein?
Das wird der Herr von Seipel sein.
Ja, ja der Seipel sein,
das wird Herr Seipel sein.

[11] Rudolf Herrmann, "Der fliegende Prälat," Bildarchiv, Österreichische Nationalbibliothek, Vienna.

design" that guided him through his whole life. Certainly Seipel's thinking and feeling were rooted in the era of Francis Joseph. His very speech—slow, dragging, relaxed, slightly nasal—gave him away as an "old Austrian," as his kind came to be called after the revolution. In a certain sense he shared this background with his later political foes, men like Johann Schober and Karl Renner. When Robert Musil observed that while the "system of government [in the Monarchy] was clerical, the general attitude of life was liberal," he characterized an inherent lightheartedness, casualness, mutual tolerance, and distrust of extreme positions which permeated the whole society.[12] Friedrich Heer called this happy blend a part of the "humanitas Austriaca."[13] Today's social scientist might feel justified in terming it a "consensus." Seipel was distinctly part of this consensus.

It is too readily assumed that the consensus in old Austria, insofar as it existed, was mainly passive, something that amounted to mere muddling through or, in Friedrich Engel's terms, to "indifference and stagnation."[14] There was nothing sleepy, aimless, or stagnant about the young priest who quietly but purposefully worked his way up from humble origins to become part of the Monarchy's establishment. In fact, he did not allow himself simply to be absorbed by that establishment, flattered for having arrived in what the Viennese used to call the "second society," which included university professors. Quite to the contrary, Seipel was one of the few explorative, creative minds to emerge from within official Austria. Not that he was a rebel. In his revealing autobiographical sketch such adjectives as "reasonable" and "moderate" are significantly recurrent.[15] But without doubt

[12] In this connection see the delightful and perceptive essay by Mark Twain, "Stirring Times in Austria," in *The Man that Corrupted Hadleyburg and Other Stories* (New York and London, 1901), pp. 284-341.

[13] Friedrich Herr, "Humanitas Austriaca," in *Spectrum Austriae*, ed. Otto Schulmeister (Vienna, 1957), pp. 478-522.

[14] Quoted in Albert Fuchs, *Geistige Strömungen in Österreich 1867-1918* (Vienna, 1949), p. 89.

[15] "Ignaz Seipel," *Encyclopaedia Britannica*. Seipel's own draft of the

11

he was a renovator who consistently urged both Church and society to rethink their premises and practices in the light of modern political and social realities. Suffice it here to emphasize the fact that the conservative, supposedly reactionary, "fascist" Chancellor started out as a progressive force in both Church and Monarchy. This fact is crucial to an understanding of Seipel's political career. He was, it has been said, the first important thinker in the Austrian Church to abandon its extreme conservatism and to promulgate the message of adjustment to the modern world that emanated from the encyclicals of Leo XIII.[16] As a moral theologian he put his mind on state as well as Church: he undertook a major review of the meaning and function of supranational rule, emerging in the middle of the war with a striking critique of Austria's imperial policies. At the eleventh hour, he challenged the dual base of the Monarchy and drew up an imaginative plan for reform that would solve the nationality problem—a plan which, by the way, invites comparison with similar ones devised by the Social Democrats Karl Renner and Otto Bauer, his later opponents. In keeping with his rejection of modern nationalism, Seipel became a fearless opponent of the wartime alliance with Germany. In fact the man who on his deathbed would allegedly exclaim "One must shoot, shoot, shoot!"[17] was, during the earlier phases of his career a pacifist. He once wrote that he considered himself "a pacifist from the very beginning, not merely a pacifist of the prewar or the postwar period, but a pacifist of the war period as well."[18] It has been observed that, had the Austrian

---

article, designated "Lebenslauf" ("curriculum vitae") is in the files of the Seipel Archive.

[16] Alfred Diamant, *Austrian Catholics and the First Republic* (Princeton, 1960), p. 49.

[17] Ernst Karl Winter, "Am Beispiel Österreichs," in *Christentum und Zivilisation* (Vienna, 1956), p. 410; confirmed in an interview with Professor August Maria Knoll on April 8, 1958. Knoll was Seipel's assistant during the last months of his illness.

[18] Ignaz Seipel, "Der Weg nach Europa," Vienna, August 26, 1929. Draft, Seipel Archive.

commonwealth not fallen to pieces, Seipel would have become known as "an advocate of the most modern political and social ideas compatible with the Catholic credo."[19] Indeed it was because of these ideas and of Seipel's cautious, tactful manner that Emperor Charles drew him into his entourage and, at the eleventh hour, included him in the short-lived liquidation ministry headed by Heinrich Lammasch.

The winter of 1918-19, then, which marked the end of centuries of Habsburg rule in Central Europe, was the time of Seipel's rise to political importance. This rise was a meteoric and, admittedly, increasingly puzzling one. Early in November 1918, the neophyte imperial minister was playing a leading role in the abdication crisis. But the same Seipel, who had hoped somehow to salvage the imperial idea from the revolutionary turmoil, was largely responsible for his country's smooth transition from empire to small state and from monarchy to republic.

It has been said that Seipel was "born too late," that the new Austria was "far too small for a man of his political genius and ambition," who needed the scope of a Richelieu or a Metternich.[20] However, there was something singularly challenging about applying Metternich's statecraft and concepts to a power as insignificant as Austria was after the breakup of the Monarchy. Although Central Europe had ceased to exist as a political unit, the whole area remained his field. Seipel held to his vision of the historical, geographic, and economic viability of Central Europe and of some supranational settlement that might hold it together. If it is true that Seipel was "born too late," that he was a quixotic figure, it is also true, particularly in the light of events from the 1930s on, that he was born too early. In any case, he was and always remained an imperial figure.

The story of Ignaz Seipel's political career is essentially a chap-

---

[19] Ernst Karl Winter, *Ignaz Seipel als dialektisches Problem: Ein Beitrag zur Scholastikforschung* (Vienna, Frankfurt, and Zurich, 1966), p. 60.

[20] G.E.R. Gedye, *Fallen Bastions: The Central European Tragedy* (London, 1939), p. 28.

Introduction

ter in the intricate history of twentieth-century political Catholicism. His triple calling as priest, scholar, and statesman height-
ens his interest as a historical figure and enhances his impressive-
ness as a personality. Wearing his priestly cassock wherever he
went, he always had a singular air of authority—whether preaching or lecturing, conferring or campaigning, crossing wits with
his friends or adversaries, or again uttering, as he sometimes did,
soothing trivialities to the broad masses. The priest-politician was
not an unusual figure in Central Europe, but Seipel did have an
unusually pronounced character, and all his moves—even his
detours—seemed related to a distinct set of religious premises.

The relationship between his different callings is one of the
main themes in Seipel's diary, which he began keeping, he said,
to achieve "better self control and thus a more conscientious use
of time."[21] The priesthood was of course the central calling from
which everything else radiated:[22] "Above all should stand the
priest."[23] Ideally, at least, politics was an "indirect pastoral function"[24] that consisted of "ministering to the needs of the people
and the state."[25] But while Seipel's statesmanship was an "indirect
pastoral function," the pastoral function was indirect statesmanship. Even more than Weimar Germany's several Catholic chancellors, and even more than his predecessor as leader of the Austrian Christian Socialists,[26] Seipel typified the twentieth-century
Catholic leader who sought to integrate politics with the premises of his faith. It was precisely his attempt to follow a "uniform

[21] Rudolf Blüml, ed., *Ignaz Seipel: Mensch, Christ, Priester in seinem Tagebuch* (Vienna, 1934), p. 28.
[22] See the entry for July 29, 1920: "Today I want to think about my different offices: (1) member of Parliament; (2) Superior [of the Order of the Servants of the Sacred Heart of Jesus in the Keinergasse, where Seipel also lived]; (3) professor; (4) head of the Caritas Socialis." (Ibid., pp. 70f.)
[23] Ibid., p. 71.   [24] Ibid., p. 193.
[25] Ignaz Seipel, *Der christliche Staatsmann* (Augsburg, 1931), p. 17.
[26] Seipel's predecessor as party leader was Prelate Johann Nepomuk Hauser.

14

total policy"[27] and to carry out a "reform of the souls"[28] in a divided country which made him so controversial and so distrusted by those who did not share his premises.

Ideological leadership, in striving for consistency, is subject to the conflict between what Max Weber called "the ethic of ultimate ends" and "the ethic of responsibility"[29] for the immediate consequences of given actions. In Seipel this conflict was persistent. Few of his contemporaries knew that behind his cold blue eyes, his serene and imperturbable mask, there was a complex and struggling mind. Whenever, at noon or in the evening, he returned from his baroque office at the Ballhausplatz to his silent monastic residence, he resumed his battle with himself.[30] The more he threw himself into politics—and he did so with alacrity —the more the priest and the politician clashed.[31] The ethics of the Sermon on the Mount accorded ill with the exigencies of the moment and the use of power. When he faced himself in his monkish loneliness Seipel was therefore driven to self-recrimination. In his dealings with his contemporaries he laid himself open to fierce attacks from both outside and inside the Church. To his historian he exhibits the strange case of Seipel contra Seipel.

The tensions that Seipel experienced may well have been intensified by his ill-health. At the age of thirty-seven he contracted

[27] "Einheitliche Gesamtpolitik"; Ignaz Seipel, diary, June 1, 1922.

[28] "Reform der Seelen"; "Seelensanierung."

[29] Max Weber, "Politics as a Vocation," in *From Max Weber: Essays in Sociology*, ed. H. H. Gerth and C. Wright Mills (New York, 1946), p. 120.

[30] See the repeated self-reproaches for "foolish, increasing" ambition, "fantastic" vanity, impatience, nervousness, lack of self-control, bitterness, indolence, "vain" and "secular" imagination, secularism, shyness, in Blüml, *Seipel*, passim. Subsequent passages from Seipel's diary will be cited from the original.

[31] See Seipel's diary entry for January 1, 1931: "I could not repress politics without violence and dishonesty against myself." See also the diary entry by Josef Redlich for April 24, 1919, on Seipel's having "great fun" with politics, in *Schicksalsjahre Österreichs 1908-1919: Das Politische Tagebuch Josef Redlichs*, ed. Fritz Fellner (Vienna, 1954), II, 342.

diabetes; the attempt on his life on June 1, 1924, left a bullet in one of his lungs; and in 1930 he became tubercular. And though it may be fallacious to attribute his contradictory policies to the antithetical nature of his two chronic diseases,[32] it is fair to assume that his pathology cast a shadow on much of his mature life. The rigid diet, the daily struggle against physical decline, must have exacerbated his troubling though well-masked nervousness and increased his isolation. Moreover, when torn between the needs of the state and those of his health, Seipel would sacrifice the latter: "Politics first and only then health."[33] The tireless and unsparing pace to which he kept until the end of his life no doubt hastened his death. Whether there was any connection between his political failure and defeat and his surrender to disease at the relatively early age of fifty-six,[34] one can only guess. However, Seipel's death, which occurred at the crucial time when both Austria and Germany were on the road to dictatorship, raises some more definite, though certainly conjectural, questions. What would have happened to Austria had Seipel lived longer? What views would he have had on the Nazi seizure of power in Germany, and how would he, as an Austrian statesman, have dealt with this threat to his little country?

The nature of these questions should suggest the importance that Seipel's case may have for us even though the power he exercised was limited by the condition of his country. He lived in troubled times, and in every way reflected this fact. He was torn between theory and practice, Church and state, monarchy and republic, empire and small nation, democracy and dictatorship, peace and violence. Moreover, he was one of the truly transitional or unharmonious figures of our century, a son of the old Europe trying to deal with a new Europe which, between the

[32] For this argument see Julius Tandler, "Seipel," *Wiener Politische Blätter*, I (August 27, 1933), 183, and E. K. Winter, "Am Beispiel Österreichs," *Christentum und Zivilisation*, p. 409.

[33] Hofrat Professor Dr. Gustav Singer, "Aus Seipels Lebens- und Krankengeschichte," *Neue Freie Presse*, August 3, 1932, morning ed.

[34] Ibid.; also E. K. Winter, *Christentum und Zivilisation*, p. 409.

16

two wars, never assumed any real shape. He suffered from the recurrent modern predicament, "Wandering between two worlds, one dead,/The other powerless to be born." Seipel's failure to find a way out of this wilderness was his own and also his country's tragedy; this was the point, if any, at which the swastika-propelled bat with a prelate's head should have become visible over the rooftops of Vienna.

But this macabre image should not set the tone for the following chapters. To demythologize Seipel is to defer judgment on him, though not in the end to abstain from it. Seipel's personality, his ideas and policies, will always be controversial. I hope, however, to shift the basis of eventual judgment from partisanship to scholarship. In other words, I hope that the questions asked, the evidence, arguments, and conclusions presented in this study will lead to an understanding of the very intricate situation in which Seipel had to make his decisions. On this basis only is a historical judgment in order. The historian's task is not to find culprits but to retrace steps and disentangle tragedy, error, and guilt. He is bound to discover that the course of events does not generally offer a choice between a right way and a wrong one, that the choices open to statesmen are usually difficult—as they certainly were in Seipel's case. The historian must, then, acknowledge complexity and perhaps even tragedy before he can pass judgment.

One

THE FORMATIVE YEARS, 1876-1909
THE CHURCHMAN AND SCHOLAR

Politics and Society in Vienna at the Turn of the Century

SEIPEL has been presented as an imperial figure. Growing up in the last decades of the long reign of Francis Joseph, who had virtually become the symbol of everything Austrian as well as of the European monarchic order, he was taught to see his sovereign as the successor of the Holy Roman emperors, the earthly manifestations of God's universal rule on earth.[1] He thought of Austria as a kingdom of kingdoms, a nation of nations, an empire whose mission was not to conquer and subjugate but to unite its peoples, an empire which in defiance of modern nationalism could assert its claim to the cherished fifteenth-century device, *Austria erit in orbe ultima*, and was comparable only to the Roman Empire.

But to the perceptive observer the Austria of the late nineteenth century represented a diminishing empire. In spite of Austria's triumphs at the Congress of Vienna, the Habsburg Monarchy had been seriously weakened by the upheavals of 1848-1849, the strains of the Crimean War, and two unsuccessful wars in 1859 and 1866. And though the Empire reemerged after the fatal setback of 1866 in the form of a Danubian Monarchy, based essentially upon possession of the Austrian hereditary lands, of the crowns of St. Wenceslas and St. Stephen, the domestic settlement of 1867, the so-called Ausgleich, was in itself the cause of serious dissension, since it divided the Monarchy between the Germans (in Cisleithania) and the Hungarians (in Transleithania). Its double centralism was interpreted, particularly by the Slavic groups, as a setback to their aspirations. But the Aus-

---

[1] Cf. Ignaz Seipel, *Nation und Staat* (Vienna and Leipzig, 1916), p. 20.

gleich appeared as a denial and betrayal of the Austrian supra-national idea to the more thoughtful Germans also, and among others to Seipel. They tended to look back to the days of the Kremsier diet when Austria had come close to solving its nationality problem. "Since the diet of Kremsier," argued Hermann Bahr, one of Austria's leading men of letters at the turn of the century and an elderly friend of Seipel's, Austria moved about "merely as a ghost."[2] It was the nationality struggle, after all, that paralyzed much of political life within the Monarchy in the last decades before the war, and at the same time undermined its position among the European powers.

Vienna itself, where Seipel grew up, was a truly imperial city, though much of its splendor was carried over from the past, taken for granted but not tested against contemporary political realities. While remaining a "metropolis of the baroque," it had lost its political function and become the metropolis of the European "value-vacuum."[3] For better or worse it was strangely immunized against the conflicts which were agitating the nationalities of the Empire. Despite the bitterness that prevailed in the Reichsrat, the capital maintained to the end its ability to absorb the people of different backgrounds living in its confines. By the same token it had become increasingly clear that Vienna and its vast bureaucracy no longer held the Empire together.[4] The "blighting breath" of the capital smothered the vitality of the whole realm.

The reactions of late nineteenth-century Vienna to the manifestations of the social problem were equally perplexing. Naturally the effects of industrialization and the resulting friction between social classes made themselves felt in the big city. It was

[2] Hermann Bahr, "Das österreichische Staats- und Reichsproblem," *Preussische Jahrbücher*, CLXXXIII (January 1921), 10.

[3] Hermann Broch, *Hofmannsthal und seine Zeit: Eine Studie* (Munich, 1964), p. 58f.

[4] Henry Wickham Steed, *The Hapsburg Monarchy* (London, 1913), p. 206.

20

the stock-exchange crash in Vienna in May 1873, coming ironically on the heels of the World Fair, that magnified class feeling. The Viennese monied bourgeoisie, closely linked with the crash, seemed to recover quickly from this unfortunate incident. Indeed the so-called *fin de siècle* became the golden age of the *haute bourgeoisie*, who made up a new leisure class that was not unlike the old aristocracy—imitating it, but in a more creative and artistic manner. It set the tone for a seemingly carefree society, playing, as one observer wrote, on a "keyboard on which the graver notes simply are not there."[5] In this respect the wealthy bourgeoisie added its part to the somewhat deceptive, unreal atmosphere of the capital and closed its eyes to the suffering of the poor.

The Austrian capital in the last decades before the First World War had its way of coping, or rather not coping, with political and social realities. Life was pleasant and amusing, because the Viennese had a superb gift for looking away. There was a great deal of political wisdom, but no one to apply it; there was much talent, but it was untapped and purposeless, with no will to act and no sense of power. "Attached to nothing, hanging in the air,"[6] it was expressing void and disintegration rather than life and affirmation. And like his many languid and loyal subjects the "poor Francis Joseph," as Herman Bahr called the old emperor, "saw the sun set in his Empire while saying nothing."[7]

However, the 1880s witnessed the rise of three mass movements in the western half of the monarchy protesting against the spirit of the bourgeoisie and the economic policies of Austrian liberalism: the Pan-Germans, the Social Democrats, and the Christian Socialists. Indeed they came upon the scene initially in a temporary and rather strange alliance, manifested in the Linz

[5] C. A. Macartney, *The Social Revolution in Austria* (Cambridge, 1926), p. 203.

[6] Steed, *Hapsburg Monarchy*, p. 204.

[7] Bahr, "Das österreichische Staats- und Reichsproblem," p. 13; Joseph Roth, *Der Radetzkymarsch* (Hamburg, 1957), p. 159.

21

The Formative Years

Program of 1882, whose *spiritus rector* was the vigilantist Pan-German, Georg von Schönerer. Each movement aimed in its own way at some form of socialism: national, Marxist, Christian. Each one, and in particular the Pan-German, reflected the increasing anxiety of the German element in the Austrian half of the Monarchy over its future in relation to the other nationalities.

The three new movements took up distinct ideological positions, a fact which explains, after the Linz honeymoon, an increased stiffening against each other which in the long-range had a decisive bearing on the uncompromising civil-war atmosphere during the first Republic. The Pan-Germans, in their inability to cope with the ethnic problems of the Monarchy, represented a typical instance of the relationship between fear, despair, and late nineteenth-century right-wing politics.[8] Their socialism, as one of their critics accurately said, was in effect the "socialism of the stupid fellow,"[9] namely antisemitism and, in broader terms, xenophobism. The Pan-Germans so influenced the schools and universities of Austria as to make them hotbeds of a pro-German irredentist agitation in which the idea of an Anschluss was nurtured.

The Social Democrats, founded on the solid structure of Marxist doctrine, were the party of the proletariat. Led by Viktor Adler, a great mind and organizer, they followed a distinctly moderate course. Indeed, on the occasion of its congress in Brno (Brünn) of 1899, the party came out endorsing a "democratic federation of nationalities," thus implicitly accepting the Habsburg Monarchy. This so-called Austromarxism was a "positive force in the state" (*staatserhaltend*); people used to call the party in jest "k.k." (*kaiser-königlich*, "imperial and royal"). In this respect it was not as far as has been generally assumed from the Christian Socialists, who became the imperial party.

[8] Cf. Fritz Stern, *The Politics of Cultural Despair* (Berkeley and Los Angeles, 1961).

[9] Ferdinand Kronawetter (1838-1913); quoted in Albert Fuchs, *Geistige Strömungen in Österreich 1867-1918* (Vienna, 1949), p. 142.

22

The Christian Socialists were by no means an imperial party from the beginning. They were a rebellious Viennese group (originally called "United Christians") within the fold of Austrian clericalism who turned against the conservatism of the Church hierarchy as well as against liberal society. Their intellectual guide was Karl von Vogelsang (1818-1890), a convert and one of the many expatriate Germans who had moved to Vienna during the Bismarckian era. There he became editor of the clerical journal *Vaterland*, which he used as a means of publicizing social problems to the conservative-clerical circles and for elaborating Christian social theories. He managed to gather around him a circle of younger and enterprising Catholic minds, among them Alois Liechtenstein, the "red prince," one of the most distinguished personalities among the Catholic politicians who gave weight to the new movement in its struggle with the conservatives, and Prelate Franz Martin Schindler, Seipel's teacher at the university, who like Vogelsang himself was closely connected with the preparatory work leading to Leo XIII's social encyclical *Rerum Novarum* (1891). Karl Lueger was also a member of this group, and it was under his dynamic political leadership that the Christian Socialists became a mass movement. He appealed to the economic grievances of the lower bourgeoisie against capitalism and of the artisans against big industry, and turned against the Jewish segment of the population, which had gained a stronghold in the economic and intellectual life of the capital and which was held responsible for the crash of 1873 and the many dislocations of urban life.

It is indicative of the official Viennese climate that Francis Joseph and his advisers sought to silence the Christian Socialist movement three times by refusing to grant the imperial sanction for Lueger's popular election to the office of mayor of Vienna, and that powerful elements within the government and the Church twice intervened against him with the papal authorities in Rome. However they could not prevent the ultimate recognition of the movement by Leo XIII, in 1895. And finally in 1897

Francis Joseph had to accept Lueger as mayor of his capital.

With the conquest of Vienna, the Christian Socialist movement became increasingly respectable. In the first decade of the new century its members moved into cabinet positions, and in 1913, in the person of Friedrich Piffl, the Prior of Klosterneuburg, into the archbishopric of Vienna. At its congress in Eggenburg in 1905 the party had taken a strong stand on the nationality problem in supporting the non-Magyar nationalities of Hungary and urging a reorganization of the Empire to take the place of the existing "rotten form of government." This policy, which was also represented in the columns of Dr. Friedrich Funder's influential Catholic daily *Reichspost*, led to close contacts with the heir apparent Francis Ferdinand. The Belvedere castle, where the staff of the impatient archduke drew up plans for reforms of the Empire, relied strongly on the Christian Socialist leadership; in fact, the *Reichspost* became the archduke's mouthpiece.

If the party suffered a smashing defeat in the Austrian elections of June 1911, it was partly because of the vacuum left in the party leadership after Lueger's death in March 1910, and partly also because of its new profile. It had moved far from its original rebellious course. At first a party of the lower bourgeoisie, it was on the way to becoming the party of agrarian interests, supported by finance and industry.

But the crisis into which the Christian Socialists were plunged at the point of success and recognition was deeper and more consequential than its chronicler Friedrich Funder would have us understand.[10] While the Social Democratic claim that the Christian Socialists had been "torn to pieces, stamped out, exterminated" was vastly exaggerated, the loss of Vienna to the party[11]

[10] Friedrich Funder, *Vom Gestern ins Heute: Aus dem Kaiserreich in die Republik* (Vienna and Munich, 1952), pp. 448ff.

[11] If the Christian Socialists retained their mayor, Dr. Richard Weiskirchner, who had succeeded Lueger in 1912, until the end of the war, it was because of the technicality that the 1911 election was a national election and did not affect the composition of the Vienna city council.

24

inaugurated the long reign of the Social Democrats over the capital, creating a conflict with the rest of the country which plagued the first Republic. With the Social Democratic victory in Vienna the center of gravity of the Christian Socialist party shifted away from the capital, where the party had originated, to the country, from the petty bourgeoisie to the conservative peasantry. This shift explains the strong position which, later in the republican era, the Länder could maintain in the face of Seipel's leadership. The trend toward social conservatism in the provinces and thus within the party was furthered by the alarm caused by the Pan-German–Social-Democratic coalition ticket for the runoff elections in Vienna; the specter of a recurring anticlerical combination haunted the Catholic leaders and drove the party further in the direction of capitalism. Altogether the election of 1911 left the Christian Socialists defeated and divided, if not "exterminated." The trend away from social reform toward social conservatism had the immediate effect of casting doubts upon the ideological premises of the party.

It is interesting, though not surprising, that the dying Lueger in his last will should have anticipated some of the dangers which were threatening his party. He warned against its becoming a "class party,"[12] and emphatically stressed the importance of the "faultless carrying on" of the administration in the capital.[13]

No less interesting than Lueger's warning were the "end of the year thoughts" which were put down late in 1911 by a young theologian at the University of Salzburg whose name was Ignaz Seipel.[14] "In view of the events of the past year," he addressed himself to the need for unity and leadership among the Catholics of Austria. It was the second theme to which he devoted most of

[12] "Irgendeine spezifische Berufspartei"; Kurt Skalnik, *Dr. Karl Lueger. Der Mann zwischen den Zeiten* (Vienna and Munich, 1954), p. 165; cf. Funder, *Vom Gestern ins Heute*, p. 451.

[13] Funder, *Vom Gestern ins Heute*, p. 451.

[14] Ignaz Seipel, "Sylvester Betrachtungen," *Katholische Kirchenzeitung*, LI, December 28, 1911.

his attention. Though he stopped short of throwing stones at the Christian Socialist leaders, he pointed squarely to the "want of leadership equipped with the necessary authority."

> But the *leader of the Christian people*, that we . . . want is altogether different from an efficient head of party or parliamentary caucus. He must have the *conviction* that he is called to lead his people by virtue of a higher mission. This conviction should be so strong that he would make any sacrifice for it, abandon all other aspirations, and impart it in turn to his fellow combatants. The Christian people must be able to place its entire confidence in him, not because of a party decision or an electoral arrangement, but because of the simple fact that he *is* the leader.

For historical precedents the writer referred back to the Old Testament, according to which, when the "need of God's people was great," God often called upon wholly unknown men "who derived their claim to leadership neither through inheritance nor through election but through their mere *calling*." The legitimation of this leadership was brought about by its deeds. Looking ahead into the uncertain future, Seipel asked:

> Will the Catholics of Austria, or more strictly speaking those of German Austria, be favored with such a leader in the coming year or in the foreseeable future at all? We don't know it, but we wish for it. Whence will he come and how will he be recognized? . . . If he is one of those men who are already in the public eye, so much the better; if he is a new man who, like Lueger at one time, must start from small beginnings, that will nevertheless be good. How will he be recognized? By his *deeds*, his *life* and his *success*. A party leader, a head of a parliamentary caucus can be elected, a popular leader must *arise*.

The more conventional types of leadership, as defined by "organization and statute," however necessary, were clearly "makeshifts" compared with leadership *"by the grace of God."*[15]

Had these thoughts been the work of a mere observer of the political scene, they would have been dismissed as a cross between political mysticism and amateur political science. But the man who wrote this article, while at the time twice removed—both by occupation and by geography—from the political center, was clearly more than casually involved in the future of the Catholic movement in Austria. Young Seipel himself had only once met Lueger when he was already sick and half blind.[16] He was for Seipel the example of the "true leader" legitimized by *"his deeds,"* whose "grandiose unselfishness" made him "sacrifice everything in order to live for his calling of leadership." But the fact is that Lueger's death had left a void among the Christian Socialists which neither Prince Alois Liechtenstein, who succeeded in the party, nor Weiskirchner, who succeeded in Vienna, could fill. The fact is that "increasingly recurrent signs of storm," as Seipel put it, were calling for a change of guard, and the fact is that the author of these thoughts turned out to be the very man who, when the storm was at its worst, when the "need" of the people was most desperate, took over the leadership. In these terms the "end of the year thoughts" are in effect an important document, indicative of the state of the party before the war, and at the same time a portent of things to come.

Family Background

Ignaz Seipel came from the very class to which Lueger had originally appealed, a class whose roots and ways were preindustrial

[15] Seipel's italics.

[16] Cf. "Gedächtnisprotokoll Dr. Anton Julius Walter über die Unterredung mit Exz. Dr. Seipel am 4. Dezember 1929," courtesy Erika Weinzierl-Fischer.

and attitudes conservative. In fact, for more than two centuries it had found an advocate in a forerunner of Lueger's, the eccentric imperial court preacher Abraham a Sancta Clara. A good-natured, good-humored class, it had sharpened its wits in the various Viennese *Volkstheater* which had opened around the turn of the eighteenth century and listened to the popular comedies of Raimund and Nestroy. In Church and theater this class experienced a native kind of democracy which brought with it an emotional participation no less real and no less satisfactory at the time than its much later participation in the political and social democracy of the twentieth century. Certainly the lower bourgeoisie of Vienna was traditionally imperial and loyal to the crown, even in its increasingly restless mood of the late nineteenth century. Like its leader, Lueger, it was "black-yellow" to the bone.

Seipel's origins thus were lowly, but proudly Viennese. On his father's side he could claim an uninterrupted Viennese ancestry.[17] His great-grandfather Franz, who still spelled his family name "Seipl," was a cloth manufacturer (*bürgerlicher Samt-und Bandfabrikant*), his grandfather Johann Baptist a minor official (*Offizial der k.k. Finanzprokuratur*). His father, Ignaz Karl (1841-1901), known as "Deutschmeister-Karl" for his military service with the Deutschmeister regiment, was evidently a thoroughly popular character. As a coachman, customarily called *Fiaker*, he followed a favored calling in Vienna, until in 1884 he became a concierge at the Fürsttheater in the Prater. All these paternal forebears of Seipel's came from areas which by Seipel's time had become incorporated in the city—St. Ulrich-Grund, Gumpendorf, Braunkirchen.

His mother's family originated from the Danubian country upstream from Vienna which is dominated by the majestic, baroque Benedictine abbey of Melk. There, in the village of Weitenegg,

[17] The documents on Seipel's family and person are contained in the Seipel Archive.

28

Seipel's maternal grandfather, Josef Zehentner, was a boatman, and there his mother Elisabeth was born (1850-1879).[18] Although Seipel identified himself distinctly with his "thoroughly urban, metropolitan birth and ancestry"[19]—as he once confessed as chancellor in front of Parliament—his roots extended far into the Lower Austrian countryside. This background constituted a potential element of strength in a society in which friction between the capital and the rest of the country was accentuated.

Born on July 19, 1876, in one of the many grey and depressing tenement houses[20] where the poor people of Vienna live in the shadow of the resplendent elegance of the city, Ignaz Seipel belonged to what Thomas Jefferson once called the "natural aristocracy among men" based on "virtue and talent." His Spartan habits were recorded by the school principal of his *Gymnasium* in Unter-Meidling, Hofrat Josef Wastl, later one of his intimate friends. After his school days his life was marked by dedication to work and asceticism. This trait may have been accentuated by a serious case of scarlet fever which, at the age of thirteen, took him out of school for more than a year and was responsible for his premature baldness. He always stood apart; he was almost always alone. Late in his life, when he was trying to recuperate from his fatal diseases in Switzerland and preparing himself for a return to Vienna and politics, he wrote whimsically to a friend

---

[18] She died of tuberculosis a few days after Ignaz's third birthday, leaving him to the care of the paternal grandmother Karoline. His three siblings died in early youth. Seipel's father took as his second wife a widow, Sophie Thoma, née Berska, who kept house for the later Professor Seipel in Salzburg until her death in 1910.

[19] *Stenographische Protokolle,* 151. *Sitzung des Nationalrates der Republik Österreich,* I. *Gesetzgebungsperiode,* November 26, 1929, p. 4919. Also on December 27, 1931, Seipel wrote a draft of a letter in response to some prize competition in the *Kleines Volksblatt,* a Viennese tabloid, "In search of the arch-Viennese" ("Ur-Wienern") in which he proudly referred to his paternal background (Seipel Archive).

[20] Märzstrasse 48 (now 42) in the 15th district, not far from the Westbahnhof.

that "no family," "no social life," "not even a *Stammtisch*"[21] was waiting for him at home. This aloofness, begun early in his life, was his strength in many ways, and was respected by both friend and foe. His politics, his views, his judgment, his decisions may have been challenged or assailed, but never were his independence and integrity questioned. Commenting once on the relation between money and politics which plagued the Viennese political scene no less than any other, Seipel wrote to the same friend: "My life is much too simple; I come from too far below not to have primitive habits. Therefore my private life is also not interesting."[22] While as a general statement this one may contain poor psychology, it applied fully to himself.

He was ambitious, as indeed he once admitted, "childishly ambitious,"[23] striving to emerge from his plain background and "move up into the big world."[24] However, he always remained free of the affectations of the Austrian titled aristocracy; he had none of the fussy ways of the inevitable bureaucrat of whom he always was rather disdainful, none of the overrefinements of the wealthy Viennese bourgeoisie. With all his success Seipel remained throughout his life a man of the people, though in a different sense from his model Lueger. Lueger was a demagogue, a charmer, a magician. Seipel, in addressing the people, never made any concessions to their tastes. He remained aloof from the masses and detested demagoguery. His speeches were uncompromisingly logical and thorough, often inexcusably sober and colorless. But they were invariably effective. His arms raised over the crowd had the effect of a priestly blessing, his pointed finger one of fatherly admonition. Moreover, his dry, often-biting

21 Seipel to Dr. Heinrich Mataja, copy, Davos, February 19, 1931 (Schmitz Archive).

22 Seipel to Mataja, Zürs, August 16, 1931.

23 Ernst Karl Winter, *Christentum und Zivilisation* (Vienna, 1956), p. 410.

24 August M. Knoll, "Gespräche mit Ignaz Seipel," *Reichspost*, December 25, 1932.

humor always found its way to his target. In his peculiar, aloof way Seipel was a popular figure after all. And he, who rose to eminence in Church, university, and state, fittingly recalled his father: "My father was a *Fiaker,* and from him I have inherited the art of conducting the state coach."[25]

The Young Churchman and Scholar

In 1895 Seipel graduated from the *Staatsgymnasium* in Unter-Meidling with an outstanding record, though he was stronger in religion than in Latin and Greek, and his weakest field, aside from gymnastics, was philosophy. Graduating "with distinction," he moved on the same year to study for the priesthood at the University of Vienna, where he consistently received the mark *eminenter.*[26] He was ordained in July 1899.

From 1899 to 1903 Seipel served as chaplain in various congregations in Lower Austria and in Vienna. It is interesting that during these early pastoral years Seipel should have discussed in his sermons some of the important questions which agitated modern Catholicism around the turn of the century and which eventually became central to his function as a Christian statesman. Once he said, "like the individual, *the whole of society* is under the obligation to be Christian," but looking around, with a typical air of realism, he added: "But where do we find this Christian spirit?"[27] This kind of questioning took him from the elevated heights of the kingdom of Christ to the kingdom of this world,[28] to a society

[25] Rudolf Blüml, *Prälat Dr. Ignaz Seipel: Ein grosses Leben in kleinen Bildern* (Klagenfurt, 1933), p. 81; cf. also p. 188 for a slightly different version.

[26] For the records from the Volksschule Fünfhaus, the k.k. Staatsgymnasium Unter-Meidling, and the Meldungsbuch from the University of Vienna, see Seipel Archive.

[27] Rudolf Blüml, ed., *Ignaz Seipel: Im Dienste des Wortes: Der Kaplan, Katechet, Kanzler in seinen Predigten, Exhorten und Ansprachen* (Vienna and Munich, 1955), p. 30; italics in original.

[28] Ibid., p. 37.

which was marked by injustice and struggle among classes and disunion among nations.[29]

In 1903 Seipel embarked upon his scholarly career. The previous year he had moved to the capital and, while still functioning for a short while as a chaplain in the Second District of Vienna, finished his doctor's thesis for the theological faculty at the university. The university allowed Seipel to reexamine the foundations of his belief and to develop his thoughts on the precise relations between the religious and secular domains. In fact, he became a student in Vienna of Prelate Franz Martin Schindler,[30] one of the leading theologians in the country, whose influence colored both his academic and his political careers. A churchman and scholar in politics, Schindler became his model. Holding the chair of moral theology, his concerns extended beyond the confines of the university into social and political affairs. Among the leaders of Catholic Vienna who took over after Vogelsang's death, Schindler was, alongside the conspicuously aristocratic Liechtenstein and the demonstratively plebeian Lueger, the most unassuming of the three. But it was he more than anyone else who was responsible for giving direction and content to Austrian political Catholicism. If the Christian Socialist party was an "ideological party" (*Weltanschauungspartei*), as Seipel was later to stress, it was due to the Prelate Schindler, who in his circumspect way brought together the elite of Catholic politicians and thinkers for "mutual discussions of vital contemporary issues."[31] The foundation in 1892 of the Austrian Leo-Gesellschaft, a society dedicated to questions of religion and culture, assured the Christian Socialist political movement of an intellectual sounding

[29] Ibid., pp. 30, 36f.

[30] Friedrich Funder, *Aufbruch zur christlichen Sozialreform* (Vienna and Munich, 1953).

[31] The so-called *Ente* evenings, meeting at the Hotel Zur Goldenen Ente regularly on Tuesdays from 1889-1898, attracted men like Vogelsang, Lueger, Liechtenstein, Weiskirchner, Leopold Kunschak (the Catholic labor leader), and Dr. Friedrich Funder; ibid., p. 114.

32

board. Later when Seipel himself had reached leading positions in Church and state he never failed to acknowledge his debt to his learned and fatherly mentor. "If I, as man of the Church, did not confine myself to one organization, namely the Church, but sought to recognize the organizational principle of society and to administer it in the nation and the state, I owe it to the school from which I originate." This tribute to his teacher was spoken on May 9, 1931, when Seipel, "Bundeskanzler a.D.," accepted the honorary doctorate of laws from his university, the Alma Mater Rudolphina.[32]

From the first it was Schindler who steered Seipel in the direction of moral theology. This is all the more interesting since Seipel's original plans had been to take his *Habilitation* in the field of dogmatic theology. If this plan had come true it is conceivable that, in spite of his demonstrated early interests in secular matters, a very different Seipel might have developed from the one we are faced with, more confined to his priestly and scholarly world, more otherworldly, more at peace with himself.

Indeed the preoccupation with moral theology was decisive for Seipel's whole future orientation, ecclesiastical as well as political. While deepening his concern with matters social[33] and political, it also determined the mode of his concern. On the one hand Seipel opted against the perhaps comfortable but illusionary position that took for granted the immanence of Christian values in the world; the Pope himself, he conceded, was a political figure, conducting the affairs of the Church in a world that was no longer in the full meaning of the word Catholic.[34] On the other hand, Seipel avoided the pitfalls of excessive realism in ex-

[32] Quoted in Bernhard Birk, *Dr. Ignaz Seipel: Ein österreichisches und europäisches Schicksal* (Innsbruck, 1932), pp. 227ff.

[33] In fact Seipel somewhat pretentiously prided himself on having developed Schindler's moral theology into a science of sociology; cf. Seipel to Dr. Alfred Missong, Mersina (Turkey), March 31, 1932, Schmitz Archive; cf. also Birk, *Seipel*, p. 228.

[34] Ignaz Seipel, "Pius X—der Seelsorgerpapst," *Katholische Kirchenzeitung*, August 27, 1914.

ploring the secular world. In fact he explicitly rejected attempts to divorce Christian principles altogether from politics, or to separate private from public morality. This, he argued, had been the fallacy of absolutism, that it had relegated Christian morals to the private sector and subjected society to laws that were altogether divorced from ethics.[35] In this way Seipel committed himself to a position once removed from the extremes both of Christian romanticism and naked cynicism. If he was not the type of the "Platonic *politikos*," neither was he the type of the Machiavellian. He dedicated himself to the implementation of the essentially Thomist scholastic proposition that an accommodative course should be pursued in relating two realms to one another that were not identical. This course called for watchfulness and flexibility, if not virtuosity; a continuous and cautious balancing of ideal premises and real possibilities. And it also opened itself up to the sort of ethical dilemmas which later on made Seipel both controversial and misunderstood as a statesman.

Through his teacher Schindler, Seipel got involved in the "struggle of orientation" which had broken out among German Catholics around the turn of the century. The problem over which the struggle took place was not a new one. Throughout its history Christianity has been faced with the task of defining its relationship to human civilization. The argument was bound to become acute again in the nineteenth century with its unprecedented acceleration of cultural and social change. Within Catholicism the main positions taken on this issue were the conservative, "integralist," or, as it has been fittingly called, the "cautious" one, and the "liberal" or "confident" one.[36] The first

[35] Ignaz Seipel, *Neue Ziele und Aufgaben der katholischen Moraltheologie* (Vienna, 1926).

[36] For a discussion of the overall problem see H. Richard Niebuhr, *Christ and Culture* (New York, 1951); the distinction between the "cautious" and the "confident" has been used by Robert D. Cross, *The Emergence of Liberal Catholicism in America* (Cambridge, Mass., 1958). See also Joseph N. Moody, ed., *Church and Society: Catholic Social and Political Thought and Movements, 1789-1950* (New York, 1953), p. 465.

considered secular civilization to be inherently hostile, and therefore insisted upon a rigorously Catholic approach to cultural, political, and social problems; while the latter, viewing man's achievements more benignly as creations of God's children and therefore redeemable, argued the case for maximum cooperation between Church and civilization. On the level of the social issue the struggle of orientation had left Catholics correspondingly divided between the "cautious" ones who indulged in dreams of a restoration of a wholly Christian order (*Sozialreform*) and those who were ready to solve the social problem and assert their ideas within the framework of the existing industrial order (*Sozialpolitik*).

It was during the pontificate of Leo XIII (1878-1903) that the Roman Church boldly ventured into the highly controversial political and social issues of the times, thus making the "liberal" position respectable. From his elevated position Leo attempted to reach and encompass areas which the Church had tended to ignore. One of his earlier encyclicals, *Immortale Dei* (November 1, 1885), dealt with the problem of civil authority, stating that, while its origin was divine and there was "no power but from God," the right to rule was not necessarily tied to any special form of government. "It may take this or that form, provided only that it be of a nature to insure the general welfare." In matters political then, "a difference of opinion is lawful."[37] The Leonine position signified a clear departure from the inflexible policies of his predecessor on the papal throne. The new policy was clearly based on Thomistic premises of accommodation to the modern secular state. It was to have a decisive effect on Austria during the revolutionary turmoil of 1918 when the Austrian Catholics, largely upon Seipel's prodding, chose to shift their allegiance from monarchy to republic.

A more immediate influence upon Austrian Catholicism was Leo's great encyclical on the social question, *Rerum Novarum*

[37] Cf. Etienne Gilson, ed., *The Church Speaks to the Modern World: The Social Teachings of Leo XIII* (New York, 1961), pp. 161ff.

(May 15, 1891). Coming out half a year after Vogelsang's death, it incorporated many of the conservative notions of the great Catholic social thinker. However on the whole it encouraged the cause of *Sozialpolitik*, that is, of those who were willing to adjust to the existing modern society.[38] While Germany in the nineteenth century became fertile ground for the development of a "liberal" Catholicism (inspired by such men as Franz Hitze and Heinrich Pesch), Austria remained the stronghold of a somber, integralist position. Vogelsang's conservative theories dominated the Austrian Catholic scene. He nailed Catholic social theory down to an essentially medieval, precapitalist, romantic position.[39] His "social monarchy," which was to be corporatively organized, resurrected an ideal Christian society without making any concessions to the secular state or to the separation of Church and state.

But the controversy eventually spilled over into Austria. The younger, more progressive elements within the Church, and also within the Christian Socialist movement, resented "the smell of Byzantium."[40] And even if they were cautiously steering away from the outright "modernism" which Pius X so vigorously indicted in 1907 and again in 1910, they liked to think of themselves as advocates of a reforming Catholicism (*Reformkatholizismus*) which through a newly gained flexibility and openness was to be in a better position to resist the pressures of the Pan-German "Los von Rom" movement as well as the anticlericalism of the growing Social Democratic movement.

Seipel's first major scholarly work, his *Habilitationsschrift* on

[38] Cf. Alfred Diamant, *Austrian Catholics and the First Republic: Democracy, Capitalism and the Social Order, 1918-1934* (Princeton, 1960), pp. 23ff.; August M. Knoll, *Katholische Kirche und scholastisches Naturrecht* (Vienna, 1962), pp. 105f.

[39] Cf. Diamant, *Austrian Catholics*, pp. 41ff. and Joh. Christoph Allmayer-Beck, *Vogelsang. Vom Feudalismus zur Volksbewegung* (Vienna, 1952).

[40] Funder, *Vom Gestern ins Heute*, p. 343.

the Church fathers' teachings on social ethics,[41] ought to be viewed in the context of the struggle of orientation. While examining one of the earliest phases in the development of Christian ethics, Seipel probed into the duties of the churchman in society and so indirectly into the exact nature of the relation between Christian ethics and politics. The striking discovery resulting from Seipel's investigations was that the fathers, in their concern with secular matters, had been far from attempting to control economic life. They had neither rejected nor condoned the owning of property. In other words, the Church, belonging to all races, nations, and classes, to all economic and political orders, to all times, was neither communist nor capitalist. "There are," Seipel explained elsewhere, "no ecclesiastical norms for science, literature and art, there is no political, social or economic program of the Church. There are only those norms . . . which insist on the assertion of the laws of Christian ethics in all these areas of human endeavor."[42] Somewhat more pointedly Seipel stated later that "there are no 'economic doctrines of Christianity' because Christ the Lord has not become man in order to teach economics; there are only 'Christian doctrines concerning economic ethics.' "[43] Thus a fairly insignificant dissertation had the effect of preparing the ground for an unprecedented latitude on the part of the Austrian church.

There is one other facet of Seipel's dissertation which deserves comment because it offers a key to his thinking and especially to his later political argument. Since the Church, according to his

[41] Ignaz Seipel, *Die wirtschaftsethischen Lehren der Kirchenväter* (Vienna, 1907).

[42] Ignaz Seipel, "Kirchliche Autorität und persönliche Freiheit," *Über den Wassern*, VI (1913), 181.

[43] Seipel's comments of April 13, 1925, on the draft by P. Ferdinand Frodl, S.J., for the pastoral letter on social issues of the Austrian episcopate of November 29, 1925, Archive of the Archdiocese of Vienna, quoted in Erika Weinzierl-Fischer, *Die österreichischen Konkordate von 1855 und 1933* (Vienna, 1960), p. 143.

findings, had no economic doctrine of its own, Christians were in the precarious position of seeking to translate the ethical premises of Christianity into all other areas, including the economic one, and of seeking at all times the order most nearly conforming to them. Thus Seipel derived from the writings of the Church fathers a two-level theory of property: he distinguished between "higher" or "true" property on the one hand, which, in complete conformance with the spirit of justice and love, may be claimed by those who are "wise, just, and good," and "earthly" property on the other, which is not the highest of goods, which, in the hands of the miser, indeed turns into poverty.[44]

But beyond serving a mere theory of property, this two-level view of reality came to shape Seipel's approach to all political matters; in fact it came to offer a key to his thought and action. Everything in the realm of reality, he once observed, has its counterpart in an "idea emanating from God."[45] Throughout Seipel's political argument, then, ran the opposition between higher (true, genuine) and lower (wrong, surrogate, vulgar, formal) forms of peace and war, of leadership, patriotism, republic, and democracy. The higher level in every case was the ideal, the norm which should penetrate the real, but with which the real could not be expected to be identical. Here, no doubt, the Augustinian,[46] if not the Platonic, influence came to the fore in Seipel. The Augustinian dualism between the ideal and the real, between the City of God and the earthly city, called for a right ordering of values and served therefore to control and direct Seipel's bold venture in accommodation.

While the Church was, according to Seipel, an *ecclesia accommodititia* that could adjust to the secular order, it was by no means indifferent to the nature of that order. It was, as Seipel pointed out, no Spartacus aiming at setting slaves free, but a Paul

[44] Seipel, *Lehren*, pp. 62ff.

[45] Ignaz Seipel, *Der christliche Staatsmann* (Augsburg, 1931), p. 19.

[46] Cf. August M. Knoll, "In Memoriam Ignaz Seipel," transcript of address over Radio Vienna, August 1, 1933, Knoll Archive.

who admonished bad slaves to be good, and bad masters to be good.[47] Above the realm of politics there was clearly a higher one over which the Church stood as a guardian. Meanwhile, however, the political reality, while of a lower order, was the only tangible one. Accordingly, Seipel saw fit to emphasize the importance of recognizing "realities." Any neglect of these realities Seipel castigated as "romanticism," and he noted that he had a "great fear" of romanticism in politics. The "realities" were the "language of God," and indicative of the "ideas and the will of God."[48]

Addressing the Catholic delegates of the League of Nations in 1930 on the subject of St. Augustine, Seipel said that he looked at the creations of this world "both with pleasure and with skepticism."[49] It can be said both of him and of Pope Leo XIII that while they aimed at sanctifying the modern world, they embraced it and loved it despite all its imperfections. The political scene was the setting for a morality play, a *Welttheater*, in which man, with all his faults, acted out allegorically the drama of sin and redemption.

It is indicative of the gulf separating the Austrian Catholic intellectual scene from Germany that at a time when German sociology made strides in the direction of a value-free and empirical discipline under the guidance of Max Weber, a brand of sociology should have asserted itself at the University of Vienna, and not only in the faculty of theology, which was entirely ideological in orientation. By the turn of the century German thinking in the fields of social studies, including history, was facing up to hard and fast facts that were in irreconcilable conflict with ultimate values. Weber's awareness of the "ethic of responsibility,"

[47] Cf. August M. Knoll, *Katholische Kirche und scholastisches Naturrecht* (Vienna, 1962), p. 16.

[48] Ignaz Seipel, *Wesen und Aufgaben der Politik* (Innsbruck, 1930), p. 17.

[49] Ignaz Seipel, "Der Völkerbund im Lichte des Augustinus-Jubiläums," September 14, 1930, *Im Dienste des Wortes*, p. 161.

The Formative Years

Troeltsch's assertion of the nonabsolute nature of Christianity as a religion, Troeltsch's and Meinecke's discovery of historicism as an inescapable reality which challenged the traditional notion of absolutes, of universal values, led this generation of German scholars into a sea of disenchantment and skepticism. It was a generation which had lost the sense of wholeness. In one sense it was enriched by its knowledge; in another impoverished by its doubts. It was a "disinherited" generation. By comparison, Seipel's emphasis on the Christian law of nature seems, however generous, strikingly removed from the mainstream of twentieth-century thought. While proposing to make Christian ethics enter into areas which the Church itself had long ignored, he was not sufficiently aware that Christian ethics no longer had universal value. A century earlier Seipel's "sociology" might have exercised a truly revolutionary influence on Catholic thought and politics. The twentieth century made it illusionary. The *res publica Christiana* was dead, even in Austria after 1867. If twentieth-century Austria did not produce a Max Weber, it gave birth to Freud and Karl Kraus, Rilke and Kafka, all "disinherited" minds.[50] But with none of these did Seipel have any contact. And what would Seipel's Christian offensive have meant to the many liberals, to the growing army of Social Democrats, and to the many increasingly disaffected nationalties? No doubt, the young Viennese theologian set out on a dangerous course. The richer he was in certainties, the poorer he was in practical insights. In his first Declaration of Policy in 1922 he prided himself on "never" having been a pessimist.[51] Seipel's very optimism left him unprepared for the storm that was ahead. His scholarly work, then, while setting up the framework for his statesmanship, did not prepare him sufficiently for adversity. He therefore ran the risk of reacting violently out of disillusionment and fear, of becoming impatient and fierce. For the tenuous connections between the real and the

[50] Cf. Erich Heller, *The Disinherited Mind* (New York, 1959).
[51] Josef Gessl, *Seipels Reden in Österreich und anderwärts* (Vienna, 1926), p. 18.

40

ideal might break down altogether, prompting the disappointed idealist to abandon the partial and contingent virtues of a secular order and to espouse the absolute values of a transcendent one to which all practical considerations would be subordinate. Seipel ran the risk, in other words, of forsaking the concrete and relative for a pure truth. In this case, "true peace" might turn out to be actual war, "true democracy" dictatorship, and the whole "rat's tail" of concepts,[52] as E. K. Winter put it, marked by the epithet "true" might merge into their opposites.

[52] E. K. Winter, "Österreich und der Nationalsozialismus," *Wiener Politische Blätter*, I, December 3, 1933, 198; cf. Charles Gulick, *Austria from Habsburg to Hitler* (Berkeley and Los Angeles, 1948), II, 806ff.

41

Two

THE MAKING OF A CHRISTIAN STATESMAN: THE SALZBURG YEARS, 1909-1917

The "Grand Rehearsal": The Salzburg Cultural Scene

THE ASSIGNMENT in Salzburg, where Seipel was appointed Professor of Moral Theology in 1909, took him to one of the historical centers of Western civilization. Just a few years earlier Roman mosaics had been unearthed beneath the Domplatz, recalling the fact that the city had been a prosperous trading center in imperial days. At the foot of the steep cliffs of the Mönchsberg was the site of the Benedictine monastery of St. Peter from which modern Salzburg took its origins. Made a bishopric in 739, it became an archbishopric in 798, almost ten centuries before Vienna. The archbishopric of Salzburg, which in 1225 became a duchy as well, controlled a large area and was the ecclesiastic, political, and cultural heart of Central Europe, a bridge between west and east, and in particular, since the baroque period, between north and south. Hermann Bahr, for many years a resident of Salzburg, once wrote, "We Austrian Germans are called upon to become north-southerners and west-easterners."[1] In this sense Salzburg, though never formally a Habsburg possession until the early nineteenth century, was an Austrian city par excellence. It was moreover the city whose head, the archbishop, was Primate of Germany, even though the title had little more than symbolic significance. Through its university, founded in 1622, it became an important intellectual center. Whereas Vienna since Maria Theresa, and more so since Joseph II, had increasingly taken on the character of a secular city, the center of a bureaucratic empire, Salzburg had remained the seat of the "old" Austria. There

[1] Hermann Bahr, *Tagebuch 1918* (Innsbruck, 1919), p. 252.

43

was a grain of truth in Bahr's statement that he "who knows Vienna, as yet knows nothing about Austria."[2] Seipel's move from Vienna to Salzburg, then, took him from the metropolis to the mighty archepiscopal citadel over the Salzach river. Among the baroque spires of the "German Rome," as Salzburg has often been called, he would have the leisure to travel back in time and review his thoughts on the meaning of Christian rule. During the crucial time of the immediate prewar period and of the first three years of the war he could thus, at a distance from the turmoil in Vienna, rethink the needs and purposes of imperial policies.

Salzburg, like any other city, was what one made of it; and young Seipel, well-grounded in his faith, well-trained in his discipline, brought his whole ingenuity to bear on the resources of this center. Since the old Alma Mater Paridiana had been closed in 1810 when Salzburg had become a province of Bavaria, the university had never been able to regain the status and the prosperity which it had enjoyed in the seventeenth and eighteenth centuries. In 1850 a lone theological faculty was reestablished. As a member of this faculty, Seipel taught courses on moral theology and "Christian sociology" and another, oddly enough, on "the foundations of economics." Among the ten scholars on this small faculty Seipel found only a few congenial minds, and he had good reason to remark on the "narrowness of conditions";[3] but for Seipel this narrowness was nothing more than a challenge. In fact, there had been attempts under way in Germany as well as Austria since the late 1840s to reconstitute a "free Catholic university" in Salzburg, but the agitation and fund-collecting had become bogged down in the course of the German Kulturkampf. When in 1884 a Catholic "Universitätsverein" was founded alongside a liberal "Hochschulverein," the university question had clearly become a political issue and the positions of

[2] Hermann Bahr, "Österreichisch," *Die neue Rundschau*, XXVI (July 1915), 917.

[3] Seipel to Hermann Bahr, December 18, 1916. Hermann Bahr Archive, Nationalbibliothek, Vienna.

the two groups sharply opposed, with the former agitating for a Catholic university and the latter for a secular one. Seipel became a driving force and leading spokesman for a compromise solution. In effect, this whole university struggle between Catholics and liberals became but another chapter for him in the "struggle of orientation" within the Catholic Church. The compromise protocol, which was finally signed on April 17, 1917, and which provided for a fully fledged university in Salzburg called "k.k. Kaiser Karl Universität,"[4] constituted a healthy reminder to the Austrian Catholics of the advantages of cooperation with the non-Catholic world. In his summary article for the *Reichspost* Seipel concluded: "We welcome with genuine pleasure every move which promises to lead to a closer connection and undisturbed cooperation with our fellow citizens of other persuasion (*Weltanschauung*), and we gladly contribute, even at the price of sacrifices, towards cementing such a connection."[5] In spite of many years of preparation and negotiation, this settlement never saw the light of the day. The strongest reasons for its failure were of course the war and defeat; but even later Chancellor Seipel never abandoned the project for a university in Salzburg.

Seipel's efforts to come to an agreement with the liberals reflected not only his interest in Salzburg, but also a willingness to minimize and overcome the effects of the nineteenth-century Kulturkampf. "The time of religious wars," he once stated, "is over."[6] He thus set a precedent during the Salzburg years for the coalition between Christian Socialists and Pan-Germans (the successors of the liberals), which in republican Austria became the basis of his government. He proved that he was a man who could think in terms of the "bonum commune."[7] Certainly his role in the

---

[4] For the documents on this matter cf., Archive of the Archdiocese, Salzburg.

[5] Ignaz Seipel, "Die Wendung in der Salzburger Universitätsfrage," *Reichspost*, May 6, 1917.

[6] *Reichspost*, September 23, 1920.

[7] Seipel later used the concept of "bonum commune" as a rationale for the alliance with the Pan-Germans; "Grundsätzliches zur Reform des

negotiations helped establish his reputation as a man of moderation, patience, judgment.

There was hardly an area of Church life in Salzburg in which Seipel did not play a leading part. Back in 1907 he had become a director of the Leo-Gesellschaft in Vienna. In 1912 he established a branch of this association in Salzburg.[8] At first he seems to have had minor difficulties with the Archbishop Johannes Katschthaler, who feared that the new venture might compete with the Universitätsverein. Indeed, when in 1913 Seipel planned the general convocation of the whole Austrian association in Salzburg and scheduled one of the sessions for 9 A.M., he was taken to task by a "high ecclesiastical source." "Yes, the Social Democrats would do it this way; a Catholic event ought not to take place while the service still goes on in the Cathedral."[9] This was probably the first and last time in his life that he was so closely equated with his archenemies. Nevertheless, the general convocation turned out to be a great success, with dignitaries of both Church and state participating. No less successful was the work done in the regular biweekly meetings in the Hotel Zum Wolf-Dietrich, which were often addressed by such leading Catholic thinkers as Richard von Kralik and Heinrich Lammasch. Seipel's work on behalf of the Leo-Gesellschaft brought his name more and more into circulation in ecclesiastic as well as political circles; it added up to a "grand rehearsal" for him.[10]

Seipel's public activities during the Salzburg years were impressive. In 1910 he joined the editorial board of the official *Katholische Kirchenzeitung* and soon afterward, in 1913, of the

---

Wahlgesetzes," November 1, 1930, Seipel Archive. Cf. *Das Neue Reich,* XIII (November 29, 1930), 178.

[8] For Seipel and the Leo-Gesellschaft see the informative article by August M. Knoll, "Ignaz Seipel und die österreichische Leo-Gesellschaft," *Jahrbuch der österreichischen Leo-Gesellschaft,* ed. Oskar Katann (Vienna, 1933), pp. 183-204.

[9] Seipel to Theodor Innitzer, undated; ibid., p. 197.

[10] Ibid., pp. 197, 200.

cultural biweekly *Über den Wassern*. His contributions to the former were profuse, but uneven in quality. A somewhat excessive self-assurance made him move into all sorts of fields from ethics to aesthetics, from history to political theory, with results ranging from the trivial to the penetrating, an inconsistency which continued to characterize his public addresses, but which to some extent always served him well.

Through his work with the Salzburg cultural journal *Über den Wassern* Seipel got involved in the so-called literary controversy (*Literaturstreit*) which was yet another offshoot of the "struggle of orientation." It raged over the issue of whether Catholic culture should be self-contained, pure, and integral, or freely opened to secular influences. The challenge came from Germany, from Karl Muth, who had founded the magazine *Hochland* to broaden the horizon of Catholic literature. He called upon Catholics to break out of the "fortress" or "ghetto" of their self-imposed mediocrity and isolation. He found his most formidable antagonist in Richard von Kralik, dean of the Viennese Catholic intellectuals, who preached a romantic-conservative point of view through his magazine *Gral* (1906) and his rather cultic group of followers, the "Gralbund."

Über den Wassern[11] was to be the Austrian equivalent of *Hochland*. It served Seipel as a base from which he could attack the position of the *Gral* "integralists." Just as the Church fathers had studied the works of classical antiquity, he argued, so Catholics ought to read their own national literature.[12] The *Gral*, to be consistent with its own position, ought not to carry an article on Goethe. He defended vigorously the right and duty of a Catholic journal to carry articles by and about non-Catholic authors such as Thomas Mann, Gerhart Hauptmann, Stefan Zweig, Alfons Paquet. The purpose of such liberality would be, Seipel

[11] From "Und der Geist Gottes schwebte über den Wassern" ("and the Spirit of God was moving over the face of the waters").
[12] Ignaz Seipel, "Literarische Polemik und katholische Moral," *Über den Wassern*, VII (December 1914), 686.

conceded, to expose secularism and the preponderance of a "Jewish literary clique."[13]

Seipel's part in the literary controversy, then, clearly marked him as a "liberal" Catholic, although he never applied that label to himself. No doubt, he was an anti-integralist. He disliked the narrowness, militancy, and fanaticism of the integralists. In his diary he once compared them to the radicals among the socialists. After reading Lily Braun's *Memoiren einer Sozialistin*, he noted in September 1916: "There radicalism against revisionism, here integralism against us."[14] This entry is an unusually interesting one, since it projects some light on the by no means unambiguous relationship between Seipel and the Social Democrats. It suggests that maybe there were some points of comparison after all between Seipel's Catholicism and Socialism. At least the diary entry exposes Seipel as a fundamentally moderate man, opposed to doctrinaire positions within the Church as well as without. Indeed radicalism as such was his foe. With his experience in the literary controversy clearly in mind, Seipel stressed later, while defining his concept of "Catholic policy" in 1923, that "one-sidedness is never truly Catholic and every form of fanaticism is un-Catholic." "Constructing artificial differences" without being able to show how they could be overcome, was no less "un-Catholic."[15] That is why even in this literary controversy Seipel always remained somewhat above the fronts, while not lacking the courage to speak his mind openly. Like his contemporary, and later his close associate, Friedrich Funder, he was not sufficiently interested in a controversy which, they thought, largely agitated an older generation of Catholic thinkers.[16] Seipel saw himself in

---

[13] Ibid., 685.   [14] Seipel diary, August 16, 1916.

[15] Ignaz Seipel, "Katholizismus und Gegenwart" (May 14, 1923), in Josef Gessl, *Seipels Reden in Österreich und anderwärts* (Vienna, 1926), p. 133. Cf. also Seipel's address to the Congress of German Catholics, Dortmund, September 5, 1927, in which he accused the fanatic in politics of "blasphemy"; *Neue Freie Presse*, September 6, 1927, morning ed.

[16] Friedrich Funder, *Vom Gestern ins Heute* (Vienna and Munich, 1952), p. 347.

the position of mediator in this troublesome affair. Above all, he hoped to be instrumental in reconciling the two groups and thus furthering unity among the Catholics.[17] It was undoubtedly due partly to the influence of Seipel that the two feuding journals buried the hatchet during the war and combined into one to form the "new" *Gral.*

Once again the Salzburg professor had displayed a marked sense of liberality and moderation. He quite clearly had a talent for rising above issues, for bringing people together, for compromise. But even from this unpolitical phase of his life it became quite evident that he had a way of settling questions on his own terms. He had the gifts of patience and persuasion, and with all his moderation he did not lack shrewdness and a sense of power. In various ways, then, the Salzburg experience was a rich and wholesome one for Seipel. It turned out to be his proving ground, and we are told by a man who knew Seipel well during those years that after the merger of the two journals Seipel wrote to a friend that he considered his literary mission fulfilled and could now dedicate himself to a new sphere of activity.[18]

The Sulking Corner by the Salzach River

Heinrich von Treitschke once called Jacob Burckhardt's Basel the "sulking corner" of Germany. Burckhardt had turned his back on the lure of the hustling and power-crazy German capital, withdrawing to the University of Basel and expounding the priority of culture over politics and power. Basel, he explained, had

---

[17] Ibid., 673; also the letters from Seipel to Richard von Kralik, July 7, 1913, September 25, 1913, October 1, 1913, July 13, 1914, and July 23, 1914, which convey Seipel's deep esteem for Kralik as well as his emphatic desire to conciliate (Manuscript collection, Vienna Stadtbibliothek). Cf. also Ignaz Seipel, "Die beiden Richtungen in der katholischen Literaturbewegung," *Über den Wassern*, VII (December 1913), 130-34.

[18] Werner Thormann, *Dr. Ignaz Seipel der europäische Staatsmann* (Frankfurt, 1932), p. 14.

become for him "not only desirable for earthly reasons, but metaphysically necessary." In a similar way, it might be suggested, Salzburg became for Seipel and his friends the "sulking corner" of Austria. In the course of his stay in Salzburg Seipel was drawn into a circle of congenial minds which, since the outbreak of the war, had concerned themselves intensely with political issues and become increasingly critical of imperial policy, particularly in connection with the question of war and peace. While there was nothing emotional in their position toward the capital, as there was in Burckhardt's case, there was a good deal of uneasiness over the idea of Vienna. The distance from it affected Seipel and his friends as more than a merely geographic one. Their separation gave them perspective and accentuated their independence of thought in the midst of a war frenzy that had gripped public opinion.

The people with whom Seipel was associated were like-minded men who worked and walked together, who corresponded and visited each other. The war and the problems which it raised drew them even closer together and gave them a certain cohesion and identity. While loyally supporting the Monarchy, they saw their function as that of critics of official policy rather than apologists for it. If they wrote about the "ideas of 1914," as did so many German writers in exaltation of German *Kultur* and martial virtues, they addressed themselves to praise not of the nation but of what Hermann Bahr called the "union of peoples."[19] The "Catholic cathedral of mankind,"[20] he reminded his readers, arises over the various nations. Altogether these men veered, as the war dragged on, in the direction of a native Austrian brand of pacifism rooted in the time-honored experience of peaceful cohabitation of different peoples. They preferred love to force and culture to unrestrained power. They stood for the old supranational baroque Austria, as Hermann Bahr liked to highlight it,

[19] Hermann Bahr, "Ideen von 1914," *Hochland*, XIV (January 1917), 448.
[20] Ibid., 418.

against the new Austria that had become engulfed in an alien world of nationalism and power conflicts.[21]

Among this group was Heinrich Lammasch (1853-1920), one of the most remarkable personalities of the late Monarchy. An authority in the fields of penal and international law, he was a passionate partisan of peace, and one of old Austria's great scholars. Holding a chair at the University of Vienna, he gained a wide reputation and well-earned recognition. In the course of his career he distinguished himself as Austria-Hungary's representative at the Hague Peace Conferences in 1899 and 1907 and as a member of the International Court of Arbitration at The Hague after 1900. After his return from the first Peace Conference he was called by the Emperor into the Upper House, which henceforth he used to take an active part in public affairs and to voice his convictions. After 1910 he also acted as adviser to the Archduke Francis Ferdinand, and this willful, impatient heir apparent could hardly have had a better counterbalance than the firm, cautious, and honest lawyer. When Lammasch retired to the Salzburg area in 1914 for reasons of health, he withdrew in effect from his teaching obligations to dedicate himself fully to his concerns about the immediate political issues of the times. This learned, cultivated, devoutly religious man was a passionate fighter for his cause, and his cause was law and peace. It was the ethos of his profession as well as his understanding of the Christian message and the Austrian tradition that impelled him to devote the rest of his life to stemming the tide of nationalism, fanaticism, and war. Here was a man, a "perfect Austrian" as Hermann Bahr called him,[22] who in the last years, and virtually the last hours, of the Monarchy became its conscience.

Through Lammasch, in turn, Seipel met the German educator

[21] Cf. Hermann Bahr, *Kritik der Gegenwart* (Augsburg, 1922), p. 202.

[22] Hermann Bahr, "Sein Wesen," in *Heinrich Lammasch, seine Aufzeichnungen, sein Wirken und seine Politik*, ed. Marga Lammasch and Hans Sperl (Vienna and Leipzig, 1922), p. 5.

The Salzburg Years

Friedrich Wilhelm Foerster (1869-1966), a dedicated Christian pacifist and untiring foe of Bismarckian Germany. An outspoken, fearless man, Foerster taught briefly in Vienna before the war and then moved to Munich, where in 1916, because of his upright advocacy of peace and criticism of governmental policies, he became the center of an "Affaire Foerster." Among Seipel's acquaintances Foerster was the most militant pacifist. The rougher climate in Germany, which would not tolerate dissent, left Foerster's spirit undaunted though not uninjured.

Then there was Hermann Bahr (1863-1934), one of the liveliest men of letters in the German-speaking world around the turn of the century. He was one of the leading expressionist poets and critics, and was also passionately interested in history and politics. In France one would call him a "politique et moraliste." Though his political concerns were more reflective of the main currents of the time than they were original, they were always voiced with vehemence and epigrammatic persuasion. Thus Bahr, after having gone through a Pan-German irredentist, a socialist, an antisemitic, and a prosemitic phase, a Marxist, Nietzschean, and Barrèsian period, became one of the vociferous and convincing interpreters of Austrian self-consciousness. It was at that point that he suddenly remembered the city where he had been brought up, "the old German city of Salzburg, a wholly Italian city, in which the Gothic and Baroque converge . . . , rightly a symbol of Austria."[23] Salzburg remained Bahr's second home during a restless life in which he moved from one European capital to another. In 1912 he returned to live in the Salzach city. It was then that he met Seipel, whom he ardently, perhaps too ardently, came to admire, and in whom he saw the savior of Austria.

As for Seipel himself, he served during the war years as military chaplain of the Salzburg Reserve Hospital and attended

[23] Hermann Bahr, "Österreichisch," *Die Tat*, vi (September 1914-March 1915), 588.

wounded soldiers in the Red Cross hospital.[24] In this capacity he found himself called upon to explain the position of the Church in the life-and-death struggle of the empire. The war, which stirred up patriotic fervor, gave rise to all sorts of attacks, both overt and covert, against the Church, and specifically against the clergy. Seipel's pamphlet on "The Catholics in the Present World War"[25] was a "rebuttal to a variety of accusations." And while Seipel somewhat pointedly extolled the old Emperor as "Emperor of peace" and explained the war as a defensive war, indeed a "just war,"[26] and while he declared love of the fatherland and of the people to be "a religious duty" and denied any "serious conflict between religion, patriotism, and national fervour,"[27] he left no doubt that there was an area of conflict between Catholicism and nationalism. Resorting to a distinction between "true patriotism" and "true national sentiment" on the one hand and "excesses of nationalism" on the other,[28] he designated the manifestation of nationalism, which was a value in itself, as a threat to religion. And not only did he turn on the irredentist nationalism of the non-Germans within the Monarchy, which was a clear threat to the latter's existence, but he spelled out the dangers which came specifically from a German nationalism. In the midst of the war frenzy of 1914 Seipel pleaded for self-examination. Quite unmistakably Seipel thus entered the public arena in 1914 as a dissenter. To be sure the dissent was a cautious one, but it was grounded in the very promises of a Christian position concerned with safeguarding the prerogatives of religion against the excessive claims of the state and of modern nationalism.

[24] Ignaz Seipel, *Kriegsbrief an den Vater des Kriegers; Kriegsbrief an den verwundeter Krieger* (both Vienna and Salzburg, 1914).

[25] *Die Katholiken im gegenwärtigen Weltkrieg, Kriegsflugblätter* (Salzburg, 1914).

[26] Seipel, *An den verwundeten Krieger*, p. 7.

[27] Seipel, *Die Katholiken*, p. 1.

[28] Ibid., pp. 5, 8. Cf. also Ignaz Seipel, "Vaterland, Nationalismus und Religion," *Katholische Kirchenzeitung*, October 15 and 20, 1914.

53

The Salzburg Years

Nation und Staat

The early wartime pamphlets and articles, though not very important in themselves, offer significant clues to the turn that Seipel's mind took during the war. They were sketches of sorts for Seipel's major work, *Nation und Staat*.[29] The appearance of this book, with its focus on political problems, was surprising to his friends.[30] But it was not really so new, representing, as it did, the logical result of Seipel's preoccupation with moral theology. The pressing issues in the nineteenth and twentieth centuries, Seipel once said, were the "social problems" and the "international problems."[31] His dissertation on the Church fathers was Seipel's first venture into the social aspect of these issues, and *Nation und Staat*, written under the impact of the war, his first study of their international aspects.

Though it was in its way an Austrian version of the "ideas of 1914," *Nation und Staat* set out to make distinctions rather than to obliterate them, as had been the objective of much of the German literature on the subject. *Clarae notiones, boni amici*, the motto of the book, introduced the claims of the Catholic position amidst a wave of patriotism and nationalism. It was a sober book rather than a stirring one, cautious rather than eloquent; but in this sobriety and caution, in its refusal to become engulfed in wartime passions, lay its distinction. Like Seipel's shorter wartime publications, *Nation und Staat* was an expression of dissent —a sort of grand review of the Christian position in an increasingly nationalistic Europe.

Rather than a swan song, as some have suggested,[32] *Nation und Staat* was a scholarly reminder of the relevance of the supranational tradition in Austria. Seipel reflected none of the nostalgic pathos of a Novalis, the great German romanticist who a good

29 Vienna and Leipzig, 1916.   30 Thormann, *Seipel*, p. 19.

31 Seipel, *Neue Ziele und Aufgaben*, n.p.

32 Cf. Alfred Diamant, *Austrian Catholics and the First Republic: Democracy, Capitalism and the Social Order, 1918-1934* (Princeton, 1960), p. 100.

54

century before had looked back in his *Christenheit oder Europa* to the "beautiful and glorious time, when Europe was a Christian land, inhabited by one Christianity." Seipel was less panegyrical about the Austrian "mission" than his colleague Friedrich Wilhelm Foerster.[33] Neither did he indulge in tortured, baroque, apocalyptic visions like his friend Bahr, whose zest for old Austria after his earlier checkered intellectual career was somewhat excessive and unconvincing. Bahr had every reason to look up to Seipel's "cautious and discriminating intellect."[34] *Nation und Staat* was the work of a realist.

Indeed *Nation und Staat* was a Thomistic rather than an Augustinian work. St. Augustine had had to dissociate himself from the Roman Empire, which represented the *civitas terrena* and was doomed to failure through its essentially pagan character. Seipel could look back upon the Roman imperial tradition renewed and sanctified by the medieval Christian Empire and the Habsburg Empire.[35] The "mission of Austria" became therefore an essentially Christian one; it "strangely converges upon the Catholic Church."[36] For Seipel then, the *civitas terrena* and the *civitas dei* somehow converged upon each other in the Habsburg Monarchy. The mere fact of the convergence, which was Thomistic by nature, made Seipel confident about the *civitas terrena*. That is why he thought he could renew the time-honored motto *Austria erit in orbe ultima*.[37] That is why *Nation und Staat*, as a study of the idea and reality of the Christian commonwealth, was a testament to Seipel's indomitable and "exaggerated" optimism.[38] In the setting of the late years of Francis Joseph, however, it was an autumnal optimism.

The distinction of the book lies more in its polemical and politi-

[33] Cf. Friedrich Wilhelm Foerster, *Das österreichische Problem vom ethischen und staatspädagogischen Gesichtspunkt* (Vienna, 1914).

[34] Herman Bahr, *1917* (Innsbruck, 1918), pp. 175ff.

[35] Seipel, *Nation und Staat*, pp. 12, 17.

[36] Ibid., p. 19.   [37] Ibid., p. 20.

[38] "Übertriebener Optimismus," quoted in Thormann, *Seipel*, p. 27.

cal than in its scholarly aspects. The chapter on the fundamental law of organization,[39] for example, discusses tribe and race, folk and nation, state and empire—subjects which more than a hundred years earlier were covered more thoughtfully and far more beautifully by Herder. As a dissertation on the relationship between nation, state, and universal values it hardly compares in historical grasp and incisiveness with either Lord Acton's essays, written more than fifty years before, or Meinecke's monumental *Weltbürgertum und Nationalstaat*, which was published in 1911. The very fact that Seipel knew neither Acton's or Meinecke's work is proof of the isolation of Austrian Catholicism from the main currents of European culture. And if with this book Seipel was attempting to break out of this isolation by parading a vast bibliography of Austrian and German works both Catholic and non-Catholic, then his effort was a failure. The literature remained largely unabsorbed and unevaluated, and the strain of triviality which appeared in Seipel's earlier writing was by no means missing from his magnum opus.

Nevertheless, in spite of its weaknesses, *Nation und Staat* was a work of first importance. Its creative strength lay in the application of Catholic social theory to the Central European experience. The discussion of the various forms of organization reflected the map of Central Europe in which the dimensions of folk, nation, and state hopelessly overlapped, defying any obvious rational order. The idea of a Christian commonwealth had a legitimate testing ground in Central Europe, and in the year 1916 it had more than a theoretical relevance, especially if it represented, as it did to Seipel and his friends, an "attempt at organizing many peoples in freedom."[40]

The affinity of Seipel's basic approach to Lord Acton's thought is sufficiently striking to call for some comment. Both combined an affirmation of the modern world with an apology for one of

[39] Seipel, *Nation und Staat*, pp. 20-64.
[40] Hermann Bahr, "Der Augenblick Österreichs," *Neues Wiener Journal*, September 26, 1916.

the oldest supranational institutions in Europe. Lord Acton the liberal was well aware of the fact that "in Austria everything smacks of decline and fall."[41] However, Lord Acton the Catholic came to look toward Austria. Its multinational structure alone assured recognition of the "rights of nationality," while it defied what Lord Acton called the "theory of nationality,"[42] which made the state and the nation commensurate with each other. Because he rejected the nation-state, he came out after all in support of the Austrian Monarchy, since it offered the "conditions necessary for the highest degree of organization which government is capable of receiving." "Christianity," Lord Acton stated, "rejoices in the mixture of races."[43] Austria was therefore the model for a Christian commonwealth.

Seipel was only a little less ambivalent about the Monarchy than Acton. In principle it appeared to him as the "older and higher idea of state,"[44] and he set himself apart from the whole tradition of the nineteenth-century German unification movement. He maintained that by aiming at overcoming the separation of nation and state it led to an extreme form of nationalism and represented the idea of a "lower order" of state. Seen in this light, Bismarckian Germany was a child of the French Revolution, an "Eastern France," as one of the leading critics of Bismarck once put it.[45] Certainly, Seipel argued, "the new German Reich is not the resurrected old one."[46]

Seipel became associated with the tradition of the "enemies of Bismarck." It is on this level that Burckhardt's Basel, Acton's Munich, and Seipel's Salzburg converge. In one way or another

[41] Lord Acton, "Notes on the Present State of Austria" (1861), *Essays on Church and State* (London, 1952), p. 349.

[42] Lord Acton, "Nationality," *Essays on Freedom and Power* (Boston, 1948), p. 192.

[43] Ibid., p. 186.

[44] Seipel, *Nation und Staat*, p. 17.

[45] Constantin Frantz, *Die nationale Rechtseinheit und das Reichsgericht* (Augsburg, 1873), pp. 2, 7.

[46] Seipel, *Nation und Staat*, p. 13.

they were identified with the older Germany, the European Germany. As Salzburg was a bridge between west and east and north and south, Austria and Germany were to be a "bridge from one nation to another,"[47] and Austria in particular, as the "frontier,"[48] was conditioned to keep alive the idea of a Christian Empire.

At the same time, Seipel and his friends, like Lord Acton earlier, were critical of the actual structure of the Monarchy. The dualism of 1867, "invented by the Magyars and carried through with the help of the Germans" was "arbitrary and artificial."[49] And the Magyar and German pressure had the effect of precipitating a counterpressure from the Slav nationalities which threatened to break up the Monarchy.

A reform of the Monarchy—and Seipel's *Nation und Staat* was meant to serve as the outline for a last-minute reform—was to be based on the distinction between nation and state, which was, as he claimed, vital to the Central European experience. In the absence of identity between nation and state he saw the decisive difference in modern history between the German and Central European world on the one hand and western Europe on the other. His version of the "ideas of 1914" thus amounted also to a juxtaposition of the German world and the West, and to the assertion of the superiority of the former over the latter. The basis of his judgment, however, was not nationalistic but practical (in view of the Central European nationality structure) and religious. The nation-state, Seipel admitted, might be the most practical organization in some cases (that is, in Western Europe),[50] but "from the point of view of humanity" it was deficient.[51] In its exclusiveness it tended to negate the rights of other nations and

---

[47] Ibid., p. 17; cf. also p. 94.   [48] Ibid., p. 81.

[49] "Gewalttätig und gekünstelt," ibid., p. 133.

[50] Interesting is Lammasch's dissent on this point. In his copy of Seipel's *Nation und Staat*, which is in the possession of the Harvard Law School, he commented in a handwritten marginal "never and nowhere" ("niemals und nirgends"); ibid., p. 14.

[51] Ibid., pp. 13, 57.

to lead to "hatred among nations";[52] and it encouraged the formation of a self-sufficient unit which would assume the higher functions reserved for religion.

Like Acton, Seipel came to make an essential distinction between the creative "national self-consciousness,"[53] the equivalent of Acton's "rights of nationality," and the stifling "nationality principle,"[54] the equivalent of Acton's "theory of nationality." It should be added, though, that while Lord Acton used the necessity of safeguarding of the "rights of nationality" in relation to the state to press the prerogatives of religion, as well as to demonstrate an important test case for political liberty, the political dimension was less pronounced in Seipel's thought. Nevertheless it is important to note that in the middle of a war which marked the heights of the nationality principle, a Catholic clergyman should have taken the trouble to demonstrate its inapplicability to Central Europe and to stress its pernicious character.

In theoretical as well as political terms *Nation und Staat* constituted a significant breakthrough in spite of its obvious weaknesses as a work of scholarship. Jacques Droz, one of the leading authorities of our time on the nationality problem, hardly exaggerates, therefore, when he attributes to this work the merit of having "set the stage for a veritable transvaluation of values."[55]

In the first place, Seipel, with his emphasis on the distinction between Western European and Central European conditions, was on the brink of setting up models for the study of the theory of nationality that were to become the basis of the study of that problem between the two wars. These models, one derived from Renan's nation-state concept and the other from Herder's stress on the nation as a "natural organization" in contrast to the "artificial" state,[56] he later called the "French" and the "German" na-

---

[52] Ibid., p. 17.   [53] "Nationale Gesinnung," ibid., p. 70.

[54] "Nationalitätsprinzip," ibid., pp. 72f.

[55] Jacques Droz, *L'Europe Centrale: Évolution historique de l'idée de "Mitteleuropa"* (Paris, 1960), p. 270.

[56] Seipel, *Nation und Staat*, pp. 76, 11.

tionality concepts. The latter was based upon an "inalienable cultural and linguistic community."[57] It could not find its realization in a centralized, leveling state, but only in some form of supranational organization.

Secondly, by separating the nation from the state and the cultural realm from the realm of the state, Seipel echoed Lord Acton's concept of freedom and at the same time reinterpreted Thomistic and Leonine pluralistic social theory in terms of the freedom of nationalities. A plurality of nations within one state might turn out to be not a burden to the state but an asset, helping it to climb "hitherto unknown heights."[58]

Thirdly, the separation of nation and state allowed Seipel to develop the theme of an "exaggerated nationalism" in conflict with the universal Church.[59] A cautious pacifism winds itself through the whole of Seipel's argument, climaxing in the plea to keep the doors open between nations during the war between states.[60] As unrealistic as this argument may appear, it was a plea, under the watchful eyes of wartime censorship, for a disassociation of the Church from the war, and particularly from the increasingly troublesome German alliance. *Nation und Staat* was designed to achieve for the Catholic world what the conference of Zimmerwald had accomplished the year before for the Socialist International—namely, self-examination and commitment to peace.

Fourthly, *Nation und Staat* was an imaginative and extremely interesting contribution to the argument on imperial reform. While the book was meant to serve primarily as a statement of principles, it raised the concrete question of alternatives to the

[57] "Der französische Nationsbegriff"; "der deutsche (Fichtesche und übernommene tschechische) Nationsbegriff" based on "unveräusserlicher Kultur- und Sprachgemeinschaft"; "Aufzeichnungen von Unterredungen mit Seipel (16.6.32)"; Knoll Archive.

[58] Seipel, *Nation und Staat*, p. 80.   [59] Ibid., p. 70.

[60] Cf. in particular Seipel, *Nation und Staat*, pp. 140ff.

dualistic settlement of 1867 by disassociating itself from the stock answers of centralism and federalism. The former did not acknowledge the multinational character of the Monarchy and ignored the rights of nationality, and the latter, which was the magic word in Christian Socialist circles, Seipel did not consider feasible.[61]

Seipel, along with Lammasch, distinguished himself from the Catholic ranks by attempting to face up to the immense practical problems of imperial reform. In lieu of the "territorial principle" inherent in federalism, he advocated the "personal principle."[62] This would allow all members of a given nationality to join a national association of their choice, which would administer their national cultural affairs. He also proposed, after the pattern of the successful local "compromises" in Moravia in 1905 and Bukovina in 1910, that the number of representatives to be sent from each national group to the Reichsrat in Vienna be settled proportionately before the election on the basis of the national census. In this way he thought that the issue of centralism versus federalism could be reduced to a secondary and purely administrative one.

The question of the models which served Seipel in the definition of the personality principle, the boldest feature in his scheme, is pertinent here. There is no doubt that he fell back upon the work of Wenzel Frind (1843-1932), a German-Bohemian churchman and scholar, who in an elaborate treatise had emphasized that within a multinational framework the right to use one's language was based upon the law of nature and was attached not to a territory but to the person.[63] Furthermore, it is

[61] Ibid., pp. 127ff.
[62] "Territorialsystem," "Personalitätsprinzip," ibid., p. 138; for Lammasch cf. Heinrich Lammasch, *Europas elfte Stunde* (Munich, 1919), pp. 119-24.
[63] Wenzel Frind, *Das sprachliche und sprachlich-nationale Recht in polyglotten Staaten und Ländern mit besonderer Rücksichtnahme auf Österreich und Böhmen vom sittlichen Standpunkte beleuchtet* (Vienna, 1899).

distinctly ironic that Seipel should have followed the precedent set by the Social Democrats Karl Renner[64] and Otto Bauer. It was Renner (1870-1950), a Moravian by background, who, as librarian of the Reichsrat at the turn of the century, had thrown himself into the study of the nationality problem and published, under various pseudonyms, a number of important studies on the subject,[65] in which he developed the concept of "national autonomy" as a basis for imperial reform. He argued that "nationality by its nature is not primarily related to a territory."[66] As a socialist he maintained that the territorial principle was autocratic, but the personality principle would lead to the transformation of the Monarchy into a democratic federation of nationalities, as was envisioned by the Brno Party Congress in 1899. Similarly, Otto Bauer (1881-1938), his younger colleague, infinitely more aggressive and doctrinaire, a Jew whose parents had migrated from Bohemia to Vienna, suggested in his brilliant work on the nationality question and Social Democracy[67] that a haven be built for the workers on the basis of personal autonomy within the framework of the Monarchy. Unlike Renner he had little traditional reverence for the old Monarchy as such. Nevertheless he conceived of it as a convenient means at that point to help the worker subordinate his national self-consciousness to class interest. He therefore endorsed Renner's scheme as the "most perfect form of national autonomy."[68]

Renner's constant concern with the renewal of Austria and

[64] Cf. Kurt Adamus, "Die Theorie Ignaz Seipels über Nation und Staat und ihr Verhältnis zu Karl Renners Theorie über Staat und Nation (diss., Graz, 1952).

[65] In particular Synopticus (pseud. for Karl Renner), *Zur Österreichischen Nationalitätenfrage* (Vienna, 1899); *Staat und Nation* (Vienna, 1899); Rudolf Springer (pseud. for Karl Renner), *Der Kampf der österreichischen Nationen um den Staat. Erster Theil: Das nationale Problem als Verfassungs- und Verwaltungsfrage* (Leipzig and Vienna, 1902).

[66] Springer, *Der Kampf*, p. 35.

[67] Otto Bauer, *Die Nationalitätenfrage und die Sozialdemokratie* (Vienna, 1907).

[68] Ibid., p. 363.

Bauer's searching and more cold-blooded analysis of the nationality problem overshadowed in thoroughness and imagination the rather half-hearted efforts from the conservative camp. Seipel's lament, late in 1911, about the state of the Christian Socialist party certainly becomes more understandable in the light of this fact.[69] Clearly the Social Democrats had taken the lead in the exploration of the intricacies of the nationality problem; and Seipel, writing in the Monarchy's eleventh hour, stood to gain from their thinking.

The propinquity between Seipel's *Nation und Staat* and the Austromarxists ought not to appear too surprising, extending as it did into areas other than the technical one of the personality principle. In spite of the ideological gulf which separated the Catholic and the Marxist positions, there were some striking points of convergence. Both had supranational perspectives. Each was committed to a framework that was prepared to hold together a multinational flock threatened by the nationality struggle. For this reason particularly Austromarxism had grown into the Monarchy, under the leadership of Viktor Adler. In effect, through Renner's and Otto Bauer's works, it had explored ways of holding the Monarchy together. From very divergent points of departure then, Seipel and the Marxists converged upon the practicality of supranational organization, a convergence on a question that was no minor matter. It is reasonable to argue that, had the Monarchy held together, it might have led to a more comprehensive cooperation between the Christian Socialists and the Marxists. In any case, *Nation und Staat* was above all an argument against the Pan-German movement—its race concept, which was "erroneous" and "not to be taken seriously," and its irredentism, which was defeatist.[70] By contrast, Seipel quoted

---

[69] It is interesting to note in this connection that the Reichspost Bookstore turned down the publication of *Nation und Staat*, which was finally brought out by Braumüller (Rudolf Blüml, *Prälat Dr. Ignaz Seipel* [Klagenfurt, 1933], p. 247).

[70] Seipel, *Nation und Staat*, pp. 28f., 132, 125.

Renner in support of his position concerning the viability of supranational government.[71] And in turn the *Arbeiter-Zeitung* lost no time in coming out with an enthusiastic review of Seipel's book.[72] It noted that few other works had coped quite so "clearly and sharply" with the tedious nationality struggle, and singled out Seipel's emphasis on the "international" aspect of the problem —the crisis of cosmopolitanism and internationalism based on a fallacious identification of the nation with the state. As if to stress the irony inherent in the review, it concluded: "Who has written these splendid lines? A 'fellow without fatherland?' 'A Social Democrat of the most radical persuasion?' No, the author is a *Catholic clergyman* and professor at the theological faculty in Salzburg."

There was an additional aspect of this convergence in the thought of Seipel and the Social Democrats that only the review in the *Frankfurter Zeitung* touched upon. Singling out the Church, the nation, and class as "competitors of the state," it came to the conclusion that the nation-state was not an ideal solution, an argument which went beyond Seipel's explicitly stated one. However, Seipel was aiming at disentangling Church interests from excessively close ties with the state; and in agreement with the Austromarxists he stressed the separation of the nation from the state. Could this argument not be extended to include the prerogatives of class? *Nation und Staat* was an important document serving, in the Thomistic and Leonine tradition, the cause of a pluralistic society in which the various social organs would have their basic freedom from state interference. Certainly class as a "competitor of the state" could have a place in Seipel's scheme.

The affinity between Seipel and the Social Democrats, as sug-

[71] Ibid., p. 67.

[72] As was to be expected, most of the reviews appeared in Catholic papers. Notable among the exceptions was the review in the *Arbeiter-Zeitung*, written by "H.L.," which came out within a month of the book's publication, and another in the *Frankfurter Zeitung* of April 22, 1917, morning ed. ("H.L." turned out to be Heinrich Lammasch, who wrote repeatedly for the *Arbeiter-Zeitung*; Seipel diary, November 7 and 27, 1916.)

gested earlier, should not be exaggerated. Certainly it should be viewed in the context of the basic ideological opposition between Catholicism and Marxism which proved decisive after all and determined the political pattern of republican Austria in the twenties. Nevertheless, the common concern with imperial reform and pacifism, and the parallelism of interest vis-à-vis the state between the two internationals, the Church and socialism, are striking to the historian. If Seipel, in his book on the Church fathers, proved himself open-minded on the "social problem," he also proved himself open-minded on the "international problem" in *Nation und Staat*. In its tone and message *Nation und Staat* was a conciliatory work—a call for peace—but it also helped clear the ground for cooperation between the Catholic and Marxist camps in the first two years after the revolution, a cooperation which helped set up the Republic and whose collapse was altogether fatal to the future course of Austria.

Even though the world for which *Nation und Staat* was written soon collapsed, the book did not lose its relevance, certainly not for Seipel. More than a mere reform plan, it was after all a general statement of principles. It gave a Catholic view, and an unusually imaginative one, of peace between nations, and tackled specifically the thorny nationality problem in Central Europe. The book therefore remained relevant even after the Monarchy had collapsed. In fact, *Nation und Staat* was Seipel's favorite book, summarizing his theology and scholarship and anticipating his statesmanship. It was a link, not a break, between his *vita contemplativa* and his *vita activa*. It remained his guide throughout the last two years of the war, and in an even more challenging way after 1918.

The Plan for Imperial Reform and Seipel's "Personal Peace Policy"

During the months following the publication of *Nation und Staat* Seipel was almost feverishly active on behalf of imperial reform and in the cause of peace. He had become a public figure, and now traveled often to Vienna to give lectures and attend meetings. In March 1916 his teacher Schindler, about to retire from his chair at the university, had convinced him that his "time of probation"[73] in Salzburg was almost over. When Seipel was in Vienna in February 1917 conferring with the Cardinal and Max von Hussarek, the Minister of Education, the latter praised *Nation und Staat* warmly and asked him pointedly whether he was satisfied in Salzburg. Although Seipel replied in the affirmative "out of politeness," as he somewhat ruefully put it,[74] a sense of national urgency did draw him to Vienna. Old Francis Joseph had died in November 1916, and his successor and great-nephew, Charles, was known to be distressed by the increasingly disastrous effect of the war on his peoples, by the threat of the breakup of his Empire, and by the troublesome consequences of Germany's domination of the alliance of the Central Powers. Furthermore Charles was deeply religious, and it soon became evident that he was to be an "emperor of peace" who would miss no opportunity to enter into negotiations with the Entente powers and put an end to the fighting.

Seipel's draft of August 1917 for imperial reform owed its impetus largely to the accession of the new Emperor.[75] Among the many reform plans, official and unofficial, circulating during the last decades of the Monarchy's existence, Seipel's was distinguished by its unquestionable absence of special pleading, explicit or implicit, for any one nationality; it was aiming at "building Austria anew, organizing Austria in such a way as to quiet all centrifugal tendencies of the different population groups."[76] Going beyond *Nation und Staat*, Seipel set about implementing the principle of national autonomy, and even went as far as to affirm

[73] "Wartezeit"; Seipel diary, March 21, 1916.

[74] Seipel diary, February 14, 1917.

[75] Ignaz Seipel, "Gedanken zur Reform der österreichischen Verfassung 1917," *Der Kampf um die österreichische Verfassung* (Vienna and Leipzig, 1930), pp. 3-29.

[76] Ibid., p. 12; italics in original.

the Emperor's duty to break his oath to the existing constitution on the grounds that it would be immoral to maintain a poor constitution, and no one can be committed to immorality by an oath.[77] Thus the moral theologian, upon entering the political scene, was concerned with moral issues rather than procedural ones. In view of Austria's inexperience, rigid adherence to constitutionality smacked to him of "doctrinarism."[78] Seipel's commitment to constitutionality depended, then, not on principle, but on the possibility of achieving substantial goals. He was able to dispose of the struggle between ends and means in politics with the trite phrase, *salus publica suprema lex.*[79]

Along with the reform of empire Seipel concerned himself a great deal with the question of peace. These were twin issues not only for him but also for his friends. At this time he had a casual connection with Para Pacem, an Austrian association created before the war to further "understanding among the peoples" in which Schindler and Lammasch were active.[80] In fact, when early in 1916 the organization circulated an inquiry concerning the "mutual relation among the peoples after the war" among high dignitaries of the state and the universities, Seipel came up with the shortest and most succinct answer: "I lead a continuous fight against the artificial stirring up of animosity against the members of other nations, and I advocate, wherever possible, the maintenance of the cultural community among the European nations."[81] More important, he was in touch with the circle that was active on behalf of peace, formed in the capital around the solicitous Viennese merchant Julius Meinl (1869-1944). Meinl stood in close relation to Lammasch and Josef Redlich (1869-1933), an internationally recognized authority on law and political sci-

---

[77] Ibid., p. 13.   [78] Ibid., p. 26.   [79] Ibid., p. 13.

[80] Cf. Heinrich Benedikt, *Die Friedensaktion der Meinlgruppe 1917/18: Die Bemühungen um einen Verständigungsfrieden nach Dokumenten, Aktenstücken und Briefen* (Graz and Cologne, 1962), p. 56.

[81] "Rundfrage des Verbandes 'Para Pacem' über das gegenseitige Verhältnis der Völker nach dem Kriege," *Para Pacem* (May 1916), p. 24.

ence and one of Austria's keenest political observers, and also to Friedrich Wilhelm Foerster in Munich. To give his circle a public outlet, he founded in December 1915 the Österreichische Politische Gesellschaft,[82] which brought together the political and professional elite of Vienna.

Yet in looking back on the war years later in his life, Seipel could refer to his "personal peace policy."[83] For in the pursuit of peace he had indeed been a loner of sorts. Once removed from the urbane, informal activism of the Viennese group, the Salzburg theologian, somewhat dogged and parochial, insisted on outlining a specifically Catholic approach to peace and dismissing those of other persuasions. While he did not concur with the Quakers' unconditional rejection of war, he directed most of his criticism against the progressive, secular peace movement. The "liberal" Bertha von Suttner, Austria's winner of the Nobel Peace Prize, was to him an "unpleasant literary figure" who, together with her friends, made herself "ridiculous."[84] The democratic forces of peace emanating from the U.S. and France were "superficial."[85] In May 1917 he published an important article on the problem of peace in the influential Catholic newspaper *Reichspost*.[86] His argument, juxtaposing the right and the wrong—that is, the Catholic and the Wilsonian—answers to the problem, was homespun, and its vocabulary awkward, but it was nevertheless a strikingly perceptive critique of Wilson's peace formula, for it did suggest that the Wilsonian model of self-determination was inapplicable to Central Europe. Democracy—that is, majority

---

[82] Cf. Benedikt, *Die Friedensaktion*, pp. 13ff.

[83] "Meine persönliche Friedenspolitik"; letter to Professor Dr. Josef Zuck, Vienna, July 2, 1919, in Alexander Novotny, "Ignaz Seipel im Spannungsfeld zwischen den Zielen des Anschlusses und der Selbständigkeit Österreichs," *Österreich in Geschichte und Literatur*, VII, no. 6 (1963), 265.

[84] Ignaz Seipel, "Der Pazifismus und die Katholiken," *Kultur*, XVII (1916), 6.

[85] Ibid., 7.

[86] Ignaz Seipel, "Wege und Irrwege in der Weltfriedensfrage," *Reichspost*, May 27, 1917.

rule—was not the answer for an area in which language was the source of the nationality struggle, and Wilson had not recognized this stubborn fact. Self-determination would lead to the suppression of the rights of minorities rather than to the "reconciliation of nations." Seipel therefore felt that he had to warn his fellow Catholic pacifists, especially Lammasch, against the Wilsonian "fallacy"; indeed Lammasch complained that this warning was "insufficiently polite toward Wilson."[87] Seipel's fears were borne out after the war when Wilson's prescriptions could not be applied consistently and when they did not in any case bring about the "reconciliation of nations."

The contrast between the "right approach" of the Catholics and the "wrong approach" of the Quakers, liberals, or Wilsonians enabled Seipel to differentiate between "true peace" and "false peace," in keeping with his two-level view of political reality. Seipel realized, however, that he could not favor the Catholic peace movement which he had advocated at one point.[88] To do so would have meant engaging in basic controversy with the progressive peace movement, and this was against the wishes of Pope Benedict XV, who wanted to call upon the help of "friends of peace all over the world."[89] In any case, this realization was in keeping with his conciliatory position on the university question and with his involvement in the "struggle of orientation," and he therefore saw the need of falling into line with the general peace effort.

Toward the summer of 1917 Seipel's Salzburg friends were more and more drawn to the capital. Salzburg was too remote. They were attracted by the climate created in Vienna by the Emperor Charles, who was determined to set Austria on a new course and after the resignation of the Prime Minister Clam-

[87] "Aufzeichnungen von Unterredungen mit Seipel (16.6.32)"; Knoll Archive.

[88] Seipel, "Der Pazifismus," p. 9.

[89] Seipel to Baron Angelo de Eisenhof, Salzburg, January 25, 1917; Nationalbibliothek, Vienna.

Martinič on June 18[90] had begun a search for a new peace cabinet which drew the Lammasch-Meinl-Redlich-Foerster group into his orbit.

Three times, on June 22, July 10, July 21, Lammasch was called upon by the Emperor to form a government; but the sickly, modest old man, fully aware of his lack of political experience, declined each offer. Moreover, on July 5, after two audiences with Emperor Charles, the ambitious Redlich, the only one of the group with any political sense, was asked to form a government; but he failed in his negotiations with the party leaders. Occasionally the name of the impetuous Friedrich Wilhelm Foerster appeared on cabinet lists, but Foerster in his boundless idealism had overestimated the Emperor's determination and exaggerated the chances for a government led by his friend Lammasch.

All in all the story of this search reveals a high-minded, weak, and vacillating monarch in negotiation with equally high-minded but almost wholly inexperienced and politically weak men. Foreign Minister Count Ottokar Czernin was not far wrong when he emphasized in a memorandum that the purpose of forming a new government was to form not a "League of Virtue" (*Tugendbund*) but an able cabinet to direct Austrian policy.[91] The *Tugendbund* did not materialize, for the time being at least. The brief and futile search for a peace cabinet drove home the fact that at this critical moment Austria was headed by an idealistic monarch, all too gentle and vacillating, and that the men closest to him lacked the political acumen as well as the will and ability to act.

Seipel, who among his group of friends had the greatest gift for politics, had not figured in these negotiations. As yet he had not sufficiently proved himself as a politician, but he was moving close to the center of things. In the middle of May he heard that

[90] It was understood that his immediate successor, von Seidler, was to serve only in a caretaker capacity.

[91] Reinhold Lorenz, *Kaiser Karl und der Untergang der Donaumonarchie* (Graz, Vienna and Cologne, 1959), p. 386.

he would be proposed as Schindler's successor at the university.[92]
During a ten-day trip to Vienna at the end of May he attended
to old business and new, busily shuttling between the Ministry
of Education, the university, the Leo-Gesellschaft, peace groups,
and the headquarters of the Christian Socialist party. A letter
from Lammasch to Meinl on September 5 ended with the news:
"Bahr is also active. Seipel has already moved to Vienna (address: university)."[93] From then on Seipel's name figured regularly in the communications between Lammasch and Meinl on
behalf of the "peace action" which culminated in Lammasch's
negotiations with George D. Herron, Woodrow Wilson's unofficial emissary, in February 1918, which, however, remained
inconclusive.

At about the time that Seipel moved to the capital, the influential Vienna daily, *Neues Wiener Journal*, carried the following
profile by his friend Bahr:

> Already from his fine work *Nation und Staat* . . . we know
> Seipel as a conciliatory man. . . . He is a man of varied and
> mutually complementary gifts, among which moderation to
> a point almost of pedantry, distrust of all extremes, and the
> need to discriminate sharply are as little lacking as is a nat-
> ural instinctive caution against violent decisions. Such a
> well-advised, circumspect man will best know how to help
> us. He neither ignores the fact that our whole history speaks
> against centralism, nor does he conceal his doubts concern-
> ing federalism . . . and he expects justice for all and domestic
> peace only on the basis of national autonomy. . . .
>
> This man must be strong enough to make our peoples see
> at last with their own eyes. No such man has as yet fallen
> from heaven. It must be a man who comes from below [*aus
> der Tiefe*]. It must be a man in whom the people recognizes
> itself, the Austrian people which lives in all our nations. It

[92] Seipel diary, May 16, 1917.
[93] Benedikt, *Friedensaktion*, p. 162.

must be a man in whom our whole need [*Not*] and our whole longing has found expression. And much as fools may now malign our Commonwealth [*Volkshaus*], I have the faith that it will produce this man, the husband of Austria.[94]

Six years before the young theologian Seipel had expressed his thoughts on leadership in the *Kirchenzeitung*. And now a well-known man of letters was introducing the same theologian, on the verge of a great career, to the public in an extravagant panegyric. The crisis of leadership within the Christian Socialist party had meanwhile widened into a crisis of leadership in the Monarchy. And did Emperor Charles's indecision and his inability to find a forceful and imaginative prime minister not indicate the more fundamental troubles of the Monarchy? But these were dimensions which evidently did not touch Hermann Bahr. At the time it was said of him that, alongside Redlich and Renner, he was the only person who believed in the necessity of Austria.[95] He carried the proverbial Austrian sense of unreality to the point of aggressively mystical faith in the Austrian mission and indeed in the cleric whom he had elected to represent it.

If Hermann Bahr had been foolhardy in his indomitable faith in Austria's resurrection, he was not mistaken about the man on whom he banked. He had had the opportunity of observing the *homo novus* from nearby. The Church had given more scope to this priestly scholar than the bureaucracy of the late Empire could have done. Within the Church Seipel had developed his style, and at every crossroad so far he had chosen the forward and "confident" way. Above and beyond this he had consistently played the role of mediator, and following the example of St. Ambrose, the "practical Roman" type,[96] he had demonstrated the

[94] *Neues Wiener Journal*, October 14, 1917.

[95] Redlich diary, July 22, 1917, in Fritz Fellner, ed., *Schicksalsjahre Österreichs 1908-1919* (Vienna, 1954), ii, 223.

[96] Ignaz Seipel, "Der heilige Ambrosius von Mailand. Ein literarisches Charakterbild," *Über den Wassern*, vi (August 1913), 445.

need for moderation and compromise. "The civilization of mankind calls for compromise,"[97] he stated in his review of the function of the Austrian Empire. The "husband of Austria," as Bahr glowingly called him, seemed committed to the Austrian tradition, which he himself later defined as "governing and administering with gentle means, of waiting patiently and experimenting."[98] The author of *Nation und Staat* promised to carry this tradition into the future, whatever that future was to be.

The Salzburg years were clearly years of preparation for Seipel. In the light of his 1911 article and his preoccupation with St. Ambrose as a "born adviser and pastor of the great," as "bishop and statesman,"[99] it can be safely assumed that it was quite a conscious preparation. When Seipel, then forty-one years old and in the prime of life, moved to the University of Vienna, it was evident to those who knew him that he was destined for still greater responsibilities, whether in Church, party, or state. With amazing equanimity and confidence he moved into a position that was likely to test all his notions concerning the working of Christian ethics in the hard-and-fast realities of politics.

[97] "Die Kultur der Menschheit verlangt nach Ausgleich," Seipel, *Nation und Staat*, pp. 94f.

[98] Ignaz Seipel, "Österreichische Tradition," *Winkelried*, Eger/Cheb, Czechoslovakia, viii (December 1920).

[99] Seipel, "Der heilige Ambrosius," 436.

Three

REVOLUTION BY CONSENSUS
AND THE POLICY OF
ACCOMMODATION: 1918-1920

". . . Guarding the Exit of Habsburg"

THE capital to which Seipel returned in the autumn of 1917 had lost much of its traditional gaiety. The clouds of war hung over it and the specter of disillusionment was increasingly evident. The reconvening of Parliament in May 1917 emphasized the fact that the *Burgfriede* of August 1914 was no longer a reality. Neither the reestablishment of constitutionalism nor the July amnesty were able to prevent the increasing disaffection of the non-German delegates to Parliament, particularly the Czechs and Southern Slavs. Vienna was no longer an effective capital of the Empire. Since the failure of Emperor Charles in July to turn over the affairs of the Monarchy to Lammasch and his friends, all hopes in this direction had vanished; it was increasingly evident that he did not have the strength to make decisions, being, according to an entry in Redlich's diary, "too undistinguished a man,"[1] and Seidler, his Prime Minister, was a bureaucrat from whom no decisive policy could be expected.

Seipel had no illusions about the situation. He did not shield himself against the "very unfavorable news"[2] and registered in his letters to Lammasch his unrelenting opposition to the Prime Minister for his "weakness and inefficiency."[3] His removal was for Seipel an imperative necessity if Austria was to survive, and in January 1918, when weariness and hunger caused two hundred

[1] "Zu wenig, ein zu unwesentlicher Mensch," Redlich diary, April 6, 1922, at the occasion of the Emperor's death, "Politische Tagebücher 1920-1936."

[2] Seipel diary, September 17, 1917.

[3] Seipel to Lammasch, Vienna, January 21, 1918.

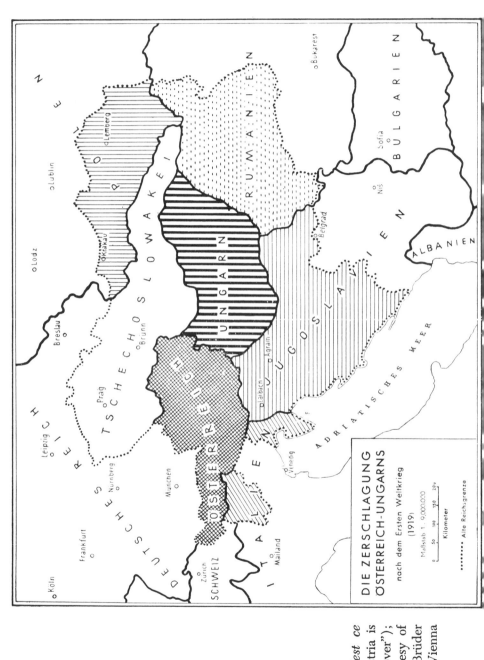

L'Autriche c'est ce qui reste ("Austria is what is left over"); 1919. Courtesy of Verlag Brüder Hollinek, Vienna

thousand Viennese workers to strike, the "helplessness, lack of ideas, and weakness of the government and all parties including the Social Democrats"[4] became painfully evident to Seipel; he reported back to Salzburg that in Vienna one continued "dancing on top of the volcano."[5]

Although the new *Ordinarius* in Vienna therefore had reason enough to look back with a certain nostalgia to the "good hours"[6] spent with Lammasch in Salzburg, his overriding reaction to Vienna was one of satisfaction in being closer to the center of action. He had lived long enough in the protective calm of Salzburg, and was now eager to face the challenge of a new sphere of activity. In Catholic circles he became virtually a vogue, which he himself explained whimsically by the fact that while there were very few people who were confidence-inspiring and at the same time accessible, he himself had been in Vienna too briefly to have betrayed anyone's confidence;[7] and it was then that Schindler remarked to the cautious Dr. Funder, "You will see: he [Seipel] is a man of the future."[8]

His continued preoccupation with imperial reform and peace took Seipel further into the tempting world of politics. He sat in on numerous discussions on constitutional reform, which brought him close to the Christian Socialist party, whose parliamentary club elected him in February 1918 to a fifteen-member commission to explore the subject. It is interesting to note that even in these first direct encounters there was a certain coolness between Seipel and the party which he was eventually to lead. He later recalled that he had entered the party as an "outsider"[9]—as a priest rather than as a party man. And as the Christian Socialist party continued to lose its *élan*, as the Imperial party, so-called, was

[4] Ibid.   [5] Ibid.
[6] Seipel to Lammasch, Vienna, December 24, 1917.
[7] Ibid.
[8] Friedrich Funder, *Vom Gestern ins Heute* (Vienna and Munich, 1952), p. 334.
[9] Seipel to Bahr, Vienna, June 19, 1920; Bahr Archive, Nationalbibliothek, Vienna.

turning into a party of petty ward politicians, Seipel had reason to complain about its "lack of direction."[10] Indeed his six-point program, which he presented in February 1918 to the parliamentary caucus of the party, was not too well received.[11] It amounted to a reformulation of his earlier memorandum and was only partially adopted by the party, which balked on two essential points —the personality principle and the reorganization of the Upper House along lines of nationality; so the party draft, which otherwise incorporated the bulk of Seipel's proposals, concluded with this statement: "The Christian Socialist Association of the House of Representatives will see to it that at the occasion of the constitutional reform the position of the German population group in Austria which was obtained by virtue of its political, cultural, and economic contribution to our commonwealth, will not be disadvantageously affected."[12] The party after all could not free itself from the notion of German preponderance, and no statement could have been more in conflict with the spirit of Seipel's reform efforts.

Seipel's sense of urgency over the peace issue and his vigilance concerning "rampant militarism within" as well as "all German efforts" to "ruin" the peace[13] took him from mass meeting to lecture platform and, together with Lammasch, to a peace mission in Zurich where a meeting of the International Catholic Union was called late in January 1918 with the purpose of coordinating

[10] He also claimed that a man like Funder, who had come to see the need for a peace settlement, was "prevented by the party" from taking an overt stand on the issue; Seipel to Lammasch, Vienna, January 21, 1918.

[11] Ignaz Seipel, "Grundgedanken für die Reform der österreichischen Verfassung," in *Der Kampf um die österreichische Verfassung* (Vienna and Leipzig, 1930), pp. 38-41. Cf. "Prof. Dr. Ignaz Seipel unterbreitet nachstehende Grundlagen für die Reform der österreichischen Verfassung," n.d., Seipel Archive.

[12] Franz Sommeregger (Constitutional Commission, Christian Socialist Parliamentary Club), "Verfassungs- und Verwaltungsreform," n.d., Seipel Archive.

[13] Seipel to Lammasch, Vienna, January 21, 1918.

78

Catholic peace efforts.[14] There Seipel met some of the German Catholic leaders, including Erzberger, Heinrich Held of the Bavarian Center party, and Karl Muth, the editor of *Hochland.*

At the same time the forceful and outspoken Count Botho Wedel, German ambassador to Vienna, was reporting to Berlin that "the Emperor consults preferably with pacifists, clergymen, and other irresponsible persons."[15] Lammasch in particular was singled out as a "pernicious influence at court."[16] Lammasch's and Seipel's trip had, indeed, been made at the Emperor's behest, and Lammasch continued his journey from Zurich to Berne for secret meetings with George Herron on February 3 and 4. Seipel, however, returned to Vienna and faced his first encounter with the Emperor. All we know is that on February 15 he reported on the Zurich conference at the supreme headquarters in Baden for an audience.[17] Another audience followed on June 1 in the park of the Laxenburg Castle.[18] It was a hurried affair covering the whole range of foreign policy and including the fatal case of the Foreign Minister Count Ottokar Czernin, who for his role in the Sixtus Affair had been forced to resign in April 1918.[19] Altogether

[14] Seipel to Lammasch, Vienna, January 21, 1918.

[15] Kaiserliche Botschaft in Wien, Strictly Confidential Dispatch A6567, Wedel to Count Georg Hertling, February 10, 1918; German Foreign Office (G.F.O.), S.A. (Saint Antony's College), Roll 24.

[16] Kaiserliche Botschaft in Wien, A9743 Wedel to Hertling, "Stimmung in Österreich," March 2, 1918, S.A., Roll 24.

[17] Seipel diary, February 15, 1918; cf. also Seipel Memorandum to Emperor Charles, Vienna, February 5, 1918, Archive of the Archdiocese, Salzburg.

[18] Seipel to Lammasch, Vienna, June 2, 1918; cf. Fritz Fellner, ed., *Schicksalsjahre Österreichs 1908-1919: Das politische Tagebuch Josef Redlichs* (Graz, 1954), II, 277.

[19] It was Seipel who, after a conference with the Prelate Johann Hauser, Governor (*Landeshauptmann*) of Upper Austria and head of the Christian Socialist caucus in Parliament, had prevailed upon the *Reichspost* to take the side of Emperor Charles in this matter; *Reichspost*, April 20, 1918; Seipel diary, April 21, 1918; cf. Redlich diary, June 6, 1918, *Schicksalsjahre*, II, 277.

The Policy of Accommodation

Seipel found the monarch, while consciously engaged in playing for time, still strongly, too strongly, optimistic.[20]

In the summer of 1918, Seipel got an official inquiry from Salzburg whether in view of the Archbishop's death he would be willing to be considered as his successor.[21] In the midst of the rapidly deteriorating political situation, it looked as though this was a last chance for Seipel to withdraw and return to the peace of Salzburg, this time as its spiritual head. As was to be expected, Seipel answered in the affirmative. His program of action in case of his election evidenced a realistic, practical mind at work and aware of the "princely," that is political, aspects of the office which included promoting "peace among the states as well as within the Monarchy."[22] Was it God's will that he be elected, or would He prefer the "calmer ways" of the Suffragan Bishop, Ignatius Rieder?

Rieder was elected and even if, unlike Seipel, we cannot attribute this decision to a direct interference of God, it was somehow in line with the whole development of Seipel's recent life. He had moved steadily toward a broader political life and was committed to it. What had he meant when he wrote to his friend Lammasch in June that there might still be a chance to "interfere" in things and that he still was hoping for "the salvation"?[23] In any case, by midsummer of 1918, Seipel had gone past the point of no return and was definitely launched into politics. And he may have felt that after long years of preparation he was on the threshold of a challenging career, though certainly stormy compared to the one which Salzburg had promised. Was it modesty alone that prompted the entry in his diary at this moment that he felt himself best suited after all to "completely quiet desk work"?[24]

[20] Seipel to Lammasch, Vienna, June 2, 1918.
[21] Rudolf Blüml, *Ignaz Seipel, Mensch, Christ, Priester in seinem Tagebuch* (Vienna, 1934), pp. 53ff.
[22] Ibid., p. 56.
[23] Seipel to Lammasch, Vienna, June 17, 1918.
[24] "Eine ganz stille Schreibtischarbeit," Seipel diary, August 14, 1918.

80

"Guarding the Exit of Habsburg"

In the light of what we know of the strains which existed in the Habsburg Monarchy during the war, it is surprising how little sense of urgency there was in Vienna. But in crises societies have an understandable tendency to cling to old-established and familiar ways and to reject thoughts of doom and catastrophe. Francis Joseph's Austria, for better or worse, had also developed a talent for muddling through, minimizing hard facts that tended to disturb the customary sense of reality and saying, as Robert Musil whimsically recorded, *"Es ist passiert,* 'it just sort of happened' . . . when other people in other places thought heaven knows what had occurred."

Even the dissenters in the Monarchy, such as Lammasch and his friends, shared this self-deception. They prepared memoranda, gave speeches, wrote articles warning of possible castastrophe, but even so, in retrospect, they can be accused of too much lethargy, too much confidence and civility, and finally of having failed to take over the direction of the state in the summer of 1917 when there was still some hope of reform and survival.

But the mood in Vienna changed radically in the summer of 1918. At the front the combined impact of the ill-fated battle of the Piave against the Italians in July and the crumbling of the Bulgarian front leading to the Bulgarian armistice of September 29 finally reduced Vienna to a state of panic. At home the stirrings of the non-German nationalities, particularly the Czechs and Southern Slavs, backed up by exile committees, and the activities of the German parties themselves in turning their backs upon the Imperial idea were a clear reflection of the degree to which a sudden sense of emergency had taken over.

It was about this time, in the late summer of 1918, that Lammasch moved to Vienna to be closer to events, as they took a rapid turn for the worse. The hour had come for Lammasch and his friends, but alas it was the eleventh hour of the Monarchy. But Lammasch moved gingerly into position, unimpressed by the various cabinet lists put before his eyes by the Prime Minister Max von Hussarek or circulated at court, which invariably in-

The Policy of Accommodation

cluded him, frequently Redlich, and once also Seipel.[25] As though time was not a factor in a fast deteriorating situation, he continued to let himself be guided by his personal modesty and professorial aloofness.

Not even the issuance of the Imperial Manifesto of October 16 prevailed upon Lammasch to abandon his reserve. The Emperor, addressing himself to his "Austrian peoples," announced that the "reconstruction of the fatherland" was to be brought about with their free cooperation. The beautiful language of the document, with its vision of a Habsburg commonwealth reborn in the form of a "federation of free peoples," only dimly disguised the fact that at best it was a desperate move by the young sovereign to bring about an "honorable peace" on essentially Wilsonian terms and thus to salvage his Empire.[26] And only after Wilson's long-delayed answer to the Austrian request for negotiations had become known in Vienna on October 20, dashing all chances for a settlement on the basis of the Fourteen Points and spelling the death sentence of the dynasty, did Lammasch, the *cunctator*, having reserved for himself the role of *liquidator*, take over the helm of the state. After Hussarek's resignation on October 22 the selection of his successor was a foregone conclusion. Lammasch became Prime Minister almost by elimination. Unworldly though he was, he was the one person of prominence in the vast Empire who was not in one way or another politically compromised; he

[25] For a Hussarek-Lammasch-Redlich-Seipel combination (October 20) cf. Josef Redlich, "Heinrich Lammasch als Ministerpräsident," in *Heinrich Lammasch, Seine Aufzeichnungen, sein Wirken und seine Politik*, ed. Marga Lammasch and Hans Sperl (Vienna and Leipzig, 1922), p. 168; Redlich diary, October 20, 1918, *Schicksalsjahre*, II, 305; Z.703-Präs. Seipel to "Lieber hochw. Kollege," December 17, 1918, Haus-, Hof-, und Staatsarchiv, Vienna, Neues Politisches Archiv 1918-1938 (St.A.), Präsidialakten des Staatssekretärs Dr. Otto Bauer, K.262. Seipel was supposed to take over the Ministry of Social Welfare.

[26] For an exemplary monograph disentangling origins, purposes, and effects of the Manifesto cf. Helmut Rumpler, *Das Völkermanifest Kaiser Karls vom 16. Oktober 1918* (Munich, 1966).

82

was the one man to whom friend and foe, within the Monarchy as well as without, could look up as a moral authority. Finally, upon Redlich's insistence, Lammasch accepted, and together they drew up the list of ministers which included most of those from the Hussarek government. But the new look was provided by the new Prime Minister himself, by Redlich, who was to be Minister of Finance, and after special urging on the part of Lammasch, by Ignaz Seipel, who was chosen to direct the Ministry of Social Welfare.[27]

Lammasch, Redlich, and Seipel, all formerly from the "sulking corner" then took over the affairs of state. Foerster had retired to Munich to teach, and emerged in November 1918 as Minister Plenipotentiary to Switzerland, representing Kurt Eisner's Bavarian People's Republic.[28] Meinl, it was thought, lacked the necessary authority to be considered seriously for a political position. While earlier he had been respected by his friends for being a singularly "far-sighted merchant,"[29] as time passed he had revealed himself to be a dabbler in politics, a somewhat irrelevant person whose ideas were adjudged "foolish,"[30] and even his motives questioned. Was he really concerned with peace and peacemaking, or was his political activity only a "front" for "purely commercial purposes"?[31] In short, Meinl had not worn well with his friends. As for Hermann Bahr, he had reached the apex of his personal ambition when he had become the over-zealous director

[27] Initially, Lammasch had some misgivings concerning Seipel because of his connections with the Church, and at one time had given thought to forestalling anticlerical criticism by the appointment of Dr. Julius Tandler, a distinguished Jew and Social Democrat and an authority on public health. But when it was called to his attention that Josef Redlich himself was of Jewish origin he was satisfied with the balance in the new government.

[28] Allan Mitchell, *Revolution in Bavaria 1918-1919: The Eisner Regime and the Soviet Republic* (Princeton, 1965), pp. 129f.

[29] Seipel to Baron Angelo Eisner de Eisenhof, Salzburg, January 25, 1917, Nationalbibliothek, Vienna.

[30] Redlich diary, October 24, 1918, *Schicksalsjahre*, II, 308.

[31] Seipel to Lammasch, Vienna, January 21, 1918.

of the famous Burgtheater in Vienna and dedicated himself entirely to what Redlich called "mere theater politics."[32]

Lammasch, having taken over the burden of leadership, had no illusions. Knowing well how desperate things were, his decision actually amounted to a grandly stoic act. And while Redlich and Seipel shared this sense of dedication, as younger men they also saw the situation as a greater challenge. Redlich was intrigued at the thought of being perhaps the "last old-Austrian Minister of Finance,"[33] and Seipel, as he later stated in his usual colloquial manner, was pleased to be "on the team" rather than a mere spectator having to witness all the shattering events "from afar."[34] What for the saintly Lammasch was a final sacrifice, for the zealous Seipel was a new challenge, where the politician overshadowed the priest. Out of his deep feeling and concern for his country came his great opportunity.

After the swearing-in ceremonies of the new ministry amid all the "proud splendor" of the Hofburg's Alexander Apartment, the Emperor received each cabinet member individually in private audience. Redlich staying almost three-quarters of an hour, found the Emperor worn and pale, and left with a sense of being "empty and tired."[35] To Seipel the Emperor pointed out that he was the first clergyman to act as an Austrian minister, and admonished him to take a firm hold on his office, lest those having little fear of the clergy seek to dominate him.[36] Little did the young ruler know his new minister and of what stuff he was made.

The new cabinet met continuously, but it was helpless in the face of oncoming castastrophe. The first cabinet meeting in the

[32] Redlich diary, October 25, 1918, *Schicksalsjahre*, II, 308.

[33] Ibid., p. 309.

[34] Z.703-Präs. Seipel to "Lieber hochw. Kollege," December 17, 1918, St.A., K.262.

[35] Redlich diary, October 28, 1918, *Schicksalsjahre*, II, 309f.

[36] Seipel diary, October 28, 1918.

84

afternoon of October 28, dedicated to a statement of policy phrased upon Lammasch's request by Seipel, was interrupted by news of a Prague coup and then by the arrival of representatives of the German National Council, a shadow government which soon was to replace the imperial government in German Austria. Lammasch presided "amicably but without real energy."[37] The statement of policy, while calling for the creation of "independent national states," conjured up in a "cautious form" for the last time before the fall Lammasch's and Seipel's imperial vision of the possibility of a "coordination," whether on the basis of constitutional or international law.[38] In fact, however, the one function left to the cabinet was to wind up affairs in a dignified and orderly manner. Even Lammasch's label "peace cabinet"[39] was a euphemism; it was no more than a liquidation cabinet. It was confronted with the hard-and-fast realities of secession, of the surrender and the collapse of the imperial armed forces.

The two items left to the discretion of the cabinet were its own resignation and the Emperor's abdication. It was in connection with these morbid issues that Seipel, the political novice among experts, displayed his toughness, skill, and ingenuity and was catapulted into a position of decisive importance. "There was a presence about him," reminisced the man who kept the minutes of the cabinet meetings, "which elicited a kind of special confidence one has toward a personality of unusual significance."[40] Seipel took the lead in vigorously opposing the cabinet's resignation, which came up for discussion on November 1,[41] thus disagreeing with his friend Redlich.[42] "The Minister of Social Welfare," so read the minutes of the cabinet meeting of November 6,

[37] Redlich diary, October 28, 1918, *Schicksalsjahre*, ii, 310.
[38] Allgemeines Verwaltungsarchiv, Vienna (A.V.A.), Ministerrats-Protokoll 64 (M.R. 64), October 28, 1918.
[39] A.V.A., M.R. 69, November 1, 1918.
[40] Robert Ehrhart, *Im Dienste des alten Österreich* (Vienna, 1958), p. 407.
[41] A.V.A., M.R. 69, November 1, 1918.
[42] Redlich diary, November 1, 1918, *Schicksalsjahre*, ii, 312.

once again speaks up against the resignation of the cabinet on grounds both of principle and the following considerations. . . . One should not oneself anticipate the course of events. There was no dignified great occasion that would justify the resignation. In want of such an occasion it would be regarded as a demonstration, be it in the sense of an abandonment of hope for the Monarchy or in the sense of a kind of protest against German-Austria.

Besides, the resignation was not in the best interests of German-Austria which has not even been granted international recognition and therefore, by the terms of international law, is not capable of negotiating. It was the task of the present government to function as trustee for German-Austria as well as for the other national states.

Furthermore, the name of the Prime Minister signified an important consideration in the peace question, which one should not forego. Finally the government should make all efforts to prevent His Majesty from irrevocably breaking his ties with the state; it certainly could, in this respect, not take the initiative.[43]

Thus spoke the man who two days before, on the Emperor's name day, had attended the traditional Emperor Mass in St. Stephen's Cathedral with the rest of the cabinet and the dignitaries of state and Church, and, when removed from the turbulence outside, had sent to heaven his "God save, God guard our Emperor" to the tune of Haydn's time-honored melody.

Seipel's brief was most impressive for its dispassionate tone concerning a question charged with emotion. It was not sentimentality which bound him to the House of Habsburg but, for the moment at least, a sense of loyalty, of dignity, and of statesmanlike reasoning with which one might agree or disagree. And in these days of crumbling events and values, a certain impressive independence was evident in Seipel, who was following his

[43] A.V.A., M.R. 73, November 6, 1918.

own conscience and who seemed willing even to swim against the stream if necessary. While some colleagues urged resignation in order to preserve their public image,[44] as a priest, Seipel could disregard such considerations. After a sharp argument in the council of the cabinet, in which Baron Karl von Banhans, the senior member and Minister of Railroads, led the opposition to Seipel, it was decided that on the following day a delegation consisting of the Prime Minister, Banhans, and Seipel should submit the problem to the Emperor. In a long audience in Schönbrunn on November 7, Seipel's point of view prevailed, and it was decided that for the time being the cabinet, particularly Lammasch, Redlich, and Seipel,[45] was to stay in office. The Emperor, reaffirming his confidence in Lammasch, asked his ministers, in a language once again evoking the bonds of Habsburg overlordship, not to "desert him."[46]

Immediately afterwards, the problem of the Emperor's abdication became acute, precipitated in part by the German Kaiser's abdication on November 9. On the evening of the following day, the Socialist leaders Renner and Seitz approached Lammasch with the urgent demand that the Emperor abdicate lest the revolutionary situation get out of hand. On November 9 a republic in Germany had been proclaimed by the Social Democrat Scheidemann partly to prevent a Spartacist take-over. In German-Austria the problem, as Redlich put it, was a similar one of preventing "the street" from proclaiming the republic and the Red Guard from marching on Schönbrunn.[47] The threat from "the street" did not exclusively come from the extreme Left. The *"pereat* Lammasch" calls outside the building in the narrow Her-

[44] Redlich, "Heinrich Lammasch," *Heinrich Lammasch*, ed. Marga Lammasch and Hans Sperl, p. 177.

[45] Seipel diary, November 7, 1918.

[46] "Nicht fahnenflüchtig zu werden"; Paul Mechtler, "Erinnerungen des Dr. Karl Freiherrn von Banhans (1861-1942)," *Mitteilungen des Österreichischen Staatsarchivs*, xii (Vienna, 1959), 394.

[47] Redlich diary, November 12, 1918, *Schicksalsjahre*, ii, 317.

rengasse where the Provisional National Assembly met came from youthful academic Pan-Germans.[48] The pressure was on the Christian Socialist party in particular, which, as its parliamentary leader Prelate Hauser told the Cardinal as late as the morning of November 10, was still committed to the monarchic idea.[49] But even within the Christian Socialist party, among its agrarian and provincial elements, the republican tendencies made considerable headway and Hauser himself was sensitive to them.

In this situation Seipel once again assumed a prominent role. Moving back and forth between cabinet meeting and "Parliament," consulting the Cardinal on vital issues, as he invariably did[50] in negotiating the arduous problems of abdication and proclamation of the Republic, he showed that he had the necessary qualities of firmness, steady nerves, and flexibility of mind. In his diary on November 10 he entered that he was engaged in a "fervent delaying action"[51] and the following day, which turned out to be the decisive one, he wrote: "I declared in Parliament as well as in the cabinet meeting, that my nerves were strong enough to justify holding out on the part of the Emperor as well as the government."[52] His reasons were once again plausible and practical, and his aim was to remain until the start of peace negotiations to assure the existence of an internationally recognized government, as the new German-Austrian government did not yet enjoy such recognition by the Entente Powers. The Emperor, represented by Lammasch, could in this way take part in the peace conference. But he added with calm resignation, that he would submit, if necessary, to the weight of all the arguments that might make such a cause impossible.[53]

[48] Mechtler, "Erinnerungen," p. 393.

[49] "Die christlichsozialen Führer während der Umsturzzeit," *Reichspost*, June 8, 1923; cf. also Oswald Gschliesser, *Von der Monarchie zur Republik in Österreich* (Vienna, 1957), pp. 24f.

[50] Seipel diary, November 10, 1918.

[51] Seipel diary, November 10, 1918.

[52] Seipel diary, November 11, 1918.   [53] Ibid.

"Guarding the Exit of Habsburg"

The document which he finally submitted to the Emperor for signature in the morning hours of November 11 read as follows:

> Since My accession to the throne I have ceaselessly endeavored to lead My peoples out of the horrors of the war for whose outbreak I bear no responsibility whatsoever. I have not hesitated to restore constitutional order and have opened up to the peoples the road towards their independence. Impelled now as ever by unchanging love for all My peoples I do not want My person to be an obstacle to their free development.
>
> In advance I recognize the decision which German-Austria will make about its future form of government. The people through its representatives has taken over the government. I renounce all participation in the affairs of state. At the same time I relieve My Austrian government from office. May the people of German-Austria in unison and harmony create and consolidate the new order. From the very beginning the happiness of My peoples has been the aim of my most ardent desires. Only internal peace can heal the wounds of this war.[54]

The Emperor signed as usual with pencil and Lammasch countersigned.

The document was vague. The Emperor, while speaking of "all" his peoples in fact addressed himself solely to the German Austrians; but in this case vagueness suited a situation in which there was as yet no legal reason to prejudice the fate of the non-German areas of Austria. If furthermore the key passage was vague, it was deliberately and skillfully so: "I renounce all participation in the affairs of state." It must be remembered that the Manifesto was the work of many hands. An original draft by Renner, aimed at abdication, was carefully reworded by the old cabinet, and it is generally agreed that the key passage was

[54] *Neue Freie Presse*, November 11, 1918, evening ed.

The Policy of Accommodation

phrased by Seipel.[55] In contrast to the German example of November 9 it was not to be construed as a formal abdication, which in any case Emperor Charles refused to sign. Only if German-Austria should decide upon a republican form of government would the renunciation become an abdication; otherwise, if the monarchic form of government were maintained, the formula would protect the House of Habsburg-Lorraine in its claim to legitimacy.[56] "A typical piece of Jesuitry," charged

[55] The most authoritative statements on the somewhat clouded issue are:

1. The memorandum from Hans Kelsen to Charles A. Gulick, which includes the following sentence: "I remember correctly Dr. Seipel told me later that he personally had formulated the decisive words"; Charles A. Gulick, *Austria from Habsburg to Hitler*, 2 vols. (Berkeley and Los Angeles, 1948), I, 47.

2. Redlich's diary entry of November 12, 1918, recording that "the majority of the controversial sentences were worded partly by Seipel, partly by myself"; *Schicksalsjahre*, II, 317.

3. Ehrhart's emphasis on his own "modest role," which in its modesty is also confirmed by Redlich, and his de-emphasis of Seipel's role: he had "featured little in the consultations"; Ehrhart, *Im Dienste*, p. 407.

4. Banhans's claim that, upon Lammasch's and Seipel's request, he and the Minister of Education, von Hampe, worked it out; Banhans predates the elaboration of the manifesto to November 9; Mechtler, "Erinnerungen," p. 396.

5. Glaise-Horstenau's attribution of the drafting to von Hampe; Edmund von Glaise-Horstenau, *The Collapse of the Austro-Hungarian Empire* (London, Toronto, and New York, 1930), p. 326.

6. Reference to "the initiative of Minister Dr. Seipel" in the official Christian-Socialist correspondence, "Austria"; "Die christlichsozialen Führer," *Reichspost*, June 8, 1923.

7. General attribution of the major role in the question of the manifesto to Seipel in the secondary literature; cf. Walter Goldinger, *Geschichte der Republik Österreich* (Vienna, 1962), p. 19; Reinhold Lorenz, *Kaiser Karl* (Graz, Vienna, and Cologne, 1959), p. 553; Gordon Brook-Shepherd, *The Last Habsburg* (New York, 1968), p. 212.

[56] Cf. Hans Kelsen, *Die Verfassungsgesetze der Republik Deutschösterreich*, part 1 (Vienna, 1919), p. 9.

Gulick, who was not one of Seipel's admirers,[57] and he added erroneously that it paved the way for the Emperor's attempts at restoration. Seipel argued on the contrary that his formula had enabled the conservative circles to make the transition from monarchy to republic and thus to contribute toward the construction of the new state. With this in mind he wrote that his party had received the Manifesto with "great relief."[58] Indeed it was largely because of Seipel's role in the abdication crisis that he never again became fully *persona grata* with the exiled monarch's family and its diehard supporters.

The Manifesto of November 11, the last official act of the House of Habsburg-Lorraine concerning Austria, whose destinies it had directed for more than six hundred years, was a dignified document. By stressing peace and not war, love and not defiance, healing rather than the wounds, it reviewed appropriately the short rule of Emperor Charles, and somehow, for many of his Austrian subjects at least, stressed the long rule of his dynasty and underscored the tragedy of his life. The "poor young Emperor,"[59] Josef Redlich described him during these last days of disillusion. His gentle, not too forceful ways may have been, from a political point of view, his great weakness. But in the two shattering years of his reign little was left for him but to go down with dignity. And this he did. He left in style. He gave his Empire a last government that was worthy of the best traditions of old Austria. Lammasch was its moral force, recognized throughout the world for his humanity and his fight for peace. Together with Redlich and Seipel he could claim that his broad, generous ideas concerning a Christian commonwealth were not merely a concession to defeat, last-minute attempts to stave off disaster, but rooted in deep conviction. The part which these three men

[57] Gulick, *Austria*, I, 61.
[58] Ignaz Seipel, "Der neue Staat und sein Aufbau nach dem christlich-sozialen Programm," *Volkswohl*, x, no. 1 (1919), 5.
[59] Redlich, *Schicksalsjahre*, II, 315.

played in the last two weeks of the Monarchy was their service to these convictions.

The Emperor's intention to avoid bloodshed and civil war was fully supported by his cabinet. In this respect, Seipel's influence proved decisive. He turned out to be politically more gifted than the bulk of the good old bureaucrats in the cabinet—shrewder certainly than Lammasch, and more effective, after all, than Redlich. Being younger than both his friends, he had a more watchful eye on the future. Hermann Bahr later wrote in a letter to Seipel, "You were"—and he meant the troika Lammasch-Redlich-Seipel—"the last ministers of Austria." With a not surprising vanity, he added, "and I was the last Burgtheater director of old Austria. Our figures guard the exit of Habsburg."[60] But for Seipel these two weeks were both an end and a beginning. No doubt, his "period in 'government,'" as he once put it, had been "crushing."[61] No doubt he felt acutely, as he admitted when Chancellor in front of the Republic's Parliament, that he had fought "from one day, indeed hour, to another" for the survival of the old Monarchy and then had to "leave the scene defeated."[62] However, there was a challenge for Seipel in this situation. As a young theologian he had trained himself to be flexible, adjustable, and this training had stood him in good stead.

What followed the proclamation of the Manifesto, as far as the Lammasch government was concerned, was merely an aftermath, and not altogether a handsome one. Tears ran down Lammasch's white beard during his moving farewell address, and tears, we are told, were in everyone's eyes. But then, as so often in history, the ridiculous followed the sublime. The inevitable *Hofrat*, as Hermann Bahr had repeatedly labeled him in his writings, celebrated a macabre comeback, and the wrangling began over dec-

[60] Hermann Bahr to Seipel, Munich, July 30, 1923, A.V.A., Bundeskanzleramt Inneres, Korrespondenz Seipel, K.79.

[61] Seipel to Lammasch, Vienna, December 30, 1918.

[62] Seipel, "Die erste Regierungserklärung," May 31, 1922, in Josef Gessl, ed., *Seipels Reden in Österreich und anderwärts* (Vienna, 1926), p. 18.

orations, titles, and pensions. Lammasch was awarded the Great
Cross of the Stephen's Order, Banhans, as senior minister, the
Great Cross of the Leopold's Order, and Redlich, Seipel, and
Hampe were made Privy Councillors; two others, to their overwhelming sorrow, were refused this title.[63] Redlich recorded the
"terrible procedure of the last cabinet meeting."[64] *Sic transit
gloria mundi.*

The following day, after the Republic had been proclaimed,
a letter reached Seipel addressed to "My Minister for Social Welfare, Dr. Ignaz Seipel." The typewritten contents read as follows:

> Dear Dr. Seipel:
>
> By relieving you according to your wishes from the posi-
> tion of My Minister of Social Welfare, I express to you for
> your outstanding service My gratitude and My full recogni-
> tion. On this occasion I grant you free of tax the title of Privy
> Councillor.
>
> Vienna, November 11, 1918
> Karl [in pencil] Lammasch [in ink][65]

A separate letter of the same date, addressed to Seipel as "k.k.
Minister for Social Welfare, k. and k. Privy Councillor" awarded
him a yearly pension of twenty thousand crowns, or slightly more
than four thousand dollars.[66] In the republican years, Seipel was
generally addressed as "Your Excellency" in honor of his imperial
service. The bureaucratic title "Privy Councillor" was not in
keeping with his personal style, and he never used it. But the
state pension, which in later years was adjusted to the inflationary spiral and to currency reforms, gave him a secure income for
the rest of his life.

[63] Cf. Ehrhart's not very dignified account of the refusal, Ehrhart, *Im
Dienste*, pp. 403f.

[64] Redlich diary, November 12, 1918, *Schicksalsjahre*, ɪɪ, 317.

[65] Seipel Archive.　　[66] Ibid.

The Policy of Accommodation

The Revolution: Monarchy or Republic?

In the years 1917-1918 the long-delayed and long-suppressed revolution came to Eastern and Central Europe, and, if the revolutionary year 1917 in Russia was a sign of things to come, forces of political and social revolution in Central Europe might well burst out with a violence dwarfing even that of the French Revolution. It would sweep out the old classes with a vengeance and substitute for them the rule of the people.

However, neither the German nor the Austrian revolutions of November 1918 conformed to this pattern, and they have, as a consequence, been found wanting by the historical guild. They have been properly labeled "improvised revolutions";[67] that is, the democratic changes they brought about were not a response to long-term domestic pressures but by-products of defeat. One might call them revolutions by default, or revolutions *manquées*. Indeed the German revolution was essentially the result of defeat and collapse; it was carried through by honorable men like Friedrich Ebert, who hated social revolution "like sin," and after a short-lived, wholly unrealistic period of euphoria saw itself confronted with the ugly reality of Versailles, which deprived the new democracy of its political legitimacy. For the rest, democracy in Weimar Germany fought a losing battle against the old reactionary forces. The experiment of "improvised democracy," which Hugo Preuss had still given a fighting chance late in October 1918, had failed; and all too soon the revolutionaries who re-

---

[67] The term "improvised revolution" is borrowed, with a slight variation, from the well-known but much misunderstood article by Hugo Preuss ("Die Improvisierung des Parlamentarismus," *Norddeutsche Allgemeine Zeitung*, October 26, 1918, reprinted in Hugo Preuss, *Staat, Recht und Freiheit* [Hildesheim, 1964], pp. 361ff.), in which he pleaded the case for a transition in Germany from the *Obrigkeitsstaat* to the *Volksstaat* by means of a peaceful revolution. The pejorative use of the term "improvisation," as popularized by Theodor Eschenburg (Theodor Eschenburg, *Die improvisierte Demokratie: Gesammelte Aufsätze zur Weimarer Republik* [Munich, 1963], pp. 11ff.) and meaning a process inevitably leading to failure, adds up to a misreading of Preuss.

94

jected extremist experiments and chose "law and order" became transformed into counterrevolutionaries. The result was the painful postrevolutionary history of Weimar Germany—in effect a civil war between the divided and dispirited revolutionary tradition and the obstructionist reactionaries allied with the new forces of fascism.

There is no doubt that the revolution in Austria, that rather insignificant country "left over" after the partition of the Austro-Hungarian Monarchy, was improvised. But it might be suggested that the very lack of a distinct revolutionary tradition is hardly a liability in a country which, like the old Austria (I am here thinking of the western half of the monarchy), had granted universal male suffrage; which could pride itself on progressive social legislation; which had allowed the great socialist movement to grow into society rather than away from it; and in which both socialists and conservatives—for example, the librarian of Parliament, Karl Renner alias Rudolf Springer, and the Salzburg theologian, Ignaz Seipel—had worked on plans for imperial reform that were astonishingly similar. Anyway, the revolution, when it came, was unleashed by the combined impact of war, defeat, and the secession of the nationalities.

The Austrian revolution was in fact the last act of the agony of Empire, and ironically it was the Emperor himself who released its forces. Its first phase, the outbreak of national revolutions in the various centers of the Monarchy, legally followed the Imperial Manifesto of October 16. It coincided with the convocation of the Provisional National Assembly on October 21, which proceeded to elect three presidents, one from each major party, and a Council of State (*Vollzugsausschuss*) composed of twenty deputies chosen from the same parties. All this happened in a spirit of consensus and unanimity. Josef Redlich commented on the rather *gemütlichen* tone of this first act of revolution; it proceeded in a "sloppy" (*salopp*) manner.[68] "Revolution in Kakania,"

[68] Redlich diary, October 21, 1918, *Schicksalsjahre*, II, 305.

he might have added. The sloppiness, the lack of fanaticism of "that misunderstood" revolution (Musil), may after all have been an asset. Even the impetuous Otto Bauer prided himself on the fact that the new Austrian state was "fundamentally the product of a *contrat social* . . . arrived at between the various classes of the German-Austrian people, as represented by the political parties."[69]

The revolution was marked by a singular continuity between the old and new forces, notably by unique coexistence and cooperation between the Lammasch-Redlich-Seipel government and the revolutionary Chancellor, Renner. In all the central offices an Austrian state secretary appointed by the new revolutionary government sat beside an imperial minister,[70] and both officials invariably communicated in the most correct if not amicable of terms, a state of affairs that has been described variously as anomalous, untenable in the long run, and comical.

One might, in light of this evidence of concession, consensus, and continuity, be led to question the revolutionary nature of the revolution. The Austrian revolution, unlike Germany's, did not even have its equivalent of the Kiel revolt. Did it amount only to a "national revolution" or the formal "legal revolution" which, according to Hans Kelsen, occurred on October 30 when the German-Austrian state was proclaimed, Renner's provisional constitution adopted without reference to the old constitution, and the continuity thus formally "interrupted"?[71] Did it add up to a political revolution, or, indeed, a social revolution?

The revolutionary situation was not lacking in Austria, in particular after "the ninth of November" in Germany, which had a contagious effect.[72] The minutes of the National Assembly betray

[69] Otto Bauer, *Die österreichische Revolution* (Vienna, 1923), p. 96.

[70] Cf. ibid., p. 100, and Friedrich F. G. Kleinwaechter, *Von Schönbrunn bis St. Germain: Die Entstehung der Republik Österreich* (Graz, 1964), pp. 89f.

[71] Kelsen, *Die Verfassungsgesetze*, part 1, p. 10.

[72] Cf. Bauer, *Revolution*, p. 100, and Viktor Adler's last address to the

a sense, amid general collapse, of the abdication of an old world, and of a new beginning in the name of democracy, which, Renner stated in the meeting of November 12, had become "the fundamental law of the whole world."[73] And if the "law concerning the form of state and government of German-Austria" was passed unanimously "to the accompaniment of stormy applause of the whole House and galleries,"[74] it does not suffice to attribute this event to an "outmaneuvering" (*Überrumpelung*)[75] of the Christian Socialists by the Socialists. The Christian Socialists, like the Pan-Germans, were swept along by the public elation that arises in revolutionary situations where the old almost automatically gives way to the new. When Prince Alois Liechtenstein lamented that the other parties had looked on "shaking their heads" while the Social Democrats engineered the overthrow of the monarchy,[76] he was aptly corrected by the witty Hermann Bahr: "Oh no, not at all shaking their heads but nodding their heads, and how lively, with what enthusiasm! . . . *No, the other parties by no means merely 'looked on,' they made haste to 'participate.'* "[77]

In the early afternoon of the same November 12, upon Renner's motion the National Assembly marched in solemn procession through the majestic doors of the House of Parliament toward the balustrade to greet the people of German-Austria and proclaim its decisions to them. When President Seitz began to

---

revolutionary government on November 9, 1918, in Ludwig Brügel, *Geschichte der österreichischen Sozialdemokratie* (Vienna, 1925), v, 390ff.

[73] *Stenographische Protokolle, 3. Sitzung der Provisorischen Nationalversammlung für Deutschösterreich*, November 12, 1918, p. 65.

[74] Schulthess' *Europäischer Geschichtskalender, 1918*, II, 105.

[75] This term was used by one of the leaders of the pro-Habsburg legitimists, H. K. Zessner-Spitzenberg. See Ruth Werner, *Die Wiener Wochenschrift "Das Neue Reich" (1918-1925): Ein Beitrag zur Geschichte des politischen Katholizismus* (Breslau, 1938), p. 62.

[76] "Der Anfang des Endes in Österreich," *Das Neue Reich*, October 5, 1919, p. 2.

[77] "Hermann Bahr, über Alois Liechtenstein," ibid., November 2, 1919, p. 82; italics in original.

read the text of the constitution, members of the assembled crowd seized the newly adopted republican red-white-red flags, the old colors of Babenberg Austria, which were about to be hoisted on the two large flagpoles, and cut out the white pieces, leaving only patched-up red flags, the symbol of the proletarian revolution. Shots were fired, causing two deaths and many more casualties, and the Austrian revolution had its modest baptism of fire.

It was at this point that, for the first time since the mass strike of January 1918, the masses, the "street," again came into the picture and the specter of social revolution emerged. The masses waiting outside Parliament cheering Renner were made up mostly of Social Democrats, their presence contributing no doubt to the predominant role in government councils played by the Social Democrats, the weakest of the three parties. From their ranks came Renner the Chancellor; Viktor Adler the Foreign Secretary, who after his death on the eve of the revolution (November 11) was replaced by Otto Bauer; and also the competent and enterprising Ferdinand Hanusch, Seipel's "successor" in the Secretariat for Social Welfare. But still more important was the fact that the Socialists through Julius Deutsch managed to build up a republican army, the Volkswehr, which put the Austrian revolution, in comparison with the German one, into a singularly advantageous position. Otto Bauer saw in the creation of the Volkswehr "a revolutionary act," indeed "the first act of the proletarian revolution which was beginning to overshadow the national revolution."[78] However Deutsch was not spared the task of having to defend the new Republic against a further radicalization. During the first half of 1919 the new Austrian Republic had to defend itself against the determined uprisings from the extreme Left on April 17 and June 15.

The acid test of revolution lies in how it develops and what it achieves. The course taken by the Austrian revolution lacked the

[78] Bauer, *Revolution*, p. 99.

acceleration and surge of the French-Russian model, but it was not completely without momentum. There was something impressive about its development and about the way the Austrians managed it. What was begun in cooperation between Lammasch and Renner was, after November 12, carried on by singular cooperation among the three parties. While the historian of this period would be foolish to underplay divisions in the population along lines drawn by class, ideology, or religion, he cannot help noticing that steady consensus rather than conflict marked the events of the revolutionary months. Was this, after all, what the dying Viktor Adler, the self-styled "*Hofrat* of revolution," had meant when he said, "We Germans will give an example to the world of how to make and carry through revolution in the smoothest, the most classical and simple way"?[79]

Now, there are types of consensus. There is the consensus rooted in the common life, habits, institutions, and experience of generations that Benjamin F. Wright attributes to the American Revolution.[80] The Austrian consensus was predominantly, though not entirely, a consensus of crisis. It was born not out of "contentment and success"[81] but out of misery and suffering. "Our people bleeds from a thousand wounds," Chancellor Renner said to the National Assembly on November 12, when he called for "free cooperation of all forces."[82]

How otherwise could the Socialists, whose stronghold was Vienna, have coped with the more conservative peasantry, on whom in time of blockade and food shortage the capital doubly depended? How otherwise could the new government have asserted itself against rising unemployment, against an army which streamed back into the country with no plan or discipline, with-

[79] Quoted in Hanns Leo Mikoletzky, *Österreichische Zeitgeschichte* (Vienna, 1962), p. 62.

[80] Benjamin F. Wright's masterly lectures, "Consensus and Continuity—1776-1787," *Boston University Law Review* (Winter 1958), pp. 1-52.

[81] Ibid., p. 50.

[82] *Sten. Prot., 3. Sitzung*, November 12, 1918, p. 64.

out abandoning the country to Bolshevism? How else could the Republic have kept itself immune from the questionable Eisner experiment in Bavaria and later from the Soviet republics in Bavaria and Hungary? How, finally, could the Republic have expected to support its plea for the retention of the German Bohemian territories and the South Tyrol within the frontiers of Austria? To meet all of these problems, Renner had stressed in his address to the Provisional National Assembly of November 12 the need for unity among the three main groups of the population, "burghers, peasants, and workers."[83] Politically the revolution found its expression in a combined tripartisan approach— not always an easy one in the first two years of the Republic—to the problems of governing and administrating the country, to the framing of a constitution, and to the problems of peace and foreign affairs.

For the Social Democrats the tripartisan policy meant restraint. At their party convention which met in the midst of the revolution on October 31, Otto Bauer reported that the masses were pressing to drive the revolution further on and to transform it from a purely political into a social upheaval. "We however must remain prudent and firm; we must act like a general who, after an enemy position has been taken, does not let his troops storm further, but who first of all seeks to fortify the conquered territory to establish the basis for further advances."[84] In fact, the party did not immediately press for the formal proclamation of a republic.

In retrospect, surveying the course of events, and in particular the failure of the republic, one might accuse the old Adler of carelessly procrastinating and missing the opportunity to establish democracy in Austria by a clear revolutionary act. But no undue procrastination was involved, only an awareness that precipitate action would from the very start have ruined the revolution. The "improvised revolution" had to be based on a

[83] Schulthess, *1918*, II, 105.
[84] Quoted in Brügel, *Geschichte*, v, 363.

consensus. And the strength of the undivided Austrian Social Democracy, by this reasoning, would be better employed guiding and broadening the revolutionary effort than wasting it prematurely in an unsuccessful explosion.

It was in particular the threat of Bolshevism from within and without that prompted the Socialists to pursue a policy of order. Professor Archibald Cary Coolidge reported from Vienna on January 10, 1919: "The authorities are . . . proud of the order they maintain and contrast the quiet of Vienna with what happened in Berlin, Warsaw, Budapest, and elsewhere."[85] Otto Bauer wrote of necessary "sacrifices" for the national and social revolution.[86] This was not due to cold feet, but was a piece of pragmatic statesmanship of the highest order, giving the "improvised revolution" its only chance to succeed. It carried the republic safely through the first two years of its shaky existence and enabled it to deal with the problems of governing and administering the country, framing the constitution, and negotiating the peace.

We must also understand that the other groups lived up to the bargain. In this respect the contrast with the German situation is marked. The Ebert-Groener pact, however necessary it may have been, led to an instant revival of the German military. But the Austrian army was disintegrating and no longer constituted a threat to the republic. Thus, Austria's military weakness turned out to be its potential political strength. The new Austrian government could proceed with the formation of a republic without obtaining and keeping the support of the old army, as the Germans had found necessary.

The traditional monarchic loyalties of the *Bürgertum* and the peasantry gave way almost imperceptibly to a pragmatic republicanism. The Austrians' adaptability, compared with that of the Germans, was startling. Neither monarchy and democracy nor monarchy and republic appeared as antitheses. In fact, there

[85] *Papers Relating to the Foreign Relations of the United States 1919. The Paris Peace Conference* (Washington, 1942), II, 229.

[86] Bauer, *Revolution*, p. 142.

existed a grass-roots republicanism in the provinces and in the country, namely, in Upper Austria, Carinthia, the Tyrol, and Vorarlberg, which became manifest in the course of the revolution and moved the various political groups. For the Pan-Germans, in short, the republic became concomitant with their chief objective, the Anschluss.

Of course for the Catholic camp the position of the Church hierarchy was vital.[87] Cardinal Piffl, whose Habsburg loyalty was beyond doubt, fell into line once he was confronted with the Emperor's renunciation, with revolution and the proclamation of the Republic. As promptly as November 12 the Archbishop issued instructions to the Viennese clergy. They were followed by a pastoral letter to Austrian Catholics on January 23, urging Catholics to serve the new state loyally. Leon XIII's advice of 1885 to the French Catholics (*Immortale Dei*) was now made applicable to the Austrians. The Church was not identified with any one form of government and could accept any provided that it served the common good. This was in striking contrast to the predominantly negative attitude of German Protestantism.

However it cannot be overlooked that the Christian Socialist party went into the revolution divided. Unlike the Church, its structure was not a hierarchic one. Unlike the Social Democrats, the Christian Socialist party had not enjoyed a strong leadership since the death of Lueger, and it had no Viktor Adler. Unprepared as it was for the revolution, it turned out to be a critically divided party, a fact which the unanimous vote in the Provisional National Assembly could not obscure.[88]

[87] Throughout the years there had been monthly meetings in the palace of the Archbishop between Piffl and the leaders of the Christian-Socialist party; Robert Prantner, "Katholische Kirche und christliche Parteipolitik in Österreich im Spiegel der katholischen Presse der Erzdiözese Wien unter der Regierung Kardinal Piffls von der Gründung der Republik Österreich bis zum Tode des Kirchenfürsten (1918-1932)," (theol. diss., Vienna, 1955), p. 21.

[88] Not only did monarchists led by Wilhelm Miklas and the Catholic labor leader Franz Spalowsky oppose republicans, who were represented by some

Monarchy or Republic?

It was over the burning issue of the party's position toward revolution and toward monarchy and republic that Seipel, encouraged by Dr. Funder of the *Reichspost*, proved decisive. Like Piffl he had been a proponent of an anti-integralist "liberal" Catholicism. Now, in the midst of crisis, the man who had proven his shrewd sense of accommodation and ability to mediate as a scholar was called upon in the last hours of the Monarchy to save the unity of political Catholicism in Austria.

On the particular subject of revolution, Seipel had already published a little-noticed article in the *Hochland* which, particularly in retrospect, was striking in its message.[89] A dissertation on the problem of legitimacy, which Austria had defended over the ages, it raised the question whether a revolution "in all circumstances" had to be assessed as a "violation against the moral world order." Seipel proceeded from the proposition that a revolutionary regime (alas, that of Soviet Russia) can be recognized to the one that revolution itself, under certain conditions, can actually be justified. The scholar of the socioeconomic doctrines of the Church fathers stressed that authority, like property, was only a trust from God for man to administer. Just as political revolution was sometimes defensible, as in certain cases of self-

---

influential peasant leaders such as Josef Schraffl (Tyrol) and Jodok Fink (Vorarlberg) along with the Upper Austrian Prelate Hauser; but the more conservative and centralist "Viennese wing" set itself off against the more progressive, federalist, Länder. There was a right wing, vigorously anti-Marxist, and a left wing, more disposed to cooperate with the Socialists. Finally the increasingly controversial and urgent issue of the Anschluss divided the party into friends and foes of union with Germany. The example of Seipel himself, who, belonging to the so-called Viennese wing, was initially at least a champion of cooperation with the Social Democrats, showed that lines could not be arbitrarily drawn and that positions often overlapped; cf. on alignments within the party the fine discussion by Adam Wandruszka in *Geschichte der Republik Österreich*, ed. Heinrich Benedikt (Vienna, 1954), pp. 320f.

[89] Ignaz Seipel, "Das Problem der Revolution," *Hochland*, xv (October 1917–March 1918), 543-552.

defense (*Notwehr*), so social revolution was justifiable if at the same time it aimed at a more equitable redistribution of property. Indeed Seipel argued that the revolution could create a "new legitimacy."[90] Here the moral theologian for the first time translated domestic accommodation into terms of a Catholic version of *Realpolitik* which he was soon to practice himself. Here Seipel went as far as he ever did in justifying the Russian Revolution, though with great caution and some reservations. But to speak of Seipel as left-oriented would be misleading. He was writing as a churchman, and with the detachment of a churchman toward the secular world he was staking out the ground which the Leonine Church considered legitimate. Political and social revolution was, under certain circumstances, a part of that ground.

It was clear then that Seipel entered the inner-party controversy from without; that is, he brought his Thomistic-Leonine perspective to bear on an issue which after the *fait accompli* of revolution and Republic threatened to cause division. He entered this highly charged atmosphere with sovereign detachment, and as he once said, politics was to him "not merely a matter of feeling but of coolly calculating reasoning."[91] The catastrophe of 1918 certainly did not invalidate the principles for which he stood, but it probably complicated their pursuit, and this Seipel saw as the greater challenge.

The party itself rather bored and irritated Seipel, and there were moments when its "indolence" made him seriously think of "quitting."[92] In fact immediately after the revolution he gave some thought to the founding of a new one,[93] but then he figured that the party was only a vehicle to influence public life, and in

[90] Ibid., p. 552.

[91] Ignaz Seipel, "Die zweite Regierungserklärung," November 21, 1923; Gessl, *Reden*, p. 78.

[92] Seipel to Lammasch, Vienna, September 14, 1919.

[93] Ignaz Seipel, "Die unpolitischen und politischen Vereine in der christlichen Volksbewegung," *Reichspost*, January 5, 1920.

spite of all its shortcomings "the only useful instrument of politics,"[94] and for this purpose must be unified.

Only an outsider like Seipel could step before the Catholics of Austria and be unsparingly frank and at the same time extremely convincing. Indeed the first of his "programmatic" articles commissioned by Dr. Funder for the *Reichspost* added up to a vehement indictment of the old regime: "Something in the old regime has caused the great misfortune in which we find ourselves, therefore the regime must disappear."[95] For the rest of his argument Seipel relapsed into his schoolmasterly manner and chose as his chief targets bureaucratism, remnants of feudalism, capitalism, and absolutism.[96]

His singling out of bureaucratism is particularly indicative of his image of Austria as well as of his own future role. Might we not assume that in the long walks which Seipel took with Hermann Bahr in the Volksgarten during the winter of 1918-1919[97] Bahr's favorite theme of the conflict between the historical baroque Austria and the mechanical bureaucratic state created by Joseph II featured prominently? Seipel agreed with his friend that the predominantly German administration had been in conflict with the best traditions of the Habsburg Monarchy. With its centralizing Josephinist outlook it had imposed an alien, western European pattern on a multinational Empire. Seipel now moved into the political arena as an anti-Josephinist. If he was not a party man, he was even less a bureaucrat. He was a man of the Church.

While Seipel's charge against the "remnants of feudalism"— meaning the tenure of leading positions by the high nobility— might be understood as a time-conditioned and never-to-be-

[94] Seipel to Hermann Bahr, Vienna, June 6, 1920; Hermann Bahr Archive.

[95] Ignaz Seipel, "Das Recht des Volkes," *Reichspost*, November 19, 1918, in *Kampf*, p. 51.

[96] Ibid., pp. 52f.

[97] Cf. Hermann Bahr to Seipel, Munich, June 3, 1922; Seipel Archive.

repeated outburst on the part of the *homo novus*, his attacks on "capitalism" and "absolutism" served to stake out the common ground between Catholicism and social and political democracy. All Catholic writers were more or less in agreement on the issue of capitalism, and if anything the integralist school of Vogelsang felt more strongly on the subject than the "liberal" Catholics, who, like Seipel, cautiously opposed the laxity of "mammonist" capitalism. At this point Seipel translated the argument from his dissertation on the Church fathers into political terms by raising his voice not against property as such, but against the wrong use of property, which had been fostered by the "system." The rejection of absolutism grew out of Seipel's understanding of the function of moral theology; later he developed this theme more elaborately.[98] The age of absolutism had caused a split between public and private morality which was overcome only by revolution. But while Seipel conceded that Catholics were not likely to take the lead in revolution, he believed they ought not to leave to others the reconstruction after revolution. They had become too easily used to playing the "brave subjects" (*Untertanen*). Democracy essentially meant moral and political responsibility.

The subsequent *Reichspost* articles were dedicated to elaboration on the Catholic understanding of democracy.[99] In a "free democratic state," as opposed to an "autocratic state,"[100] the people would exercise their right to universal and equal suffrage[101] as well as the right to participate in the leadership of the state and in local administration.[102] Pleading for cooperation among the political groups as well as the social classes, he concluded his

[98] Ignaz Seipel, *Neue Ziele und Aufgaben der katholischen Moraltheologie* (Vienna, 1926); cf. Ignaz Seipel, *Der Friede: Ein sittliches und gesellschaftliches Problem* (Innsbruck, 1937), pp. 48f.

[99] Ignaz Seipel, "Das Wesen des demokratischen Staates," *Reichspost*, November 20, 1918; "Die demokratische Verfassung," *Reichspost*, November 21, 1918; "Das Volk und die künftige Staatsform," *Reichspost*, November 23, 1918, *Kampf*, pp. 54-66.

[100] Seipel, *Kampf*, p. 54.   [101] Ibid., p. 59.

[102] Ibid., pp. 57, 61f.

appeal to his fellow Catholics: "The Emperor in advance has recognized the decision which German-Austria will make concerning its future form of government. *We do not want to be more imperial than the Emperor and therefore we submit to the will of the people. But let it be understood clearly: only to the will of the people, not to a dictatorship. Freedom above everything!*"[103]

To the well-trained observer there were many reservations built into Seipel's democratic republican credo. To begin with—and here we touch upon the inevitable weakness of the "improvised" revolution—what value is there in an advocacy of republicanism or democracy which does not come from the heart? Seipel himself had in the last month of the Monarchy made the distinction between "the Empire [*Kaisertum*] for which all hearts beat," and "democracy which reason proposes to us as being desirable and the only possible solution in the future."[104] Seipel, who emerged as the leading figure within political Catholicism after the war, was in this respect representative of most Austrian Catholics of his generation. Having lived under and identified himself with one dispensation for more than forty years, how could he ever become committed to the new one? Even allowing for his exceptionally critical stand toward some of the institutions and policies of the old Monarchy and his accommodative disposition, was he not bound to remain in conflict with himself, plagued by an inevitable lack of commitment? Moreover, might one not take exception to Seipel's insidious distinction between the "truly democratic" state and the "formally democratic" Republic?[105] Did not this formulation carry a mental reservation toward the same democracy which Seipel pretended to embrace? His conception of the democratic constitution was permeated with corporative notions. He associated universal suffrage after all with an "atomistic" state consisting of isolated individuals, and declared himself in favor of the "organic" state based on groups

---

[103] Ibid., p. 66; italics in original.
[104] Ignaz Seipel, "Kaisertum und Demokratie," *Kampf*, pp. 43f.
[105] Ignaz Seipel, "Das Volk und die künftige Staatsform," *Kampf*, p. 64.

such as families and estates (*Berufsstände*).[106] As a counterbalance to excessive politicization he proposed that certain cultural and economic questions be turned over for expert decision to special professional commissions.[107] Finally, did not the detached flexibility displayed by the Church and the Christian Socialist leadership during the revolution open the doors toward indiscriminate cooperation with any secular regime, whether democratic or antidemocratic, socialist or antisocialist, and was not Seipel's accommodation after all only a temporary concession, a deceptive maneuver to screen the counterattack?

All these questions have a compelling relevance, especially in the light of Seipel's later political course. For the moment, however, his accommodative position allowed him an unusual degree of flexibility toward the revolutionary changes in Austria, and the "programmatic" articles had the effect of swaying his readers. It is argued, and with good reason, that this course prevented the dissolution of the party over the issue of Monarchy versus Republic; but even more was accomplished. The very idea of counterrevolution was quashed. While it might be argued from a leftist point of view that he planted the seeds of counterrevolution by salvaging the Right, it is certain that he effected on his part what the Social Democrats did on theirs: a nonviolent transition from Monarchy to Republic. In answer to attacks from within his own ranks and especially from the aged Prince Alois Liechtenstein,[108] Seipel later justified his position in this way:

> We have been reproached for having evaded the issue of the form of government. . . . In our fatherland . . . the new form of government, which came about almost by itself, cannot be changed without . . . civil war. . . . What would have hap-

[106] Ignaz Seipel, "Die demokratische Verfassung," *Kampf*, pp. 60f.

[107] Ibid., pp. 62f.

[108] He denounced the party's policies during the revolutionary period as a "fiasco"; Alois Liechtenstein, "Politische Streiflichter," *Das Neue Reich*, II, January 18, 1920, 245.

pened had our party not recognized the Republic and not tried to cooperate with it? What would have happened had the only conservative party of Austria . . . counted itself out? It would be forced today to try to assert itself outside the floor of Parliament. But then we would have civil war.[109]

In this way Seipel contributed to the consensus of the critical winter months of 1918-19 and was largely responsible for the fact that republican Austria, unlike Weimar Germany, suffered no basic division over the form of government and experienced no so-called *Flaggenstreit*. While the conservatives in Germany, with their narrow, dynastic view of legitimacy of the kind which Seipel dismissed as "useless,"[110] became disaffected with the Republic and thus weakened its foundation, Seipel opened up the possibility of a constructive conservative function within the new Austrian Republic.

Campaigning

In the winter of 1918-19 when the new Austrian Republic braced itself for its first general election on February 16, Seipel became a candidate. The Provisional National Assembly, having carried through the revolution in an impressive spirit of prudence and calm, was winding up its business to make way for the Constituent National Assembly, whose chief task was to draft the constitution. But while the Church had, soon after the revolution, unequivocally endorsed Seipel's party, the Christian Socialists,[111] he himself, being a clergyman, needed special permission from

[109] Ignaz Seipel, "Österreichs wirtschaftliche und politische Lage," *Reichspost*, October 24, 1921.

[110] *Reichspost*, April 3, 1922.

[111] It admonished the Catholics to cast their vote in a "Catholic spirit" and not for "agnostic or anti-Church representatives"; pastoral letter of the archbishops and bishops of German-Austria, January 23, 1919, quoted in A. Diamant, *Austrian Catholics and the First Republic* (Princeton, 1960), p. 118.

Church authorities to run for office. Quite apart from the fact that the electoral campaign could be expected to unleash bitterness and recrimination and to be a real test of the consensus so carefully guarded during the initial weeks of the revolution, Seipel himself now risked being drawn into the public argument from the somewhat Olympian position he had so far always maintained. As a clergyman and former imperial minister he was bound to become the symbol of clericalism and reaction. But he was more than likely to find himself shot at from his own ranks as well. Mayor Weiskirchner, the grand old man of the Viennese party, led those in a rearguard action who tried to prevent the new man from seizing the party leadership, thus also giving expression to a basic distrust among Catholic politicians of "clericals"[112] and of a too direct involvement of the Church in politics. All these issues were understandably thrashed out when Seipel submitted his request to the Cardinal in a personal audience;[113] and it was not until the end of the year that a letter from the archbishopric to "His Excellency, the Most Reverend Doctor Ignaz Seipel, Privy Councillor and former Minister" allowed "His Excellency to be a candidate for the National Assembly and after election to accept and exercise a mandate."[114]

The electoral issues which overshadowed all others were those concerning the form of government and Anschluss, with socialization running a poor third. Early in December the question of a formal abdication of the Emperor became acute once again. With the Social Democrats, especially Seitz, doing the pushing,[115] and the Christian Socialist party, in spite of its official acceptance of the Republic, divided down the line, Seipel steered a tenuously cautious course. But what earlier may have passed for cau-

[112] Cf. Seipel to Lammasch, Vienna, December 30, 1918.

[113] Seipel diary, December 10, 1918.

[114] Fürsterzbischöfliches Ordinariat to Seipel, Vienna, December 31, 1918; Seipel Archive.

[115] Seipel diary, December 10, 1918; cf. also Redlich diary, December 11, 1918, *Schicksalsjahre*, II, 324.

tion and prudence growing out of theological detachment, now in the heat of battle looked increasingly like ambiguity and deception. The Left might well have been loath to recognize the same man who refused to cooperate in the Emperor's abdication as a bona fide republican. But Seipel's own camp was left no less perplexed concerning his stand on this issue. To some, like Weiskirchner, he was the "chieftain of the monarchists";[116] to others, such as Richard von Kralik, the integralist dean of Catholic intellectuals, and Joseph Eberle, the no less influential and reactionary editor of the Catholic weekly, *Das Neue Reich*,[117] he seemed to have betrayed the Emperor. Hermann Bahr, of whom Seipel saw much during these days, was "emphatically" warned by the Dominicans in Graz against Seipel, who was held responsible for preventing a restoration.[118] In fact, Seipel was caught here in a crisis of conscience which in his usual manner he submitted to the Cardinal.[119] It involved on the one hand his loyalty to Emperor Charles and the House which he continued to consider legitimate,[120] and on the other hand his own realism. What-

[116] "Monarchistenführer," "Monarchistenhäuptling"; Seipel to Lammasch, Vienna, February 16, 1919, and September 14, 1919; cf. Seipel diary, January 12, 1919: "vehement Christian Socialist agitation against me as former minister."

[117] Joseph Eberle, like Vogelsang, who served him as example, had emigrated to Austria (from Württemberg in 1913) to become a spokesman for a Catholic-conservative position. After working for five years for the *Reichspost*, in 1919 he took over the monthly *Monarchie*, whose new title, *Das Neue Reich*, indicated a commitment to the Catholic pre-Bismarckian imperial tradition. Under Eberle's editorship the circulation of *Das Neue Reich* went steadily up from four thousand copies after the first year to fifteen thousand by December 1924, of which a good third was in Germany; cf. the fine and helpful monograph by Ruth Werner, *Die Wiener Wochenschrift "Das Neue Reich" (1918-1925): Ein Beitrag zur Geschichte des politischen Katholizismus* (Breslau, 1938).

[118] Seipel to Lammasch, Vienna, January 5, 1919.

[119] Seipel diary, December 10, 1918.

[120] Seipel to Lammasch, Vienna, January 5, 1919; Charles made a point of keeping in touch from his place of seclusion with the rising star of the Christian Socialist party; Seipel received his first greetings from Charles

ever his emotional attachment, he had come to see in the Republic the form of government that divided Austrians least; it was "the best one to carry through the reconstruction of the fatherland as a free democratic state."[121] Finally, both his refusal to support the formal abdication and his advocacy of the Republic were contingent on the terms of the imperial formula of renunciation, which had been of his own making and which had deferred the final decision on the form of government to the people.[122]

The unanimous resolution of the Provisional National Assembly on November 12 declaring German-Austria "a constituent part of the German Republic" was above all a counsel of despair. It was a spontaneous reaction on the part of a population deprived of its empire and rejected by the other nationalities. Used to thinking in terms of a large political unit and broad, generous horizons, the Assembly overwhelmingly dismissed independence as a valid alternative. The very thought of it was inconceivable, and to those who gave it consideration the lack of viability of a small Alpine republic during the cold and hungry winter of 1918-19 was all too obvious. While the idea of some sort of a Danubian confederation to take the place of the Habsburg Monarchy was widely discussed in Vienna, it was immediately quashed by the unwillingness of the Succession States to join. Thus the Anschluss, almost by elimination, became the general prescription. It offered Austria the renewed prospect of broad horizons—different, however, from those of the Habsburg era; to the west rather than to the east, national and not universal. But if somehow the grandeur of the vision that had marked the Anschluss idea at its inception in 1848 could be renewed—and

---

since the latter's "move to the country [Eckartsau]" the day before the election; Seipel to Lammasch, February 16, 1919.

[121] *Reichspost*, February 6, 1919.

[122] Cf. Seipel's reaffirmation of this position in the *Reichspost*, February 6, 1919.

Renner in his proclamation to the German-Austrians of November 12 referred to the democratic ideals of 1848, now "happily" realized—the Anschluss might, in the midst of general collapse, serve as a new rallying point. It came to assume, then, the role of a "universal panacea,"[123] and, conforming to the Wilsonian formula of self-determination of peoples, it even gave a sense of a new legitimacy to the Austrian step.

The initiative in the Anschluss question, as in the one concerning the form of government, came from the Socialists. But while the revolutionary events brought the Pan-Germans and the Social Democrats together on the Anschluss question, the Christian Socialists were less disposed to fall into line on this issue. The party which had been one of the chief pillars of the Monarchy and the supranational order was not entirely prepared to accept national unity as an objective; its own understanding of a projected union with Germany was distinctly colored by the vision of a Catholic idea of Empire under Austrian, not German, direction. But ill-prepared as the party was for the revolution, it had no clearcut position on the Anschluss and gave itself up to the pressures of the moment, which came largely from the provinces where the Christian Socialist press overwhelmingly endorsed the Anschluss.

But once the first shock of military and political collapse had subsided, it became evident that the hasty Anschluss declaration was built on quicksand, and with this realization the Christian Socialists were the first to have second thoughts on the matter.[124] Vigorous opposition to the Anschluss was expressed in the columns of *Das Neue Reich* by men like Prince Alois Liechtenstein,

[123] C. A. Macartney, *The Social Revolution in Austria* (Cambridge, 1926), p. 91.

[124] On the deceptive nature of the initial unanimity in Austria on the Anschluss question cf. S. W. Gould, "Austrian Attitudes toward Anschluss October 1918–September 1919," *Journal of Modern History*, XXII (September 1950), 220-231, and Frederick Dumin, "Das Problem eines deutsch-österreichischen Anschlusses 1918-1919," *Österreich in Geschichte und Literatur*, IX (October 1965), 403-418.

The Policy of Accommodation

Joseph Eberle, and Richard von Kralik, whose charge that the Anschluss declaration was precipitate and that the Christian Socialists had been outwitted by the Social Democrats came close to the truth.[125]

Between the emotionalism of the Anschluss advocates and the doctrinaire position of the conservative opponents around Liechtenstein stood Seipel, cautious, judicious, enigmatic. Addressing one electoral assembly after another, he introduced himself as one who under the old system had never been among the "super-patriots,"[126] adding that he had no intention of changing his style and of abandoning the independence and composure that he expected of a politician.

Even in his public addresses Seipel was defensive about the Anschluss: "I am neither against the Anschluss nor against the Republic,"[127] and "yes, the union of German-Austria with the bulk of the German people is one of our ideals."[128] What followed was generally a string of carefully reasoned pros and cons, with a distinct emphasis on the cons. The hard-and-fast questions that had to be asked about the Anschluss were its possible effect upon German-Austria's hold over Sudeten Germany and the South Tyrol, and also upon Germany's hold over the left bank of the Rhine, German-Austria's part in the reparation payments, the future of Austria's industry and agriculture, and indeed German-Austria's constitutional position within a larger Germany.[129] In fact, Seipel's electorate found out that his interpretation of "Anschluss" did not mean only "union with Germany." Certainly Austria should not abandon itself to a "pseudonational intoxication"[130] and allow itself to be degraded to a province. Anschluss

[125] Minor, "Bedenken gegen den Anschluss," *Das Neue Reich*, I, January 2, 1919, 229-231.

[126] *Reichspost*, February 9, 1919.   [127] Ibid.

[128] Ibid.

[129] Ignaz Seipel, "Der neue Staat und sein Aufbau nach dem christlichsozialen Programm," *Volkswohl*, x, no. 1 (1919), 10f.

[130] Ignaz Seipel, "Minoritätenschutz und Judenfrage nach dem christlichsozialen Programm," *Volkswohl*, x, no. 2 (1919), 49.

114

was not antithetical to a Danubian confederation which would also include non-German states.[131] Austria, so his somewhat involved and ambiguous argument went, was committed to the Anschluss with both west and east, and only thus might she again become what she supposedly had been in the old days and what Seipel in his *Nation und Staat* had meant it to be, "the great bridge among cultures and among peoples."[132]

An invaluable source for Seipel's early views on the Anschluss question is a long, private letter which he wrote to an unnamed German colleague late in 1918. As it was confidential, the letter allowed Seipel to be far more outspoken than he tended to be in his public utterances.[133] To start with, Seipel squarely hit the Anschluss proclamation of November 12 for belonging to the realm of "politics of sentiment" and containing "*platonic* declarations of a far away ideal." He further observed that the German reaction had been, on the whole, indifferent: "*We shall not force ourselves on you. Your rulers from now on have the word.*" Among all the practical reservations against the Anschluss, which Seipel recited in great detail, he came down heavily on the uncertitudes of the German political scene:

> . . . in Germany of today in which the terror of soldiers' councils and a *socialist dictatorship* prevails, in which a *Kurt Eisner* can rule and so forth, *we have no business.* With us there was an agreement among the parties not now to raise the question of republic or monarchy but to leave it for

---

131 Ibid.   132 Seipel, "Der neue Staat," 11.

133 Z. 703-Präs. Seipel to "Lieber hochw. Kollege," December 17, 1918, St.A., Präsidialakten Otto Bauer, K.262. Ironically the letter fell into the hands of Ludo Hartmann, Austria's new emissary in Berlin, and through him into those of his Foreign Secretary, Otto Bauer. Indeed it seemed so explosive that Bauer asked for permission to "use" parts of the letter, but Hartmann was unable to obtain this from his informant; telegram (in cipher) Z. 703-Präs. Otto Bauer to Ludo Hartmann, Vienna, February 6, 1919; secret telegram Z. 865, Ludo Hartmann to Otto Bauer, Berlin, February 8, 1919; St.A., Präsidialakten Otto Bauer, K.262.

the future Constituent National Assembly. . . . *The party coalition has remained valid up to the present and no disorders worth mentioning have disturbed the public [bürgerliche] order,* but we live under the continuous threat lest the new order in Berlin and Munich might infect us. . . . *As long as order has not been secured with you, union means a great danger. You must not overlook that with us the National Assembly, in which all parties cooperate, has not for a moment been displaced,* whereas you have no Reichstag and no legal government.

Projecting the Anschluss question against the background of Austria's historical past, he added, "It is by no means certain as yet, *where* God wants us German-Austrians, and this after all matters vitally. The old Austria is by no means dead as yet. The 'Danubian confederation' will certainly come and renew it."

Anschluss with Germany, then, would have closed the books over Austria's supranational mission. But, he concluded,

it looks dishonorable if we stuck by Austria as long as it was great and now since a more modest role has been indicated for it, we would make haste to part with it. Only once Austria has definitely disappeared shall we be morally free to enter into other ties. Before the conclusion of the peace, however, there is no way of knowing what will happen.[134]

"Jesuitry," charged Bauer's envoy to Berlin,[135] and from his point of view Seipel's arguments might well have appeared devious and tortured and more dangerous even than the openly hostile line of Liechtenstein's hard-core reactionaries. In the light of this letter, were not his public protestations of fraternal feelings

[134] Z. 703-Präs. Seipel to "Lieber hochw. Kollege," December 17, 1918; italics in original, St.A., K.262.
[135] Strictly Confidential letter Z. 23/Res. Hartmann to Bauer, Berlin, January 14, 1919, St.A., Präsidialakten Otto Bauer, K.262.

exposed as blatantly dishonest? In fact, Seipel was no friend of the Anschluss, but he risked appearing ambivalent by removing the issue from the scope of political passions. He was right in refusing to see in it a panacea. Instead of stereotypes he offered alternatives, instead of emotionalism he offered pragmatic statesmanship. By his elaborate reasoning Seipel fully exposed the fact that almost everyone was agreed upon an initial position—the Anschluss—without really being agreed upon its practicality.

What is particularly impressive about Seipel's argument, however, is his combination of the ability to size up a concrete situation with a long-range vision of a supranational order in Central Europe. While accommodating himself to realities, however unpleasant, he never let the broader perspectives out of his sight. Hewing to a "straight line" in politics was Seipel's "favorite sport."[136] For the first time since Metternich, or perhaps Schwarzenberg, Seipel appeared as a conservative statesman with scope and vision, who could interpret the Austrian experience persuasively in terms of past, present, and future. However, in comparison with Metternich and Schwarzenberg who had the backing of a large and still powerful monarchy, Seipel, deprived of it, maneuvered in a power vacuum, a fact which lent his course a singularly visionary, but at the same time, quixotic note.

Apart from the impact of his argument, there was the impact of his personality, which came at the very time when Austria bled from a thousand wounds. While on the Left postmortems for the great Viktor Adler were still sung, on the Right the priestly figure of Seipel had come forward—the man for whom Hermann Bahr had called during the previous year, the man who came "from below," in the hour of "need." But entering the electoral campaign as a cleric he was to begin with a controversial and deeply mysterious candidate. It must be added that his whole strategy was not devised to discourage controversy or to dispel mystery. All in all, Seipel rather enjoyed being thought of as "the

[136] Interview with Lothar C.F. Wimmer, April 2, 1958; cf. also Seipel to Heinrich Mataja, Vienna, November 21, 1930.

most hated man of Vienna." This controversy about his person, he figured, would cost his party votes, but, in turn, would add "beyond measure" to his own stature.[137]

It was at this time, early in February 1919, that Seipel visited Dr. Gottfried Kunwald. The entry in his diary, somewhat less cursory than usual, read: "Evening at Dr. Kunwald's, very important conversation on financial questions."[138] The two men continued to meet, at times weekly and even daily, until Seipel's death.

What little is known about the person of Dr. Kunwald merely deepens the mystery surrounding him. A heavily set man with a tall "head of a thinker," bald, red-bearded, he was paralyzed from his waist down and supported by the "sadly twisted thin legs of a five-year-old child." He was repeatedly observed being wheeled for his encounters with Seipel into the elegant Sacher Hotel or into Parliament; more often, however, Seipel after an arduous day's work went to see him in his dark three-room apartment in the Schulerstrasse. Dr. Kunwald was a Jew and allegedly a Freemason. He held an important position in the Biedermann Bank, one of the many small Viennese banks to go bankrupt in the course of the twenties. He had a brilliant mind and was regarded as something of a wizard. But if he ever did write on "universal philosophy," the work never saw the light of day. And only a few people succeeded in meeting him—"a few ministers, a few scholars of distinction."

Seipel's and Dr. Kunwald's relationship evidently went back to the wartime when Dr. Kunwald had been, like Seipel, an admirer of Lammasch's peace policy. However, the intimacy could hardly have been based on shared ideas. It can be assumed that the topics discussed by the two men were primarily of a financial nature. Seipel understood little about finance and may have been leaning heavily for advice on Dr. Kunwald, who most likely acted

[137] Seipel to Lammasch, Vienna, February 16, 1919.
[138] Seipel diary, February 7, 1919.

as financial adviser to the Christian Socialist party. But even from the sketchy entries in Seipel's diary it is evident that he and Kunwald discussed other than financial topics. It had been suggested, not without reason, that Dr. Kunwald often had a decisive influence on appointments of state. In brief, he was Seipel's, if not the Christian Socialists', gray eminence.[139]

Only a few people knew what was transacted between the two men, and Dr. Kunwald's name was "whispered from mouth to mouth,"[140] anxiously, suspiciously. Certainly the mystery about him added to the mystery surrounding Seipel. Among Catholic politicians especially the connection between the priest, the rising star in the party, and the old freemasonic Jew caused a good deal of rumormongering, which even connected Seipel himself with the freemasons. Once again, Seipel did not choose to respond to any such gossip.

If in the crossfire of charges and countercharges, ranging from Jesuitry to Freemasonry, Seipel reported whimsically to Lammasch, who had again retired to Salzburg, that politics did not show its "best side," he had for better or worse entangled himself in its web.[141] He was ready and eager to cope with the challenge ahead, and according to his friend Redlich, had at just this time "great fun with politics."[142] Years later Seipel himself revealed, in a letter to a friend, how consciously he was engaged in shaping his own public image: to "let people guess at you" was a way of "collecting a possibly great following."[143]

[139] Cf. Ernst Benedikt, "Der Berater. Eine Figur aus den Hintergründen der österreichischen Politik," *Neue Freie Presse*, April 6, 1924, morning ed. Cf. also the novel by Robert Neumann, *Macht* (Berlin, 1932), in which Dr. Kunwald features prominently under the pseudonym of "Herr Direktor Dr. Lassalle."

[140] *Neue Freie Presse*, April 6, 1924, morning ed.

[141] Seipel to Lammasch, Vienna, December 30, 1918.

[142] Redlich diary, April 24, 1919, *Schicksalsjahre*, ii, 342.

[143] Seipel to Mataja, Vienna, April 28, 1930.

119

The Policy of Accommodation

The Coalition with the Left; Socialization

The election of February 1919, which initiated Seipel into his parliamentary career, brought about a balance between the two major parties, the Social Democrats and the Christian Socialists.[144] Since neither was eager to enter a coalition with or to depend upon the decimated Pan-Germans, a red-black coalition, so-called, was indicated. The government formed on March 15 was under the chancellorship of Karl Renner and the vice-chancellorship of the Christian Socialist peasant leader from Vorarlberg, Jodok Fink. Its main function was the negotiation of the peace treaty. In his address to the newly convened Constituent National Assembly, Renner emphasized that the new government was based upon parties which, according to their ideologies and political programs, were at a great distance from each other, and in order to serve the common task, each had to put aside some of its political objectives.

The first coalition stood under heavy pressure from the Left as well as from the Right. Among the Social Democrats a small but vociferous minority on the Left, encouraged by the proclamation of Soviet republics in Hungary (March 22) and Bavaria (April 7), hoped to push forward the process of social revolution in Austria, bring the Austrian revolution in line with the world revolution, and establish a dictatorship of the proletariat there. The majority among the Marxists, however, led by Chancellor Renner, was fully aware of the dangers which bolshevization of Austria would have meant to the country as well as to the Social Democracy, and even Otto Bauer grudgingly tolerated the coalition as a temporary expedient.

The Christian Socialists, the junior partners in the new govern-

[144] The Social Democrats emerged with 72 seats, followed closely by the Christian Socialists with 69. The Pan-Germans, who in the Provisional National Assembly had constituted by far the strongest bloc, now could muster only 26 seats. Three representatives of minor groups completed the roster of delegates. See Alfred Kasamas, *Österreichische Chronik* (Vienna, 1948), p. 476.

ment, had no less reason for having mixed feelings about the coalition. While it is right to talk, as Braunthal does, of a "workers' and peasants' coalition,"[145] it ought to be understood that the "identity of mood" between the two classes, while it made the alliance possible, was a very passing one. There were more compelling reasons than a temporary mood on the part of the peasants for the commitment of the Christian Socialists to the coalition. These we find operative in the much maligned "Viennese wing" of the party, as represented by Dr. Funder's *Reichspost*, and, if by any other person, by Seipel. Only an excess of hindsight, which is not conducive to historical accuracy, could, in connection with Seipel's role in the coalition question, mark him as the "architect of Catholic counterrevolution."[146] He became one of the architects of the coalition with the Left not out of disingenuousness but in consistency with his whole previous thought and action.

There were, of course, purely pragmatic reasons why the Christian Socialists should have entered the coalition. It was largely a "sense of duty," the *Reichspost* claimed, that led the party to take this course.[147] Seipel approved of the first coalition because, as he later explained, "it allowed for the very establishment of a parliamentary government, and thereby prevented a Soviet dictatorship."[148] Just as in November 1918 he had been consciously instrumental in keeping the Christian Socialist party from maneuvering itself "outside the floor of parliament," he now was trying to prevent the Socialists from breaking out of Parliament. The potential backing which the Social Democrats had from the labor organizations as well as from the street, and moreover the threat of Bolshevism from Hungary and Bavaria, clearly

---

[145] Cf. Julius Braunthal, *The Tragedy of Austria* (London, 1948), chapter 5, pp. 69ff.

[146] Ibid., p. 80.

[147] *Reichspost*, March 16, 1919.

[148] Ignaz Seipel, "Die Christlichsozialen in der Nationalversammlung," *Reichspost*, September 16, 1920.

indicated the dependence of the Christian Socialist party on parliamentary government.

Strangely connected with the first coalition was the drive towards socialization. "Everybody speaks of socialization," wrote Professor Schumpeter.[149] As in Germany's "dreamland of the armistice period," socialization in Austria became a formula that seemed to give positive meaning to times that were otherwise subject to collapse and suffering. It was an integral part of the Austrian revolution.

While in 1919 almost everybody spoke of socialization, there was, even among the Marxists, a wide margin of disagreement over what it actually meant, how far it was to go, and whether it was feasible. Like the Anschluss, it was projected into the void. The Social Democrats had good reason to look back with pride on the extraordinary achievement of Ferdinand Hanusch, Seipel's "successor" in the State Department of Social Welfare, who had, in the initial phases of the revolution, pushed through legislation on the eight-hour day, a vacation act, a child labor law, and a revision of the social insurance statutes. But from there on they moved, with varying degrees of doctrinairism, in the direction of a socialization which was to accomplish what Bauer called the "revolution in the factories."[150]

The Christian Socialist coalition partners, though less concerned with the social revolution, nevertheless joined in good faith in the general debate.[151] Seipel, arguing as a moral theologian, recalled that it was an "old Christian idea" that man was merely the administrator of the wealth he obtained from God. Socialization, then, was an ethical proposition since it was to reaffirm Christian values.[152] The Christian Socialist party, the party

[149] Joseph Schumpeter, "Sozialistische Möglichkeiten von heute," *Archiv für Sozialwissenschaft und Sozialpolitik,* xxxxviii (1920-1921), 307.

[150] Bauer, *Revolution,* pp. 161ff.

[151] For the Christian Socialist official stand on socialization see *Neue Freie Presse,* February 28, 1919, morning ed.

[152] Ignaz Seipel, "Die Christlichsoziale Partei und die Sozialisierung," *Reichspost,* April 10, 1919.

of Karl Vogelsang, could look back after all on an outspokenly anticapitalist tradition and could invoke, furthermore, as Seipel did, the precedent of Lueger's municipal socialization, which now was to be extended to a wider area. As a spokesman for socialization among the Christian Socialists, Seipel reemphasized the original reformative orientation of his party. Upon the initiative of "Seipel and colleagues" the Constituent National Assembly adopted a law creating a socialization commission on March 14, and on the following day proceeded to appoint Bauer its president and Seipel its vice-president.

Seipel's insistence on an orderly procedure was matched by his awareness of the danger of a Russian-style "wild socialization."[153] And at the point of "impending danger,"[154] the very man upon whose motion the socialization commission had been instituted demanded its dissolution. On October 17 the National Assembly was told that both Bauer and Seipel had resigned their positions in the commission. This, in fact, was the end of socialization in Austria.

Seipel's strange role in the socialization issue cannot be explained as a mere tactical move aimed at boring from within to wreck the chances of the program. Even though he constituted a "retarding element" on the question in the first coalition, as E. K. Winter has observed,[155] he approached it in good faith. If anything, he should be criticized for an excessive lack of realism. But on the pursuit of socialization depended the coalition, and on the coalition depended the new republic. Seipel's decision to back socialization was an eminently political one.

As sober and as expert a man in financial and economic matters as Josef Redlich saw from the start that "no one expects that the Social Democrats . . . will seriously aim at 'La Sociale'; the problems which now exist do not admit a 'socialist' solution at

---

[153] *Reichspost*, April 10, 1919.

[154] *Reichspost*, September 16, 1920.

[155] E. K. Winter, *Ignaz Seipel als dialektisches Problem: Eine Beitrag zur Scholastikforschung* (Vienna, Frankfurt, and Zurich, 1966), p. 63.

all."[156] Professor Joseph Schumpeter, who had initially championed socialization and had even criticized the Social Democracy for its "lack of vigor,"[157] quickly came to see that it was not feasible;[158] the problem of Austria was essentially Vienna, and the preservation of Vienna as a commercial and financial center of Central Europe was *"the* task of Austrian politics."[159] It is very likely that Seipel, who saw a good deal of Schumpeter during the spring of 1919[160] and who considered himself on good terms with the Secretary of Finance,[161] adopted his sobering thoughts. Even the Marxists did. Bauer saw that the revival of capitalism in Western and Central Europe had dealt at least a temporary blow to the expropriation of private industry.[162] The often quoted phrase, "One cannot socialize debts," goes back, it must be remembered to Renner.[163]

Hence within less than one year socialization had proved a grand illusion. But even though it failed, it had distinct political repercussions. Both Seipel and Otto Bauer saw the connection between socialization and the Bolshevik danger; like the coalition itself, socialization appeared as a device to prevent the "full breakthrough"[164] of communism, and moreover Otto Bauer had to acknowledge that the collapse of the Soviet dictatorship in Hungary reduced the pressure for socialization.[165] While it is not wrong to argue, as Charles Gulick does, that "the historical importance of the socialization attempts in Austria lies chiefly and almost solely in their relation to the struggle against Bolshe-

[156] Redlich diary, February 17, 1919, *Schicksalsjahre,* II, 333.
[157] Bauer, *Revolution,* p. 179.
[158] Cf. his article, "Sozialistische Möglichkeiten von heute," pp. 305-360.
[159] Ibid., p. 355; italics in original.
[160] Seipel diary, March 18, April 1, April 30, May 31; these meetings took place generally in company of Dr. Kunwald and Heinrich Mataja.
[161] Seipel to Heinrich Lammasch, Vienna, May 1, 1919.
[162] Bauer, *Revolution,* p. 181.
[163] *Neue Freie Presse,* October 11, 1919, morning ed.
[164] Ignaz Seipel, "Das Entscheidungsjahr," *Reichspost,* January 7, 1920.
[165] Bauer, *Revolution,* p. 181.

vism,"[166] this statement requires a shift of emphasis. Socialization did not hold back Bolshevism, but the illusion of socialization served to maintain the vital coalition;[167] and when it was finally exposed as a failure, it was dropped by common consent of both parties.

The Peace Treaty

Actually the main lines of the Parisian treaty system were already settled by the national revolutions which had taken place in October 1918. Each nationality had gone its own way and set up its own state. The Succession States were there to stay. The "oppressed nationalities" of Central Europe had proceeded in the direction of establishing their New Europe and the German Austrians and Hungarians had followed suit. So by the time the peace treaties had been negotiated, the breakup of the Central European unit was accomplished.

The Treaty of St. Germain was a draconic peace. The Austrian delegation arrived completely empty-handed. Austria-Hungary, by contrast to the German Reich, had surrendered unconditionally. It could therefore make no claim to the Wilsonian principle of self-determination, even though the latter had become generally invoked as a morally binding commitment and as a legitimation of territorial settlements. Also the Great Powers themselves were committed in some instances, as in their relation to Italy and Rumania, to secret treaties arrived at in the course of the war, which in many ways violated self-determination. The much dreaded transfer of two hundred and fifty thousand Tyrolians from the South Tyrol to Italy and of more than three million German Bohemians to Czechoslovakia could be effected with the stroke of a pen. On the other hand, the Austrian delegation staged a distinct success in persuading the victors to allot Western Hungary (the later Burgenland) to Austria as well as

---

[166] Gulick, *Austria*, I, 143.
[167] Seipel, "Das Entscheidungsjahr," *Reichspost*, January 7, 1920.

stretches of southern Styria, and to provide a plebiscite for Carinthia, the outcome of which was bound to be favorable to Austria.

Altogether the territorial transfers of the Peace Treaty system only replaced the multinational Empire by the nation-state in principle. The New Europe, in effect, was not divided into nation-states. The principle of self-determination was not and could not be consistently carried out. The peace settlement left approximately twenty-four million Central Europeans in the minority status out of a total population of about one hundred and ten million. A large *Europa Irredenta*, as a German scholar pointed out,[168] was left. The minorities of postwar Europe were left dependent on Minority Treaties which were an integral part of the peace settlement, but to which the big powers, including Italy, did not subject themselves, the small powers only grudgingly signed, and the League administered conscientiously but, inevitably, with little effect. It was this situation which, among other things, kept alive Seipel's continued interest in the old Austria and nourished his active concern for the minority problem.

The most grievous and perplexing problem that Austria inherited from the dismemberment was the one of its identity. Whereas Germany after Versailles, in spite of revolution and territorial decimation, maintained its unquestioned identity to the point of continuing to call itself "Reich," and also, with the exception of the Polish Corridor, its territorial integrity, defeat and the treaties eliminated the Austrian Empire's territorial integrity and jeopardized the identity of little Austria.

The uncertainty and controversy over the name of the new state is indicative of the uncertainty over its identity. Actually the very name German-Austria, officially adopted by the Provisional National Assembly of October 21, 1918, was meaningless in terms of historical precedent and the political reality after November 1918. But in spite of a host of other more or less artificial alterna-

[168] Max Hildebert Boehm, *Europa Irredenta: eine Einführung in das Nationalitätenproblem der Gegenwart* (Berlin, 1923).

126

tive designations, the name "German-Austria" nevertheless asserted itself as a gesture toward the Anschluss idea. The designation "German-Austria" indicated that the new state from the very start had no will to live, that it was a "state against its own will,"[169] eager to become part of the German Republic.

The fact that the Allied and Associated Powers, largely upon French insistence, from the very start of the peace negotiations used the nomenclature "Austrian Government" in addressing Renner's government[170] was indicative of their position on the Anschluss question. Certainly the German treaty, handed over to the German delegation on May 7, contained a clear veto of the Anschluss, which only remained to be transferred to the Treaty of St. Germain. After all this, however disappointing, it was not surprising to the Austrians that the final draft of the treaty decreed in its Article 88 that "the independence of Austria is inalienable except with the consent of the Council of the League of Nations." Furthermore the new state was forced to change its name from "German-Austria" to "Republic of Austria."[171]

The outrage following the presentation of the Peace Treaty was unanimous among all parties in Austria. "The Peace Treaty imposes upon us the most bitter national sacrifices," Renner told the National Assembly on September 6, "and every heart is therefore filled with mourning and bitterness." Hauser seconded him: "We are forced by the conditions to sign our own death warrant."[172] Much was said, in particular by Renner, about the economic plight of the new state. Whereas Germany had been only weakened economically, Austria had been destroyed. What was left of Austria was a decimated Alpine area surrounding an over-

[169] Reinhold Lorenz, *Der Staat wider Willen. Österreich 1918-1938* (Berlin, 1940).

[170] Cf. "Invitation of the French Government," Vienna, May 2, 1919, in Nina Almond and Ralph Haswell Lutz, *The Treaty of St. Germain: A Documentary History of its Territorial and Political Clauses* (Stanford, 1935), p. 39.

[171] Almond and Lutz, *St. Germain*, pp. 248-253.

[172] Schulthess, *1919*, I, 540f.

size capital, mountainous land without sufficient arable soil, industries without outlets and without access to the sea, and a bureaucracy large enough to serve a vast empire. Moving words were spoken about the losses of Austrian land and peoples. But however relevant, however justified these outcries, the underlying theme was one of lamentation over a lost identity which was, after all, the gravest problem bequeathed by the Treaty of St. Germain to Austria, the "land without name," as Renner recalled years afterward.[173] Hauser did not shy from calling the new state a "cripple" before the Assembly, and he continued, "We are torn to pieces, and the many unhappy ones, who still crawl through the streets as sad reminders of the terrible war, will be a symbol of our poor Republic."[174] Hermann Bahr wrote some years later, "What is now called Austria irritates me, because it carries wholly without title the name dearest to me."[175]

The treaty had buried the Empire beyond resurrection, and even thoughts of a Danubian confederation, which immediately after the collapse had continued to occupy many politicians' minds,[176] faded into the background. The Anschluss as an alternative was also dashed by the terms of the treaty. Only the most incorrigible optimist would find encouragement and hope in the clause of the Anschluss articles of Versailles and St. Germain which referred to the consent of the Council of the League of Nations. The more the Anschluss ceased to be a realistic political alternative within the framework of the Paris treaties and postwar power relations, the more the continuing Anschluss agitation became a direct challenge to the whole international order established in 1919.

For the moment, therefore, the unwanted state had to become a state. The idea of Austria's independence was born not only of

[173] Karl Renner, "Austria, Key for War and Peace," *Foreign Affairs*, xxvi (July 1948), 595.

[174] Schulthess, *1919*, i, 542.

[175] Hermann Bahr to Seipel, Munich, June 3, 1922 (copy); Seipel Archive.

[176] Cf. above, p. 112.

the will of the Allies but also of the insight of responsible Austrian statesmen into her terrible human and economic plight; they saw, with another winter ahead, the country's complete dependence on the victorious powers. In an atmosphere in which passions ran high, in which the counsel of desperadoes was higher in the order of things than sober reflection and action, it was by no means an easy task to advocate moderation and steer a basically unpopular course. The National Assembly, with its Social Democrat–Christian Socialist majority prevailing against the voices of the Pan-Germans, bowed to the inevitable by voting overwhelmingly for the Peace Treaty. But it cannot be denied that the two parties gave good leadership to their people. "Work, work, not despair," were Renner's final words to the National Assembly on September 6, endorsing a similar appeal by Hauser: "Believe in the future, believe in the community of our interests within the frame of this state."[177]

It was Seipel, along with Renner (still overshadowing Bauer in the Social Democratic party) who chose the course of *Realpolitik* and thus started the new little republic off on the arduous road toward a new identity. Once again his pragmatic approach to politics allowed him to adjust to a new situation. Time and again, in public and in private, he repeated his *Hic Rhodus, hic salta!* He said that he loved the new state "because it is and because it could not be unless God after all wanted it, and because something could still come of this state if God helps us and if we make the utmost effort."[178] This did not imply that he had lost sight of the broader horizons of "the old great supranational state."[179] Rather he faced up to being, as he later phrased it, "condemned to live, for awhile, the hard life of a small state."[180] To

---

[177] Schulthess, *1919*, I, 553.

[178] *Sten. Prot., 73. Sitzung d. konst. Nationalversammlung*, April 20, 1920, p. 2122.

[179] Ibid.

[180] Letter to Dr. W. Bauer, in Sweet, "Seipel's Views on *Anschluss*," *Journal of Modern History* (January 1947), p. 322.

The Policy of Accommodation

keep working for a supranational Central European order within the framework of a Balkanized order, with only a small, powerless state to fall back on, became a challenge for Seipel as he began to shape his thoughts on foreign policy in the early 1920s.

The domestic political situation in Austria explains why no "stab in the back" legend arose in Austria, as it did in Germany. In the first place, the Austrian Right, thanks to Seipel, had accepted the Republic. The government which sent the delegation to St. Germain was a coalition government of Left and Right, the delegation itself being tripartisan. The vote for acceptance was carried by a Social Democrat–Christian Socialist majority, which unlike the Social Democrat–Centrist majority in Germany represented a broad political spectrum. The mood of Austria was resigned. "With sad heart," said Weiskirchner during the ratification debate on October 17, "we resign ourselves to this terrible necessity."[181] But the vital background for the quiet, dignified acceptance, uncontested by emotional outbursts, was the governmental coalition of which Seipel was one of the main architects. A good deal of the credit for the Austrian Republic's first year of existence without any domestic upsets should go then to Seipel's circumspect guidance.

Renewal and Breakup of the Coalition

With the ratification of the Peace Treaty the coalition had accomplished its main task, and on the very day of the National Assembly's decision Renner offered the resignation of his cabinet. The termination of the first coalition reflected a certain shift in the political balance of the country. The threat of Bolshevism, which had hung over Austria and had to a large extent held the coalition together, receded with the failure of the experiments in Bavaria and Hungary. Conservative circles in particular took heart from this. Having so far made concessions to the Social Democracy as a welcome rampart against the common enemy, they now

[181] Schulthess, *1919*, I, 559f.

recovered their own identity. But many arduous tasks remained to be settled before the frail Republic could stand on its feet. The Constituent Assembly was still to accomplish its main objective, the drafting of a constitution. Under these circumstances the renewal of the coalition was recognized by its former members as essential. The new government, then, was formed once again under Renner's chancellorship and Fink's vice-chancellorship, but its composition was an indication of the strengthened position of the Christian Socialists.

The second coalition, which the new government represented, was this time based on a formal pact whose architects were Seipel and Bauer. It was a fragile and tenuous coalition, and after St. Germain and with the receding threat of bolshevization the problems that remained tended to be divisive. While Renner saw the coalition metaphorically as the "snow pit"—in which two strange wanderers caught in a storm find temporary protection[182]—Seipel justified it as a continued protection against the extreme Left as well as a means of avoiding civil war such as threatened in Germany with the Kapp *Putsch* of March 1920.[183] Certainly, the new constitution had still to be finished before the coalition would have accomplished its objectives.[184]

Once the coalition had overcome one of its chief hurdles by the passing of the Army Law (*Wehrgesetz*), which represented a compromise between the two major parties, in the National Assembly on March 18, it stumbled over a relatively subsidiary matter. It is not unusual in history that major upsets are precipitated by relatively minor causes, but it should be remembered that the minor issues are generally the outward symptoms of deeper disturbances. The control of the army was in itself no

[182] Cf. Funder, *Vom Gestern ins Heute*, pp. 638f.

[183] In his discussion of the Kapp *Putsch* Seipel made sure to emphasize, not without a certain pride and indeed malice, that little Austria, in contrast to Germany, had so far escaped civil war; Ignaz Seipel, "Die Märzrevolution im Reiche und wir," March 16, 1920, *Kampf*, pp. 80-82.

[184] Cf. Ignaz Seipel, "Heraus mit der Verfassung," *Kampf*, p. 86.

minor matter, as the army law had favored the Social Democrats by providing for the institution of so-called soldiers' councillors (*Soldatenräte*), a matter on which the coalition partners were extremely sensitive. During the debate Seipel had explicitly given notice that the law depended on loyal administration without which an "incurable wound" would be inflicted upon the people.[185] The actual breakup of the coalition occurred over the issue of a decree concerning soldiers' councils by the Secretary of the Army Deutsch, which the Pan-Germans and Christian Socialists claimed was the prerogative of the whole government. When in the National Assembly session of June 10 the Social Democrats and Christian Socialists added fuel to the fire by sending into the battle their most hot-headed speakers, Karl Leuthner and Leopold Kunschak, the hour of the coalition had struck. The breach seemed irreparable and Renner reported the resignation of the cabinet to the President of the National Assembly.

A short but important phase in the history of the Austrian Republic which has been generally overlooked by historians ended with the coalition. Between October/November 1918 and June 1920 Austria, no more than a shadow of a once powerful Empire, was a struggling state, searching for its identity and uncertain of its future. Nevertheless the political achievement of that period, especially if compared with the situation in Germany during the same period, was impressive. There had been no violence. There was neither an obstructionist Right nor a strong Communist movement. There was no enemy, so to speak, on the Right or on the Left. Under the pressure of the blockade, of hunger, and cold, and of the Communist threat from without, the politicians of all major parties, however far apart ideologically, joined hands to guide the new Republic through its infancy. The coalition between the Social Democrats and Christian Socialists, the socialization initiative, and the general agreement on the unpopular

---

[185] Quoted in Funder, *Vom Gestern ins Heute*, p. 644.

peace served the same purpose. During these two short years a body of goodwill was built up which had all the markings of at least a temporary consensus and which might well have extended to a more solid permanent one.

But in the long run the store of goodwill and moderation was not able to withstand the forces of divisiveness. As happens so often, the release of pressure from without lessened the sense of urgency at home. And at home the parliamentary tradition was all too young. Therefore, it is not altogether incidental that the coalition should have fallen apart, as Funder puts it, "in open session."[186]

It should be remembered here that in itself a coalition government is not a good thing. A great coalition such as the Christian Socialist–Social Democratic one tends to remove the government from the people and absolve the parties from responsibility for their policies. Decisions, agreements, deals are being made between the parties—in this case in the *camera caritatis* of the coalition's executive committee, strictly speaking an outer-parliamentary body—and for these decisions all parts are responsible and none. Parliament, in this case the National Assembly, is left without a vigorous opposition. The country, in short, is being administered rather than governed; the emphasis is upon law and order rather than parliamentary responsibility.

Such considerations may explain why, leaving aside mere hotheadedness, tendencies may have existed in both camps which, with the best of intentions, would have led to impatience with the cumbersome coalition. *Packeln*, to make deals behind scenes, had been an old practice in the days when the Austrian Reichsrat was immobilized by the nationality struggle, a subterfuge for parliamentary rule. It is no surprise then that Otto Bauer should have been sensitive to this practice.[187] He also was keenly aware of the responsibility of the Social Democrat leadership to the pro-

[186] Ibid., p. 646.
[187] Cf. Jacques Hannak, *Karl Renner und seine Zeit* (Vienna, 1965), p. 415.

letariat, and the latter had come to look upon the "sterile" coalition as an obstacle to its political and social aspirations. "Ever greater sectors of the working class demanded the dissolution of the coalition,"[188] and Bauer candidly stated that the decision for the breakup had been reached within the Social Democracy, and it was only a question of choosing the opportune time for it.[189] It was on this vital matter that Bauer gained the ascendancy within his party over the cautious, patient, less ideological, and much more statesmanlike Karl Renner. The decision then on the Social Democratic side was only to a small extent made on the floor of Parliament. It was largely premeditated. In some ways it was understandable, but in others it appears as an irresponsible decision. In the light of subsequent events it became clear, even from a Socialist view, that Otto Bauer's course had been a "political mistake"[190] and that the Republic was not healthy enough to be plunged into an open political struggle. This factor the all too doctrinaire Otto Bauer failed to reckon with.

On the Christian Socialist side counsel was no less divided on the merits of the coalition, and as a result frustration and impatience gained the upper hand over statesmanlike restraint. But not even Seipel's somewhat reluctant statement to his friend Bahr that at the time of the coalition's formation in October 1919 he had foreseen its breakup in June 1920 "by us"[191] can lend any substance to the blanket charge that it was due to the "determination of the bourgeois, capitalistic, ecclesiastical, legitimistic reaction led by Prelate Seipel to exclude the Social Democracy from every influence over the state."[192] Prelate Seipel—he had been elevated to this ecclesiastical dignity by Benedict XV in Au-

---

[188] Bauer, *Revolution*, p. 219; cf. also Hannak, *Karl Renner*, pp. 111f. and Julius Braunthal, *Otto Bauer: Eine Auswahl aus seinem Lebenswerk* (Vienna, 1961), p. 78.

[189] Bauer, *Revolution*, p. 220.

[190] Cf. Karl Renner, *Österreich von der Ersten zur Zweiten Republik* (Vienna, 1952), p. 43; cf. Hannak, *Karl Renner*, pp. 410ff., 417.

[191] Seipel to Bahr, Vienna, June 19, 1920; Bahr Archive.

[192] Braunthal, *Otto Bauer*, p. 79.

gust 1919[193]—was, as we have seen, one of the chief architects of coalition. At the dramatic session of June 10 he was not even present. The assumption is correct that had Seipel, who was not apt to indulge in grand and expensive public gestures, been present in Parliament, the parting of the ways would at least have been different.[194] Like Bauer, however, Seipel miscalculated the ability of the country to enter into political battle. The pacifist was preoccupied with the specter of civil war, and he specified a "bloody one."[195] But he did not sufficiently think through the corrosive effects of a bloodless civil war.

Viktor Adler is reported to have said shortly before his death, "We can start the wrangling only once we have gained some ground underneath our feet."[196] The Republic was not healthy enough to be plunged into open political struggle. An enormous burden lies on those who made the mutual decision to break up the coalition in June 1920. After two promising years, the Republic was thrown into a creeping civil war. Lightheartedly, thoughtlessly, the switches were set which sent the train of events into almost inevitable disaster. Certainly the decision on both sides— and in each case the element of decision and error outweighs the often attenuating element of tragedy[197]—spelled the beginning of the end of the Republic. There were moments in its subsequent history when short-termed agreements could be reached, but these were not substantial enough; there were moments when

[193] The document is dated August 2, 1919; Seipel Archive.

[194] Cf. Funder, *Vom Gestern ins Heute*, p. 647, and Josef A. Tzöbl, "Ignaz Seipel," In Hugo Hantsch, ed., *Gestalter der Geschicke Österreichs* (Innsbruck, Vienna, and Munich, 1962), p. 584.

[195] Seipel to Bahr, Vienna, June 19, 1920; Bahr Archive.

[196] Johann Nepomuk Hauser; *Stenographische Protokolle, 138. Sitzung des Nationalrates der Republik Österreich, I. Gesetzgebungs Periode*, October 12, 1922, p. 4425.

[197] Unlike Renner, who unmistakably speaks of the "political mistake" on either side (Renner, *Österreich*, p. 43), Hannak, in his discussion of the Socialist camp, is too readily swayed in the direction of "tragedy" (Hannak, *Karl Renner*, pp. 410ff.).

it became evident that a great coalition needed after all to be re-constructed, but the two great parties never came together again.

Consensus, tenuous as it had been, was replaced by division, compromise by struggle: struggle between social classes, between Church and anti-Church, between increasingly rigid party positions and also between personalities. In this respect the change of guard in the Social Democracy was decisive. With Bauer's ascendancy over Renner, a titanic contest began to shape up between Bauer and Seipel under which the Republic was finally crushed. In Bauer's case, a highly doctrinaire version of Austromarxism replaced Renner's pragmatism. In Seipel's case, a defensive rigidity of principle (which E. K. Winter has, not without reason, called "Austro-Scholasticism")[198] increasingly replaced his customary moderation and pragmatism. Between the two versions, both exclusive, both aspiring to universality, there was little room for adjustment and compromise.

The Constitution

When the coalition was dissolved the country had no constitution, but one was finally agreed upon in the autumn of 1920, when it sprang like a newborn child out of a dissolved wedlock. Late in 1918 Dr. Renner had commissioned Hans Kelsen, a distinguished constitutional lawyer at the University of Vienna, to prepare a constitution, and when in October 1919 a special secretariat was established for this purpose under Michael Mayr, a Tyrolean Christian Socialist, Kelsen moved into this office.[199] It was indicative of the urgency of the constitutional question that after the breakup of the coalition, when the parties could not agree upon any regular government, Mayr was put in charge of

[198] Ernst Karl Winter, *Christentum und Zivilisation* (Vienna, 1956), p. 405.

[199] Hannak, *Karl Renner*, p. 403; Kelsen's "pure theory of law," according to which the legal order is a set of formal norms independent of value systems, became in effect the basis of the Austrian constitution of 1920.

a makeshift proportional government (*Proporzkabinett*). It was composed of all three parties, proportional to their representation in the National Assembly, with each party assuming responsibility only for its own ministers. This strange caretaker government was to finish the constitution and see through new elections scheduled for October 17.

There was agreement at least among the major parties upon the need to proceed to a final constitutional settlement. The overriding concern, particularly on the side of the Socialists, was the increasing role on the part of the Länder. The Social Democrats were particularly fearful lest the Constituent National Assembly should fail to produce a constitution and it would have to come about by agreements between the Länder, leading in effect to a confederate solution in Austria.

The Christian Socialists, having their strength in the Länder, were naturally identified with the federalist position. But certainly the "Viennese wing" came to regard the excessive claims of the Länder with apprehension. Thus Seipel, while in many ways having to go along with provincial particularism, focused on the danger of separatism which threatened from the Tyrol and Vorarlberg. The fault, he attributed to "Red" Vienna, indeed to its—and implicitly his own—socialization policy.[200] Even if later he saw fit to soft-pedal the threat of separatism as belonging to the "childhood diseases" of federalism,[201] he was at the time seriously concerned for the unity of the new state; the Länder, he stated cate-

[200] Ignaz Seipel, "Die Absonderung der Länder," lecture to the Politische Gesellschaft, May 14, 1919, *Kampf*, pp. 74-76. Seipel's ambiguous position on socialization is here thrown into an interesting perspective. We have seen that one major consideration in his holding on to a socialization policy was the maintenance of the coalition which, in turn, was needed for the conclusion of the peace treaty. In the case, however, where socialization seemed to affect his relation to the Länder and moreover the unity of the state, he was ready to scrap it. The pros and cons of socialization, then, were judged from the not altogether extraneous point of view of the *raison d'état*.

[201] Ignaz Seipel, "Die zweite Regierungerklärung," November 21, 1923, Gessl, *Reden*, p. 76.

137

gorically "will not be permitted simply to jump out of German-Austria."[202]

The Christian Socialist interest in a constitution was clearly manifested in a series of party-sponsored public assemblies in the spring of 1920, when the coalition was still intact, with the slogan "Let's have the constitution." Seipel addressed himself primarily to the identity problem of the new state. The economy as well as future foreign relations of the country demanded a "firm domestic structure."[203]

There was an additional complex of questions which impelled the Christian Socialists and Seipel particularly to push for a constitutional settlement, and these concerned the relationship between Church and state, a matter in which the party and the Archbishop were equally interested.[204] Disagreement among the parties on this issue had most likely played a large part in the dissolution of the coalition,[205] after which a settlement seemed all the more remote. But since this was an issue which separated the Christian Socialists not only from the Social Democrats but also from the Pan-Germans, it conjured up in Seipel's mind the threat of a Social Democrat Pan-German "libertarian or antireligious" coalition.[206] The clerical faction under the leadership of Seipel, because of the deadlock over the complex question of "fundamental rights," hoped to avoid a settlement which would have called for a definite separation of Church and state similar to that prescribed by the Weimar constitution.[207]

A common concern as well as common fears for the future of

---

[202] Ibid., p. 76.

[203] Ignaz Seipel, "Heraus mit der Verfassung," *Kampf*, p. 85.

[204] Cf. Seipel diary, December 8, 1919: "Verfassungssitzung beim Kardinal"; cf. also Erika Weinzierl-Fischer, *Die österreichischen Konkordate* (Vienna, 1960), p. 140.

[205] Ibid., p. 139.

[206] "Freisinnige oder kulturkämpferische," *Reichspost*, September 9, 1920.

[207] Cf. Hans Kelsen, "Der Drang zur Verfassungsreform," *Neue Freie Presse*, October 6, 1929, morning ed.

the state brought the Socialists and the Christian Socialists together again. The constitution was bound to be a bundle of compromises expressing the tenuous balance that existed between the two large parties in the country. Much credit goes to the cautious direction of Renner and Fink, to Kelsen's expertise, and to Mayr's tactful give and take; but the decisive breakthrough after the dissolution of the coalition was due, as Kelsen observed, to Otto Bauer as head of the constitutional subcommittee of the National Assembly and Ignaz Seipel as its reporter:[208] "If the Constituent National Assembly did not go home with its mission unaccomplished, it is in the first place thanks to the fact that these two leading politicians came to terms with each other on the question of the constitution. All essential stipulations of the constitution decided upon by the Constituent . . . go back to the agreement between these two men."[209]

On September 29, 1920, Seipel, as reporter of the constitutional subcommittee, was in a position to present and justify the constitutional draft of the National Assembly.[210] It was, symptomatically, a constitution without preamble. However in this connection the beginning of Article 1 ("Austria is a democratic Republic") ought not to be minimized. In addition to the general desire of the constitution-makers to safeguard the existence of the state, there was some other, positive, agreement. Seipel reminded the House of its "unanimous" intention to give the constitution "forever" a democratic foundation.[211] But interestingly enough he saw the need for explaining, not without justification and pride, that an identification with democracy had become necessary in Austria in March 1919 in view of the threat of a "dictatorship of one single class,"[212] which was even greater than the threat of "reaction."

[208] For the minutes of the subcommittee see Felix Ermacora, *Quellen zum Österreichischen Verfassungrecht (1920)* (Vienna, 1967).

[209] Kelsen, "Der Drang zur Verfassungsreform."

[210] "Der Bericht in der Nationalversammlung," *Kampf*, pp. 90-106.

[211] Ibid., p. 90.   [212] Ibid., p. 91.

The Policy of Accommodation

Article 2, stating that "Austria is a federal state," also contained a somewhat programmatic statement, obviously a concession to the Christian Socialists—its real value lying in the form and degree of its implementation of the federal principle.

Though on both issues, the democratic and the federal, compromises were reached all along the line, the Social Democrats scored particularly on the first one. "The Austrian revolution," Otto Bauer wrote proudly, "began as a parliamentary revolution, and its result was parliamentary rule."[213] The Socialists favored legislative supremacy as a reaction against long years of absolutism in Habsburg Austria. In consequence the Nationalrat (National Council), elected on the basis of universal suffrage, emerged supreme, with only a weak presidency and a weak Bundesrat (Federal Council) by its side. The president was to be elected, by insistence of the Social Democrats, not by popular vote, but by the Bundesversammlung (National Assembly), composed of both chambers. A popular vote, the Social Democrats feared, would have given the president an independence bordering on autocracy. Otherwise the provisions for direct popular initiative were minimal. The Christian Socialists, and particularly Seipel, had urged the strengthening of the popular referendum, thus indicating a distinct leaning toward direct democracy. Seipel had pleaded for the plebiscite to be built into the new state as "the best and greatest guarantee for democracy."[214] It was above all to serve as a tool for the election of the president, with the possibility of making him independent of the parties.[215] Though there is no likelihood that Seipel would have been a disciple of Rousseau's or even a student of his work, he came close to his thinking on this matter. At the same time he was subject to some of Rousseau's paradoxes, a fact which became evident in the latter phases of Seipel's political career when his preference

[213] Bauer, *Revolution*, p. 223.

[214] "Der Bericht über das Gesetz betreffend die Volksvertretung" (March 14, 1919), *Kampf*, pp. 69f.; cf. also Seipel, "Der neue Staat," 7.

[215] Cf. Ermacora, *Quellen*, pp. 311ff.

140

for a plebiscite, supported by a vigorous antiparliamentarism, landed him in the antidemocratic camp. But the Social Democrats had feared and foreseen such a process all along.[216] Apart from parliamentary supremacy the Social Democrats succeeded in pushing through proportional representation, which they considered "the safeguard par excellence for democratic government."[217] At the same time the rule of parliament was not turned into the rule of the majority; the minority was protected by a provision requiring a two-thirds majority for any constitutional change. In the opinion of Kelsen this clause was decisive in reconciling the Christian Socialists to parliamentary rule.[218]

On the issue of federalism the prerogatives of the state and the Länder were carefully delineated, but large areas remained under the control of the federal government. The constitution also revised the legal status of Vienna, which the Socialists rightly considered the workers' bulwark in Austria, by loosening its ties with Lower Austria and preparing the ground for the formal establishment of the capital as an independent *Land*. This elevation of Vienna, finally effected on December 29, 1921, was to prove from the Social Democratic point of view "the most important innovation in the constitution,"[219] for with the subsequent shift in power away from the Socialists they still retained a stronghold in Vienna, which was no longer subject to a conservative provincial government.

In his report to the National Assembly Seipel took pains to point out and to defend the compromise character of the constitution. His defense of compromise once again reflected the spirit and latitude of Leonine accommodation and also the gap which separated him from the more rigid and conservative Catholic

[216] On the disagreement between the Christian Socialists and the Social Democrats on the issue of the popular referendum see Mary Macdonald, *The Republic of Austria 1918-1933* (London, New York, and Toronto, 1946), pp. 19ff.

[217] Macdonald, *The Republic of Austria*, p. 27; cf. ibid., p. 14.

[218] Kelsen, "Der Drang zur Verfassungsreform."

[219] Ibid., p. 222.

141

politicians such as Eberle and Anton Orel, who saw in the constitution of 1920 a violation of organic principles of social organization and rejected compromise as relativism.[220] Seipel said that the constitution could not be, "least of all in a time like ours, the work of merely theoretical considerations." A constitution cannot be construed, and then forced on those on whose cooperation it depends; it has to take account of "the existing, real power relations in the state." And he added magisterially: "One must figure on the realities."[221] This statement, far from being a mere momentary gesture, was the product of Seipel's conscious identification with a progressive, realistic policy on the part of the Church towards the modern state and modern society. The man who reported to the National Assembly was after all quite distinctly a "man of the Church"; but a flexible, accommodative Church.

There were limits to the compromise, however. There were some essential questions, such as those pertaining to marriage and education, which the Church claimed to be within its spiritual prerogative. No agreement could be reached on those matters between the Christian Socialists and the two other parties, or between a religious and a secular position, and Seipel was forced to explain that the constitution contained certain "very conspicuous gaps,"[222] notably the one on "fundamental rights"; in place of a settlement he did succeed in having the old stipulations of 1867 carried over.

"In this area," Seipel explained, "it is neither a question of varying constitutional opinions, nor of party programs, but here ideologies themselves confront each other."[223] On this matter Seipel was determined to hold the line. However pointedly progressive his acknowledgment of "realities" was, here he struck a note of warning, which was a portent of things to come. Cooperation, accommodation was possible only as long as the basic

[220] Cf. Diamant, *Austrian Catholics*, pp. 140ff.
[221] "Der Bericht," *Kampf*, pp. 91f.
[222] "Sehr bedeutende Lücken"; ibid., p. 96.
[223] Ibid., p. 96.

142

spiritual realm of the Church was not threatened. Otherwise the gap in the constitution might lead to a new Kulturkampf.

Under the circumstances, considering the tough bargaining by the two parties, the constitution was as much as could have been expected. In fact, it was a minor miracle that any agreement was reached at all, however great were its shortcomings. It was, to start with, much too complicated to be successfully interpreted by a people who had so recently attained self-government. It was too explicit on much that might better have been implied,[224] but where there was so little agreement on the important questions, there had to be a clear understanding of small details.

As in the case of the Weimar constitution, proportional representation weakened parliamentary government. The effects of this upon German politics were immediately apparent in the formation of many splinter parties which expressed all shades of opinion, made compromise difficult and a coalition necessary. And since the German constitution provided for a much stronger executive than did the Austrian one, there were, with the help of the emergency Article 48, ready constitutional safeguards to off-set a parliamentary deadlock. In Austria proportional representation had the effect of stiffening party lines. The closed list-system, which had been introduced along with proportional representation, resulted in the elected members of both Houses becoming dependent on their respective party caucuses, instead of being free agents. As a result Parliament, and specifically the Nationalrat, became "a house divided against itself, a battleground for rival groups."[225] In this instance the nonexistence of an emergency article to break the parliamentary deadlock proved as injurious as its very existence did in Weimar Germany. A weak presidency, along with a weak government, condemned Austria to government by an almost inoperative parliament, unless the ab-

[224] Cf. the cumbersome listing of federal and provincial prerogatives in Articles 11 and 12, which includes such items as steam boilers, disposal of corpses, health resorts, etc.

[225] Macdonald, *The Republic of Austria*, p. 43.

surdity of this constitutional settlement were to become sufficiently damaging to pave the way for constitutional reform.

Perhaps most important was the fact that the constitution represented transient party strength rather than a reasonably permanent outline of government. Characterized as it was by legislative supremacy and a token bow to federalism, it favored the Socialists, who were at that time the predominant factor in Austrian politics. It was inevitable, with shifts in power away from the Socialists, that constitutional changes would be necessary to adjust the constitutional imbalance. Though it was not without irony that Seipel, one of the chief architects of the constitution, should have emerged as one of its chief critics, this fact in itself casts no doubts on the sincerity of his attempt to bring about a workable compromise. Certainly he was far removed from a position like Eberle's which, in place of unsatisfactory parliamentarism, clamored for "strong dictators" who, rather than make concessions to the "shiftless masses," would follow the law of God.[226] Seipel was too much a man of the people to recognize such a juxtaposition of opposites. His criticism of the constitution was harsh but appropriate, and his attack on the "rule of parties" (*Parteiwirtschaft*) was justified. Thanks to the pressures of the Social Democrats not even parliamentarism emerged supreme in the Austrian republic; the parties were supreme. Austria, Seipel complained, with some justification after all, had been given a democratic nomenclature, but not a truly democratic constitution, or a democratic way of life.[227] This critique of the party system, this aim of Seipel's at "overcoming the parties"[228] dates back to a legitimate critique of the constitution of which he himself was the author.

[226] Joseph Eberle, "Grundsätzliches vor den Parlamentswahlen," *Das Neue Reich*, ii, September 26, 1920, 876.

[227] Karl Freiherr von Werkmann, "Seipel bei Kaiser Karl im Exil," *Neues Wiener Journal*, September 20, 1934. For the circumstantial setting in which this statement was made see the following passages.

[228] "Überwindung der Parteien," ibid.

Alarming, however, if our not disinterested source is correct, is the vehemence of Seipel's expression. The store of patience which had accompanied the Salzburg theologian in his move to the capital soon dwindled under the pressure of political affairs. As yet Seipel did not know where the "overcoming of the parties" would end. How would his detached Leonine identification with democracy stand up against an increasing temptation to improve upon the party state, and was not the road away from the parties, in the last analysis, a road away from democracy?

The Visit to the Emperor

In August 1920, shortly before the constitution was completed and two months before the general elections, Seipel made a secret trip to visit Emperor Charles in his exile in Switzerland. This visit, when publicized in 1929, added much fuel to the speculation concerning Seipel's loyalties. We should recall a few facts here. When Seipel spoke, even as Chancellor, about his attachment to the Monarchy, he thought above all of the Christian commonwealth which remained to him the model of life among nations. Like most Austrian Catholics, Seipel doubtlessly also felt a traditional attachment to the House which was so deeply a part of his country's history. But in this respect Seipel adopted what he once called a "favorite idea of [Alois] Liechtenstein," that the Habsburgs since the eighteenth century had become a French family and that with the Lorrainean blood a Western and alien bureaucratic influence had taken hold of the imperial family. "The Habsburgs were great masters [*Herren*], the Lorrainers brave bureaucrats," and when Seipel met Poincaré, "the other Lorrainer," he was reminded of Francis Joseph, who worked from morning to night, who himself studied all his files, and who provided them with marginalia.[229] Seipel had written his article

---

[229] Seipel gave various expressions to this theory, in letters as well as in private conversations. Cf. in particular "Gedächtnisprotokoll Dr. Anton Julius Walter über die Unterredung mit Exz. Dr. Seipel an 4 Dezember

The Policy of Accommodation

on "Kaisertum und Demokratie" in October 1918, he later recalled, to confront the "Lorrainese emperors with their sins
[*Sündenfall*]" and to show them a way to return to the imperial
idea within the framework of democracy. "The *Kaisertum*," he
allowed himself to speculate, "will someday again play its part in
Austria or Europe" if it were to return to the old Habsburg tradition. "Since I don't know whether or when this will happen, I
am 'uncertain.' "[230]

The question of form of government, then, was a secondary
one to Seipel, who, unlike Legitimists and Social Democrats, did
not make it a matter of principle but was realistic enough to understand the inevitability of the events of November 1918. His
role in the formulation of the Imperial Manifesto of November 11, 1918, critically received by Legitimist and Socialist critics
alike, prevented an irrevocable decision and kept the doors open
for the future.

Since the fatal days of November 1918, Emperor Charles, after
a month at the Eckartsau Castle near Vienna, had left Austria
under British protection to find refuge in Switzerland, the country of his ancestors. At the frontier town of Feldkirch on
March 24, the Emperor had issued a proud and spiteful Manifesto declaring "null and void" all dispositions concerning him
and his House by the German-Austrian government and the National Assemblies, rescinding the formula elaborated by Seipel
which had promised to recognize the decision of the Austrian
people concerning its form of government. The German-Austrian
government's motion for the proclamation of the Republic on

1929," courtesy Erika Weinzierl-Fischer; also Seipel to Regierungsrat Eduard
von Poppy (Munich), Vienna, February 28, 1930, Schmitz Archive; Seipel to
an "important personality," Vienna, November 2, 1930, *Neues Wiener
Journal*, September 4, 1932, and *Schönere Zukunft*, viii, December 11,
1932, 263.

[230] Seipel to an "important personality," *Neues Wiener Journal*, September
4, 1932.

146

November 12, 1918, had prejudged a decision which supposedly was to be made by the whole people; the Provisional National Assembly, passing this motion under the pressure of "the street," had no mandate, and so the election of February 1919 to the Constituent National Assembly had proceeded "under the sign of terror."[231]

This latest and last Manifesto of the unfortunate Emperor, which was sent to the Pope and a number of friendly heads of state, had been kept secret lest, as Charles put it, "it might bring new misfortune to my lands."[232] This meant that, in view of Bela Kun's recent take-over in Hungary, he was loath to have the Manifesto serve as a pretext for a Communist take-over in Austria.[233] Just as important to this decision, however, was the advice which came from the Christian Socialist leaders, Hauser and Seipel, not to compromise the policies of the Right in Austria.[234] This caution had not prevented the Austrian government from putting a motion before the National Assembly dealing with banishment and confiscation of the property of the House of Habsburg-Lorraine which was voted in as law on April 3, 1919.[235]

Now, on August 7, 1920, evidently by invitation of the former Emperor, Seipel stopped en route from Innsbruck to Zurich at Villa Prangins near Nyon on the northwestern shore of Lake Geneva. His diary entry, terse as usual, records two long visits

[231] Karl Werkmann, *Der Tote auf Madeira* (Munich, 1923), pp. 36f.
[232] Ibid., pp. 38f.
[233] Ibid.
[234] Brook-Shepherd, *The Last Habsburg*, p. 249.
[235] *Sten. Prot., 8. Sitzung d. Konst. Nationalvers*, April 3, 1917, p. 176. Seipel later claimed, in a letter to Dr. Funder dated February 15, 1932, that in contradiction to the official protocol a small number of Christian Socialists, including himself, had voted against it. "One group of Christian Socialists had demanded and succeeded in obtaining suspension of party discipline. Belonging to this group were, to be sure, Miklas, Mataja, Schöpfer, and myself"; quoted in Johann Auer, "Seipels Verhältnis zu Demokratie" (diss., Vienna, 1963), p. 32.

with "His Majesty" and Charles's secretary Baron Karl von Werkmann on the following day.[236]

The information on the conversations in Prangins is sparse and contradictory, and coming from the entourage of the Emperor much of it has to be read with caution. Seipel was clearly the coming man in the conservative party of Austria and we can safely assume that the Emperor wanted to know the views of his former minister. With the passing of the threat from Bavaria and Hungary, a new political stock-taking was justified, especially since a postrevolutionary "sobering up" process to which Seipel referred in his talk with Werkmann was taking place in Austria. Undoubtedly politics were discussed between Seipel and Werkmann[237] as well as between Seipel and "His Majesty,"[238] and evidently it was the Emperor's and his aide's intention to test Seipel's commitment to the Monarchy. But did Seipel really concede, as Werkmann claimed, that the Feldkirch Manifesto, being "in almost all points persuasive,"[239] superseded Seipel's own Manifesto? He may well have professed his loyalties to the House: "Habsburg has a future" or "Habsburg is a program, a convincing program." Equally well may he have added, somewhat evasively: "It is only a question of formulating it for the public in timely terms. I shall consider this my personal task. The question remains open, who will present it to the public—his Majesty, myself, the Christian Socialist party, or who else?"[240]

[236] Note the formal designation "His Majesty," in contrast to Redlich's more casual and less committal "the Emperor."

[237] The main source is a somewhat sensational article, Karl Freiherr von Werkmann, "Seipel bei Kaiser Karl im Exil," *Neues Wiener Journal*, September 20, 1934.

[238] The main source is a memorandum by August Maria Knoll, dated August 11, 1932, of a talk with "Herr Kettenburg," a confidant of Emperor Charles and his eldest son Otto; Knoll Archive. See also Knoll's talk with former Empress Zita in Cologne, October 26, 1932, referred to in August Maria Knoll, "Ignaz Seipel," *Neue Österreichische Biographie ab 1815*, ix, 120.

[239] Werkmann, "Seipel bei Kaiser Karl."   [240] Ibid.

Indeed it would not have been out of style for Seipel, once he had revealed his long-range preference, to have made clear where the initiative lay, and with all due respect to his Emperor, just who had the power to make decisions. "Presently," he is quoted as having stated imperiously, "I shall not tolerate a restoration. Only in ten years. Then I shall call the Emperor."[241] There is after all good reason to believe that the secret encounter in Prangins was not altogether successful.[242]

It was in one of his discussions with the Emperor that Seipel used the metaphor of having to wear a "mask" for another ten years.[243] In fact, he wore many masks. Emperor Charles himself, like many Austrians, must have wondered who the real Seipel was.

In the second half of September of the same year Seipel received a letter from Villa Prangins adorned with the so-called common coat of arms of the defunct Monarchy, the Austrian and Hungarian coat of arms supporting in their middle the smaller Habsburg family crest, which read as follows:

Dear Dr. Seipel,
    At the moment when the electoral campaign approaches its decisive phase I am impelled to address you, dear Dr.

---

[241] Knoll, "Seipel," p. 120; cf. Aufzeichnung, Donnerstag, 11. August 1932, erfahren von Herrn Kettenburg, Knoll Archive: "Seipel asked the Emperor to hold back for ten years."

[242] Lorenz, *Kaiser Karl*, p. 588, writes that it "seems not to have satisfied mutual expectations." The secrecy of the meeting was maintained until the end of 1929 when Seipel himself chose to refer to it in public; *Neue Freie Presse*, December 30, 1929, evening ed.

[243] "Seipel declared himself as a Monarchist; he only had, so thought Seipel, to carry a mask for the time being, which he would shed at a certain moment. Seipel mentioned, as I believe, the end of 1920 [*sic!*]. This statement of Seipel's the Emperor wanted to have in writing. Seipel declined to do this. Only upon strong urging of the Emperor did Seipel give the statement *in writing!*"; Knoll, Kettenburg Memorandum (italics in original). The date is clearly a clerical error; for 1920, read 1930.

Seipel. You participate in this struggle as one of the leaders of the voters committed to the Christian Socialist program—and therefore you are exposed to all sorts of enmity; troubles and sorrows are your lot. My greeting is intended to and should in these hard days give you pleasure.

I well know: the road leading to Austria's well-being is arduous. But I envisage Austria's people again entering this road which it has, to my pain and to its own misfortune, abandoned in the November days of 1918. I have gathered from your reports and from subsequent news which have reached me that Austria is witnessing a resurrection, that the people is endeavoring to liberate itself from the errors of the revolution, that it is seeking law and order once again, and, in this search, is increasingly remembering me, who even far from the homeland have not ceased to love the dear native country and its people.

I wish you, in view of your commendable efforts, good success in the elections, and express to you and all my faithful ones my heartfelt gratitude for this effort.

I shall be happy to hear soon again from you.

Yours affectionately,
Karl[244]

Seipel never made any use whatsoever of this letter.

Consensus Eroded

The election of October 1920 resulted in a reversal of the party strength which had prevailed since the revolution. The Social Democrats, who had been swept into a position of dominance and who in the February elections of 1919 were still able to maintain a slim leadership, now fell back into second place behind the

---

[244] Emperor Charles to Dr. Seipel, Villa Prangins, September 15, 1920, Seipel Archive.

150

Christian Socialists.[245] The postrevolutionary "sobering up," though not exactly the "resurrection" hoped for by Emperor Charles, was now clearly demonstrated by the Austrian voters. While the Christian Socialist party emerged in clear control of the countryside and the provincial towns, and while the Social Democrats continued to draw their strength from Vienna and the industrial centers, the shift to the Right reflected a defection of the disappointed middle-class following of the Socialists.[246] The result of the election, in general terms, was that the parties, which were traditionally ideological in character, now also became identified with specific classes. A party made up predominantly of peasants and the lower middle classes stood against a party of workers. This double stiffening of the party structure, along ideological and class lines, led to a stabilization of the party positions. They tended to become solid blocs, increasingly unable and unwilling to compromise. In the Austrian context, where no one party was likely to obtain an absolute majority and where compromise in Parliament was of the essence of things, the rigid

245

Party	*Seats*	
	October, 1920	*(February 1919)*
Christian Socialists	82	(69)
Social Democrats	66	(72)
Pan-Germans	20	(26)
Others	7	(3)

To these 175 seats another eight were added by the elections in the Burgenland of June 18, 1922, which were distributed as follows: Christian Socialists three, Social Democrats three, Pan-Germans one, German-Austrian Peasants' party one; cf. Kasamas, *Österreichische Chronik*, p. 486; Brita Skottsberg, *Der österreichische Parlamentarismus* (Göteberg, 1940), p. 242; Schulthess, *1922*, p. 158. The Christian Socialist party registered gains in almost all electoral districts, including those in Vienna, primarily at the expense of the Social Democrats; cf. *Wahlen und Parteien in Österreich* (Vienna, 1966), III, pp. 49ff.

246 Cf. also Mikoletzky, *Österreichische Zeitgeschichte*, p. 89.

151

alignment of parties could hardly be conducive to a wholesome conduct of the affairs of state.

Since the Christian Socialists emerged as the strongest party in Parliament, they were called upon to form a new government. However, under the prevailing circumstances the problems of forming a viable government were all the more complicated. With political victory there came an unprecedented burden of dependence upon and maneuvering in a parliamentary system which was less and less dependable and maneuverable. On November 9, at the First Conference of Austrian Bishops, "National-rat Dr. Seipel" delivered a "Report about the Political Situation," the tenor of which was distinctly sober. The only encouraging feature in the midst of victory, he saw fit to point out, was the fact that no Communist had been elected. "Communism thus is being rejected by the people."[247] Implicitly, at least, the Prelate made a distinction, so often ignored in Catholic circles, between Communists and Social Democrats. But the Social Democrats gave the Christian Socialists sufficient cause for trouble: they condemned them to a life with the parliamentarianism they had devised for themselves. Interestingly enough Seipel emphasized before the bishops that the Christian Socialists' lacked a two-thirds majority. This need of a two-thirds majority, in Kelsen's view the major protection of the minority against constitutional changes, now benefited the Social Democrats. But lacking even a simple majority, the Christian Socialists were confronted with a singularly hard task of governing.

For the moment the search for a new chancellor showed how difficult the process of forming a government was. The coalition was a matter of the past, and the revolutionary consensus had given way to an atmosphere of high tension between the parties. The solution finally found—a second cabinet under Mayr's chancellorship, consisting of four Christian Socialists and six bureau-

---

[247] *Protokoll der I. Konferenz der österreichischen Bischöfe in Wien am 9. und 10. November 1920, 9*; Cardinal Piffl Archive, Archive of the Archdiocese, Vienna.

crats—was definitely only an interim solution. The cabinet crisis was not solved, and even less the crisis of the young Austrian democracy. In the debate on November 23, Seipel, newly elected as leader of the Christian Socialist parliamentary caucus to succeed his friend Fink, appealed to the House from his position of responsibility, "to conduct above all a policy of state, while putting aside a special policy of parties."[248] Understandably Otto Bauer took him up on this issue, snapping back that the juxtaposition suggested by Seipel was "the most thoughtless addition to political terminology." What were parties but groups of people, he lectured to Professor Seipel, which merely differed on the exact definition of "policy of state"? "The whole struggle of the parties revolves around what the correct policy of state is." And did not Seipel in fact mean by "policy of parties" the control of representatives of the people, and by "policy of state" rule of bureaucrats?[249]

In October 1918 the Salzburg theologian had joined the last government of the Monarchy only to learn that his generous vision of a Christian commonwealth could no more be realized within the framework of the Empire. Seipel's step into politics brought him the realization of defeat. Instead of Christian love he found national hatred, instead of imperial openness, he found new borders and economic blockade. Central Europe, in short, was now Balkanized.

But was it not precisely this adversity which made out of Seipel a politician and a statesman? While he was committed to a Christian universalism which, as he once put it, excluded "national gods and national religions,"[250] he had trained himself to be flexible and to take the long view of things. The principles for which he stood were certainly not invalidated by the catastrophe of 1918. "We are Balkanized," he admitted squarely; but he confidently added, "We shall not let our political ethics be Balkan-

---

[248] *Sten. Prot., 4. Sitzung das Nationalrates der Republik Österreich,* I.G.P., November 23, 1920, p. 92.

[249] Ibid., p. 96.   [250] Gessl, *Reden,* p. 128.

ized."[251] While he knew that he could not "play Napoleon or Bismarck," he did know that the test of his statesmanship was his full exploitation of the Church's accommodative position in politics. Under the most disadvantageous conditions imaginable he could start on the road toward what he later was to call "higher units."[252] He would have to make detours, he would have to hedge, deceive, and bluff, he would have to act behind a mask, and above all, practice patience. And while he went serenely on his way, always preaching optimism, he was fully aware of the fact that "God's mills grind slowly."[253]

Once again, in November 1920, he saw his whole political course seriously challenged. He had worked loyally in the revolutionary days with the Socialists, he had brought the Catholic party into the Republic, he had patiently, if not enthusiastically, held onto both coalitions as he had conscientiously helped bring about an agreement on the constitution. But the elections of October 1920 and the problems of cabinet formation which followed made it clear that Seipel's democratic course had run into serious obstacles which were not primarily of his own making. To argue, as Renner does, that the "achievements"[254] of the two first years were thrown away by Seipel and Otto Bauer begs the question. The consensus broke down when the pressures from without receded. Seipel was quite correct in thinking that an ineffective constitution had its share in contributing to the polarization of ideologies. The elections brought about a confrontation of classes, and how was there to be democratic government if there was no parliamentary basis to be found for any conceivable combination of parties?

Once again Seipel, now in a position of leadership, faced the

[251] Ignaz Seipel, "Die christlichsoziale Arbeits- und Aussenpolitik," *Reichspost*, November 7, 1920.

[252] "Höhere Einheiten," *Neue Freie Presse*, June 9, 1928, evening ed.

[253] Hans Zehrer, "Der höchste Trumph," *Vossische Zeitung*, April 24, 1931.

[254] Renner, *Österreich*, pp. 42f.

154

real challenge through adversity. How carefully would he explore ways of reaching compromise; how patiently would he adhere to democratic procedure? And would his detours always bring him back to the main route?

No doubt the temptations to seek detours in the form of nonpolitical cabinets of bureaucrats were considerable, and the obstructionist opposition of the Social Democrats in Parliament was to be a hard test of Seipel's democratic course and was largely responsible for his increasingly fierce debate with Otto Bauer.

Nevertheless, it ought to be said that Seipel's commitment to democracy was not of the same kind as his commitment to supranational rule. The latter was close to the center of the Catholic universalist position; the former tangential to Catholicism, and like any form of government, expendable. The policy of accommodation is one that tends to avoid political commitment, and secular institutions remain relative. What guarantee was there that the adjustment *to* democracy might not be followed by adjustment *away* from democracy?[255] In which direction would the Church move in a situation of crisis, when democratic procedure was heavily tested?

---

[255] According to a Hungarian source, in the course of informal negotiations with Hungarian diplomats on the Burgenland question in 1920 and 1921 Seipel considered the possibility of establishing with Hungarian financial help a rightist regime backed by the paramilitary Heimwehr. It should he added, though, that this information is not conclusive. There is certainty neither about the date when the crucial proposal was discussed (March 13, 1920 or 1921) nor about the authorship of the key document; it was most likely a memorandum emanating from the Hungarian legation in Vienna, leaving uncertainty regarding the degree of Seipel's commitment to the proposition; cf. Lajos Kerekes, "Italien, Ungarn und die österreichische Heimwehrbewegung 1928-1931," *Österreich in Geschichte und Literatur,* IX (January 1965), 3-13; Lajos Kerekes, "Die 'Weisse Allianz.' Bayrisch-österreichisch-ungarische Projekte gegen die Regierung Renner im Jahre 1920," *Österreichische Osthefte,* VII (September 1965), 353-366; Gerald Schlag, "Die Angliederung des Burgenlandes an Österreich," *Österreich in Geschichte und Literatur,* XV (October 1971), 433-453; also the controversy in *Die Furche,* February 17, March 2, 30, April 20, May 18, 1968.

The Policy of Accommodation

Political crisis became inescapable in Austria in 1920. The new truncated state, whose survival depended on domestic unity, was threatening to disintegrate from within. When Prelate Seipel addressed the Second Conference of Austrian Bishops in November 1921 he struck a new note of alarm by referring to the Kulturkampf toward which the Social Democrats and the Pan-Germans were pointing. But in relation to the Kulturkampf, he stressed, "other questions are secondary."[256] The Kulturkampf touched upon matters essential to the Church—such as marriage and education—which left no room for compromise. In this area lay the certainties, the ultimate commitment of Seipel the churchman; and he would fight with any means at hand to defend those prerogatives of the Church.

To say there was a great change in Seipel's thinking at that time, as E. K. Winter does, is misleading.[257] Seipel merely spelled out, under the pressure of political crisis, the terms of his accommodative position, distinguishing between the realm in which his commitment lay and where he was not committed. He had repeatedly warned his fellow Catholics of the "great danger" of getting "wholly absorbed by politics."[258] His commitment lay beyond politics, commanding as it did the possibilities as well as the limits of a Catholic commitment to democracy. The more Seipel saw his spiritual realm threatened, the more committed he became to a departure from the previous political and social course which had led him into cooperation with the Socialists. Then Seipel the "clerical politician" superseded Seipel the "social philosopher."[259]

[256] *Protokoll über die Konferenz der österreichischen Bischöfe am 22. und 23. November 1921*, p. 12; Cardinal Piffl Archive, Archive of the Archdiocese, Vienna.

[257] Winter, *Seipel*, p. 79.

[258] *Reichspost*, January 5, 1920.

[259] These distinctions were made in a memorandum by the former German Chancellor Wirth dated June 13, 1928, to the German Foreign Office, G.F.O., 2347/4576/E173479. Cf. also Weinzierl, *Die österreichischen Konkordate*, p. 143.

156

SEIPEL AND THE PROBLEM OF
AUSTRIAN IDENTITY: 1920-1922

Conditions for an Austrian Foreign Policy

SMALL powers are not generally in a position to conduct an active foreign policy. The *Grosse Politik* is the prerogative of the great powers, which tend to bypass the smaller ones, if not actually to patronize or even to menace them. Of all countries, Austria, which Josef Redlich called "this most questionable of all creations of the Parisian treaties"[1] was incapable of playing much of a role in international politics. An early memorandum for the Foreign Office, written even before the German-Austrian delegation set out for St. Germain, candidly stated: "It may at first sight appear futile to talk today about a future foreign policy of German-Austria."[2] At the time of course the possibility of an Anschluss with Germany did actually make even the thought of Austrian foreign policy seem futile. But even aside from the Anschluss it seemed clear to the writer of the memorandum that in the foreseeable future German-Austria would be in no position to conduct an "active foreign policy."

The Treaty of St. Germain in every way verified such an estimate of Austria's impotence by leaving the little Republic prostrate and helpless—deprived of its resources as well as its markets. Now it might be argued that such a position of isolation made the need for a reestablishment of foreign ties even more urgent, and that the general dislocation of trade in Central Europe called even more for new arrangements at some future time.

[1] Josef Redlich, "Austria: A Word Problem," *New Republic*, xxv, February 9, 1921, 310.
[2] Strictly Confidential Memorandum by Konsul Maximilian Hoffinger, March 1919; St.A., Liasse Österreich 7/1, K.342, Fs.3-12.

The Problem of Austrian Identity

But with the most important initial alternatives—the Anschluss and Danubian confederation—ruled out, in which direction could Austria move? Otto Bauer's Anschluss escapade had proven futile. A fierce revisionist policy would no less have courted disaster and activated the partition plans of the neighboring powers. Self-abandonment, occasionally considered, and even threatened, would have been a desperado gesture leading to an uncertain servitude. No demonstrative gesture in any direction could have rescued the little Republic. The only road open to it was one of patient probing and of a shrewd grasping of any opportunities offered. It was a long and arduous road under any circumstances, but one likely to open up the advantages of political impotence.

To start with, there was actually next to no scope for an Austrian foreign policy. Seipel's *hic Rhodus, hic salta* applied in this area, too, as a device of supreme wisdom; in technical language this meant a "fulfillment" policy. But within this limitation there were possibilities which were left to Seipel to explore—he being the "master of the political chess game,"[3] according to one of his few German admirers. Even small powers have a maneuverable range in which to operate. In the immediate postwar situation this range was set by the uncertain balance left in Europe, and especially Central Europe, by the terms of the Paris treaty system. The Great Powers in 1918, unlike in the 1815 settlement, had agreed only on the treatment of the vanquished but not on a new order. The European balance was not redressed, and the power vacuum left in Central Europe particularly opened up some avenues for maneuvering. The European powers were not agreed upon a definite pattern for Central Europe, and not even on the Anschluss question. While no one was in favor of the Anschluss, there was a distinct variation in the intensity of feeling about it between France on one side, and England, Italy, and even

[3] Reichskanzler a.d. Dr. Josef Wirth, "Ein Logiker der Politik," *Reichspost*, August 7, 1932.

Czechoslovakia and Yugoslavia on the other. While the balance in Central Europe was thus unsettled and the situation fluid, the basic need for Austria was not to make hasty commitments, but, as Seipel repeatedly stressed, to keep doors open. In a report to the German Foreign Office of 1928, the German ex-Chancellor Wirth commented on Seipel's concept of "seeming impassivity," in view of the possibilities still open.[4] Time was working for Austria. Seen from Seipel's theological perspective this meant waiting to see what "mission" God still had in store for the once imperial Austrians. In this direction lay Seipel's ultimate commitment; and in somewhat more down-to-earth terms this did not exclude a policy of playing the Powers against each other, with flexibility, "good nerves," and even with deception. To be regarded as "dark and ambiguous" or as a "sphinx,"[5] would, under these conditions, be a price worth paying for the recovery of diplomatic flexibility. Again, God's mills grind slowly, and again there was a distinct danger that a weak country, led by as strong a leader as Seipel turned out to be, might find that the mills were not God's but Don Quixote's.

Apart from the more traditional Machiavellian devices there was still the possibility of improving Austria's position through a direct appeal to the League of Nations. This Wilsonian creation, whose Covenant had been incorporated into the Peace Treaties, could be expected to exert a controlling force over the European balance and to redress the inequities of the treaties. While it had been created by the victorious powers, it did not necessarily have to become their instrument. Through membership in the League the defeated powers could reasonably hope to obtain enforcement of general disarmament to follow the one-sided provisions of the treaties, protection of minorities, and revision of

[4] Memorandum by Josef Wirth to German Foreign Office, June 13, 1928; G.F.O., 2347/4576/E173471.

[5] Erwin Wasserbäck (Press Attaché in Berlin) to Seipel, Berlin, December 1, 1927; St.A., Liasse Deutschland I/III, Geheim, K.464, Fs.29-30.

161

some of the treaty clauses. Even on the Anschluss question reconsideration was envisaged in Article 88 "with the consent of the Council of the League of Nations." At the meeting of the League Assembly on December 15, 1920, called to decide upon the admission of new members, including Austria, the Czech foreign minister Eduard Beneš classified applicants into three groups: small states, newly created states with uncertain stability, and former enemies. Austria, fitting into each one of these categories, was admitted at the top of a long list of applicants, thus paving the way for the development of the League into a truly universal organization.[6] In these early years the character of the League was sufficiently unsettled for the small powers such as Austria to have reasonable expectations of seeing it develop into an instrument of peace, justice, and protection.

The obvious difficulties which Austria faced in establishing its position among the European powers were compounded, however, by its domestic political problems. Quite apart from the inevitable economic plight in which the country was left, there was the increasing internal division which stood in the way of the formation of a stable government. Above all, there was the question of Austria's identity, which had so little meaning to the Austrians themselves. The more the Anschluss as a concrete political alternative receded into the background, the more it surged up again as a domestic issue, an outlet for the psychological disorientation that plagued the population, particularly in the Länder. The more the European powers, following France's lead, became committed to an anti-Anschluss stand, the more did the Anschluss movement assume an irresistible force in Austria itself. It was the kind of problem that was more talked about in Austria than really considered feasible. Even the Germans, who financed it secretly, had to soft-pedal it publicly. While no one was as outspoken as Count Wedel, the Kaiser's last ambassador in Vienna, who suggested that Austria was hardly "worth a mass"

---

[6] Schulthess' *Europäischer Geschichtskalender, 1920,* II, 415f.

and pointed out the "sacrifices" which an Anschluss would mean for Germany,[7] there was no German chancellor and foreign minister who did not see the need of playing down the Anschluss as a political alternative lest it interfere with Germany's diplomatic and political priorities. In the end it was Austria who was left to feel the full impact of this explosive issue, which could in no conceivable way lead anywhere but to disaster. Its immediate effect was to deepen the split in the Christian Socialist party between the "Viennese wing" and the Länder; to prejudice the formation of a coalition between Christian Socialists and Pan-Germans; to topple governments; to deprive the country of much-needed instant credit help from abroad; and, last but not least, subject it to a continued threat of division among the powers.

These were the problems to be dealt with by those who had to conduct Austria's foreign affairs. To be sure, the domestic agitation was no less a factor than pressure from abroad, and it would take supreme wisdom and patience along with unusual dexterity and shrewdness to lead Austria out of its dilemma. A semblance of domestic stability, a workable government coalition which at the same time would give confidence to Austria's potential creditors, these were prerequisites for Austria's survival.

Moving Into Position

After the fiasco of Otto Bauer's foreign policy, it was left to Renner to take the first steps to establish ties abroad. He sent out feelers in various directions with the one tangible result of a "secret treaty" with Beneš which, apart from adding up to a reaffirmation of the unpopular Treaty of St. Germain, committed Austria to an anti-Hungarian policy.[8]

Renner's foreign policy drew harsh criticism from Seipel. He

[7] Memorandum A.3993 by Wedel, "Die Anschlussfrage," Vienna, February 6, 1919, Deutsche Botschaft, Vienna, G.F.O., S.A., Roll 25.

[8] Cf. A.V.A., 100. Sitzung, V.A.G.V., January 25, 1922. Cf. also *Arbeiter-Zeitung*, January 8, 1922; *Reichspost*, January 9, 1922.

rejected the kind of "orientation policy" which actually had no distinct orientation;[9] it was "careless, sloppy, restless," amounted to "dilettantism" and lacked—and here Seipel invoked one of his favorite principles—the virtue of keeping to a "straight course."[10] Nevertheless, Renner laid the foundations for an inevitable policy of fulfillment with which Seipel himself became identified as Chancellor. For the moment he obtained credit relief and private charity to carry Austria through the winter of 1919-20; and it took courage and even dignity for Renner to take this task upon himself, traveling, as he did, like a beggar, for his suffering country.

It was Mayr, succeeding Renner as head of the government, who felt the full impact of the unsolved domestic issues upon foreign affairs. During his tenure of office the former Emperor Charles staged his first return to Hungary in March 1921. Though Austrians of almost all shades of opinion condoned a "hands off" position and the government took pains to dissociate itself from the adventure, it had distinct domestic repercussions. When the government gave way to Socialist pressure over the issue of selection of the escort for the former Emperor on his return trip through Austria, Seipel took leave, as he frequently did in later years, suddenly and demonstratively resigning from his parliamentary functions.[11] He spent the following weeks touring Germany and studying its political problems.[12] In the area of for-

[9] Strictly Confidential "Darstellung der ersten Besprechung des Herrn Bundeskanzlers in meiner Anwesenheit [Grünberger] mit dem Herrn ungarischen Ministerpräsidenten Grafen Bethlen und dem Minister des Äusseren Daruváry in Budapest am 7. Jänner 1923"; St.A., Liasse Ungarn I/III, K.879, F.243.

[10] "Linie"; Ignaz Seipel, "Was nach den Wahlen?" *Reichspost*, October 10, 1920.

[11] *Neue Freie Presse*, April 6, 1921, morning and evening eds.

[12] Cf. Seipel diary, April 21, 1921. Cf. also Seipel's first public address after his return to Vienna; Ignaz Seipel, "Gegen eine Politik mit dem Kopf durch die Wand," *Reichspost*, May 28, 1921. Seipel's reaction to the second return of the former Emperor to Hungary was less mysterious. He

eign affairs the former Emperor's return was the main contributing factor to the consolidation of the three-power bloc consisting of Czechoslovakia, Rumania, and Yugoslavia into the Little Entente, an alliance which henceforth became a major factor in the political structure of Central Europe. Austria's relation to the Little Entente became a new issue, and a highly sensitive one, in the conduct of its complicated foreign affairs.

It was the clash between the domestic Anschluss agitation and the exigencies of foreign policy, already evident during Renner's tenure, which became a virtual nightmare to Mayr's government. Thus, while the Mayr government was negotiating for credits, preparations were made for a plebiscite. The more the government came to see the impossibility of reconciling these policies—Anschluss and credit—the more did the Länder, pushing their particular interests, go their own way and plan plebiscites of their own.[13]

The Powers, naturally, deducted from this outburst of popular opinion that the government was deceptive and using the threat of the Anschluss to extort more help from abroad, or, more charitably, that it was losing its control of the domestic situation. Their demarches threatened to cut off help and to insist upon full reparation payments. The threats of direct military intervention against Austria and even against Germany came from the French.[14] At the time the metaphor of the Austrian "artichoke"

---

rallied, as he evidently had not been able to do at the previous occasion, to an endorsement of the Republic as a "necessary" if not ideal form of government; *Sten. Prot., 61. Sitzung, I.G.P.*, October 25, 1921, pp. 2227f.; cf. Johann Auer, "Seipels Verhältnis zu Demokratie und autoritärer Staatsführung" (diss., Vienna, 1963), p. 47.

[13] The plebiscites held in the Tyrol on April 24, 1921, and in Salzburg on May 29, 1921, resulted in an overwhelming expression in favor of union with Germany; cf. Brita Skottsberg, *Der österreichische Parlamentarismus* (Göteborg, 1940), pp. 259ff.

[14] Cf. Sektionschef Richard Schüller remembers seeing telegrams by the French Minister Lefèvre-Pontalis late in 1920, inquiring about the availability of Czechoslovak and Yugoslav armies to occupy Austria; Richard

was freely circulating in diplomatic circles, suggesting that a piecemeal Anschluss of the Länder to Germany would be followed by an occupation of Vienna and eastern Austria by the Succession States.[15] Indeed, the *Finis Austriae*, as Dr. Funder recorded, seemed imminent.[16]

The government's position became untenable when on May 30 the leadership of the Pan-German party, defending the Länder's initiative, in a unanimous resolution expressed its lack of confidence in the government which, exchanging the Anschluss for foreign credit, appeared no longer to be an "adequate representative"[17] of Austria's internationally guaranteed independence. It declared its unwillingness to continue lending support to the government. Indeed, when the Styrian Diet, adding insult to injury, decided to hold a plebiscite of its own, the government, under the conflicting pressures from without and within its ranks was forced to resign on June 1.

What was explained to the country by the Chancellor primarily as a cabinet crisis, was to the Christian Socialists, above all, a party crisis. The government, as Seipel clearly perceived,

---

Schüller, "Das Erbe Österreichs," typescript, St.A., and Gottlieb Ladner, *Seipel als Überwinder der Staatskrise vom Sommer 1922* (Vienna and Graz, 1964), p. 18. Cf. Secret Telegram Eichhoff to Vienna, April 29, 1921, reporting the French threat to occupy Berlin; Anton Rintelen, *Erinnerungen an Österreichs Weg* (Munich, 1941), p. 87.

[15] Cf. Dispatch Z.48/Pol., Nikolaus Post (Austrian Chargé d'Affaires in Berlin) to Bundesministerium für Äusseres, Berlin, January 26, 1921; St.A., Fasz. 10.

In view of Austria's impotence it is not surprising that three days before the Tyrolean plebiscite an order should have been prepared in the Ballhausplatz "not to use the army for the defense of the frontier" in case of an invasion by the Entente, and to "abstain from hostile actions," Z.1619/1 "Weisung für den Fall von Gewaltmassnahmen der Entente wegen Anschlussabstimmung im Tirol," Vienna, April 21, 1921, St.A., Fasz 147, Deutschland I/1.

[16] Cf. Friedrich Funder, *Vom Gestern ins Heute: Aus dem Kaiserreich in die Republik* (Vienna and Munich, 1952), pp. 657f.

[17] *Neue Freie Presse*, May 31, 1921, morning ed.

had been "overthrown" by its own party.[18] Federalism, the preserve of the Christian Socialists, had now turned against them, and the latent split between Vienna and the Länder had come into the open. The Länder, and in particular Styria, had brought a central government to its knees.[19]

The time had come for Seipel to take the initiative. He had returned from his self-imposed German exile impressed by Chancellor Wirth's fulfillment course and confirmed in his determination to have the voices of reason prevail in Austria.[20] But he also understood that the first condition for any Christian Socialist government in conducting the affairs of state was control over its own party.

The party congress which met on June 7 with the primary task of reestablishing party unity was altogether dominated by the personality of Seipel. Confronting the party with the need for meeting the situation caused by the Peace Treaty realistically and responsibly,[21] he emerged as the one person who had a statesmanlike grasp of Austria's political needs and at the same time commanded the authority to impress upon the provincial elements the importance of deferring to them. "When one listened to him," recollected Dr. Funder, "how in his serene manner, only occasionally raising his voice, he would interweave with unfailing logic the resulting consequences for state and party, one was inclined to think of one of the classical lawgivers, whose marble statues adorn the great hall of the Austrian Parliament."[22]

[18] Ignaz Seipel, "Die christlichsoziale Partei und die politische Krise," *Reichspost*, June 8, 1921; cf. *Neue Freie Presse*, June 8 and 9, morning eds.

[19] Strictly speaking, Seipel argued, the crisis was precipitated not by the conflict between Vienna and the Länder, but between the Länder delegates in Parliament and the Länder politicians in the Länder governments and diets; *Reichspost*, June 29, 1921.

[20] Ignaz Seipel, "Gegen eine Politik mit dem Kopf durch die Wand," *Reichspost*, May 28, 1921.

[21] *Neue Freie Presse*, June 8, 1921, morning ed.

[22] Funder, *Vom Gestern ins Heute*, p. 659.

The Problem of Austrian Identity

It was a foregone conclusion that at the end of the sessions Seipel would be elected head of the Christian Socialist party. He had, in these days, performed a *"masterpiece of party- and state-policy,"* which, Funder rightly summarized, *"from a party political point of view cleared access to the great financial reconstruction* [Sanierungswerk] *which he could begin one year later as chancellor."*[23]

The way was now cleared for proceeding with the next task, the construction of a viable coalition for a new government. Already Mayr, in his exposé at the Christian Socialist party congress on his resignation, had emphasized the need for the Christian Socialists to cement a coalition policy with the Pan-Germans.[24] The Christian Socialists were ready to give parliamentarianism a chance rather than, as on previous occasions, to promote a nonparliamentary government of civil servants.

After prolonged negotiations, Dr. Johann Schober, Vienna's Chief of Police, finally emerged as the new Chancellor. Somewhat patronizingly, Seipel reminded Schober at a later date that when in the first year after Austria had obtained its constitution it had seemed opportune to put a "man of the civil service" at the head of the federal government, "we came to you and chose you as Federal Chancellor."[25] This was, in fact, the truth of the matter. Though the cabinet posts were filled predominantly with civil servants, most important was the fact that the new cabinet was based on a pact between the Christian Socialists and the Pan-Germans to which the small Peasants' party acceded; this pact included agreement on the cessation for the moment of further Anschluss plebiscites.[26] Thus the new cabinet, though having the character of a cabinet of civil servants, was backed by a parliamentary majority. With justified pride Seipel could say in Parlia-

[23] Ibid., p. 658; italics in original.

[24] Skottsberg, *Der österreichische Parlamentarismus*, pp. 265f.

[25] Seipel to Schober, Vienna, June 10, 1928, in Oskar Kleinschmied, *Schober* (Vienna, 1930), p. 114.

[26] *Reichspost*, June 21, 1921.

168

ment that the time would come when the "High House will try to govern with a parliamentary cabinet."[27] Seipel had, for the time being at least, gained control of the parliamentary scene and, at the same time, established a foundation for the conduct of a foreign policy.

In his first address to the Nationalrat, when the country's problems were still unsolved, Schober emphasized that his government was born "out of the need [*Not*] of our time, out of the need of our country."[28] In fact it was during the summer months of 1921 that the currency, after having recovered some of its value in the spring, started toward its dizzying inflationary ascent, reaching its height the following year.[29] Prices went up and the riots in Vienna on December 1 were a result of the suffering and despair of the masses. In such circumstances Schober, the Chief of Police, who was looked upon as an efficient, impartial public servant, in the best tradition of the old Austrian bureaucracy, offered the safest assurance for the maintenance of law and order. But the very fact that he was a civil servant and not a politician, that as Richard Schüller said, "his skin was too thin for politics,"[30] limited his effectiveness. Being a man of integrity and one who inspired confidence was not enough. As his predecessor in office he was in a position of having to adjust the foreign political needs of Austria to domestic pressures. He had to operate in a political, indeed parliamentary, situation. This very setting, however, proved to be his undoing.

The major tasks of his foreign policy were, aside from the incorporation of the Burgenland, the consolidation of relations with Austria's neighbors and the negotiations, initiated by Mayr, for foreign credits through the League. One of the major prob-

[27] *Sten. Prot., 40. Sitzung, I.G.P.*, June 22, 1921, p. 1480.
[28] *Sten. Prot., 40. Sitzung, I.G.P.*, June 22, 1921, p. 1463; cf. Kleinschmied, *Schober*, p. 175.
[29] Cf. "Kursbewegung der Devise Zürich nach den Monatsmittelkursen des Schweizer Franken 1919-1923," reproduced in Ladner, *Seipel*, p. 21.
[30] Schüller, *Erbe Österreichs*, p. 76.

lems to be solved in connection with the loans was to persuade the victorious powers to renounce the general mortgage which Article 197 of the Peace Treaty had given them upon all assets and revenues of Austria as security for reparations payment. One by one Schober tackled the thorny problems, traveling from conference to conference. If progress was made, even slowly, the problems were inevitably full of political implications, foreign and domestic, for which Schober was not prepared, and which in the long run he could not manage.

The most controversial of Schober's accomplishments was the Treaty of Lana, and an accomplishment it was. Concluded in December in the former imperial castle outside Prague between Austria and Czechoslovakia, it represented a recognition "urbi et orbi" of a condition born out of an "unavoidable political necessity,"[31] while in no way tying down Austrian foreign relations or operating against a third power. In fact, in a statement to the press, Schober claimed success in having freed Austria from the more far-reaching commitment contained in the earlier Renner–Beneš Treaty. Lana, then, had overcome Austria's political isolation.

The Christian Socialists and the Social Democrats, in rare agreement, came out in defense of Lana. Seipel, in the Nationalrat's Foreign Affairs Committee, welcomed an "official treaty" to take the place of the mysterious Renner–Beneš Treaty, and minimized the danger of dependence on either the Little Entente or France. Without political ties, he argued, no economic stabilization could be accomplished. Bauer followed Seipel in taking a positive stand on Lana.[32]

[31] Ad. Z.6885/1A "Promemoria über das politische Abkommen in Prag," December 30, 1921, St.A., Liasse Tschechoslowakei I/III, K.822.

[32] Sepp Straffner, reporting the meeting of the Foreign Affairs Committee of the Nationalrat of January 19, 1922, A.V.A., 100. Sitzung V.A.G.V., January 25, 1922. Cf. Ignaz Seipel, "Die Politik des Tages," *Reichspost*, January 7, 1922; cf. also Otto Bauer, *Die österreichische Revolution* (Vienna, 1923), pp. 255f.

But the decisive opposition came from the Pan-Germans. To them Lana meant "Danubian confederation" and surrender to the policies of France. Schober, according to Felix Frank, was "allegedly hoodwinked."[33] The caucus of Pan-German representatives, acting upon instructions of the party leadership, decided to withdraw its support from Schober and as a result brought on the collapse of the cabinet.[34]

A summary of Austria's international situation in the beginning of 1922 concluded that it was no longer politically a "quantité négligeable."[35] The affiliation with Czechoslovakia caused the more or less anxious powers, and Italy in particular, to court Austria,[36] and for the moment at least, partition plans gave way to various competing plans to integrate Austria into a new Central European balance.[37]

From the point of view of international finance, the main result of Lana was general confidence.[38] Long negotiations in London finally resulted in February 1922 in advance loans from England, France, and Italy. For the rest, Schober and Richard Schüller, a leading official in the Ministry of Finance and increasingly indispensable in Austria's financial negotiations, traveled to Genoa, where a general European conference had convened on April 10 to deal with major economic and financial issues and also with the reconstruction of Russia. Schober returned with promises, but no more than promises, that the general mortgage would be lifted.

But Schober had lost his control of the domestic political situation. With the Pan-Germans moving into the opposition, he was

[33] A.V.A., 91. Sitzung V.A.G.V., January 14, 1922.

[34] A.V.A., 97. Sitzung V.A.G.V., January 16, 1922.

[35] Z.456/1a, "Die Ordnung unseres politischen Verhältnisses zu unseren Nachbarn," Vienna, January 31, 1922, St.A., Liasse Österreich 7/1, K.342.

[36] Ladner, *Seipel*, p. 26.

[37] Ibid., pp. 25ff.

[38] In August 1921 Schober had concluded an overdue peace treaty with the United States, which had not ratified the Treaty of St. Germain, thus clearing the way for American readiness to lift the general mortgage.

able to command only a tenuous majority of three votes. Amidst a rapid depreciation of the currency and soaring prices it was Seipel who recognized the need for a "strong government against the Social Democrats" and negotiated tirelessly with the Pan-Germans for a reconstruction and strengthening of the coalition between the two parties.[39] However, the Pan-Germans kept attacking Schober, juxtaposing his and the Christian Socialists' "Entente policy" or "fulfillment policy" with what they called a "people's policy." Finally the Pan-Germans, fearing that Schober's policy in Genoa would lead to a closer tie-up with the Little Entente, together with the Social Democrats, denied him the needed domestic credit.[40] It was immediately following this rebuff of the Chancellor that the *Arbeiter-Zeitung*, in order to put an end to what the Socialists called the "Seipel-inspired Schober government,"[41] sounded a formal call for Ignaz Seipel to take over the government: "The situation that someone governs and dictates without formally taking over the responsibility is simply unbearable. We are unbending foes of Herr Seipel but even the most passionate opposition deals preferably with the real leader than with his puppet."[42] On May 24, 1922, Schober handed in the resignation of his cabinet. His successor was Ignaz Seipel.

The overthrow of Schober has become a subject of controversy. Though the Chancellor was brought to his knees by a combined move of Social Democrats and Pan-Germans, Seipel has been featured as the sinister plotter at work.[43] While it is hard to believe that Seipel was wholly passive and innocent in this affair,

[39] A.V.A., 112a., 112b. Sitzung V.A.G.V., March 9, 14, 1922.

[40] For a concise summary of events, cf. Schulthess, *1922*, p. 157.

[41] Cf. Karl Renner, *Österreich von der Ersten zur Zweiten Republik* (Vienna, 1952), p. 52.

[42] *Arbeiter-Zeitung*, May 20, 1922.

[43] Renner, *Österreich*, p. 52; cf. also Charles A. Gulick, *Austria from Habsburg to Hitler* (Berkeley, 1948), I, 118, and *Der österreichische Volkswirt*, XXII, February 8 and 15, 1930, 501f., 529. Cf. also Karl Ausch, *Als die Banken fielen: Zur Soziologie der politischen Korruption* (Vienna, Frankfurt, and Zurich, 1968), p. 49.

172

the assumption that he "utilized their [the Pan-Germans'] resentment . . . [over Lana] to help overthrow Schober"[44] is not supported by "evidence." Seipel had gone on record in the Pan-German caucus as being in favor of retaining Schober, "since he was a strong guarantee for the economic recovery."[45] Why should Seipel have taken the initiative upon Schober's return to Vienna to assure Schober, contrary to rumors spread, alas, by the "Jew press," that no plans were afoot among the Christian Socialists and Pan-Germans to displace him? Did Seipel want to take the credit for Schober's long spadework, as charged in Gustav Stolper's *Der österreichische Volkswirt*, in order to appear himself to be the savior of Austria?[46] It is more likely that Seipel dropped Schober when he became convinced that he was not equal to controlling both the foreign and the domestic problems. Because of the combined pressure of Social Democrats and Pan-Germans, not the Christian Socialists, he had lost his parliamentary footing. Not only did he lack the necessary footing in a political party, but having become *persona non grata* to the Pan-Germans, his very personality had moved in the way of the country's political recovery. We can assume then, that Seipel finally dropped Schober for this not so very sinister reason; and Schober's fall was not a measure of Seipel's ambition or capacity for intrigue, but of his determination to find a firm parliamentary basis for foreign policy. In this respect Schober had failed.

We are told that when Schober heard about the domestic opposition on the closing day of the Genoa Conference, he said, "If I do my duty, what can they do against me?"[47] This was a soft-skinned reaction to the hard-and-fast realities of parliamentary

[44] Gulick, *Austria*, ɪ, 118.

[45] A.V.A., 112b. Sitzung V.A.G.V., March 14, 1923.

[46] Seipel himself tried to refute the argument by asserting, in a letter to *Der österreichische Volkswirt*, that the loans which Schober obtained were small and for current expenses and not sufficient to halt the currency depreciation; Seipel to *Der österreichische Volkswirt*, Vienna, February 16, 1930, *Der österreichische Volkswirt*, xxɪɪ, February 22, 1930, 557f.

[47] Schüller, *Erbe Österreichs*, p. 84.

politics, and was, as well, the reaction of a bureaucrat who prided himself on his "expertise" (*Sachlichkeit*),[48] but who neglected and was not equal to the realities of politics. If one wants to regard the episode of late May 1922 as a clash between Schober and Seipel, one must also recognize it as much more than a personal conflict, and also more than the tiresome machinations of a sinister intriguing prelate. Actually, the old Austrian administrative tradition clashed with the political realities of the Republic, and Seipel was more keenly aware than Schober of the need to acknowledge these realities, if only to have them serve as a basis for the conduct of foreign affairs. Schober had not seen this need, and his pride and perhaps a touch of vanity had removed him from the degrading parliamentary scene. Therefore while all parties were agreed that Schober was an honorable man, they were also agreed, in May 1922, that Seipel was the one to unravel the political tangle. In this task the Christian Socialists and Pan-Germans wished him well, but the Social Democrats wished him to fail.

Chancellor

Even though during this time Seipel was acutely aware of his deteriorating physical condition,[49] he threw himself feverishly into political activity. Two days before Schober's resignation, on May 22, he had already composed a program for his forthcoming government.[50] However, the decisive event which paved the way for Seipel was the resolution reached by a large majority vote at the "Imperial" party convention (*Reichsparteitag*) of the Pan-

[48] Cf. Kleinschmied, *Schober*, p. 233.

[49] Cf. Seipel diary, May 9, 1922: "In the evening at Kunwald's. He strongly advises me to relax since my decay is already generally visible. Indeed in the Foreign Affairs Committee I have hardly been able to speak coherently."

[50] Seipel diary, May 22, 1922; cf. *Neue Freie Presse*, May 26, 1922, morning ed.

174

Germans of May 26-28 in Graz[51] in favor of the party joining in a government with the Christian Socialists. It led to the formulation of a coalition pact between the two partners which carefully spelled out the terms of their cooperation. The section on domestic affairs, as a concession to Seipel, deemphasized the "programmatic" or ideological differences, stipulating that questions pertaining to Church and state relations be left untouched. As a concession by Seipel, the section on foreign affairs, on the other hand, called somewhat euphemistically for a "continuation" (*Festhalten*) of the Anschluss policy and gave the Pan-German partner full freedom to pursue his Anschluss propaganda.[52]

It is interesting to note that, at this point, the coalition partners rejected the obvious *bürgerlich* ("bourgeois") label which, not without reason, was attached to them by the Left, and which came to characterize the coalition. Wishful thinking made them see themselves as "people's parties" (*Volksparteien*) rather than class parties.[53] Certainly nothing could have been further from Seipel's intention than to see the new alignment in terms of class struggle.[54] Considerations not of class but of cultural policy, and above all the aggressive stand of the Social Democrats on the sensitive questions of Church and state relations, loomed increas-

[51] Franz Dinghofer delivered the main address; he had been all along a proponent for a coalition with the Christian Socialists; A.V.A., 106. Sitzung V.A.G.V., February 21, 1922.

[52] It was during his Salzburg years that Seipel had begun to establish ties with the Pan-Germans. At a later date, in a Salzburg speech of 1926, he stressed that he considered as the particular achievement of his "personal policy" the Christian Socialist–Pan-German coalition, rather than the Geneva Protocols for which it had paved the way; Seipel, "Fragen der europäischen Wirtschaft" (Salzburg, March 11, 1926), Josef Gessl, *Seipels Reden in Österreich und anderwärts* (Vienna, 1926), p. 304.

[53] Cf. *Reichspost*, May 29, 1922.

[54] As late as 1928, in a private conversation with the former German Chancellor Wirth, he defended himself vigorously (*scharf*) against the "accusation" (*Vorwurf*) of being an adherent of the "Bürgerblock" idea; Memorandum by Joseph Wirth to German Foreign Office, June 13, 1928; G.F.O., 2347/4576/E173479.

ingly large in Seipel's mind.[55] In other words, it was not so much Seipel the "social philosopher" as Seipel the "clerical politician" who determined the increasingly anti-Socialist orientation of the new coalition.

The new cabinet included a large group of Christian Socialists and three Pan-Germans, among whom Felix Frank acted as Vice-Chancellor and Minister of the Interior. It was immediately assailed by the Social Democrats, who labeled it a "prelate's government" and called it the "shame" of the bourgeoisie, with a Roman prelate for its chancellor.[56] The magisterial *Neue Freie Presse* merely recorded the ironic fact that "a priest under patronage of the Pan-Germans" had taken over.[57] Even Dr. Funder, one of Seipel's closest political associates, reacted skeptically to the prospect of a priest taking over the leading position in the state. In his quiet, friendly, but firm way, he expressed his misgivings to Seipel: "Excellency, this is a misfortune."[58]

On May 31 in the afternoon Seipel faced the assembled Chamber to deliver his first Declaration of Policy. The galleries were packed, ready to focus on the man who, surrounded by legends and rumors, had for so long, almost too long, been the power behind the throne and was now to step into the limelight. He started his address on this self-assured and solemn note: "Rarely has a government been called for as long and as loudly as this one which has been elected today."[59] There was no suggestion of emotion in his speech, no visible passion. With a professorial

[55] In fact, during the intricate deliberations among the Christian Socialist leadership which lasted from May 29 through the morning of May 31, one of the chief demands of Seipel's was that a Christian Socialist be appointed minister of education; minutes of the caucus of the Christian Socialist party, May 30, 1922, "Seipel-Lueger," K.VIII, Schmitz Archive.

[56] *Arbeiter-Zeitung*, June 1, 1922.

[57] *Neue Freie Presse*, May 31, 1922, morning ed., welcomed Seipel, the "clever, cautious priest."

[58] Friedrich Funder, "Dr. Ignaz Seipel, sein Leben und sein Werk," *Reichspost*, August 3, 1932.

[59] "Die erste Regierungserklärung," Gessl, *Reden*, pp. 17-23.

irony he reminded the opposition that they were the ones who had insistently called for him, and asked them whether it was because of their clamor or because of the rules of parliamentarianism that the leader of the strongest party was now about to take over the constitutional responsibilities of the government.

The new Chancellor's tone was relaxed and intimate. He had all the worldly honors and titles and all the influence he wanted, and in the past months he could have taken on the chancellorship at his pleasure. Ambition had not prompted him to take office, but rather his sense of duty and his faith during times of need.

After this introduction there followed a measured, carefully balanced analysis of the country's needs. A "Roman calm"[60] emanated from the speaker paying tribute to Lammasch, the last Prime Minister of old Austria, as this "noble man," alluding to his own role in the time of revolution, and noticeably toning down the divisive potential of the political issues concerning monarchy or republic and the Anschluss. A careful listener might even have found in the address a gracious gesture on the part of the Chancellor toward his one-time coalition partners, the Social Democrats.[61]

Seipel's oration was honest, shrewd, and courageous, and particularly so in his declaration of the viability of Austria. "In order to be able to work for a state, one must believe in its viability."[62] Whatever doubts he may privately have harbored about this matter, as chancellor he had to put up a show of confidence—hence his "policy of the as if."[63] It was precisely in this respect

[60] Birk, *Seipel*, p. 231.

[61] He stated that he would have preferred his government to be supported by all parties; Gessl, *Reden*, p. 22.

[62] Ibid., p. 19.

[63] The Vienna correspondent of the *Frankfurter Zeitung* observed later in the same year that the need for "primum vivere" had made for an "as if" existence of Austria as a state; *Frankfurter Zeitung*, November 30, 1922, morning ed. Seipel himself said a number of years later to the German ex-Chancellor Wirth; "in spite of our inner conviction about the untenability of the present situation, one ought to *suggest* [*suggerieren*] to the Austrian

that he differed from Schober.[64] Seipel, more shrewd, cunning, and aware of the psychological effect, was willing to play the game in order to carry Austria into the time when, under any conditions, she could stand on her own feet. "The fact that there is one man who still believes that things can change, this is the innovation."[65] Seipel concluded with a reemphasis of his belief in the democratic process, but also with the hint, certainly ominous to the opposition, that he was willing to carry through the program with special plenary powers, if necessary.[66]

Even though the new government was based on a coalition, it had a distinct style, imposed upon it by its head. Seipel's guidelines were the same as those that had served him some four years before when he had outlined an elaborate schedule to go into effect in the eventuality of his election as Archbishop of Salzburg; they stressed leadership, self-discipline, efficiency, and hard work. In fact he had exchanged the quiet majesty of Salzburg for the troubled misery of Austria. Seipel well knew what kind of chancellor he was to be; that he had to play the parliamentary game and at the same time assert his authority. The very first cabinet meeting reflected his clear concept of how to rule: "The Cabinet must make an effort in effect to exercise the executive powers [*Regierungsgewalt*] itself. . . . It goes without saying that each parliamentary minister is to remain in close touch with his party. Beyond this, the political parties are to be contacted only when the cabinet has approved such a step."[67] The very evening after the first cabinet session Seipel entered in his diary the strangely portentous and not unalarming words, "uniform all-

---

people that it accommodate itself for good to the present political and economic realities and take care of its livelihood always within the framework of the prevailing conditions," Wirth Memorandum, June 13, 1928, G.F.O., 2347/4576/E17372; italics in original.

[64] Kleinschmied, *Schober*, p. 233, on Schober's aversion to such a policy.
[65] "Das ist das Neue," Gessl, *Reden*, p. 22.
[66] Gessl, *Reden*, p. 23.
[67] A.V.A., M.R. 191, June 1, 1922.

over policy."[68] The following day he went to pay his respects to the Cardinal and the Nuntius.[69]

Whither Austria?

With the country on the brink of disaster the new Chancellor faced staggering problems. The value of the Austrian crown was deteriorating alarmingly. The Swiss franc, which early in 1919 had been worth approximately three crowns, by the time of Seipel's accession brought 2,151 and soon after, on June 12, 4,110 crowns.[70] Of course this inflationary spiral drove the cost of living up tremendously. According to the index of *Der österreich-ische Volkswirt*, Gustav Stolper's influential and belligerent journal on economic affairs, by October 1922 it was more than ten times what it had been in May of the same year.[71] The price of a loaf of bread on June 12, 1922, went from 940 to 1,230 crowns,[72] and soared further throughout the month of August to 5,670 crowns.[73]

When Seipel had become minister in 1918 the country had faced political dismemberment, but now it was confronted with the much more concrete threats of physical extinction, hunger, and bankruptcy. Inflation threatened the bare livelihood of the working classes and no less so some large groups among the middle classes, particularly those with fixed income. While Seipel himself, in an earlier address to Parliament, had stressed the importance of "economic policy"[74] there was no doubt that he had had a less than inadequate economic schooling. How could he,

[68] "Einheitliche Gesamtpolitik"; Seipel diary, June 1, 1922.

[69] Seipel diary, June 2, 1922.

[70] Cf. F. G. Kleinwaechter, *Von Schönbrunn bis St. Germain* (Graz, 1964), p. 196; Gottlieb Ladner, *Seipel als Überwinder der Staatskrise vom Sommer 1922* (Vienna and Graz, 1964), pp. 21, 46.

[71] *Der österreichische Volkswirt*, xv, January 6, 1923, 367-368.

[72] Schulthess, *1922*, p. 158.   [73] Ladner, *Seipel*, p. 72.

[74] "Wirtschaftspolitik," *Sten. Prot. 4. Sitzung, I.G.P.*, November 23, 1920, p. 95. In 1928 Seipel recalled that "six to eight years ago" he had

with his homespun wisdom, master problems of an intricately technical nature? "A people," he once said with his peculiarly supreme self-confidence, "does not just perish, however desperate its economic situation." "Spend less, and save more"[75] was his economic remedy. Not without reason did the Social Democrats characterize Seipel as a man "who had not studied economics, but the Church fathers."[76] And the *Neue Freie Presse* pointed out quite soberly that for his economic and financial policies he would have to depend heavily upon others.[77]

The financial reconstruction carried through by Seipel in 1922 has been interpreted as indicative of his "conversion" from a socialist to a capitalist course. Among the Social Democrats it was Karl Seitz who gave eloquent expression to this argument during the great debate in Parliament on the Chancellor's Declaration of Policy. Seipel's "conversion" to "Manchester liberalism," he charged, with an undisguised anti-Semitic accent, was backed up "by the grace of the Jew press."[78] To the Socialists Seipel was but a living example of the course which the Christian Socialist party had taken since its "heroic" days under Vogelsang and Lueger; indeed they charged Seipel with having been effective in leading the party into capitalism, the coalition with the bourgeoisie, and the struggle against the workers.[79] The critics in his own camp also took him to task for having shifted soon after the revolution from a Socialist course to a "consciously and deliberately capitalistic" one.[80]

---

advocated the "primacy of the economy and of economic policy." Ignaz Seipel, *Der Kampf um die österreichische Verfassung* (Vienna and Leipzig, 1930), pp. 125f.

[75] "Eine Stunde mit Msgr. Seipel," *Österreich in Geschichte und Literatur*, VI, December 1962, 450f.

[76] Friedrich Funder, "Dr. Ignaz Seipel," *Reichspost*, August 3, 1932.

[77] *Neue Freie Presse*, May 31, 1922, morning ed.

[78] *Sten. Prot., 112. Sitzung, I.G.P.*, May 31, 1922, p. 3705.

[79] Cf. Otto Bauer, "Ignaz Seipel," *Arbeiter-Zeitung*, August 3, 1932.

[80] Cf. Bernhard Birk, *Dr. Ignaz Seipel: Ein österreichisches und europäisches Schicksal* (Innsbruck, 1932), p. 100; cf. also E. K. Winter, *Ignaz*

In coping with this problem it must be recalled that Seipel was as little committed to any one position in the conflict between capitalism and socialism as he was to any one form of government. His study of the Church fathers, however ridiculous to his opponents, was relevant in this question, and allowed him a good deal of latitude on economic and social issues. If he initially followed a leftist course, it was not without a certain detachment, and with the understanding that his policy at this specific time was most concordant with the demands of Christian ethics. To maintain, as Winter does, that Seipel's original leftist orientation was "deeply rooted" in his "mentality," that he stood on the left "out of an inner necessity"[81] evades the very problem of Thomistic accommodation, which provides for flexibility in either direction. Indeed flexibility in matters such as socioeconomic policy or the form of government is essential to maintain the independence of the Church in secular issues and at the same time to assure its survival. One might even go one step further and claim that it is a function of the Church to accommodate itself to a given situation in order to uphold amidst the latter's imperfectness its own perfect vision.[82] In any case, if the Church could live within the framework of a socialist society it could also live within the framework of a capitalistic society, and considering the predicament of Austria in 1922, a capitalistic course was certainly laid out for Seipel. But this was less a matter of a conscious change of direction than a full exploitation of the potential of his Thomistic position for flexibility and accommodation.

Seipel als dialektisches Problem (Vienna, Frankfurt, and Zurich, 1966), p. 64; and August Maria Knoll, "Ignaz Seipel," *Neue österreichische Biographie ab 1815* (Vienna, 1956), IX, 123. Seipel first indicated his shift of position early in 1920, when, after assessing the merits of the coalition with the Socialists, he called for a "change of system"; Socialism had failed in Austria and the only hope for the future, he argued, lay in bourgeois ("gut bürgerliche") ideas; Ignaz Seipel, "Das Entscheidungsjahr," *Reichspost*, January 7, 1920.

[81] Winter, *Seipel*, p. 59.   [82] Cf. Knoll, "Seipel," p. 123.

The Problem of Austrian Identity

The controversy concerning stabilization has generally been misrepresented; it is not quite true that the Social Democrats, supported by Stolper's *Der österreichische Volkswirt*, advocated self-help, while Seipel, seeing its limitations, advocated the need for foreign aid. Actually the first step in financial reconstruction, the domestic financial plan (*Finanzplan*) as presented to the Nationalrat on June 21, was basically backed by all parties, including the Social Democrats. Its Social Democratic provenance, as claimed by Otto Bauer,[83] allowed Redlich, an increasingly distant and saddened observer of the political scene, to quip about the "financial policy of Dr. Bauer draped in the soutane of Seipel."[84]

The controversy concerning stabilization raged in reality not over the *Finanzplan* itself, but over the broader context within which it was to become effective. For had not the Social Democrats repeatedly acknowledged the need for foreign credit for the stabilization of the currency?[85] Was it not Otto Bauer who on June 9 had come out with the proposal for a currency union between Austria and Germany;[86] and was it not Seipel who—rightly as time was to prove—had rejected this opinion as erroneous and also refuted it as a threat to Austria's independence?

Indeed Otto Bauer's project was irresponsible. Had he not, when he was still in a position of responsibility as Foreign Minister, seen the need for soft-pedaling Ludo Hartmann's enthusiasm for the Anschluss? He had at that time stated to his Minister to Berlin: "I fear that you are not sufficiently aware of the degree of our economic dependence on the Entente."[87] This situation certainly had not changed by June 1922. The frustrations of Mayr and Schober had sufficiently demonstrated that the Anschluss

[83] Bauer, *Revolution*, p. 258.

[84] Redlich diary, June 20, 1922, Josef Redlich, "Politische Tagebuchnotizen, 1920-1936."

[85] Cf. Gulick, *Austria*, I, 169.

[86] Ibid., p. 165; Richard Schmitz, *Ignaz Seipel* (Vienna, 1946), p. 8.

[87] Secret letter, Z.2026/Präs., Otto Bauer to Hartmann, Vienna, July 15, 1919; St.A., Fasz. 262, Präsidialakten Otto Bauer, 2.

182

agitation was a dead-end affair. If Germany at no point since the Anschluss negotiations in February 1919 was really willing to meet Austria's overtures, it certainly was not able to do so now. The German Chancellor Wirth was quite correct when in his confrontation with his Austrian colleague in August 1922 he said "we are one to one and a half years behind you."[88] Sooner even than he had figured the German mark began to topple and Germany was faced with the Ruhr occupation and a threat of civil war.

Seipel in turn, while he felt that he could "in good conscience" step before the public with the declaration that the *Finanzplan* would save Austria,[89] had to continue exploring the possibilities of foreign credit at the same time. He was partly influenced by his economic advisers[90] in steering his policy toward this exploration. Indeed it was the kindly and helpful Sir William Goode, chief of the Austrian section of the Reparations Commission, who urged Seipel to follow up the "alternative course of action" to the domestic plan and seek an external loan.[91] The disagreement between the opposition and the government, then, was not really one between self-help and foreign aid, between Austrian independence and dependence upon international capitalism, but between two kinds of dependence. Austria faced the choice between Anschluss with an old friend and ally with an insolvent

[88] Z.2845a, Wildner, "Aufzeichnung über die Reise des Bundeskanzlers Dr. Seipel noch Prag, Berlin und Verona 20. bis 27 August 1922," St.A., Liasse Österreich 8/IV, K.471.

[89] A.V.A., M.R.199, June 17, 1922, Secret Appendix.

[90] Viktor Kienböck, who soon succeeded August Ségur as Minister of Finance, Richard Schüller, Austria's veteran negotiator, of whom it has been said that he combined "with the foresight of a great chess player the . . . high courage and the cunning of Ulysses" (Sir George Franckenstein, *Facts and Features of My Life* [London, 1939], p. 230), and last but not least the mysterious Dr. Gottfried Kunwald.

[91] Private and Confidential Letter, Sir William Goode to Seipel, Vienna, June 30, 1922; A.V.A., Bundeskanzleramt Inneres, Korrespondenz Seipel Div. K.83a.

183

economy—Germany—and dependence upon her former enemies —the Western Powers—whose economy could be very helpful.

In August the last chance of success for Seipel's financial plan and for foreign aid vanished. The former, in spite of a partial lifting of the general mortgage, was foiled by the insistence of the French-controlled Länderbank and the English-controlled Anglobank on special guarantees on the part of the Powers. This, however, delayed the establishment of the Notenbank, a new privately financed bank of issue on which the success of the financial plan hinged. Expectations of foreign aid were finally dashed when the London Conference of the Supreme Council, which had convened in August mainly to cope with the German reparations problem, failed to agree upon financial help to Austria and relegated the investigation of its situation to the League of Nations.[92]

By all traditional standards Austria's situation on that August 15, when the text of the adverse decision of the Powers reached the Ballhausplatz, was desperate. Neither one of the possible avenues, self-help, or foreign credit, had succeeded. Referring the matter to the League seemed to many observers a mere formality.[93] The Austrian problem after all had not been the primary obligation of the Conference and Austria was a small, insignificant state. "All were agreed," wrote the London *Nation*, "in shelving the petition of the wretched Austrian government"; its position was admittedly, help or no help, "utterly hopeless."[94]

But what was to happen to this unhappy country? In early August Seipel had toyed with desperate measures, such as confiscation of foreign holdings in Austria with the objective of

[92] Secret Telegram Z.80, Franckenstein-Schüller to Gesandter Wildner, London, August 14, 1922; St.A., Liasse Österreich 8/IV, K.345; cf. also Ladner, *Seipel*, pp. 85f.

[93] Telegram Z.81, Franckenstein-Schüller to Wildner, August 15, 1922; St.A., Liasse Österreich 8/IV, K.345.

[94] *The Nation* (London), xxxi, August 19, 1922, 672.

precipitating intervention by the Allied Powers. While on second thought Seipel dismissed this step as "not to be taken seriously," he suggested in turn an open declaration of renunciation of the Peace Treaty.[95] While the London Conference was in session he confronted it twice, somewhat melodramatically, with a threat to renounce all responsibility for a total collapse, to call together Parliament to resign, and, since no other Austrian government was conceivable, to turn the destiny of Austria over to the Allied Powers.[96]

Rumors were rampant once again in the summer of 1922 concerning the possibility of military intervention by the other powers and the partition of Austria. Seipel and the British financial expert G. M. Young seemed to have agreed in the course of a long conference that the general European situation was "as critical as 1914" and that the "danger of war" and specifically of "Austria's collapse" was imminent.[97] Whether or not the rumors about Czech troop concentration along the northern Austrian frontier, Hungarian preparations for recapturing the Burgen-

---

[95] Memorandum by Wildner about the conference of August 3, 1922, between Seipel, Vice-Chancellor Frank, Foreign Minister Grünberger, Finance Minister Ségur, and others; St.A., Liasse Österreich 8/IV, K.346, Fs. 64-66.

[96] "Memorandum der österreichischen Regierung," early August 1922; St.A., Liasse Österreich 8/IV, K.345, Fs. 32-40; the text is reproduced in Ladner, *Seipel*, pp. 169-173; in Top Secret Telegram Z.77, Franckenstein-Schüller to Wildner, London, August 13, 1922, St.A., Liasse Österreich 8/IV, K.345, the senders asked the Chancellor's permission once again to impress the conclusions of the memorandum upon Lloyd George. Seipel agreed in Telegram Z.67, August 13, 1922, ibid. The interpretation of Seipel's threat as a mere "political move" ("Schachzug") as suggested by Ladner, *Seipel*, p. 89, is not fully justified in the light of the above-mentioned conference of August 3, in which equally desperate measures were discussed *pro domo*.

[97] Handwritten memorandum by Seipel on talks with G. M. Young, July 17, 1922; A.V.A., Bundeskanzleramt Inneres, Korrespondenz Seipel Div., K.83a.

The Problem of Austrian Identity

land, or Yugoslav intentions about Carinthia and Styria were well founded, they were in themselves a political reality.[98] And while in Rome Augusto Biancheri, a high official of the Foreign Office, saw fit to alert the Ministry of War to the danger of foreign invasion of Austria,[99] the Italian Foreign Minister Carlo Schanzer declared firmly at the London Conference that, in case of other powers' military intervention in Austria, Italy would reserve for itself "full freedom of action."[100] Once again, *Finis Austriae* was generally anticipated.

The "Great Trip"

As in the critical days of November 1918, Seipel, once again *in extremis*, proved that he had inexhaustive reserves of nerves, energy, and a strong political instinct, despite his physical condition. The problem of Austria was after all not purely an economic one; the logics of economic policy had clearly demonstrated that she was not a good risk and the bankers of Europe had remained unmoved by Seipel's threats. Political action was the great need—a political demonstration of the urgency of the Austrian problem and of the dangers for all of Central Europe in an unsettled Austria. It was only four years after the collapse of the multinational Empire that Seipel found an opportunity not merely to raise the Austrian problem, but to "roll up," as he liked to put it, the Central European problem. His dramatic trip to Prague, Berlin, and Verona constituted the "first act"[101] of his Central European offensive.[102]

[98] Cf. Telegram (in cipher) Z.48, Rémi Kwiatkowski (Austrian Minister to the Quirinal) to Bundesministerium für Äusseres, Rome, June 28, 1922; St.A., Liasse Österreich 8/IV, K.345.

[99] Telegram Z.62, Kwiatkowski to Bundesministerium für Äusseres, Rome, August 17, 1922; St.A., Liasse Österreich 8/IV, K.345.

[100] Memorandum by Wildner, August 17, 1922, ibid.

[101] Cf. A.V.A., M.R.224, September 11, 1922.

[102] The main sources for Seipel's trips are the official summaries Z.2845a by Wildner, "Die grosse Reise des Bundeskanzlers Dr. Seipel August 1922

It is interesting that Seipel's decision should have been precipitated by a report from his envoy in London of a conversation with Sir Basil Blackett, a high Treasury official. Reacting to the failure of the London Conference, he suggested that the British government itself would for the time being want to withdraw from its European involvement and leave the continent to itself. At the same time he anticipated that Austria, unless self-help succeeded, would have to "open up" the Central European question.[103] Did the Englishman who saw his country reverting to its imperial tasks serve as a reminder to Seipel that the time had come to resurrect the Austrian imperial position, even though *d'outre tombe*? "Austria," the liberal *Westminster Gazette* commented "now definitely abandoned by the Western Powers, is turning to the powers of Central Europe." And, in an almost grotesque emphasis on imperial affinity, it suggested that "like Canning, she is calling a new world into existence to redress the balance of the old."[104]

Seipel's diplomatic initiative was an example of his "as if" policy. Indeed it was a singular demonstration of the possibilities —and also of the limits—of small power diplomacy. He proceeded as if Austria could still play a role in Central European diplomacy, as if the League action, more than a mere formality, was still within the realm of the possible, and as if there existed a Central European common interest. To make these assumptions come true he shrewdly explored the mood of his neighbors, hop-

zur Sanierung Österreichs, Vorgeschichte," "Aufzeichnung über die Reise des Bundeskanzlers Dr. Seipel nach Prag, Berlin und Verona 20. bis 27. August 1922"; St.A., Liasse Österreich 8/IV, K.471; A.V.A., M.R.218, 220, August 17, 28, 1922 (stenographed minutes); *Sten. Prot. 134. Sitzung, I.G.P.,* September 14, 1922; Seipel facing the Foreign Affairs Committee August 31, 1922, *Reichspost,* September 1, 1922.

[103] "Auslösen"; Wildner's summary, "Die grosse Reise," states specifically that Seipel was encouraged in his venture by Sir Basil's statement as reported in Telegram Z.81, Franckenstein-Schüller to Wildner, August 15, 1922; St.A., Liasse Österreich 8/IV, K.345.

[104] *Westminster Gazette,* August 22, 1922.

ing to exploit their rivalries over Austria and, as he expressed it in the cabinet meeting of September 11, to cause "apprehension" among the Powers.[105]

Seipel's itinerary then, was carefully, though hurriedly, worked out. In his memorandum to the Western Powers on the Austrian problem, Thomas Masaryk[106] related the importance of the Chancellor's taking this unexpected trip rather than acting through his envoys and observed the significance of Seipel's confining himself to Prague, Berlin, and Rome (i.e., Verona), rather than heading for Paris or London. "For Czechoslovakia, furthermore, it is significant that he has come first to us in Prague."[107] The willingness and ability of the Great Powers had been explored to the fullest, and what was needed now was a demonstration of the urgency of the Central European problem itself. Thus the European capitals carefully noted—as Seipel wanted them to—that after stopping in Prague, he went on to Berlin and Verona. We are told that Lefèvre-Pontalis, the French Minister in Vienna, was most indignant and "irritated like a rooster" that Seipel had let him go to Marienbad in the middle of the month with no forewarning of things to come; and he became particularly indignant over Seipel's stop in Verona.[108] When he was already in Prague, Seipel was shown by Beneš a telegram from Poincaré warning against the trip to Berlin, and was repeatedly approached by Cosme, the French Chargé d'Affaires, who urged him to call off his trips to both Germany and Italy.[109] Seipel had

[105] "Beunruhigung bei den Mächten"; A.V.A., M.R.224, September 11, 1922.

[106] Thomas G. Masaryk, *Cesta Democracie* (Prague, 1933), ɪɪ, 307-312.

[107] Ibid., 307.

[108] A.V.A., M.R.220, August 28, 1922; cf. also the Strictly Confidential Report by the German Legation in Vienna, December 21, 1922; A.A., Abt. II-Ö.: Po. 2, Bd. 7.

[109] Wildner, "Die grosse Reise," stresses the French concern with the stop in Berlin, whereas M.R.220, August 28, 1922, refers to the French fears of the stop at Verona.

188

hoped to stir up precisely this kind of agitation, and he made it clear that "under no circumstances" would he change his route.[110] On the other hand, Seipel knew just how far to go. Hungary was left out because it could not have given effective help and because its inclusion would have impaired the ultimate objectives of the whole venture. Yugoslavia, in turn, was omitted in deference to Italian sensitivities; and in any case Seipel figured that it was enough to approach Beneš as spokesman of the Little Entente.[111]

At each stop Seipel asked more or less identical questions. He wanted to know what were the chances of action on the part of the League of Nations and, failing this, what alternatives were left to Austria to overcome its difficulties in conjunction with its neighbors. While in Prague he probed tactfully into the modalities of a connection with the Little Entente, in Berlin into chances of the Anschluss, and in Verona into a financial and economic union with Italy, it also must be recorded that the wily Austrian Chancellor made a point, as he later reported to his cabinet, of "varying . . . the program" in the different cities. In Prague he talked "very strongly about the Anschluss to Germany and Italy," whereas in Italy he put the South Tyrolean question on the agenda, thus hoping to put the Italians "off balance."[112] The main point was that he kept the initiative in these negotiations, and once again he had fun, even in this desperate moment. In foreign affairs he had as great a flexibility, as wide a range, as he had on the domestic scene. He could play with alternatives which would have seemed to other statesmen mutually exclusive. To him an Anschluss with Italy was almost as conceivable as one with Germany, just as monarchy and republic, socialism and capitalism were essentially equivalent alternatives. Ultimately the churchman saw all these choices *sub specie aeternitatis*. This perspective made him infinitely calm and resourceful in crises,

[110] Wildner, "Die grosse Reise."   [111] Ibid.
[112] A.V.A., M.R.220, August 28, 1922.

but it also made him appear to others as the "devil in the robe."[113]

Seipel conceded to his cabinet that, for a number of reasons, he had been most fearful of his day in Prague on August 21.[114] In the first days of planning it did indeed look as though Prague might have remained the only station on the trip, which would have invalidated its whole purpose. After all, some seven months ago an Austrian government had been toppled because of a journey to Prague. The success of this particular trip would therefore depend on the other stops, on visits to Germany and Italy. There only would the difference between Schober's and Seipel's conduct of foreign affairs become apparent.

There is no doubt that Beneš's attitude toward Austria had drastically changed in the years since 1918. Originally an advocate of the destruction of Austria,[115] he had come to see that her salvaging was an international necessity on which depended the European balance of power. The treaty with Renner and the Treaty of Lana had laid the foundations for amicable relations between the two countries; but at the same time the very controversial nature of Lana in Austria had marked out the limits of an Austro-Czech rapprochement. Meanwhile Italy's increasing interest in establishing herself as the predominant influence in Central Europe activated Beneš to find some formula for effective economic cooperation with Austria while safeguarding the political and economic independence of each state.[116] Suddenly relations with Austria became a matter of *raison d'état* for the

[113] "Der Teufel im Ornat," *Politika*, Belgrade, October 13, 1930; quoted and trans. in St.A., Liasse Österreich 2/3 Innere Lage, K.276.

[114] A.V.A., M.R.220, August 28, 1922.

[115] Cf. the excellent reports to Vienna by the Austrian Minister to Prague, Dr. Ferdinand Marek, of 1921 and 1922, in St.A., Fasz. 81; also Report Z $\frac{17/P}{764}$ Eichhoff to Bundesministerium für Äusseres, Paris, February 15, 1922, and Strictly Confidential Report Z.456/Pol, Marek to Bundesministerium für Äusseres, Prague, December 7, 1922, St.A., Liasse Österreich 8/IV, K.345.

[116] Strictly Secret Letter Z.329/P., Marek to Bundesministerium für Äusseres, Prague, June 18, 1922; St.A., Fasz. 81.

190

Czechs. Masaryk put it as follows in his memorandum to the Western Powers: "But from our point of view I declare . . . that, however regretfully and forced by events, we give preference to our connection with Austria over its connections with Germany and Italy."[117] It was ultimately the maintenance of the "order established by the Peace Treaties" that demanded such a Czech policy.[118]

Seipel's fear of Prague was partly caused by Beneš's known tendency to act quickly in his eagerness to have Austria throw itself into the arms of Czechoslovakia. But Seipel, the old fox, made a point of talking so much that Beneš had little chance to speak,[119] and, more important, Seipel's raising the "Italian solution" as a serious possibility caused a visible irritation in the Czech Foreign Minister.[120] It seemed to agitate Beneš even more than the Anschluss question, which he could safely leave for the other powers, particularly France and Italy, to cope with. For the rest, Beneš sketched out a plan of a Central Europe without its center, Germany, and also without Italy.

However, the next morning Seipel set out via Bodenbach to Berlin. Arrangements had been made for a formal reception at the Anhalter Bahnhof, but the visiting party was whisked off the train at Gross-Lichterfelde, a suburban station, because of fears of an assassination plot against the German Chancellor, Wirth, by the ominous Right-wing secret organization "O.C." Somehow this embarrassing reception cast its shadow over the whole meeting between the two Chancellors which, by comparison with the preceding one in Prague and also the later one in Verona, was, as the Austrians remarked, "short and simple."[121] This did not

[117] Masaryk, *Cesta Democracie*, II, 311. [118] Ibid., 312.
[119] A.V.A., M.R.220, August 28, 1922.
[120] Wildner, "Die grosse Reise."
[121] Wildner, "Die grosse Reise"; indeed in June 1931, during the crisis connected with the German-Austrian Customs Union project, the German Foreign Minister Julius Curtius had the Foreign Office search in vain for the records of the 1922 meeting in Berlin; letter, illegible signature, to Wirth, Berlin, May 11, 1931, A.A., Abt. II-Ö.: Po.2, Bd. 21.

mean that the Germans were unfriendly, but their country was deep in a situation of crisis and Wirth was simply preoccupied. The failure of the London Conference had hit the Germans at least as much as it had the Austrians, and Wirth reminded the visitors that there was not only an "Austrian problem," but also a "German problem," and that one should not introduce a new issue into an atmosphere already charged with unsolved ones.[122]

It is hard to imagine that Seipel would and could have had any substantial expectations from his trip to Berlin. He did not really want the Anschluss and the Germans were not in a position to offer any help.[123] However, he was clearly not averse to using the Anschluss idea as a diplomatic weapon. Georg Franckenstein, Austria's Minister to London, had once called the technique a "serious upgrading of the Anschluss idea, aimed at shaking the Powers out of their indifference and delaying passivity."[124] Seipel, the patient, used a sort of shock treatment on the Powers, the potential doctors. Besides, by this "Anschluss policy" he absolved his obligations toward his Pan-German coalition partners. By a mere raising of the Anschluss question, he accomplished his purpose toward the Powers abroad as well as toward the Pan-Germans at home, and by leaving it up to the Germans to spell out

[122] Wildner, "Aufzeichnung." Wirth confided to the British Ambassador, Lord D'Abernon, in a state of great nervous tension that he told Seipel "frankly" that "there must be no talk of 'Anschluss' as long as the reparation question was unsettled. Europe was in enough trouble about reparation without having a second problem"; Lord D'Abernon, *An Ambassador of Peace* (London, 1929), II, 89.

[123] Shortly before the "great trip," the German Minister to Vienna, in a meeting with Seipel and Vice-Chancellor Frank, had given the unequivocal answer to the question whether Germany was in a position to protect Austria militarily, should Austria have to break relations with its other neighbors: "This would mean war"; Strictly Confidential Report by Dr. Maximilian Pfeiffer, "Das österreichische Problem und die Anschlussfrage," Vienna, April 15-18, 1925; A.A., Geheimakten II-Ö.: Po.2, Bd. 1.

[124] Report Z.262/P. Franckenstein, London, June 7, 1922; St.A., Fasz. 52, quoted in Ladner, *Seipel*, p. 60.

its impracticability he was substantially satisfied. And the Germans were not a little irritated at being used as tools by the Austrian Chancellor.

In Berlin, then, no confidence materialized, no particular encouragement such as had been expected at least in "camera caritatis."[125] It was made clear to the Austrians that the "opinio communis," in particular among rightist circles in Germany, was that "under no circumstances" should the Anschluss question, at this moment, be "rolled up" directly or indirectly.[126]

When the talk turned to the question of Austria's relations with the other neighbors, Wirth abandoned his reserve, and to the obvious pleasure of his Austrian guests emphatically discouraged ties, even economic ones, with Czechoslovakia or the Little Entente, while calling an orientation toward Italy "a lesser evil."[127] When at the end Seipel once again asked what Germany would do in the event of social revolution in Austria, his German colleagues lectured him on the fact that "in politics one should not figure too many contingencies."[128] At this point it looked as though Seipel, who was a master in "juggling with several balls,"[129] had dropped one.

The answers then which Seipel received to his questions in Berlin, particularly those regarding the Anschluss, he could have easily anticipated. While it may be too harsh to follow Gustav Stolper's judgment that Seipel used the Berlin visit as a "meaningless demonstration"[130] merely to "parade" to the friends of the

[125] Wildner, "Die grosse Reise."

[126] A.V.A., M.R.220, August 28, 1922.

[127] Ibid.; cf. also Wildner, "Aufzeichnung"; cf. also Secret Telegram, Reichskanzler to Botschafter, Paris, London, Rome, Vienna, Prague, Berlin, August 24, 1922, A.A., Abt. II.-Ö.: Po.2-A, Bd. 1.

[128] Wildner, "Aufzeichnung."

[129] Walter Goldinger in Heinrich Benedikt, *Geschichte der Republik Österreich* (Vienna, 1954), p. 126.

[130] Gustav Stolper, "Prag-Verona-Genf," *Der österreichische Volkswirt*, XIV, September 19, 1922, 1187-1191.

Anschluss the helplessness of Berlin,[131] there is no reason to assume that Seipel emerged disappointed from his sojourn in the German capital, because he "honestly" had "expected more";[132] he was too shrewd a judge of what was politically feasible and what was not. And not even in this hour of despair would Seipel really have settled for an Anschluss.

All this does not mean, however, that Seipel's motives were ignoble. In general, it was part of the nature of his accommodative position to explore situations without an ultimate commitment. In this particular situation the Berlin stop was clearly not the final one. Seipel had not set out to roll up the Anschluss question but the Central European one.

In the afternoon of August 23 Seipel boarded the "D. Zug" out of Berlin for Verona. "In Verona," wrote the *Reichspost* the following morning, "the most important decisions that Austria will face in the immediate future will presumably be prepared."[133] Indeed, although the political situation in Italy was, to say the least, no more stable than the one in Germany, the reception in Verona, by comparison with that in Berlin, was ceremonious, with a guard of honor waiting at the station and a sentry of honor at the hotel; it was noticed, however, that Carlo Schanzer, the Foreign Minister, in contrast to his Secretary General, Salvatore Contarini, took trouble to soft-pedal the decisive political significance of the encounter.[134]

Austro-Italian relations had been regularized by Renner after the war. But it was not until Seipel's chancellorship that the relations between the two countries became activated to a point of seriously threatening the Central European order as established by the Treaties. Indeed in the course of repeated overtures on the part of Seipel the idea of a customs and currency union be-

---

[131] Cf. also Toni Stolper, *Ein Leben in Brennpunkten unserer Zeit. Wien, Berlin, New York. Gustav Stolper 1888-1943* (Tübingen, 1960), p. 147.

[132] Ladner, *Seipel*, p. 96.   [133] *Reichspost*, August 24, 1922.

[134] Wildner, "Die grosse Reise."

tween Austria and its "most powerful neighbor"[135] was born.[136] Although Contarini himself was reported as having dismissed the venture as a "machine de guerre,"[137] Seipel, supported by Schüller, brought up the subject again in the discussions of August 25. The Italians, Seipel later reported to his cabinet, were "very eager" for the Austrians, except for Schanzer himself, in whom Seipel saw a "timid and weak man."[138] Whatever Schanzer's personal attributes, his caution made him more sensitive to the opposition of foreign governments to the plan and more aware of the weak domestic position of his own government than the more responsive Contarini. Indeed, he was nobody's fool—not even Seipel's; and when the latter inquired into the compensations Italy might give Austria for the political and economic risks incurred by a union with Italy, Schanzer called Seipel's bluff and snapped back: "I have the impression that there is a sort of distortion of the state of affairs. It is not Italy which demands the customs union! We are ready to examine the proposals; but if you are afraid, we shall not follow it up. . . . If therefore the fear of the realization is greater than the desire, let us abandon the whole plan. . . ."[139] Seipel's overly cagey technique in diplomatic negotiations had irritated Wirth before and was a major factor in the justified guardedness of all of his successors toward the Austrian statesman. In this particular instance Seipel's approach backfired and made Schanzer all the more eager to avoid having the proposed union appear as a unilateral Italian affair. Though it was agreed that Schüller should proceed to Rome for further

[135] Confidential Telegram Z.41, Grünberger to Kwiatkowski, Vienna, June 17, 1922, St.A., Liasse Österreich 8/IV, K.345.

[136] Cf. St.A., Liasse Österreich 8/IV, K.345, passim; on the growing Czech-Italian rivalry in Central Europe, cf. Ladner, *Seipel*, p. 60.

[137] Copy of letter Z.3918/3a, Schüller to Grünberger, Rome, July 8, 1922, St.A., Liasse Österreich 8/IV, K.345; cf. Schüller, *Erbe Österreichs*, p. 87.

[138] A.V.A., M.R.220, August 28, 1922.

[139] Wildner, "Aufzeichnung."

negotiations with Contarini and Paratone, the Minister of Finance, the Foreign Minister's cautious but firm stand did in the end show Austria the road to Geneva.

There is no doubt that the stopover in Italy constituted a climax of Seipel's trip. Concerning the economic technicalities of a union between the two countries, two expert opinions stood against each other. Schüller saw the possibility for new horizons and Stolper exposed the "economic absurdity"[140] of the plan. But the Austrian Chancellor had repeatedly said that the nature of his trip, after the failure of the credit negotiations, was primarily political. In this respect Verona occupied a very different place in Seipel's plan from that of Prague and Berlin. It is evident that Seipel did not want seriously to consider a closer relationship with the Little Entente or the Anschluss with Germany. He was considerably keener on the economic and financial union with Italy. The cabinet meeting seriously reflected the tenor of public opinion in Austria in favor of the Italian alternative.[141] As far as the parties were concerned, both Christian Socialists and Pan-Germans showed an eager interest in the Italian tie, whereas the Social Democrats tended to look in the direction of Prague. Even though an Austro-Italian alignment was merely the product of a policy of despair, it opened up broader possibilities in Seipel's "imperial mind." To Masirevich, the Hungarian Minister whom Seipel would see after his journey, he suggested a similar alignment for Hungary. In the cabinet meeting he once again proposed the possibility of an inclusion of Germany in the Austro-Italian economic area.[142] There is little doubt that Seipel's vision of a "regrouping of powers"[143] anticipated some such formation of an Austro-Italian-Hungarian-German bloc.

---

[140] Gustav Stolper, "Die Kanzlerreise," *Der österreichische Volkswirt,* xiv, August 26, 1922, 1163-1166.

[141] A.V.A., M.R.220, August 28, 1922.   [142] Ibid.

[143] Memorandum "Gespräch mit dem Herrn Bundeskanzler über einzuleitende Verhandlungen mit Italien," Vienna, July 4, 1922, St.A., Liasse Österreich 8/IV, K.345, F.276.

But even if the Austro-Italian plan turned out to be a "fiasco,"[144] as Beneš said with some satisfaction, and even if any further combination would be even more of a pipe dream, Seipel thought he could claim that even in case of the League's failure he was not left "without alternatives."[145] He made no secret of the fact that, as he said bluntly to the French envoy, he would "ten times rather go to Rome than Prague."[146] Even the threat of an Italian orientation was enough to stir up the Powers. Seipel therefore had used an old maxim, "divide and rule," long established in old Austria for the benefit of the postwar Republic. He had also made at least enough "noise" to make it clear to the Powers that "empty phrases" would no longer help Austria.[147] To this extent Seipel, by his trips to Prague, Berlin, and Verona, had prepared the ground for concerted action in Geneva and had succeeded in "rolling up" the Central European question.

Between Geneva and Vienna

Austria's economic situation had further deteriorated since the London Conference had relegated the problem of Austria to the League in the middle of August, and the value of the currency continued to go down mercilessly and food prices to go up. In the hour of despair a Social Democratic "imperial conference," as Renner still referred to it,[148] called together to review the politi-

---

[144] Telegram, Z.145, Hans Cnobloch (Budapest) to Austrian Delegation in Geneva, Budapest, September 9, 1923, St.A., Liasse Österreich 8/IV, K.345.

[145] Seipel facing the Foreign Affairs Committee, August 31, 1922; *Reichspost*, September 1, 1922.

[146] Strictly Confidential Memorandum, German Legation, Vienna, December 21, 1922, based on a conversation of a "confidential authority" with Lefèvre-Pontalis and approved by the latter; A.A., Abt. II-Ö.: Po.2, Bd. 7.

[147] French Minister to Seipel, August 28, 1922, A.V.A., M.R.220, August 28, 1922.

[148] *Sten. Prot., 138. Sitzung, I.G.P.*, October 12, 1922, p. 4414.

cal course of the Left, emerged with an appeal to the "bourgeois parties" to acknowledge the complete breakdown of their policies, and with an offer to form a "government of concentration" together with the Social Democrats.[149] The condition for the coalition was not only "capitulation,"[150] but also the removal of Seipel himself. The Socialists, Renner declared, were not ready to "board" the Seipel government, and he added: "We don't like the coach, because of the coachman."[151]

However, the crown reached its nadir on August 25, and Seipel, who was returning to Vienna from Verona, had little reason at this point to sell out. Now, after his trip, he could look more confidently toward the League, the "second act" of his scheme. Though in effect the conferences with the three neighboring governments, like the London Conference, had left the decisive role to Geneva, the whole psychological and political situation had changed. The slight improvement in the value of the crown was an indication of this. Seipel had succeeded in impressing the European powers with the urgency of the Austrian problem and its connection with the general European balance. As a result the relegation of the Austrian problem to the League appeared in a new light. It had become a problem which the Great Powers had to deal with out of self-interest; it had moved into the center of attention of European statesmen.

Though originally Seipel had serious doubts about going to Geneva, fearing some "foul compromise,"[152] he was finally persuaded to go by his Foreign Minister, already in Geneva, and also by the diplomatic corps in Vienna. If the predominantly political nature of the Austrian problem was to be maintained,[153] the Chancellor himself had to speak for his country.

On the night of September 2, then, having at length consulted

[149] Bauer, *Revolution*, pp. 260ff.
[150] Ibid., cf. *Arbeiter-Zeitung*, August 26, 1922.
[151] *Sten. Prot.*, *134. Sitzung, I.G.P.*, September 14, 1922, p. 4360.
[152] A.V.A., M.R.221, September 2, 1922, Top Secret Appendix.
[153] Ibid.

with his cabinet, Seipel took the train to Switzerland.[154] His diary
entry for September 6 modestly registers only two words:
"speech delivered."[155] In reality the "appeal" was a memorable
event for him as well as for the League. The session of the Council had been deliberately scheduled for this somewhat late date
in order to enable the Third League Assembly, which had convened meanwhile, to participate. This scheduling was "an unusual tribute to international psychology,"[156] since in addition to
the ten members of the Council it allowed forty national delega-
tions to be present. In this way the Chancellor, who was the only
speaker scheduled for the meeting, could reach the whole
League membership with his appeal. Though Seipel had become
increasingly controversial in the halls of the Viennese Parliament,
"it would be hard to imagine," recorded the historian of
the League, "a more effective advocate in any international
gathering, than this quiet, ascetic, supremely intelligent priest,
whose clerical garb seemed to set him apart from the other
delegates."[157]

Speaking in German, he gave expression to "a certain emotion"
when he appeared in front of the Council to plead the cause of
his "fatherland Austria." Once again he paid public tribute to
Lammasch: "How did we Austrians . . . who loved peace, gather
around Heinrich Lammasch and speak, write, and fight tirelessly
for the League of Nations idea!"[158] At the same time the Austrian
Chancellor did not shy away from admitting the danger to the
League of becoming "an instrument of the victors of the World
War."[159] Seipel's appearance in front of the international organ-

[154] For the information derived from the League of Nations Archive in
Geneva I have seen fit, in the following pages on Seipel's negotiations in
Geneva between September 4 and October 4, to rely on the fine monograph,
Gottlieb Ladner, *Seipel als Überwinder der Staatskrise im Sommer 1922*
(Vienna and Graz, 1964).

[155] Seipel diary, September 6, 1922.

[156] F. P. Walters, *A History of the League of Nations* (London, New
York, and Toronto, 1952), I, 208.

[157] Ibid.   [158] Gessl, *Reden*, p. 25.   [159] Ibid.

ization gave him a chance, while asking for help for his small country, to help give shape to the League, to make of it a true instrument of international reconciliation and an effective protector of the weak. The Chancellor reminded his audience that Austria, a product of the Peace Treaties, was still to be proven "viable," and that the burden of the proof was up to those who had created it, lest a dangerous vacuum be created in Europe. He continued: "The eminent League of Nations faces a truly great challenge in the Austrian question. If it lives up to it, if it really possesses the authority which we gladly recognize, if it is able successfully to show the states and peoples the road to world peace, then the world will believe in it, then the League, which I am addressing today, will be the League of Nations, of which the friends of peace have dreamt for such a long time."[160]

Subsequently the Christian statesman, facing the world organization, presented the reason for his presence and for the League's action as the "need" (*Not*) of the people; but Austria could be made viable in a few years by decisive League action affecting not only Austria itself but Central Europe at large. Specifically Austria needed the lifting of the general mortgage and credit to enable her to set up her own economy. While spelling out the terms of some inevitable control over the use of the credit and indirectly over the Austrian economy, he let the fact shine through that Austria would prefer "entry into a large economic system"[161] to any infringement of its independence. The problem, he reiterated, was not merely an economic one. The "Austrian question" had become a political question of the first order. That is why he had taken his trip to visit his neighbors. And the Chancellor concluded: "Before the people of Austria in its isolation perishes, it will do all in its power to break the barriers and chains which oppress it. It is up to the League to see to it that this may be done without threatening the peace and without troubling relations among Austria's neighbors!"[162]

[160] Ibid., pp. 26f.   [161] Ibid., p. 31.   [162] Ibid., p. 32.

200

Notice here that the proud Chancellor concluded neither with a threat nor a plea. By referring to his previous trips, by alluding, even indirectly, to the Italian alternative, he kept alive this possibility of an action independent of the League, one that was so much dreaded by France and by the countries of the Little Entente. Seipel saw fit to hint at this dreaded alternative in order to strike the right balance between stressing, as he later put it, the "determination of Austria" and the "obligation of the League."[163]

In Geneva the impact of the Chancellor's appeal was striking. We are told that the "circumstances and the manner of Seipel's address to the Council, rather than his actual words"[164] produced the desired effect. The aroused Assembly[165] constituted in this situation a vital background for the work of the committees which went instantly into operation to find a solution to the Austrian problem.[166] The League had never before been confronted with such an immediate challenge, and upon its successful conclusion hung not only the fate of Austria, but, as Lord Balfour, the veteran British representative at the League, emphasized in his speech before the Assembly on September 30, that of the League itself and the "world at large."[167]

While it is quite true that Seipel's impact in Geneva was based

[163] Letter Z.24547/13 Seipel to Schober, Zürs, August 15, 1931, St.A., Fasz. 144, Deutschland I/III; cf. Gessl, *Reden*, p. 32.

[164] Walters, *The League*, I, 208.

[165] In the League Assembly of the following day, the Swiss Bundesrat Motta set the tone by an emotional peroration in which he stated that "the whole world embraced Austria." He concluded his remarks: "And thus I speak to Austria: You want to live and you will live! It is the spirit of fraternity which gives you this promise." The other delegates, starting with the Norwegian Fridtjof Nansen, followed with not much less generous statements; *Neue Freie Presse*, September 15, 1922, morning ed.; there had been a newspaper strike in Vienna between September 5 and September 14.

[166] *Monthly Summary of the League of Nations* (Geneva, 1922), II, no. 9, September 1-31, 1922, 195.

[167] Ibid., p. 210.

on his "impressive personality" and not merely on his "tactics,"[168] it would be erroneous to suggest that he had altogether left his political self at home. In order to keep the initiative and to steer the course of the proceedings, which he considered of crucial importance, he kept alive negotiations with both the Czechs and the Italians aiming at a settlement independently of the League.[169] Since he was by no means assured as yet that the League would and could get the loan, refused time and again in the past, he left himself another way out. In effect the so-called "separate action" (*Sonderaktion*) of Seipel's, particularly the ever-present threat of a union with Italy, helped to activate the League.

Though while he was in Geneva Seipel found the full support of the representatives of the nations from the first day of his appearance before the Council, in his own capital, to which he returned on September 11, he had to expect a fierce battle with the Social Democrats. After immediately reporting to the cabinet upon his arrival on September 11 and confronting the Foreign Affairs Committee on September 13, he rendered his account to the assembled delegates of the Nationalrat in the afternoon of the following day. It was as usual a sober and calm exposé. In his lucid professorial manner he rehearsed the whole background of his unsuccessful attempts toward financial reconstruction and also the particular problems connected with the Geneva action. His chief argument concerned the basic issue of the need for foreign credit as well as the related problem of an "inevitable" control. But as he was addressing his countrymen, he climaxed with an appeal for unity.

> The more difficult the times, the more must our people and must all sections and classes of this people recognize it as an absolute patriotic duty now to hold together. . . . The success

[168] Goldinger in Benedikt, *Geschichte*, p. 128.
[169] A.V.A., M.R.224, September 11, 1922, Anhang: "Bericht des Bundeskanzlers über seine Intervention anlässlich der Völkerbundtagung im Genf."

of the Government's mission in Geneva depends on the renewed cooperation in the coming days between the parties,
in order that the whole world see that the Austrian people
is ready to give the fatherland what it needs. Only then will
also the others be ready to grant us help, so that the Austrian
fatherland may remain preserved to its people.[170]

But things had changed since St. Germain and since Lana. The
"cooperation" between the parties was gone. Indeed, not without
justification did Karl Renner, at a later date, remind the Chancellor that when the peace delegation had been sent to St. Germain, he had consulted with the opposition, all parties had sent
their experts along, and all decisions had been reached in mutual
agreement.[171] It stands to reason that Seipel might have taken a
tripartisan delegation along to Geneva and that his Social Democratic colleagues, away from the heat of the domestic scene and
confronted by the economic realities as they had been elaborated
in the committees of the League, would have learned a lesson.
And Seipel might have had an easier stand at home.

The domestic alignment on the issues of foreign policy had
changed. St. Germain and Lana had been supported, with whatever reservations, by the Christian Socialists and the Social Democrats against Pan-German opposition. Now the latter, as coalition partners in the Government, admitted that "the Anschluss
with the German Reich today is not feasible,"[172] and loyally supported the Chancellor. The opposition now became increasingly
fierce, irrational and personal, emanating from the Socialists led
by Bauer and Renner. The "Seipel regime," one of the milder
catch phrases of the Left, was a tool of the middle classes and the
wealthy peasants, aiming at crushing the workers' class with the
help of Italian and Czech imperialism.[173] There was both detailed

[170] *Sten. Prot., 134. Sitzung, I.G.P.*, September 14, 1922, p. 4332f.
[171] *Sten. Prot., 138. Sitzung, I.G.P.*, October 12, 1922, p. 4413.
[172] *Sten. Prot., 134. Sitzung, I.G.P.*, September 14, 1922, p. 4343.
[173] Cf. ibid., pp. 4337, 4361.

and relevant criticism, particularly from Bauer, who for once was more controlled than Renner. No one but Seipel himself, he charged, was responsible for the failure of the financial plan, which was too easy on the capitalists and too hard on the workers. In opposition to Seipel's well-founded thesis that Austria could not be salvaged without foreign capital, he reiterated the Social Democratic prescription of self-help. However, it was not the substantial criticism on the part of the Social Democrats which was reprehensible, but their tone. Household clichés of Marxist origin, such as "capitalists greedy for a bloody subjugation of the workers' class,"[174] did not make for good politics even in the 1920s. Was the League Council, negotiating for some international financial control over Austria, really swayed by Seipel's lurid picture of his country, traversed by bloody hoardes that would justify treatment "à la Macedonia?"[175] This was wild rhetoric and real demagoguery, and Otto Bauer's finale, citing the determination of the workers' class to defend the freedom and the independence of the Republic[176] "with all its means," was an empty boast at best. It was dishonest, since the independence of Austria was certainly not Bauer's own concern. Besides, it was a thinly veiled threat of civil war.[177]

The political climate in Vienna, then, differed greatly from the one in Geneva, which could almost be described as apolitical. Good will and expertise drove the negotiations forward, in spite of difficulties which came from the Italians. The Viennese climate was charged with emotion and doctrinaire insistence, and it was Seipel's problem to adjust the two to each other and to make the Genevan decisions acceptable to the political parties.

Apart from the overall issue of self-help versus credit from abroad, the most touchy issues which came up during the negotiations in Geneva were the ones concerning a political guarantee by the Powers of the political independence, territorial integrity,

---

[174] Ibid., p. 4336.   [175] Ibid., p. 4337.   [176] Ibid., p. 4341.
[177] It was clearly understood as such by the former imperial Foreign Minister Czernin in his statement to Parliament; ibid., p. 4347.

and sovereignty of Austria, and Austria's renewed assurance that it would not alienate its independence. Other issues discussed were the plenary powers needed by the Austrian government at home to enable it to carry through actively the provisions of the Geneva decisions, and the question of control by the League and the guaranteeing Powers over the Austrian economy.

Seipel, who had returned to Geneva on September 22, took an active part in the matter of the Austrian obligation not to alienate its independence.[178] The question was whether or how reference was to be made to Article 88 of the Treaty of St. Germain. This issue closely affected Seipel's coalition partners, the Pan-Germans, who, having voted against the treaty to begin with, could not now be expected to condone it even indirectly. However, the Austrians were made to understand that the French and Czechs would press for an explicit and more far-reaching commitment on the part of Austria, should reference to Article 88 be avoided. Seipel negotiated a formulation of the Austrian obligation not to alienate its independence "in accordance with the terms of Article 88" which under the circumstances had to satisfy his coalition partners.[179]

As to the plenary powers, it will be recalled that already in his first Declaration of Policy Seipel had referred to the need for these powers. Now he found the other Powers, particularly England, pressing the issue, with himself in the position of having to express concern for getting the necessary two-thirds majority for a corresponding constitutional law at home.[180] As to the question of control, his task was limited to finding the form least offensive to the sensitivities of his countrymen.

When the Assembly of the League met for its closing meeting on September 30, Lord Balfour, on behalf of the Austrian Committee, could communicate the broad outline of impending agreement, and on October 4 the three protocols, the so-called

[178] Cf. A.V.A., M.R.231, October 7, 1922, stenographic minutes.
[179] Cf. Ladner, *Seipel*, pp. 145f.
[180] A.V.A., M.R.231, October 7, 1922.

Geneva Protocols were ready to be signed by the representatives of the governments of Great Britain, France, Italy, Czechoslovakia, and Austria.[181] In the afternoon of the same day the Council convened in its last formal meeting. The speakers, starting with Lord Balfour, emphasized the spirit of solidarity—the Marquis Imperiali even talked of Christian solidarity—in which agreement was reached. With his sense of British understatement Balfour characterized the scheme as one "not lacking in true statesmanship," designed to place Austria "in a position of prosperity, of solvency and of self-respect, and enable her to become again a great factor in European civilization."[182]

Seipel was the last speaker, and he praised the achievement as a triumph for the League: "Thank God we can say today: the League of Nations has not failed us; the great idea lives—the idea

[181] Protocol No. I contains the solemn declaration that the signatories will "respect the political independence, the territorial integrity, and the sovereignty of Austria," with the latter in turn entering into a corresponding obligation, "in accordance with the terms of Article 88 of the Treaty of St. Germain, not to alienate its independence" and to "abstain from any negotiations or from any economic or financial engagement calculated directly or indirectly to compromise this independence."

Protocol No. II spelled out the terms of the loan to Austria of 650 million gold crowns to be guaranteed by the four powers. By these terms Austria was subjected to a double control, a Commissioner-General appointed by the Council, who was to dispose of the yield of the loan, and a four-power Committee of Control under Italian chairmanship, without which Austria could accept no other loan.

Protocol No. III, signed only by Seipel in contrast to the two preceding ones, the Austrian government committed itself to drawing up within one month a program of reforms and improvements designed to enable Austria to reestablish a balanced budget within two years. The government also promised to lay before the Austrian Parliament a draft law giving any government which may be in power "full authority" for two years to take any measures within the limits of the program, without having to seek further approval by Parliament. For the full text of the protocols see League of Nations, *Official Journal*, III, no. 11 (November 1922), part III (22nd Session of the Council), 1471ff.

[182] Ibid., p. 1458f.

that a Supreme Court exists, composed of members of the nations themselves; a Court which, when a people is in such dire need that it cannot help itself, will effectually call upon the others to help, and which will perhaps by so doing unostentatiously relieve the world of burdens laid upon it by the sins of the past. Yes, this great idea lives."[183]

It was not, he continued soberly, Austria's task to make the work of the League live. He warned the Council that he would have to account before Parliament, "in accordance with the institutions of the democratic State," for his policies and decisions in Geneva, and that "there will probably be a few weeks of sharp opposition";[184] but he thought that he could assure the Council of his country's determination to make the sacrifices necessary for its rehabilitation.

In Vienna, to which he returned on October 7 from his triumph in Geneva, he received a divided reception. To some he was the savior, to others the traitor.[185] "The League of Nations first of all has decided one thing: Austria can be saved," he told Parliament,[186] and at the same time he warned them that "it doesn't matter only what will be decided here but also how the negotiations will be conducted."[187]

But this exhortation was in vain. The tone of the parliamentary debates was increasingly harsh. If the Pan-Germans lived up to Seipel's expectations by arguing, somewhat compulsively, that the Austrian commitment in Protocol No. I was made in view of danger not from an Anschluss but from the Czech-Italian rivalry over Austria,[188] they were told by the Socialists: "Take off the Black, Red, Gold, cap and show yourselves in the attire which fits you, in the Jesuit's cowl of Herr Seipel."[189]

---

[183] Ibid., p. 1461.   [184] Ibid.
[185] Cf. "Hochverräter oder Retter?" *Reichspost*, October 8, 1922.
[186] *Sten. Prot., 138. Sitzung, I.G.P.*, October 12, 1922, p. 4410.
[187] Ibid., p. 4413.   [188] Franz Dinghofer; ibid., 4428.
[189] Karl Seitz; *Sten. Prot., 147. Sitzung, I.G.P.*, November 8, 1922, p. 4673.

The Social Democrats' attack had now lost all semblance of rationality and became fiercely invective. In a melodramatic fashion Renner compared the Austrians to Rodin's "Citizens of Calais," "forced by the conqueror to turn over the keys of the city."[190] The League was but a tool of capitalists,[191] now imposing upon Austria an "economic dictator"[192] in the person of the Commissioner-General. Was not Seipel, shouted Seitz, guilty of "high treason against his own country and people?"[193] Was he not, when asking for plenary powers, making himself "Emperor of Austria?"[194]

The emphatic "no, no, and once again no"which Renner hurled at Seipel in Parliament[195] was reinforced by a massive propaganda action initiated by the Social Democratic party congress convening on October 14, which was to carry the fight against the "enslavement" of Austria to the masses. At the same time Karl Renner, as emissary for the very party that was charging the Government with "high treason," set out for Prague to establish contact with the Czech Social Democrats through Vlastimil Tusar, Czech Minister to Berlin, to urge them to attack the Czech Government on its Austrian policy.[196] He was told by Tusar that the Czech Social Democratic party could not comply, since as a member of the Government coalition it had to back up the Czech Government's policy toward Austria, and Renner's concern about the fate of the Austrian Social Democracy was essentially a domestic Austrian affair.

It is fair to talk about the "fiasco" of Renner's mission to

[190] *Sten. Prot., 138. Sitzung, I.G.P.*, October 12, 1922, p. 4414.

[191] Ibid., p. 4415.   [192] Ibid., p. 4414.   [193] Ibid., p. 4433.

[194] Seitz; *Sten. Prot., 145. Sitzung, I.G.P.*, November 6, 1922, p. 4553; Cf. also Renner; *Sten. Prot., 138. Sitzung, I.G.P.*, October 12, 1922, p. 4418.

[195] Ibid., p. 4423.

[196] Strictly Confidential Reports Z.437/Pol., Marek to Bundesministerium für Äusseres, Prague, October 21, 1922; Z.445/Pol., "Unterredung Renner-Tusar," October 28, 1922, "Zur Prager Reise des Bundeskanzlers a.D. Dr. Renner," St.A., Fasz. 81.

Prague,[197] since it merely emphasized the failure of Social Democratic policy since the party left the coalition in 1920. Renner himself had to admit this fact in his Prague talks.[198] Invective and doctrinairism had taken the place of rational argument; extra-parliamentary concerns had replaced patient parliamentary footwork; Renner's clumsy, futile, close to treacherous orientation toward the Second International had supplanted his earlier cautious, patriotic statesmanship. No doubt, the Social Democrats had played their hand poorly. They had, in November 1920, moved with alacrity into opposition, hoping to force the Christian Socialists to their knees by parliamentary means. Meanwhile, however, Seipel had patiently and shrewdly fortified his parliamentary base by his coalition with the Pan-Germans. No doubt this made the Social Democratic opposition all the more difficult.

It is ironic that the weaknesses in the parliamentary tradition in Austria should have shown their effect primarily on the one party which had been the champion of democracy and parliamentarianism all along. Once the Social Democrats had lost control of the ship of state as well as the chance for recovery by parliamentary means within the immediate future, the rules of parliamentarianism, that is the give-and-take of parliamentary debate and compromise, were readily discarded. While Seipel did assume the responsibility for governing in 1922, the Social Democrats rejected the role of a responsible opposition. This mistake was pointed out to Renner in Prague by his Czech colleague, who predicted the imminent defeat of the Austrian sister party.[199]

The Social Democratic party of the early 1920s was no more

[197] Ladner, *Seipel*, p. 162, n. 713; incidentally neither Renner himself in his autobiography nor Jacques Hannak in his biography of Karl Renner even mentioned this mission.

[198] Report Z.445/Pol., Marek to Bundesministerium für Äusseres, "Zur Prager Reise des Bundeskanzlers a.D. Dr. Renner," Prague, October 28, 1922, St.A., Fasz. 81.

[199] Report, Z.445/Pol., Marek to Bundesministerium für Äusseres, Prague, October 28, 1922, St.A., Fasz. 81.

a bona fide "democratic" or parliamentary party. Its increasingly doctrinaire orientation made political dialogue impossible. The policy of empty phrases and of phantoms and legends in the Republic of Austria came from the Left, not from the Right. In fact if Austria had been spared a stab-in-the-back legend, thanks to Seipel, it now acquired its "treasure" of legends, fabricated by the Left: the conspiracy of international capitalism against the workers; the "high treason" of the "Prelate's government"; and alas, the stab-in-the-back which, as Otto Bauer claimed, Seipel administered in October 1922 to the revolution of November 12, 1918. The national revolution of German-Austria was liquidated.[200] The Austrian experience clearly shows that political irrationalism, political legend, as well as the obstruction of the democratic process, can have roots in the political Left.

Seipel, in turn, played his hand well—almost too well. For the time being he had a viable coalition with which he could carry through the financial reconstruction of Austria. Might the moment not come again however—as in fact it did in 1931—when Seipel might need the Social Democrats? But Seipel was rigid and understandably irritated with his political foes. He was impatient with advice just because it happened to agree with Otto Bauer's self-help plan.[201] As suggested earlier, it might have been to his own advantage to have kept in closer touch with the opposition, particularly during the Geneva negotiations.[202] Even though a coalition offer as such is not necessarily a bona fide sign of willingness to cooperate, the repeated approaches by the So-

[200] Cf. Bauer, *Revolution*, p. 270.

[201] Alexander Spitzmüller, . . . *Und hat auch Ursach, es zu lieben* (Vienna, 1955), pp. 341f.

[202] Even former Chancellor Schober found occasion to convey to Seipel his feelings of deep disappointment that Seipel had made him feel his "superfluousness" by not consulting him during and after the negotiations in Prague, Berlin, Verona, and Geneva. Schober, overly touchy, even asked for his retirement as Chief of Police of Vienna, a gesture which, however, remained an empty one; Schober to Seipel, Vienna, October 11, 1922; A.V.A., Bundeskanzleramt Inneres, Korrespondenz Seipel, K.79.

cial Democrats should not have been so summarily dismissed. A greater responsiveness on the part of Seipel might have helped the Social Democrats out of the corner into which they had maneuvered themselves and encouraged them to depart from their intransigent course. The theory that "the Austrian Chancellor didn't need them anymore"[203] could have been correct for the moment, but it did not hold for the future.

Even for the moment the Chancellor depended on the Social Democrats for the passing of the law regarding plenary powers, as provided for in the Third Geneva Protocol. It was the decision over this law that became a test of government–opposition relations. While the general Reconstruction Law was passed by simple majority (98 to 60), the Law on Plenary Powers, which the Social Democrats labeled the "fig leaf of absolutism,"[204] needed a two-thirds majority and could therefore clearly not be passed in the inclusive form suggested in the Geneva Protocol. The government was thus forced to propose a compromise in the form of an Extraordinary Cabinet Council, a special parliamentary committee composed of representatives of all parties in proportion to their strength in Parliament.

In the light of the fierce opposition which the Social Democrats had put up against Seipel's policies, it was all the more surprising that they should have acceded to this compromise. Seipel, with a "boldness reminiscent of Florentine statecraft,"[205] had shifted the responsibility for the success of the Geneva settlement onto the Social Democrats who, following suit, thus indirectly gave their blessing to the Geneva "enslaving treaty." While safeguarding the full right of parliamentary criticism, they discarded the possibility of obstructing the Reconstruction Law. The majority in the Cabinet Council, which was proportionately the same as

[203] Eduard Parma, "Rakousko," *Zahranični Politica*, Prague, September 25, 1923, pp. 1205f.

[204] *Sten. Prot., 145. Sitzung, I.G.P.*, November 6, 1922, p. 4577.

[205] Gustav Stolper, "Das Ende," *Der österreichische Volkswirt*, xv, November 25, 1922, 201.

that in Parliament, would not impede the policy of the government.

Was the Social Democratic turnabout sufficiently justified by the excuse, given by Seitz, that it had successfully averted the exclusion of Parliament?[206] Could the Social Democratic party council, specially convened, honestly claim in its statement of November 22 a "part-success" for the party?[207] There may be some truth in the claim that the Social Democrats gave proof, after all, of their loyalty to the state which had been of their own creation. In the final analysis, however, the Social Democratic reversal was an acknowledgment of defeat, defeat of their policy of legend-making, and of their practice of senseless vituperation.[208] Apart from the fact that the Social Democrats had no practical alternative to offer, since they themselves did not believe in self-help, they had surely driven the Pan-Germans into the arms of the Christian Socialists. "As we did not secure the support of the Pan-Germans," wrote Otto Bauer, "we were unable to destroy the parliamentary majority which was pledged to Geneva."[209] The only other alternative, as Otto Bauer knew, was revolution, for which Austria's workers were not prepared. Besides, revolution, as Bauer also feared, would have brought the intervention of the new fascist regime in Italy.[210] Seipel's supposedly clerical and monarchistic "system" was preferable to this. The "traitor," after all, had become the savior.

In the first six months of his chancellorship Seipel stood at the height of his career. He had guided his little country out of the valley of despair and freed it from the daily threat of economic and social breakdown and from imminent invasion and partition. He had systematically fortified his control over his party, which

[206] *Sten. Prot., 149. Sitzung, I.G.P.*, November 24, 1922, p. 4752.

[207] *"Teilerfolg,"* quoted in Jacques Hannak, *Karl Renner und seine Zeit* (Vienna, 1965), p. 445.

[208] Cf. Gustav Stolper, "Das Ende," *Der österreichische Volkswirt*, xv, November 25, 1922, 202.

[209] Bauer, *Revolution*, p. 268. [210] Cf. ibid., p. 269.

212

Chancellor Mayr had lacked, and cemented a coalition which his predecessor Schober had not been able to marshal. He had hopelessly outmaneuvered the opposition, or rather let it get entangled in its own web of political legends. And if it would be excessive to back Seipel's claim that Austria through his foreign trips had again been put into a position to "enter actively into world politics,"[211] it was certainly true that Austria had regained a distinct foreign policy. Taking advantage of the rivalries of his neighbors was only one of Seipel's devices; it might, by itself, have precipitated only the dreaded division of the country. To see in Seipel merely the master of "tricky and twisted diplomatic moves"[212] hardly does him justice. It was his long-standing, vigorous advocacy of peace and of the League of Nations,[213] as

[211] *Sten. Prot., 134. Sitzung, I.G.P.*, September 14, 1922, p. 4328; Cf. Otto Bauer's challenge to this statement, ibid., p. 4338.

[212] Seitz; *Sten. Prot., 138. Sitzung, I.G.P.*, October 12, 1922, p. 4433.

[213] An important effect of the financial reconstruction of Austria was that it set a precedent for similar action on behalf of other countries hit by inflation. Sir Arthur Salter referred particularly to Hungary and Germany (speech of February 16, 1927, quoted in *Neue Freie Presse*, February 17, 1927, morning ed.). Concerning Hungary, cf. "Die finanzielle Sanierung Ungarns," *Reichspost*, January 4, 1924, and "Ministerpräsident Graf Bethlen über die Sanierungsanleihe," *Reichspost*, January 7, 1924; cf. also Count Bethlen to Seipel: "The efforts aimed at the financial reconstruction of Hungary have produced the result that the Austrian achievement . . . will serve as basis also for Hungary"; "Amtsnotiz," signed Peter, "Begegnung mit Graf Bethlen . . . (29. 9. 23), Wien," September 29, 1923, St.A., Liasse Ungarn I/III K.879, F.88. Concerning Germany, a draft for a speech to be given at the occasion of Stresemann's visit to Vienna of March 1924 is of some interest, particularly since it contains a singular tribute to the Austrian Chancellor: ". . . we ·in the North stand . . . still in midst the hard struggle for the reconstruction of our land . . . , whereas you have left the struggle behind you for the greater part thanks to the willingness to sacrifice and the exemplary communal spirit of all groups of your people and thanks to the ingenious [*genialen*] leadership which a Divine Providence has given you in the hard hours of the fall of 1922. With admiration and pride we look upon you and the enormous achievement. . . . It is understandable that specifically for us Germans in the Reich this example

well as his grasp of the broader aspect of the Central European problem, that made his diplomatic venture of 1922 a success. "What a difference, if I look at poor Germany," commented Pope Piux XI.[214] And the *Deutsche Allgemeine Zeitung* registered that "German-Austria after long years has gotten once again a statesman of great stature. . . . In the area of foreign policy he has made it possible for Austria to cast off the role of the world's beggar and to take over once again an important Central European function."[215] Gustav Stolper, one of his harshest critics and the man who late in August had triumphantly proclaimed that "the rolling up of the Central European question has failed,"[216] had to admit in the following year that "the Austrian Chancellor has become during this year an international figure. . . . The same Chancellor who in August of the past year showed an impotent Austria to the world . . . can today communicate with the representatives of foreign powers in a tone of self-confidence in which

---

[*Musterbeispiel*] should be of particular attraction, since we are confronted by the same central problems, which one and a half years ago had to be overcome in Austria [the stabilization of the currency and the balancing of the budget]"; "Entwurf für eine Rede des Herrn Reichsministers gelegentlich seines Besuches in Wien, März 1923 [sic!]," A.A., Abt II-Ö.: Po.2A, Bd.1. The *Reichspost* reported an interesting passage from the Soviet paper *Nakanune* [*On The Eve*] of September 26, 1923: "The Austrian experiment continues and we don't doubt that Russia as well as Germany will find it exemplary and worth imitating"; and, from the Polish magazine *Rzeczpospolita Spóldzielcza* (n.d.), a new version of A.E.I.O.: "Austria exemplum in orbe universo"; *Reichspost*, October 12, 1923, November 4, 1923.

[214] Friedrich Engel-Janosi, "Die diplomatische Mission Ludwig von Pastors beim Heiligen Stuhle, 1920-1928," *Österreichische Akademie der Wissenschaften, Philosophisch-Historische Klasse, Sitzungsberichte, 254. Band, 5. Abhandlung* (Vienna, 1968), p. 9.

[215] *Deutsche Allgemeine Zeitung*, December 8, 1922.

[216] Gustav Stolper, "Die Kanzlerreise," *Der österreichische Volkswirt*, XIV, August 26, 1922, 1166.

no previous government of republican Austria would have dared to speak."[217]

Through his successful negotiations abroad Seipel gave hope to his people. His accomplishment meant not a "revenge for November 12, 1918" but an affirmation of it. The new state, in which no one at first wanted to believe, had to live. By suggesting that it was viable, and that a balanced budget would lead to an intensification of the economy, Seipel laid the foundations for an identification of the people of Austria with the state.

To his critics it was precisely this accomplishment of Seipel's which was most objectionable; it seemed to them that he had bartered the chances of an Anschluss for a financial stabilization. Indeed, Austria's commitment, according to Protocol No. I, not to alienate its independence, was valid for twenty years, the duration of the loan. To Marxists and non-Marxist nationalists alike, Austria became through the Geneva Protocols a "finance colony" of Europe and the Austrians "finance slaves of Western capital."[218]

From a financial point of view the reconstruction was an immediate success. The Austrian crown was stabilized. On November 14 the government founded a new privately subscribed bank of issue (*Notenbank*) and ceased from November 18 on to issue any more notes for state purposes. As a result, savings showed a marked increase, rising during the month of November from 38,644,927 to 60,348,515 crowns.[219] With perhaps an excess of

[217] Gustav Stolper, "Sanierungskrise," *Der österreichische Volkswirt*, XVI, December 15, 1923, 314.

[218] This is the thesis of a study which appeared on Seipel's financial reconstruction in Germany; Rudolf Freund, *Die Genfer Protokolle: Ihre Geschichte und Bedeutung für das Staatsleben Deutsch-Österreichs* (Berlin and Leipzig, 1924), pp. 14, 106.

[219] Cf. Seventh meeting of the Council of the League of Nations held at Paris on February 1, 1923 (including Seipel's address); League of Nations, *Official Journal*, IV, no. 3 (March 1923), 212ff.; also Annex 458, pp. 300ff.

optimism, Sir Arthur Salter[220] wrote that the new crown, once the least stable currency in the world outside Russia, was now locally known as the "Alpine dollar" and had become the most stable one in Europe, and that the previous "flight *from* the crown" had been replaced by a "flight *to* the crown."[221] The primary objective of the reconstruction, the balancing of the budget, which involved an increase of revenue and a decrease in government spending, was accomplished by November 1923, a good half year ahead of schedule, and by early 1924 considerably less money than had been anticipated had had to be drawn from the proceeds of the loan.[222]

But the *auditur altera pars*, however irrelevant on the pros and cons of the Anschluss and on the questions of self-help versus foreign aid, is particularly relevant on the issue of how successful Seipel's government was in carrying through the reconstruction. While it would be inappropriate to apply Keynesian prescriptions, which would have called for increased government spending to follow the balancing of the budget and would have discouraged the raising of taxes, the critics of Seipel and his new

[220] Sir Arthur Salter, Director of the Economic and Financial Section of the League of Nations.

[221] Sir Arthur Salter, "The Reconstruction of Austria," *Foreign Affairs*, II, June 15, 1924, 636. During the period (August 25, 1922, to December 15, 1922) when the German mark fell from a thousand to the dollar to seven thousand to the dollar, the crown remained stable at a value of seventy-five thousand crowns to the dollar (Report by the Provisional Delegation of the League of Nations at Vienna, submitted to the Council on February 1, 1923; League of Nations, *Official Journal*, IV, no. 3 [March 1923], 306). Somewhat righteously Seipel made a point of emphasizing that Austria had remained unaffected by the inflation which had meanwhile gripped Germany, threatening it with "the greatest economic catastrophes" (*Sten. Prot.*, 145. *Sitzung, I.G.P.*, November 6, 1922, p. 4550). Even Stolper reported in December 1923 that "great German industrial concerns consider moving their seats and parts of their factories to German-Austria" (Gustav Stolper, "Sanierungskrise," *Der österreichische Volkswirt*, XVI, December 15, 1923, 315).

[222] Salter, "Reconstruction of Austria," p. 637.

Finance Minister, Dr. Viktor Kienböck, must be given credit for their charge that Seipel had cured Austria's finances, but not, after all, its economy.[223] The stabilization of the currency brought about an increase in prices which was a blow to the workers and the impoverished middle classes. Reduction of expenditure, notably the pensioning off of twenty-five thousand civil servants by January 1923, had an immediate impact on the unemployment figures, which skyrocketed from thirty-eight thousand in September 1922 to one hundred and sixty-one thousand in January 1923.[224]

The excise tax played a conspicuous role in the taxation program, as it brought in approximately one-third of the total tax revenue.[225] But it constituted a particular hardship for the poor and made the workers and employees, in the eyes of the Socialists, carry an undue amount of the reconstruction burden. In short, while inflation in its own way brought great hardships to most levels of the population, reconstruction brought new hardships to those who were already impoverished.

In these circumstances there was a particular need for an equalizing social policy on the part of the state. It was along these lines that Seipel failed. He was too far committed to the precedence of *Staatswirtschaft* over *Volkswirtschaft*[226] to change over in midstream. Renner was not far from the truth when he said that at the root of Seipel's policy was the "old liberal economic system."[227] In the present predicament, he had certainly moved far from the tradition of Vogelsang, Lueger, and Schindler,[228] and he left it to the Social Democrats to espouse the cause

[223] Cf. Paul Szende, "Klassenkämpfe und Finanzsystem in der Republik Österreich," *Der Kampf*, xxii (July 1929), 325; cf. also Hannak, *Karl Renner*, pp. 448f.; Goldinger in Benedikt, *Geschichte*, p. 130.

[224] Cf. the statistical table in Gulick, *Austria*, i, 685.

[225] Ibid., i, 383f.   [226] Gessl, *Reden*, p. 61.

[227] *Sten. Prot., 138. Sitzung, I.G.P.*, October 12, 1922, p. 4420.

[228] Cf. the interesting article by Karl Renner, "Die Christlichsoziale Partei und ihr veränderter Charakter," *Der Kampf*, xvi (September-October 1923), 293-303.

of the downtrodden. In this way those who had suffered a startling defeat over the Geneva Protocols could hope to regain new ground by an intense agitation.

However, the elections of October 1923[229] showed that the Socialists could not break out of their own ideological confinement; they were unable to exploit significantly the weakness of Seipel's position and absorb the disinherited Austrians of all social classes in a progressive movement. Both major parties registered some gains at the expense of the Pan-Germans and the other smaller groups, and even though this result slightly shifted the balance between the governmental coalition and the opposition, the former once again emerged safely in control of all nonproletarian elements of the population. Seipel even felt "quite satisfied"[230] with his party's majority, though it was not an absolute one. In addition to the propertied classes he had won over the growing and increasingly vociferous element of the disinherited middle classes, those who, though hit by inflation, deflation, and then inflation again, were too *bürgerlich*, too proud, to vote for the proletarian party. These were the kind of people who, partly in compensation for their lack of social position, would be most susceptible to anti-Semitism and nationalism. Most of them would tend to regard the Chancellor as one of their own, as their leader in the common struggle against Marxism. The question was whether or how in this struggle Seipel would be able to cope with and control these forces and check an almost inevitable

[229] They proceeded on the basis of a new electoral law, which reduced the seats in Parliament from 183 to 165. In the new chamber the distribution of seats was as follows:

Christian Socialists	82
Social Democrats	68
Pan-Germans	10
Landbund (formerly German-Austria Peasants' party)	5

Cf. Alfred Kasamas, *Österreichische Chronik* (Vienna, 1948), p. 493.

[230] Redlich diary, October 31, 1923, Josef Redlich, "Politische Tagebuchnotizen."

218

tendency on their part to drift further to the Right. But at least in the period immediately following the financial reconstruction, Seipel remained the uncontested master in his camp. The right-wing Heimwehr was as yet far too weak and divided to have much weight on the political scene, and Seipel, though willing to build it up as a potential paramilitary support for his regime, was unwilling to grant it control of the state. He maintained a stranglehold on the Heimwehr leaders by both procuring and cutting off their financial support by Austrian industry.[231]

While the Austrian reconstruction was an accomplishment in the annals of international diplomacy as well as in those of the Austrian Republic, it left much unfinished business. As yet the Central European question was merely "rolled up." Would the "third act," the Central European conference envisaged by Seipel, ever really come off? Economic reconstruction was still to be accomplished; would it ever succeed? Though the country, thanks to Seipel's achievement, had at least obtained the basis for a sense of national identity, it emerged from the reconstruction even more deeply divided. Sir Arthur Salter quoted a "well-known financier" as saying to him that "if Austria is now suffering, it is no longer from 'poor man's gout' but from 'rich man's gout.'"[232] Both Sir Arthur and his friend probably looked at the transformation of Austria after 1922 in a too glowing light. But in any case, Austria still had the gout.

[231] The story of the relations between the Heimwehr and Seipel in the months following financial reconstruction is documented in Ludger Rape, "Die österreichische Heimwehr und ihre Beziehungen zur bayerischen Rechten zwischen 1920 und 1923" (diss., Vienna, 1968), and in C. Earl Edmondson, "Heimwehr and Austrian Politics, 1918-1934" (diss., Duke University, 1966).

[232] Salter, "Reconstruction of Austria," p. 640.

Five

SEIPEL AND THE CRISIS OF
AUSTRIAN DEMOCRACY: 1923-1929

The Handicaps of Austrian Democracy

THE CRISIS of democracy was a general European phenomenon between the two wars, when the rule of reason, of moderation, and of discussion was challenged even in the older democracies of Western Europe. The aftermath of the war left them all beset by disillusionment as well as illusion; and plagued by economic setbacks and class conflicts, they were impatient with parliamentary government and nursed thoughts of dictatorship. They also had their private armies, which moved the political argument from the parliament to "the street." But while the older democracies succeeded in overcoming or controlling these problems, the new "improvised democracies" in Central Europe did not. These countries started with parliamentary democratic institutions mostly borrowed from the West, and they moved in the 1920s and 1930s toward some form of authoritarianism, dictatorship, or fascism.

Among the Central European states only Czechoslovakia, with its pronounced democratic tradition and balanced social structure, was an exception to the rule; but this country in turn was threatened by its unsolved nationality problem. In all other European countries, including Germany and Austria, formal democracy was not matched by a democratic way of life. The Western constitutional models—in particular the English one—to which they aspired could not be automatically transplanted without the social ethos that supported them. The problem of building parliamentary democracy on a soil that was traditionally authoritarian proved to be formidable, if not in the last analysis insuperable.

The Crisis of Austrian Democracy

At the same time, the borrowed model of parliamentary democracy was no longer adequate in Germany and Austria to the needs of an industrial mass society and, particularly, to the appetites of a self-conscious proletariat, less impressed by adherence to parliamentary rules than by substantial benefits, and clamoring not for representation but for direct participation in the governmental process, if not vigorous leadership. In Germany and Austria, then, an essentially feudal and authoritarian tradition coincided with the reality of industrialization and a mass society. In their historical development, both countries had skipped the phase in which parliamentary democracy corresponded to and satisfied the needs of the politically predominant middle class. In brief, the "improvised democracies" in Germany and Austria were—in terms of their tradition—unprepared for the democratic model which they took over, and at the same time —in terms of their social structure—ahead of it. The latter consideration suggests that parliamentary democracy was challenged not only by the traditionalist element in society, but also by the radical and populist element. It was indeed crushed by the pressure of both.

Austrian democracy stood, then, like most of the new democracies of Central Europe, on unstable foundations. There was only a tenuous tradition of democratic life in Austria. Nineteenth-century Austria was neither democratic nor antidemocratic. It was essentially nondemocratic, evading political conflict, minimizing relationships between friend and foe. During the period of Francis Joseph, after the flare-up of political passions in 1848, the country settled back into the contrapuntal pattern of feudal aristocratic rule and the more or less benevolent politics of bureaucracy. But the effect was the same—to neutralize political struggle. This situation was singularly reflected in the history of Austrian parliamentarianism. Parliament was overshadowed by dynasty, army, and in particular by bureaucracy.

Of course, in Austria the nationality struggle accentuated the impotence of Parliament. The latter became the scene of fistfights, desk-banging, and obstruction, thus setting an unfortunate precedent for the parliamentarians of the republican era. Josef Redlich's statement that "bureaucracy gained as the sterility of Parliament began to be apparent"[1] applies to the last decades before the war as well as to the first Austrian Republic.

Finally, however, the malfunctioning of Parliament was dictated as much by the very nature of political life since the late nineteenth century as it was by the nationality struggle. The new political movements which arose at that time were the chief manifestation in Austria of the political self-consciousness of the masses and their rejection of liberalism and its political forms. It was their strongly ideological orientation in particular that discouraged parliamentary give-and-take, debate, and compromise.

Except for difficulties caused by the nationality struggle, the handicaps of Austrian parliamentarianism were carried over from the Monarchy into the Republic. The "low order of politicians," on whom Mark Twain had remarked after witnessing one of the most turbulent scenes in the Reichsrat late in October 1897,[2] also bothered Hermann Bahr, who, grooming Seipel for political leadership, complained of the "terrible shortage of non-illiterate politicians" in republican Austria.[3] The "foul style" in the old Reichsrat certainly made itself felt again during the debates over the Geneva Protocols, and it should be said that the proponents of parliamentarianism, the Social Democrats, were the worst offenders against parliamentary decorum.

It can be argued that in imperial days the "foul style" had been of less consequence; at its worst it had been an expensive extravagance under the protective umbrella of the establishment

[1] Josef Redlich, *Austrian War Government* (New Haven, 1929), p. 39.

[2] Cf. the delightful and perceptive description of the Austrian parliamentary scene in 1897 in Mark Twain, "Stirring Times in Austria," *The Man that Corrupted Hadleyburg and Other Stories and Essays* (New York and London, 1901), pp. 284-341.

[3] Hermann Bahr to Josef Redlich, n.p., n.d., "Unveröffentlichtes von Hermann Bahr," *Die Furche*, April 4, 1953.

223

allowing the protagonists to emerge from parliamentary ink battles as though nothing had really happened after all.[4] But during the Republic,[5] in which the legislature had been given such a prominent position in the constitution, this "style," whether we call it "good" or "foul," could not be continued without penalty. Earlier on Mark Twain may have been right in saying that obstructionism had no "consequence" and that there was therefore no "danger line"; but now there was. If Parliament was immobilized after the war, so too was the state. If parliamentary democracy did not work, alternatives to it had to be sought. Thus the shortcomings of the democratic and parliamentary tradition in Austria persisted into the Republic with a vengeance, because much more depended upon the proper functioning of parliamentarianism and also because alternatives to it were now more commonly envisaged. Apart from a reversion to an essentially non-democratic neo-Josephinist *Hofratsstaat* or a return to some form of authoritarian rule, they included varieties of dictatorship and of the antidemocratic radicalism of the Left as well as of the Right. The democratic age, which was finally ushered into Austria with the fall of the Monarchy, brought with it the promise of self-rule as well as the specter of varieties of authoritarian and dictatorial rule, backed by popular despair and dissatisfaction.

In the light of all this, the surprising part of the history of republican Austria came in the first two years, when democracy seemed to work, when party conflicts and class antagonisms were in abeyance, and when a basic consensus, albeit a consensus of crisis, still prevailed among all shades and variations of political leadership. But when the coalition broke down in 1920, when the domestic armistice was over and political strife was resumed within the context of self-doubt and economic depression, the structure of the young democracy began to crumble. For better

[4] Cf. Mark Twain, "Stirring Times in Austria," pp. 329ff.

[5] Cf. Josef A. Tzöbl, "Vom guten Ton unter Republikanern," *Forum*, VII (July/August 1960), 266.

or for worse, Austria more than Germany was made to feel the vacuum of authority left by the exit of its dynasty. It had no *Ersatzkaiser*, as Germany did in its president who, elected by the whole people, had a strong position according to the constitution. Unlike Germany it had no Article 48, which allowed the executive to act in emergency situations. While the German compromise between presidential authority and parliamentary democracy, as stipulated by the Weimar Constitution, had its own serious deficiencies in the form of the revival of forces of old and the weakening of the position of Parliament, Austria by the prescription of the Social Democrats and their court constitutional lawyer, Hans Kelsen, was abandoned to the pluralism of political and social forces as represented in Parliament. However these forces, represented by the parties, dependent in a parliamentary situation on discussion and compromise, actually discussed and compromised less and less. The speeches in Parliament consisted less and less of rational argument, and served more and more to hammer out slogans directed at hearers beyond the walls of Parliament and to indoctrinate the already converted. Not wit but insult prevailed in the House, not urbanity but boorishness. And if we glance once again over the debates on Seipel's financial reconstruction, we find that the Social Democrats were the worst offenders against the parliamentary rules and against rationality. Seipel's speeches, compared to those of his Social Democratic counterparts, excel by calmness and restraint, by rationality and parliamentary decorum. But thanks to the Social Democrats and, to be sure, to some of Seipel's more vulgar party friends, parliamentarianism in Austria reflected a house divided. The one force in Parliament which might have built bridges between the two big blocs, the Christian Socialists and the Social Democrats, was the Pan-Germans. They agreed on economic matters with the former, and on cultural issues and the Anschluss question with the latter. But they were not in a position to perform an intermediary role. The 1923 elections left their party reduced by almost one-third of its previous popular votes, and more than half of its parliamentary representation. The potential middle party was thus reduced to ineffectiveness, and it became increasingly dependent on the Christian Socialists. "What difference did it make," quipped Otto Bauer "that part of the Christian Socialists called themselves Pan-Germans?"[6]

A two-party system had in effect evolved by 1923, but it had little in common with the one in England; it emphasized division rather than debate, doctrinaire positions rather than the weighing of concrete issues. Parliament in Austria, then, instead of nursing a basic consensus, as it generally does in Western democracies, emphasized the divisions in the country and contributed to the destruction of consensus.

Two Parties: Christian Socialists and Social Democrats

The deteriorating relationship between the two large parties, which was a cardinal factor in the Austrian scene from 1920, owed much to the very nature of the party structure. It will be recalled that in their origins both parties were strangely connected through the Linz Program of 1882, and both represented different branches of a populist rebellion against bourgeois liberalism. By background the parties were essentially mass movements rather than representative bodies; both were committed to "the street" at least as much as to the austere halls of Parliament. And while neither one produced in the republican era a tribune of the people of the kind of Viktor Adler and Karl Lueger, both carried on their work among the masses. Otto Bauer emerged as the educator and manipulator of the proletariat. Interpreting universal suffrage, elections, and Parliament essentially as instruments of the bourgeoisie, he emphasized the struggle of the working class against formal parliamentary democracy and in turn espoused the ideas of "functional democ-

[6] Quoted in Charles Gulick, *Austria from Habsburg to Hitler* (Berkeley and Los Angeles, 1948), I, 693.

226

racy" that brought the government into constant touch with the people.[7]

Even in Seipel there were vestiges of his party's populist background. This helps explain why the busy statesman was willing to make so many speeches,[8] mostly on public occasions before popular audiences. The Chancellor felt at home with the common man and, no doubt, in his didactic and serene way, reached him. The populist component in Seipel also considerably influenced his thinking. He was not laboring the obvious when he emphasized that he was responsible, as head of the government, not only to Parliament, but "directly" to the people,[9] and in his progressive disillusionment with parliamentarianism he was more and more ready to consider supplementing indirect democracy with direct democracy.

Both parties, as we have seen, also represented *Weltanschauungen*, a fact which distinguished them from parties in the Anglo-Saxon democracies and which set distinct limits on their ability and willingness to venture into compromises and coalitions. In addition, the Socialist party was also a class party. Its primary concern with and appeal to the proletariat gave it a degree of coherence which the Christian Socialists always lacked; but it nonetheless constituted a handicap for the party, limiting it to a well-defined electorate beyond which it could make no conquests, as the period after the 1923 election proved.

Ernst Karl Winter once properly characterized the ideological positions of the two parties as "Austromarxism" and "Austro-Scholasticism";[10] both were locked in combat, without much hope

[7] Cf. Otto Bauer, *Die österreichische Revolution* (Vienna, 1923), p. 187; also Norbert Leser, *Zwischen Reformismus und Bolschewismus: Der Austromarxismus als Theorie und Praxis* (Vienna, Frankfurt, and Zurich, 1968), pp. 304ff.

[8] He delivered 110 speeches in 1922, 305 in the election year 1923, 164 in 1924; Seipel diary, October 21, 1923, and at the end of 1923 and 1924.

[9] *Reichspost*, December 29, 1922, morning ed.

[10] Ernst Karl Winter, *Christentum und Zivilisation* (Vienna, 1956), p. 405.

for working compomises. The Social Democrats, when they took the fatal step of leaving the coalition in 1920, abandoned the course set by Viktor Adler and continued during the revolutionary period by Karl Renner of combining doctrinal commitment with practicality. Bauer's ascendancy in the party over Renner, reflecting a general awareness of the failure of past policies, meant a reorientation of the party from a policy of pragmatism to a policy of ideology. The revolutionary aim then, the victory of the proletariat, became everything to Otto Bauer. The party assumed the function of an "instrument of iron and steel,"[11] withdrawn from the arena of the struggle for influence and power in the "bourgeois" state; under Otto Bauer's leadership it adopted a position of a rigid Marxist integralism.

The ideology of the Christian Socialists, the party of "Austro-Scholasticism," was, strictly speaking, not a political but a religious one. It can be argued that this very fact allowed the party a considerable latitude in politics. Seipel after all was the leading advocate in Austria of Leonine accommodation, and it cannot be denied that he had explored it generously and had even found a *modus vivendi* with the Social Democrats. During the revolutionary period Leonine accommodation and Marxist accommodation had combined in building the foundations of the Republic.

But the religious premise of the Austro-Scholastic position also had confining aspects. The concept of the "Regeneration of the Souls" itself,[12] not merely that of financial or political regeneration, became central to Seipel's political philosophy, and, however beautiful and meaningful, was an implied challenge to the live-and-let-live attitude of the modern pluralistic society, and was understood as a direct challenge to the Socialists.

But furthermore the Christian Socialists were committed to

[11] Cf. Leser, *Zwischen Reformismus*, p. 155.

[12] Ignaz Seipel, "Die geistige Arbeit im Wiederaufbau" (February 14, 1924), in Josef Gessl, *Seipels Reden in Österreich und anderwärts* (Vienna, 1926), p. 13. Cf. also Seipel's concept of the "reform of the souls," *Reichspost*, December 6, 1921.

making a stand for the defense of the spiritual realm of the Church. "To the inviolable conditions for a coalition government with the Christian Socialists," Seipel had said in October 1919, "belongs the assurance that the religious and moral ideals will be safeguarded."[13]

The clash of ideologies was almost inevitable, and indicated how tenuous the consensus of the previous years had been, touching, as it did, upon the very heart of Catholic sensitivities. The challenge clearly came from the Socialists, who issued the call for a separation of Church and state through one of their more radical deputies in Parliament.[14] Concretely, the sensitive areas were school reform and the question of civil marriage.[15] Most aggravating, however, to the relationship between the two camps was the Socialists' appeal to their followers in February 1923 to leave the Church. The Social Democrats, instead of attempting to disentangle the relations between Church and state, carried the war far into enemy territory by interfering with the fundamental prerogative of the Church—its hold over souls. "One cannot be at the same time a Socialist and churchgoer! Therefore, leave the Church! Become disaffiliated!"[16] As a result of this agitation defections from the Church rose sharply in Vienna from 9,268 in 1923 to 22,888 the following year.[17]

[13] *Reichspost*, October 3, 1919.

[14] Karl Leuthner; *Sten. Prot., 47. Sitzung, I.G.P.*, July 12, 1921, p. 1716.

[15] Particularly controversial and a continued point of friction between the two camps in the Kulturkampf was the practice to which the Social Democrat Albert Sever had resorted as governor of Lower Austria in the immediate postwar years: on the basis of a vague paragraph in the *General Law Book* (A.G.B.G., §83), he had granted so-called dispensations (divorces) to those whose marriages had broken up, thus clearing the way for remarriage of either or both partners. Cf. the exhaustive treatment of the subject in Erika Weinzierl-Fischer, *Die österreichischen Konkordate von 1855 und 1933* (Vienna, 1960), pp. 151ff.

[16] Robert Prantner, "Katholische Kirche" (theol. diss., Vienna, 1955), p. 201; Weinzierl, *Konkordate*, p. 141.

[17] Prantner, "Katholische Kirche," pp. 286f.

The Crisis of Austrian Democracy

The Socialist agitation was a direct challenge to Seipel, chief of the "politicking priests,"[18] a challenge which found an echo even in some more progressive Catholic circles. It was at about this time that a Social Democrat crowd outside Parliament intoned the well-known song about the "gas lantern" and "Herr von Seipel."[19] But instead of being hung, "Herr von Seipel," on June 1, 1924, was shot at and seriously wounded by a worker, Karl Jaworek. Though the assailant turned out to be a psychopath who blamed the Chancellor for his misery, though there was no direct connection between the assailant and the party, the party's militant spirit, its rabble-rousing technique, had nonetheless borne its ugly fruit in this act of the unfortunate Jaworek.

It should be recorded that the "mercy" which became more and more an issue in Austrian politics during the increasingly rough climate of the twenties was still the priest's prerogative. The wounded Chancellor protected the assailant, who had also turned the pistol against himself, from being lynched by the crowd by twice exclaiming "don't strike him," and when at Christmas time he heard that the man's wife was in financial distress he sent her a gift of 100 schillings.[20] The wounds from the attempted assassination put the Chancellor out of commission for four months. Although their connection with his death in 1932 has generally been exaggerated,[21] they certainly disturbed the balance of his already precarious health.

[18] "Politisierenden Pfaffen"; Karl Leuthner, *Religion und Sozialdemokratie* (Vienna, 1923), quoted in Weinzierl, *Konkordate*, p. 141.

[19] Cf. *Sten. Prot., 171. Sitzung, I.G.P.*, March 2, 1923, p. 5304.

[20] That is roughly one-twentieth of his monthly pay as chancellor.

[21] Cf. Hanns Leo Mikoletzky, *Österreichische Zeitgeschichte* (Vienna, 1962), p. 95. According to Dr. Gustav Singer, who had been Seipel's doctor for eleven years, the bullet which remained stuck in the diaphragm of Seipel's right lung had no effect upon his tuberculosis, which developed in the left lung years later in connection with a pleurisy contracted after a celebration of St. Leopold's Day in Klosterneuburg on November 15, 1930; cf. Hofrat Professor Dr. Gustav Singer, "Aus Seipels Lebens- und Kranken-

230

In the long run the Socialists' ideological offensive was decisive for Seipel in hardening his views on socialism and Marxism. In any case, his actual acquaintance with Karl Marx's work was, by all indications, no more than fragmentary and secondhand.[22] But as he viewed the Marxist movement from afar, he stopped seeing it in terms of accommodation, and regarded it more and more, in all its doctrinairism, as anti-Church. A pragmatic, and on the whole open-minded, attitude on the part of Seipel and the Christian Socialists gave way to tight, defensive, dogmatic rejection. Their anti-Marxism became in its increasing rigidity a mirror-image of the Marxist rigidity. There was left virtually no common ground that the two camps could share.

The polarization between the two parties was augmented, particularly on the side of the Social Democrats, by a tight party organization. In fact, in this area lay one of the marked differences between the Socialists and the Christian Socialists. Viktor Adler's party had always distinguished itself by its emphasis on "unity at all cost," and had built up a whole network of social organizations, from Marxist kindergartens, sports clubs, and trade unions to funeral clubs, which immunized the proletarians from the "bourgeois" world and created a wholly self-contained proletarian subculture. Otto Bauer's integralist course reinforced this separatist trend. To the patriot's "my country right or wrong!" he opposed the Socialist's "my party right or wrong!"[23] and he went

---

geschichte," *Neue Freie Presse*, August 3, 1932, morning ed., and Dr. Gustav Singer, "Worte der Erinnerung an den Patienten Dr. Seipel," *Neues Wiener Tagblatt*, August 3, 1932.

[22] In Seipel's library, insofar as it was still being kept together in the Keinergasse in the spring of 1958, I found not a single work by Karl Marx, not even the Communist *Manifesto*. That Seipel was unfamiliar with Marx was confirmed in an interview with Dr. Friedrich Schreyvogel, May 13, 1958. Cf. also E. K. Winter, *Ignaz Seipel als dialektisches Problem* (Vienna, Frankfurt, and Zurich, 1966), p. 87, who maintained that Seipel knew Marxism through such references as appeared in the encyclicals of Leo XIII and in the writings of Jesuit authors.

[23] Quoted in Leser, *Zwischen Reformismus*, p. 155.

so far as to assert at the party convention of 1927 that "it is a hundred times better to go a wrong way united—for errors can later be corrected—than to split in search for the right way."[24]

The Christian Socialist party was admittedly no match in this respect for the Marxists.[25] Under the umbrella of the Catholic faith it included many interests and opinions: "liberals" as well as integralists, monarchists as well as republicans, conservatives as well as social reformers, friends and foes of a coalition with the Left and also of the Anschluss, centralists as well as federalists, anti-Semites as well as Jews. Though it was a relatively small party in comparison with the Socialists,[26] it lacked cohesion and depended all the more on firm leadership. In an interesting exchange of letters between Heinrich Mataja and Seipel the whole question of the function and organization of the Christian Socialist party was raised,[27] with Mataja pleading for a strong organization along the lines of the Socialists. Seipel responded, however, that the question was not whether an imitation of the Social Democratic organization was possible, but whether it was at all "beneficial" to state and society.[28] And his answer was decidedly in the negative. The chief obstacle to the Christian Socialist party's paralleling the Social Democratic effort lay in the realm of "principle."[29] "Our religious position *wholly* precludes our placing the party above the Church, our national orientation *al-*

[24] *Parteitag, 1927* (Vienna, 1927), p. 128; cf. also Mary Macdonald, *The Republic of Austria 1918-1933* (London, New York, and Toronto, 1946), p. 72; Julius Braunthal, *Otto Bauer* (Vienna, 1961), p. 73; Gulick, *Austria*, I, 694.

[25] Mataja to Seipel, Vienna, April 3, 1928.

[26] For figures for the Social Democratic membership, see Gulick, *Austria*, I, 698. The figures for the Christian Socialist membership, for good reasons, were not publicized. According to expert opinion they must have been even less than one-third of the Social Democrat figures.

[27] Mataja to Seipel, Vienna, April 3, 1928; Seipel to Mataja, Karlsbad, April 10, 1928.

[28] Seipel to Mataja, Karlsbad, April 10, 1928.

[29] Ibid.

232

most excludes our placing the party above the common good [*Volksgemeinschaft*], and our concept of state is and remains wholly different from the one of the Social Democrats. . . . We cannot engulf the whole man by the party because we should not do so."[30]

Interesting in this statement, though not surprising, is the order of precedence: Church, state, party. Indeed "the Church alone,"[31] which in her sovereign way was uniquely capable of subordinating to herself all kinds of movements, was called upon to overcome Marxism. "It would mean the greatest and final victory of the Social Democracy, if it became the example for everyone, including the other political parties, and if we accepted its concept of the state and society. Any force which is still somehow healthy, or at least in hope of recovery, is opposed to it."[32] The Christian Socialists' overt weaknesses then, which gave Seipel a great deal of trouble as Chancellor, also contained distinct elements of strength. It must be added, however, that Seipel's seemingly libertarian argument ended after all on a resigned and ominous note: "Every other decade the parties must be pushed aside to free the Church and to allow the peoples and states to live. Naturally the new parties will instantly follow."[33]

The Leaders: Seipel and Otto Bauer

It has often been suggested that it was an unfortunate development which brought the "extremist wing" in each of the two parties into the dominant positions under the leadership of both Seipel and Bauer.[34] Actually, neither Seipel nor Otto Bauer represented an "extremist wing," and neither was himself an extremist. Coming from positions fundamentally wide apart, the

[30] Ibid.; italics in original.   [31] "Ausschliesslich die Kirche," ibid.
[32] Ibid.   [33] Ibid.
[34] Cf. Macdonald, *Austria*, p. 64; cf. also Klemens von Klemperer, "Chancellor Seipel and the Crisis of Democracy in Austria," *Journal of Central European Affairs*, XXII (January 1963), 474.

Drawing by Max Sandor made after Seipel's recovery from the attempt on his life, 1924. Courtesy of Österreichische Nationalbibliothek, Vienna

Otto Bauer. Courtesy of Österreichische Nationalbibliothek, Vienna

Catholic Church and the Marxist anti-Church, their paths had variously converged. Had Seipel's efforts in the last years of the Monarchy on behalf of the nationality problem not come close to Otto Bauer's prescriptions? Was it not their common distaste for political extremism in the form of Communist despotism that brought Seipel and Otto Bauer together to form the postrevolutionary coalition? Had it not been their common concern with social justice that had brought the disciples of Schindler and of Viktor Adler together to chart out a course of democratic socialization? There was a moment after the war when Seipel's vision of a Christian commonwealth of nationalities, which had crumbled in November 1918, seemed to lend itself to translation into terms of the grand synthesis, on the smaller scale of little Austria, between Christianity and democracy, Christianity and socialism.

After all that has been said about the almost titanic struggle between these two men during the 1920s, it must be remembered that there remained some common ground between them. If indeed Seipel's "ecclesia" seemed to lack, in Bauer's view, the mildness of the message of the Sermon on the Mount, and if Bauer's "synagogue" was, for Seipel, still blindfolded and excessively rational and given to "theory,"[35] it is also true that what separated the two men also brought them together. They were peers in their ascetic commitment to Church and anti-Church, peers in their intensity of commitment, peers in their wide and generous horizons, which lifted them above the mediocrity that otherwise marked the political scene in republican Austria. Bauer honored Seipel as "the only statesman of European stature" whom the bourgeois parties of the Republic had brought forth,[36] and Seipel in turn acknowledged his "respect" for Bauer's "character and

---

[35] Josef Redlich, diary, August 6, 1927, Redlich, "Politische Tagebuchnotizen 1920-1936."

[36] Otto Bauer, "Ignaz Seipel," *Arbeiter-Zeitung*, August 3, 1932.

knowledge" at the height of the battle in 1927.[37] He appreciated Bauer as one of the few "independent"[38] men on the Austrian scene, and he pondered over the question why it was Bauer rather than Renner among the Social Democrats with whom he could best get along on a personal level.[39] Seipel liked, perhaps even loved, his foe.

Though the fight was fierce, it was guided by distinct rules. Bauer's radical stance in effect was an "alibi for inaction"[40] rather than an incitement to revolution. While the Chancellor brought the Social Democrats to their knees, the priest entered in his diary: "Pray for the Social Democrats."[41] A "sublimated ceremonial" kept reminding the two antagonists that both were after all pacifists, men of good will, and men of the vital center.

If, therefore, it is true that Seipel and Bauer, the chief antagonists on the Austrian scene, were essentially moderate, conciliatory men, fighters almost against their will, the conclusions to be drawn for the breakdown of democracy in Austria are all the more startling. The Austrian situation is in this respect analogous to the German one. Even in Germany the role of extremism, that is Communism and National Socialism, has been exaggerated. Whatever their part in undermining free life and institutions, it

[37] Redlich diary, August 6, 1927, "Politische Tagebuchnotizen 1920-1936."

[38] Seipel to Eduard von Popper-Podhragy, Vienna, May 31, 1931, in *Wiener Politische Blätter*, I, August 27, 1933, 186.

[39] Seipel broached the question to Renner during a chance encounter after Jodok Fink's funeral early in July 1929; cf. Karl Renner, *Österreich von der Ersten zur Zweiten Republik* (Vienna, 1952), p. 80. Renner's response was as unsentimental as Seipel's question was sentimental: "The explanation is simple. Both of you, one consciously, the other one perhaps unconsciously, are absorbed by the idea of a class struggle. No doubt it is a valid idea. But you two exaggerate it, and this does not suit me." He thus indicated pointedly the course that the two parties had taken since he and Jodok Fink had held them together.

[40] Leser, *Zwischen Reformismus*, p. 103.

[41] Seipel diary, August 10, 1927.

should be recalled that one of the decisive events in the eclipse of German parliamentarianism, the breakup of the Great Coalition in 1930, occurred because of the inability of the parties of the "vital center," to get together. In Austria the decisive struggle occurred between two parties and two men who were well within the vital center. In fact in Austria there was no sizable enemy on the far Left or on the far Right, no sizable Communist and National Socialist parties when Seipel and Bauer fought their fratricidal duel. The critical break occurred not by design but by wastefulness and carelessness, not by wickedness but by default. While in Weimar Germany there was not enough leadership, in republican Austria there was too much, in the towering personalities of Seipel and Otto Bauer.[42] In both cases, though, the result was the same. The squabbling parties gave way to a *tertium gaudens* in the form of National Socialism.

Fortress Vienna

The Social Democrats' withdrawal from cooperation in the state strengthened their reliance on the party organization, which gave them a substitute sense of community, and on ideology, which allowed them to think in long-range terms and to rationalize a growing record of demonstrable political setbacks as a mere "period of transition between two revolutionary processes"[43] which led, in the course of dialectical evolution, to a "higher stage." In this Marxist limbo the city of Vienna was assigned a particularly important function. Vienna, the once proud "imperial capital and residence," became, after the war, a Red citadel which allowed the Socialists to realize their bold and long-standing municipal reform program,[44] antedating the war, and also to establish a po-

[42] See Leser's interesting summary of Seipel's and Bauer's impact upon Austria, "Ergänzung zum Unheil"; they joined forces in its destruction, Leser, *Zwischen Reformismus*, pp. 414ff.

[43] Bauer, *Revolution*, p. 275.

[44] Cf. Felix Czeike, *Liberale, christlichsoziale und sozialdemokratische*

238

litical stronghold to offset their minority position in the country at large.[45]

But the dualism between the "Red" capital and the "Black" federal government proved fatal. Federalism itself, as Seipel came to understand, had turned into one of the chief obstacles to good government in Austria.[46] The double position of Vienna as capital and province made it possible for the magistrate to erect a state within a state. The medieval ramparts of the city had been torn down long ago, as had been Prince Eugene's, but Socialist ramparts were now erected in defense against the "bourgeois" world. Vienna, the "Red island in the middle of Austria,"[47] governed against the *Bund*, and vice versa; proletarians against the bourgeoisie, and vice versa.

The achievements of the Social Democratic administration of Vienna in bringing reform to the people were considerable. Let it be said that the Socialists' municipal policy was not entirely new, that it had antecedents in the municipal policy of Karl Lueger, and that rent control itself, which became such a vital issue, went back to imperial times.[48] But such considerations tend all the more to highlight the fact that the Social Democrats rather than the Christian Socialists carried on the social policy of

---

Kommunalpolitik (1861-1934): Dargestellt am Beispiel der Gemeinde Wien (Vienna, 1962), pp. 83ff.

[45] The first municipal election of May 4, 1919, registered the change in the political balance precipitated by the revolution by giving the Social Democrats a sweeping majority of 100 out of a total of 165 seats in the Municipal Council and thus bringing to an end twenty years of Christian Socialist control of the Rathaus. The exact distribution of seats in the Municipal Council was as follows: Social Democrats 100, Christian Socialists 50, Czechoslovaks 8, Pan-Germans 3, Jewish Nationals 3, United Democrat 1; Schulthess' *Europäischer Geschichtskalender, 1919,* i, 529.

[46] Wirth Memorandum, June 13, 1928, G.F.O. 2347/4576/E173477.

[47] Seipel's speech, April 13, 1927, *Neue Freie Presse,* April 14, 1927, morning ed.

[48] Cf. Adam Wandruszka in Heinrich Benedikt, ed., *Geschichte der Republik Österreich* (Vienna, 1954), pp. 453, 462.

Lueger and that the Christian Socialists under Seipel's leadership had become captives of capitalism. The names of Karl Seitz, who was Mayor of Vienna and Governor of Lower Austria; Hugo Breitner, Vienna's finance tsar; Julius Tandler, Vienna's expert on public health, are all connected with an elaborate municipal housing program,[49] cooperative stores, public kindergartens and recreation facilities financed by a vigorous tax system.

The conflict with the federal government was unavoidable. The main points at issue were the taxation policy of Hugo Breitner, which hit hard at the propertied classes, and the public building program. Quite understandably Seipel remarked that the citizens of the city were abandoned to the "almost unlimited" powers of their almighty Mayor-Governor; and concerning the federal government, he added whimsically, "the sky is high and the federal government is far," even though the latter had its seat in Vienna.[50]

The housing naturally gave Vienna an altogether new face. While the aristocratic palaces in the center of the city were obsolescent, while the villas and gardens of the elegant bourgeoisie in the outer districts rested uneasily behind protective walls, there were impressive new dwellings going up in the workers' districts—new centers of life and hope—gradually displacing the grey proletarian tenements which still lined the streets. But there were also those who noticed that the Karl Marx-Hof in the Nineteenth District with its five thousand inhabitants was built along the railroad leading into the city from a northeasterly direction, and who saw in it, not without some justification, "in effect a fortress, a construction with fortifications."[51] The new municipal

[49] During one decade the city built about sixty thousand apartments geared to the low income of the workers; cf. Czeike, *Kommunalpolitik*, pp. 103ff.; Gulick, *Austria*, I, 449ff.

[50] Seipel, "Die Stellung Wiens," *Der Kampf um die österreichische Verfassung* (Vienna and Leipzig, 1930), p. 231.

[51] *Gemeinderat, Sitzungsprotokolle, 1927*, p. 7427, quoted in Czeike, *Kommunalpolitik*, pp. 103f.

240

buildings were the most impressive monuments to the ingenuity and reforming zeal of a great party which in many ways represented what was most lively in Austria after the war. At the same time they were a visible expression of an impatient party, a desperate party, which after decades of opposition and the ill-managed interlude of 1918 to 1920 thought of them as new ways of gaining power. This party was now following Otto Bauer into a contest which it hardly stood to win.

Obstruction

In their struggle for survival the Social Democrats found a powerful weapon—which proved double-edged—in *Obstruktion* or obstruction, a version of the American filibuster which the Austrians had brought to perfection. In the Monarchy, obstruction had become common practice among the nationalities for immobilizing Parliament. But the Social Democrats had refrained from using it—as Otto Bauer pointed out, with some pride, to the Nationalrat.[52] They had not needed it then. In the 1920s, however, Bauer departed from his party's past practice and resorted to obstruction, arguing that any available political procedure, even an admittedly abnormal one, could be used when basic political questions were at stake. He passed obstruction off as mere "intensified parliamentary struggle,"[53] as a practice hardly worth a special name.

The issue which precipitated this change of tactics was that of *Mieterschutz* or rent control. Whereas wartime rent controls had been discontinued or relaxed in most European countries, the Austrian Parliament in 1922 passed new rent-control legislation. This legislation acknowledged the low wage-levels of Austrians as compared with other Europeans; at the same time it hurt landlords and tended to devaluate all urban real estate, enabling the city of Vienna to buy up land cheaply for its own purposes.

[52] *Sten. Prot., 167. Sitzung, I.G.P.,* February 8, 1923, p. 5224.
[53] Ibid.

It was at this point that Seipel stepped in, at a mass meeting in Wiener Neustadt, saying that an extreme form of rent control could not endure forever and suggesting that rents should, with the agreement of tenants and landlords, revert gradually to "normal conditions." His immediate aim was, of course, to check the city of Vienna's building monopoly by normalizing the price structure of rents and real estate and thus encouraging private initiative. This was in keeping with the Geneva agreements, through which he had committed Austria to an open economy which would be consonant with the world economy. By the end of 1923 rents were the only area in which Austria had not yet caught up with world price-levels.

From the standpoint of domestic politics, however, Seipel was no doubt making a mistake which, as Gulick has suggested, cost him his dream of a two-thirds majority in Parliament.[54] His policy on rent controls threatened the Socialists' hold on the city of Vienna, but it also offered them a welcome means of extending their appeal to the impoverished middle classes, who needed protection against the landlords. The Socialists were interested not in settling the rent-control issue, but rather in using it as a political weapon. It was perfect stuff for Marxist demagoguery.

The chief weapon used was obstruction, and this came to displace negotiation and debate in the mid-twenties. Nothing, so it seemed, had been learned since the days of the Monarchy. It became customary in the committees of the Nationalrat to deliberate to the accompaniment of trumpets and automobile horns, and the endurance record in filibustering was achieved by one Josef Winternigg, who spoke for forty-two hours.[55]

[54] Gulick, *Austria*, I, 465.

[55] It should be added that, inspired by the national model, the Christian Socialists followed suit in the Viennese Municipal Council and obstructed with an improvised orchestration. Also, the deliberations in the Lower Austrian Provincial Diet were so chaotic, the epithets so vulgar, that the

In such conditions it is hardly possible to argue that obstruction had "succeeded"[56] in any but the narrowest and most negative of objectives. The issue was no longer rent control or the budget but the structure of democracy in Austria. Obstruction turned out to be one of the main arguments against parliamentarianism in Austria. It disgraced an institution whose record there had been a tenuous one at best. Obstruction was one of the chief factors, as Renner himself had to concede, that discredited democracy in Austria[57] and furthered the cause of fascism.

Though the odds then in the Austrian situation were heavily against the successful workings of parliamentary democracy, Seipel insisted on trying to work through Parliament. There is no reason to doubt the sincerity of his assurance to his colleagues in the cabinet as late as October 1926 that "every way should be tried to make Parliament workable." Only if this failed would he have to explore other avenues of action.[58]

Clearly the crisis of Parliament was not Seipel's plot; it was his challenge. The question for the historian to decide is how Seipel met this crisis. If a policy shift in the direction of the much-dreaded "strong hand"[59] was indicated, how could he effect it while preserving basic constitutionality, basic liberties, without giving way to the counsel of despair, or to the policy of extremism?

---

only fitting comment was "scandal in permanence," *Neue Freie Presse*, November 18, 1926, evening ed.

[56] Gulick, *Austria*, I, 470.

[57] Cf. Karl Renner, "Grundsätzliches zum Kampf der österreichischen Sozialdemokratie gegen den Faschismus," *Die Gesellschaft*, I (February 1930), 132. It should be recorded, however, that in retrospect and in reply to questions put to him by Charles Gulick, Renner tended to minimize the role of obstruction: it was "not a general policy," was used "only for particular purposes," and the whole matter had become "greatly exaggerated"; Gulick, *Austria*, II, 992f.

[58] A.V.A., M.R.466, October 21, 1926.

[59] Cf. Seitz in *Sten. Prot., 112. Sitzung, I.G.P.*, May 31, 1922, pp. 3709f.

The Crisis of Austrian Democracy

Withdrawal

An interlude in Seipel's political career occurred in the period between November 1924 and October 1926, precipitated by his resignation as chancellor on November 7, 1924. The reasons for this step can be traced to the course of the country's reconstruction in its most inclusive sense. It was precipitated by a strike of railroad men for higher pay; but the Chancellor saw in these demands a threat to successful reconstruction. He expected the railroad men or public servants to subordinate their own good to the good of the whole.[60]

No less closely connected with the reconstruction was the issue that was brought forth by Seipel's unsuccessful attempt to form a new government. Considering himself committed to a recent League exhortation to administrative reforms[61] in the form of savings in the provincial administration, he ran into opposition of the provincial governors. Prelate Hauser, Seipel's old colleague, emerged as the spokesman of the federalists against Seipel, who now was pushed into the position of an ill-disguised centralist.[62] Subsequently, in a hastily convened conference, the Christian Socialist party decided by a two-thirds majority that it would prefer to dispense with Seipel's forming a new cabinet. In an odd way history seemed to repeat itself. Like Mayr, back in November 1920, Seipel was overthrown by the federalists in his own party. He had, for the time being at least, lost his control over it.

[60] Schulthess, *1924*, p. 129. The strike was settled by compromise on November 12.

[61] "Sixth Meeting (Public) held at Geneva on Tuesday, September 16, 1924, at 6:00 p.m." and "Annex 676, Joint Report by the Financial Committee and the Commissioner-General at Vienna, submitted to the Council on September 16, 1924," League of Nations, *Official Journal*, v (October 1924), 1304ff. and 1552ff. Cf. also Schulthess, *1924*, p. 449; and Seipel's report at the occasion of his first appearance before Parliament, *Sten. Prot., 57. Sitzung, II.G.P.*, September 30, 1924, pp. 1598ff.

[62] See Hans Schmitz, "Von Seipel zu Ramek," *Volkswohl,* xv, no. 10-12 (1924), 191.

But Seipel's resignation was quite different from Mayr's—the men were different, as well as the situation. An initiate in the party circles seemed to think that a more energetic attitude on the part of the Chancellor could have brought his following back into line, but that "apparently he didn't want this."[63] It is quite conceivable that there was purpose in Seipel's departure. He repeatedly mentions in his correspondence with intimates that he had a habit of choosing the right time of resigning from office as, he quipped, he also chose the time to get sick.[64] It might be reasonably inferred, then, that both the strike and the unwillingness of the governors were but outward manifestations, almost excuses, for Seipel to "roll up" the reconstruction problem in all its dimensions. As political problems they were of slight importance. As symptoms for the "spirit"[65] which had made them possible and for the "laxness"[66] among broad sections of the population, they were central to Seipel. And the more rigidly inclusive his concept of reconstruction, the more he must have felt, for the moment at least, incapable of realizing it. Something had to give. Seipel's resignation became a reemphasis of the moral side of reconstruction, of the "Regeneration of the Souls" to which the coming years were to be so largely dedicated.

In effect Seipel shifted gears. For the time being he left the narrow, confining political atmosphere in Vienna behind him. In politics he was likely to spend himself; indeed politics had

[63] Josef A. Tzöbl, "Ignaz Seipel," in Hugo Hantsch, ed., *Gestalter der Geschicke Österreichs* (Innsbruck, Vienna, and Munich, 1962), p. 593.

[64] ". . . to choose myself the moment of 'getting sick.' . . . It is like resigning from office: you choose the moment yourself"; Seipel to Lothar Wimmer (Presidial Secretary of the Austrian Chancellery, 1919-1926, later a leading Austrian diplomat), Meran (not Vienna), February 21, 1932, in Lothar Wimmer, *Zwischen Ballhausplatz und Downing Street* (Vienna and Munich, 1958), p. 188. Cf. also an almost identical passage in a letter from Seipel to Regierungsrat Franz Xavier Zimmermann (Rome), Vienna, March 7, 1932; Schmitz Archive.

[65] *Reichspost*, November 9, 1924.

[66] *Reichspost*, November 18, 1924; cf. also Hans Schmitz, "Von Seipel zu Ramek," *Volkswohl*, xv, no. 10-12 (1924), 193ff.

brought him close to death. But in spite of an intense commitment to politics, Seipel remained the professor of moral theology and the priest—and in these vocations lay the sources of his strength. The need for a "Regeneration of the Souls," as he saw it, called for a going back to these "sources," for an elaborate preparation of the ground for a new, more basic, more ambitious return. In Arnold Toynbee's terms, it amounted to "withdrawal" preparatory to "return." It was to take Seipel far away from his original political course and start him off on a new search for order and authority, a search for the "true" republic and "true" peace. In this sense Seipel's resignation marked a distinct divide in his career.

As early as February 1925 Seipel admitted to a friend that his efforts to achieve a considerable "reduction of the work load" by his resignation had failed.[67] The two years out of office merely shifted his activities from the office at the Ballhausplatz to Parliament and party headquarters, and even more to the lecture platform and conference hall in almost all parts of Europe and in the United States. He became a "never resting motor"[68] as he moved from city to city, capital to capital, country to country, and indeed from continent to continent to deliver what he called his "great speeches"—that is, those with "spiritual content."[69]

Seipel, no longer a prophet in his own country, used his travels to sketch the problems of his little country in broad strokes in relation to other countries, and particularly to Germany. He talked about the war coming to an end with no peace; about inflation and "increasing luxury-mindedness"; about the "turmoil in politics" and the "crises of the new democracy and of parliamentarianism"; about the "futile search for new forms of government," the "toying with dictatorship of individuals, parties, or

[67] Seipel to Marga Lammasch, Hütteldorf, February 20, 1925; Schmitz Archive.

[68] Seipel to Marga Lammasch, Vienna, December 24, 1926; Schmitz Archive.

[69] Seipel to Dipl. Ing. Dr. A. Chwala, Hütteldorf, August 5, 1929; Schmitz Archive.

classes," and the "corruption in public life"—all sequels of the war.[70] Above and beyond the disillusionment of the new democracies of Central Europe he projected a bold vision of a "reconstruction of Europe": "However one may think about the roads to the reconstruction of Europe, the aim should be nothing short of Europe: a united, peaceful Europe, a conscious unit, formed out of the diversity of its peoples, with enormous spiritual and economic strength, provided it will be and remain one."[71] As the Church under Leo XIII had moved the social question into the foreground of Christian thought and endeavor, it was time that it paid attention to "the other, the greater social question,"[72] that is, the question of world peace.[73]

Among the foreign destinations of the traveling prelate, the most memorable, apart from the Eternal City, was undoubtedly the New World.[74] The American trip of June and July 1926 took him to the Eucharistic Congress in Chicago. After his arrival in New York, the ex-Chancellor visited the Nation's capital, taking

[70] Ignaz Seipel, "Der Weg zum Frieden im Volk und unter den Völkern," Essen, March 1, 1925, Gessl, *Reden*, pp. 166f.

[71] Cf. Ignaz Seipel, "Die Neugestaltung Europas," March 2, 1925, ibid., p. 187.

[72] Ignaz Seipel, "Katholische Liebe und Völkerfriede," Stuttgart, August 25, 1925, ibid., p. 241.

[73] It is indicative of the direction of Seipel's thinking that he took pains to outline the limits of the secularized international law. Its father, Hugo Grotius, facing a "world of dissenters," had done mankind a service, but Seipel urged a return to its "moral foundations"; Ignaz Seipel, "Die sittlichen Grundlagen des Völkerrechtes," Vienna, March 20, 1925, ibid., pp. 190f.

[74] Seipel's foreign travels, mostly devoted to lecturing, included the following, omitting minor trips to Germany: in 1925, Holland (February and April–May), Konstanz (June, for the Bodenseekonferenz), Switzerland (June and August), Czechoslovakia (June–July), Paris (August), Bologna (September), Rome (October, as head of a group of Austrian pilgrims composed largely of parliamentarians); in 1926, Berlin (February; a visit including calls on President Hindenburg, Chancellor Luther, Foreign Minister Stresemann), Stockholm (March; Hermann Göring attended the lecture), Paris (June; a visit including calls on President Doumergue and Prime Minister Briand), America (June–July).

in Mount Vernon and calling on Secretary of State Kellogg and President Coolidge.[75] In Chicago in the course of the Eucharistic Congress Seipel addressed the session of German-speaking Catholics; under the "tent," the "tabernacle of the all-saintly Eucharist," it was proper for the Germans of the world to meet in their search for a peace.[76]

In his vision of this tabernacle, to which Seipel alluded five times in his speech, he overcame the despair of politics. That the New World should have been the setting for this vision was not wholly incidental. Seipel took to it at once; its very friendliness struck him.[77] Perhaps the Austrian traveler, who himself had come "from below," upon visiting the home of Abraham Lincoln in Springfield, Illinois,[78] felt a sense of affinity with America's great President. Somehow he saw in the New World an extension of his ideal image of Europe. The imperial horizon was translated into an overwhelming spaciousness,[79] a supranational setting into an anational one.[80] If Seipel in his Chicago address spoke of the overcoming of hatred and reasserted his faith in the cause of peace, he owed something to his environment. It was, he said, "full of new vistas and new revelations" and, besides the many sources of discord, it appeared to him as a "source of peace."[81]

[75] Seipel diary, June 17, 1926.

[76] Ignaz Seipel, "Eucharistie und Frieden," *Im Dienste des Wortes* (Vienna and Munich, 1955), pp. 143ff.

[77] Seipel at St. Joseph's Auditorium, 87th Street, east of First Avenue: "If the rest of America is as cordial as New York has been, we shall all have been Americanized by the time we sail back home"; *The New York Times*, June 14, 1926.

[78] Seipel diary, June 26, 1926.

[79] "In our economic as well as our political life we want to learn from the great, spacious America, which also makes its inhabitants farsighted"; Ignaz Seipel, "Die Zukunft Europas," Krems, July 30, 1929, *Kampf*, p. 193.

[80] Ignaz Seipel, "Die geistigen Grundlagen der Minderheitenfrage," Vienna, January 14, 1925, Gessl, *Reden*, p. 160.

[81] Seipel, "Eucharistie und Frieden," *Im Dienste*, p. 145.

"Government by Telephone"

It would be almost an understatement to say that while Seipel was on grand tour the country proceeded in low gear. Seipel himself designated Rudolf Ramek his successor as Chancellor in a party caucus.[82] Politically he was a nonentity. His government was generally considered to be but a continuation of the old. In fact it was what Seitz called a "government by telephone,"[83] taking constant directives from Seipel.[84] And if the Pan-German leader, Leopold Waber, Vice-Chancellor in the new cabinet, said in a party caucus that the government would be "not weak" because Seipel stood behind it,[85] he was mistaken only in the assessment of its strength. The government was weak. While a report by two League-appointed experts of August 1925 emerged with a distinctly favorable assessment of the Austrian economy, affirming its viability,[86] the country was plagued by the collapse of a number of savings institutes. The fact that these bankruptcies were caused at least in part by faulty speculation with the French franc, and moreover implicated some cabinet members, undermined public confidence in the government. The Foreign Minister, Heinrich Mataja, one of Seipel's closest political associates, was suspected of too close connections with Dr. Kunwald's Biedermann Bank, which was also in trouble; and the Minister of Finance, Jakob Ahrer, allegedly took bribes from Sigmund

[82] Cf. Josef A. Tzöbl, "Ignaz Seipel," in Hugo Hantsch, ed., *Gestalter der Geschicke Österreichs* (Innsbruck, Vienna, and Munich, 1962), p. 593.

[83] *Neue Freie Presse*, October 21, 1926, morning ed.

[84] It was also symptomatic that a lengthy report by Pfeiffer, the German Minister to Vienna on the domestic and foreign policy of Austria, dated April 18, 1925, dealt elaborately with the views and policies of "Federal Chancellor" Seipel without even once mentioning Ramek, the actual head of the government; Strictly Confidential Memorandum, Dr. Maximilian Pfeiffer, "Das österreichische Problem und die Anschlussfrage," Vienna, April 18, 1925, A.A., Geheimakten II-Ö.: Po.2, Bd.1.

[85] A.V.A., 48. Sitzung V.A.G.V., November 17, 1924.

[86] The so-called Layton-Rist Report; League of Nations, *The Economic Situation of Austria* (Geneva, 1925).

Bosel, a shady financier who had amassed a fortune at the expense of the average Austrian saver. Both Mataja and Ahrer had to resign, and the latter slipped off to Cuba.

While no social or political order is wholly immune from such irregularities, a developing democracy like the Austrian one is singularly vulnerable to them. An authoritarian or dictatorial system has ways of covering them up; a well-functioning and established democracy has ways of weathering them; but in postwar Austria, as in the unsteady French Third Republic and the Weimar Republic, scandals or even suspected scandals had a way of seriously threatening the whole fabric of democracy. The Staviskys in France, the Barmats and Sklareks in Germany, the Castiglionis[87] and Bosels in Austria, all in their destructive ways have made history, and so have those who helped them in their endeavors, as well as those who have blown them up out of all proportion in order to make political capital. Bosel, it might be said, was a symptom of an unhealthy society.

Seipel, since he was the man behind the political scene, cannot wholly be absolved of all responsibility. Personally he would not have been so much as suspected by even his worst enemies; but there was his close relationship to Dr. Kunwald of the Biedermann Bank, and also to Mataja, to consider. He was now put into a position which all public figures have reason to fear, where not his enemies but his friends might let him down. The Social Democratic party, which was itself not wholly immune from corruption, can hardly be blamed for having exploited the situation; for once it exercised its function of opposition properly. Seipel, who throughout the period of his withdrawal had remained party head, was himself caught in a conflict between party interests and the interests of the whole, personalities and principles, politics and morals. The man who had resigned demonstratively to fight moral laxness was now put in a position of having to soft-

[87] Camillo Castiglioni, financier of the interwar period, with a questionable reputation.

pedal his colleagues' questionable activities.[88] His studied passivity in the corruption involving his party associates may have been "good politics" in a narrow sense, but it served little to enhance democracy in Austria.

Shortly before the end of the Ramek interregnum and Seipel's comeback, the statesman-priest was once again confronted with the possibility of a high Church appointment. The bishopric of Seckau in Styria was about to become vacant. Dr. Funder, proceeding at the Cardinal's request from the Archbishop's palace in the Rotenturmstrasse to party headquarters at the Schwarzenbergplatz to break the news to Seipel, was determined at the same time to persuade the former Chancellor that he was needed in the capital. But the decision was Seipel's, and though it was not an easy one, it was an inevitable one. Deeply sighing, the man who had never really left said finally, "I shall remain."[89] In October 1926 then, when Ramek's government ran into difficulties, the time had come again for Seipel officially to take over control of the affairs of state.

Return

Seipel took office with an often quoted statement that epitomized his assessment of the general state of affairs as well as his self-esteem: "Austria is neither sufficiently badly off to force me to take over the chancellery, nor sufficiently well off to allow me to refuse it."[90] In fact, the first day in Parliament came off well. In

[88] The elaborate study which he undertook of the Ahrer affair (Ignaz Seipel, "Der Fall Ahrer: Ein abschliessendes Wort," n.d., 10 pp., Schmitz Archive; cf. also *Das Neue Reich*, xII [1931], 317-320, 343-344) makes it clear that, while he was well aware of Ahrer's failings, he was prepared to shield him. Cf. also, on Seipel's continued shielding of Ahrer, "Dr. Seipel über Besuch Ahrers," *Neue Freie Presse*, April 1, 1927, morning ed.

[89] The only source for this episode is Friedrich Funder, *Vom Gestern ins Heute* (Vienna and Munich, 1952), pp. 682f.

[90] Goldinger in Benedikt, *Geschichte*, p. 144.

one of his most skillful addresses[91] the new Chancellor could remind the opposition of the fact that the League of Nations' control over Austrian finances had just a few months to run before its termination. To the federalists in his own party, who had been partly responsible for his resignation, he lectured that federalism was not an "aim in itself" and was not to conflict with the interests of the whole. Having previously backed his own party while it was under attack for irregularities, he now felt free to urge a reform of political ethics which would serve to restore parliamentary dignity in the country. With some fervor, he appealed to the House: "Let us draw a line between the past and a new time, and we shall do it well if we draw it not between this or that land, not between this or that group, not between this or that party."[92] Even though the opposition, with Seitz holding the floor five times longer than the Chancellor himself, responded with sarcasm and vituperation, calling for a "regeneration of the soul of the Christian Socialist party," and labeling Seipel's return a "misfortune for Austria,"[93] the *Neue Freie Presse* detected a certain basic agreement among the speakers of the three parties. "A day in which the word 'scoundrel' has not featured," it commented in its editorial, "is therefore a memorable day in the annals of political life." The Chancellor had impressed the House with the "authority of his word."[94]

Two Party Programs and the Specter of Civil War

When the Social Democratic party convention met in Linz in the autumn of 1926 to chart its future course, it had to come to terms both with its basic predicament that in Austria, as in all of Central Europe, the "bourgeoisie" had consolidated their position, and also with the fact that in Russia a form of socialism had established itself which had no affinity with the democratic ideals for which the Austrian Socialists stood. The Linz Program had to

[91] *Sten. Prot., 161. Sitzung, II.G.P.*, October 20, 1926, pp. 3890f.
[92] Ibid., p. 3891.   [93] Ibid., pp. 3899, 3904.
[94] *Neue Freie Presse*, October 21, 1926, morning ed.

find a formula that would show a way out of the bourgeois hold, while steering clear of the terrorist violence used by the Bolsheviks.

Among the various factions within the party, Renner continued to plead for practical socialist work among the masses to bring about a strengthening of the party within the framework of the constitution, while Max Adler urged the adoption of the Marxian prescription, the "dictatorship of the proletariat." The "great debate" within the party was over the issue of "dictatorship or democracy."[95] Once again, as in the days of Viktor Adler, a compromise was reached, this time under the influence of Otto Bauer. It was a tortured and twisted compromise. Announcing that it was the aim of the party to "conquer the control of the democratic Republic, not in order to abolish democracy, but in order to place it at the service of the working class," it acknowledged the hard-and-fast fact that the bourgeoisie would "not voluntarily abandon its position of power."[96] Dodging the vital question of whether and how the party could become reconciled to the situation, it shifted the argument to the question of whether and how the bourgeoisie could reconcile themselves to the "democratic Republic" of the working class. This approach allowed the party to conjure up the specter of a "monarchist or fascist dictatorship," or "counterrevolution," which in turn justified the party's speaking in terms of "civil war" and "dictatorship." Even though Bauer in his speech at the congress warned against violence and stressed that "whoever takes to violence is the prisoner of violence,"[97] the decisive fact was that the threat of civil war and dictatorship was included in the compromise formula.

The Linz formula accurately reflected the predicament of the Socialists, as Leser formulated it, "between Reformism and Bolshevism": their unwillingness, on the one hand, to match the

[95] *Neue Freie Presse*, November 2, 1926, morning ed.

[96] Klaus Berchtold, *Österreichische Parteiprogramme 1868-1966* (Munich, 1967), p. 252.

[97] Quoted in Jacques Hannak, *Karl Renner und seine Zeit* (Vienna, 1965), p. 474; Braunthal, *Otto Bauer*, p. 64.

Bolshevik terror, and their need, on the other, to appeal to the workers and hold their allegiance by means of the "radical phrase." Those sufficiently initiated and patient to follow Otto Bauer's mental acrobatics should have understood that the threat was far removed and indeed a hypothetical one. Yet the party, operating in the realm of politics and not dialectics, must have been aware of the effect of the wording. Within the Socialist leadership itself warnings were voiced.[98] At best the Linz Program was ambiguous, at worst it was dangerous. The critical passages were included in the program at the risk of alarming the bourgeoisie, and this is what they accomplished. What was a compromise for the Social Democrats had the impact of a threat on the rest of the country.

Lastly, Otto Bauer's phraseology can be explained exhaustively neither in terms of the allover predicament of the Austrian Social Democracy, nor in terms of the particular circumstances of the convention. The very coupling of democracy and dictatorship was orthodox Marxism. A perfectionist vision of society, and that is what Marxism was, tended to justify means in terms of the end, the pragmatic reality being easily sacrificed for the benefit of the ideal. Otto Bauer gave a public demonstration of this dangerous thinking in Linz, and his historians ought not to explain it away. They might add, though, that the position of Seipel, his antagonist, was not inherently different. Both men were ideologists; both men were perfectionists ready to juggle means and ends, a fact which subjected both to the criticism of being "ambiguous."[99] If anything, Seipel, though not less human than Bauer, was more able to exercise power and willing to act. In the duel between the two, Otto Bauer's challenge, however harmful, remained a mere threat. But Seipel's response was likely to be more hard-hitting, more political, and more geared toward victory.

[98] Julius Deutsch, *Ein weiter Weg. Lebenserinnerungen* (Zurich, Leipzig, and Vienna, 1960), p. 163.

[99] *Verklausuliert*; Renner about Seipel in Renner, *Österreich*, p. 42; Deutsch about Bauer in Deutsch, *Ein weiter Weg*, p. 164.

The Christian Socialist program, formulated under the chairmanship of Seipel shortly after the Socialist one on November 29, 1926, was just about the reverse of the latter, unsure of itself in substance, but taking for granted the "state" within whose framework it was to be realized. It was the program of a party which had left behind its one-time reforming zest without being ready to acknowledge this fact in any way. The *Neue Freie Presse* rightly called it "antiquated."[100] It was full of commonplaces based on the premises of Christian policy and of evasive compromises on major controversial economic and social issues, as also on the Anschluss question. Its explicit passages were chiefly negative, like the one opposing the "predominance of the decomposing Jewish influence" and the one rejecting the call for a "class dictatorship."[101]

On these two latter points some comment is in order. There was nothing new, Seipel emphasized, in the party's anti-Semitic position:

> The Christian Socialist party . . . is . . . known as an anti-Semitic party. . . . This party combats . . . not the Jews and not the influence which the Jews exercise in the intellectual and economic sector, but the "predominance of the decomposing Jewish influence." . . . The fact that the leaders and propagandists of Russian Bolshevism and the . . . Communist movement in Germany and Austria, and also of the very radical Austrian Socialism, committed to the materialist theory of history and . . . to the Kulturkampf, are mostly Jews, explains sufficiently the anti-Semitic bent of popular opinion.[102]

[100] *Neue Freie Presse*, January 4, 1927, evening ed.

[101] Cf. Richard Schmitz, ed., *Das christlichsoziale Programm* (Vienna, 1932); Berchtold, *Österreichische Parteiprogramme*, pp. 374ff.

[102] "Dr. Seipel über die antisemitische Wendung im christlichsozialen Parteiprogramm," *Neue Freie Presse*, January 14, 1927, evening ed.; this statement was made to the Vienna representative of the Jewish Telegraph Agency.

Seipel thus expressed candidly the position of Austrian political Catholicism toward the Jews:[103] it was hostile. But in contrast to the Pan-German racists, its anti-Semitism was essentially defensive[104] and "ethical," directed at the secularizing impact of Judaism and the pointedly anti-Christian agitation of modern political movements like Socialism and Communism in which Jews played a predominant role. Also, the party of Lueger, while always distinctly anti-Semitic, had never been as wildly aggressive and consistent in its position toward the Jews as had the racists.

Seipel's own views on the matter reflect this restraint and ambiguity. The statement attributed to him that anti-Semitism was "for the street"[105] is distinctly in keeping with his attitude. He never allowed himself a public anti-Semitic outburst; unlike the founder of his party he was little given to carrying the Jewish question to the people and making capital of it. "His Excellency" did not engage in vulgarity, and anti-Semitism was vulgar.

Seipel's approach to the Jewish question was essentially professorial. The scholar of the nationality problem saw in it a related, though singularly complex issue, and he repeatedly suggested that it be solved by granting a minority status to the Jews.[106] For the rest, he was torn over whether the Jews were distinguished by religion or by class—and occasionally he would

[103] On the subject of Catholic anti-Semitism, see the fine article by Erika Weinzierl-Fischer, "Österreichs Katholiken und der Nationalsozialismus," I, *Wort und Wahrheit*, XVIII (June–July, 1963), 422.

[104] Seipel once talked about the "anti-Semitism of self-defense" (*Notwehrantisemitismus*); Ignaz Seipel, "Die Kulturpolitik der Christlichsozialen," *Reichspost*, September 23, 1920.

[105] *Für die Gasse*; quoted without reference in Peter G.J. Pulzer, *The Rise of Political Anti-Semitism in Germany and Austria* (New York, 1964), p. 319.

[106] Cf. Ignaz Seipel, "Minoritätenschutz und Judenfrage nach dem christlichsozialen Programm," *Volkswohl*, X, no. 2 (1919), 49-53; for the program, see Berchtold, *Österreichische Parteiprogramme*, pp. 359ff. Cf. also what was probably Seipel's first statement on the Jewish question, "Zum Kampf um die öffentliche Sittlichkeit," *Katholische Kirchenzeitung*, August 3, 1911.

say, in a rather loose fashion, "race."[107] He succumbed to the usual indecision: were the Jews, as he put it, "representatives of mobile big capital," or were they the leaders of international socialism and communism?[108] However alien the Jewish world appeared to him, however intensely he felt its "decomposing" effect upon the Christian world, Seipel acknowledged that occasionally it produced some "great and noble men."[109]

There is clear evidence that Seipel used his influence to tone down public attacks on Judaism, and in the course of time he soft-pedaled attacks on Jewish capitalism in particular. He thus reflected in his action the increasing entanglement of his party with the forces of capitalism. Not only had Seipel as chancellor been forced to rely on them, but his closest financial advisers had been Jews.[110] Indeed, when in November 1925 Archbishop Piffl had sent to Seipel for comment a draft of the forthcoming pastoral letter of the Austrian episcopate on the social question, which had included phrases such as "the Jewish finance world" or "the Jewish spirit," Seipel had pointed out quietly and tactfully that the phrasing was redundant and the text as clearly understandable without the word "Jewish," that indeed the "most reverend" bishops might leave "this," that is Jew-baiting, to the politicians. Besides, Seipel had added that the danger came not from "plutocracy" and "capitalism," but from "excesses of capitalism." For now, the enemy was on the Left. Seipel's advice in this matter was followed; the pastoral letter incorporated these suggestions.[111]

[107] Ibid.

[108] Seipel, "Minoritätenschutz," pp. 51, 53.

[109] Ibid., 53.

[110] Josef Redlich and the mysterious Dr. Gottfried Kunwald. Seipel's Minister of Finance, Viktor Kienböck, was half-Jewish by origin.

[111] "Hirtenbrief Entwurf," and Seipel to Piffl, Vienna, November 8, 1925; file "1925 Bischofskonferenz 24.XI," Cardinal Piffl Archive, Archive of the Archdiocese, Vienna. "Lehren und Weisungen der österreichischen Bischöfe über soziale Fragen der Gegenwert," *Wiener Diözesanblatt*, LXIII, December 31, 1925.

Similarly Seipel's comment on the anti-Semitic passages of the party program identified the decomposing "Jewish influence" with the enemy on the Left. He hastened to add that in his capacity as chancellor he would protect the equal rights of all citizens, irrespective of their religious faith.[112]

The Christian Socialist opposition to "class dictatorship" was a direct response to the Linz Program. Its mere mentioning of the words "civil war" and "dictatorship" now prompted the Catholics to resort to dubious terminology. "What is dictatorship?" asked Seipel's intimate Richard Schmitz in the commentary to the Christian Socialist program, and he juxtaposed, subtly but ominously, "genuine dictatorship" to "rule of force" and the "dictatorship of the proletariat."[113] Seipel himself reciprocated to the Socialist sophistry by an elaborate jesuitry of his own. "True" democracy and dictatorship became less and less distinguishable in his argument, and his search for order, authority, and workable government took him further and further in the direction of dictatorship.

The programs of the two big parties were indicative of the political climate in Austria since Seipel's return to power. They, and notably the Linz Program, were manifestos rather than working papers, and they addressed themselves to the militant rather than political instinct of the masses. The Linz Program, anticipating the mood of the bourgeoisie, had become a self-fulfilling prophecy. The tense climate of the country was reflected in the newspapers—in headlines invariably announcing some scandal, horrible crime, or public demonstration. Almost every Sunday was taken up by one or the other political parade or demonstration. Some of these public events passed by, luckily, without any immediate disturbance of the public peace, others did not.

One with serious consequences occurred on "Bloody Sunday," January 30, 1927, in Schattendorf, a village in the Burgenland,

[112] *Neue Freie Presse*, January 14, 1927, evening ed.; cf. also "Dr. Seipel über die Judenfrage," *Neue Freie Presse*, April 12, 1927, morning ed.
[113] *Das christlichsoziale Programm*, pp. 27f.

when two opposing political formations, the Socialist Schutzbund and the right-wing Frontkämpfer, clashed and the latter managed to kill an unemployed war veteran and the seven-year-old son of a worker. The mass demonstration of workers the following day along the Vienna Ringstrasse and a fifteen-minute general strike all over Austria on the day of the funeral were only mild portents of things to come. But Seipel underestimated this evidence of popular agitation. He merely complained that the parliamentary "peace" had been disturbed,[114] instead of roundly condemning the evil of citizens playing at soldiers. Had he done this with all the authority at his command, the political situation might not have gotten out of hand in the summer of the same year.

Under these circumstances the calling of new elections could only deepen the division in the country and stiffen the impasse. Seipel threw himself into the electoral campaign, his aim being to consolidate all non-Socialist forces under the slogan of anti-Marxism. He was now ready to accomplish what he once had called the "removal of the revolutionary rubbish."[115] The result was a "Unity List," also called in military fashion "Unity Front," which included Pan-Germans and various smaller political groups. It was now openly a "bourgeois bloc."[116] Seipel had indeed moved far off his original pro-Socialist course in the direction of capitalism. "Jure Romano vivit Ecclesia Catholica," he later explained in an interview to a French Jesuit: "On pourrait dire, aujourd'hui: Modo capitalistico vivit Ecclesia Catholica!"[117] He was now able to justify his capitalistic course, which had been forced upon him by the foreign as well as domestic developments

[114] *Sten. Prot., 178. Sitzung, II.G.P.,* February 3, 1927, p. 4496.

[115] Seipel in the Bundesrat; *Sten. Prot., 69. Sitzung des Bundesrates der Republik Österreich,* February 29, 1924, p. 926.

[116] Cf. Seipel addressing the general assembly of the Hauptverband der Industrie Österreichs, *Neue Freie Presse,* April 5, 1927, morning ed.

[117] "Monseigneur Seipel parle de la France," *Le Correspondant,* October 25, 1931, p. 189, quoted in August M. Knoll, "Gespräche mit Ignaz Seipel," *Reichspost,* December 25, 1932.

since 1922, as consistent with the needs of the Church and indeed consistent with his original interpretation of the Church fathers.[118]

More perturbing, particularly in the light of things to come, was the fact that the Unity List represented another step in the direction of the polarization of the country into Marxist and anti-Marxist camps, and that Seipel, moreover, succeeded through the mediation of the Pan-Germans in recruiting even the National Socialists into the Unity List. Indeed when one of their leaders, Dr. Walter Riehl, was put on the third place in the Unity List of the Leopoldstadt, the foremost Jewish district of Vienna,[119] a great outcry ensued even in the press which otherwise supported the Chancellor's policy, causing the candidate to be shifted to a less conspicuous place in a less conspicuous district. We are told, however, that Seipel was rather amused at the grotesque Leopoldstadt situation and laughed heartily.[120] In any case, even the electoral alliance with the anti-Semites raised the important question of the range of accommodation. If the Church could be "indifferent," as Seipel once put it, toward economic systems such as socialism or capitalism as long as they corresponded to its

[118] By contrast, however, the Graz theologian Johannes Ude, refusing to go along with the new Unity Front, founded a party of his own to fight corruption and to salvage the socialist orientation of political Catholicism. He was not only opposed by Seipel, but had to withdraw his candidacy because of pressure from the Church hierarchy. The *Neue Freie Presse* dismissed this saintly but also cranky man as "the fool in Christ." This "Graz Savonarola" became for a short while at least an antitype within the Catholic camp to the "realistic" Seipel; *Neue Freie Presse*, April 14, 1927, morning ed.

[119] In a letter to Riehl of April 7, 1927, Seipel even offered him the support of the Christian Socialist party organization; Riehl Papers, Diary, 1927, Institut für Zeitgeschichte, Vienna, mentioned in Ludwig Jedlicka, "Das autoritäre System in Österreich," *Aus Politik und Zeitgeschichte*, B30/70 (Bonn, July 1970).

[120] Karl Anton Rohan, *Heimat Europa. Erinnerungen und Erfahrungen* (Düsseldorf and Cologne, 1954), p. 197.

"moral principles,"[121] should it remain indifferent to a movement such as National Socialism, whose racism was in obvious violation of the Christian brotherhood of man? Austrian political Catholicism, under Seipel's direction, thus in the 1927 election came up for the first time against the problem of its relation to National Socialism, which turned out to be one of the most perplexing and controversial ones in the recent history of the German-speaking world.[122] And it seems very likely that Seipel was from the start not fully aware of the seriousness of all the implications of the problem.

The elections of April 24 did not bring the expected majority to the Unity List, but gains to the Socialists.[123] While the latter clamored for a change in government, Seipel, skillfully maneuvering, found a way out of his predicament and turned near-defeat into victory by bringing the Landbund into the government and turning over to it the vice-chancellorship. His new government was now a complete bourgeois coalition, brought together, as the speaker for the opposition reminded the House, chiefly by fear of the Social Democracy.[124] He got special ap-

[121] Seipel's comments of April 13, 1925, to the draft by P. Frodl for the pastoral letter of the Austrian episcopate on the social question of November 29, 1925, quoted in Weinzierl-Fischer, *Konkordate*, p. 143, n. 65.

[122] For Austria, see Erika Weinzierl-Fischer, "Österreichs Katholiken und der Nationalsozialismus," *Wort und Wahrheit*, xviii (June–July–August–September 1963), 417-439, 493-526; xx (December 1965), 777-804; for Germany, see Ernst-Wolfgang Böckenförde, "Der deutsche Katholizismus im Jahr 1933," *Hochland*, liii (February 1961), 215-239; Günter Lewy, *The Catholic Church and Nazi Germany* (New York, 1964); Saul Friedländer, *Pius XII and the Third Reich. A Documentation*, New York, 1966.

[123]	Votes	Percentage	Seats
Unity List	1,756,761	48.2	85
Social Democrats	1,539,635	42.3	71
Landbund	230,157	6.0	9
Others	114,973	3.0	0

Cf. Alfred Kasamas, *Österreichische Chronik* (Vienna, 1948), pp. 496f.

[124] *Sten. Prot., 2. Sitzung, III.G.P.*, May 19, 1927, p. 19.

proval from the left side of the House when he referred in his stirring address to his party's strength outside Parliament.[125]

Civil War

The flare-up which finally occurred on July 15, 1927, when the Palace of Justice in Vienna went up in flames, can hardly be ascribed wholly to the acquittal by jury of the defendants of Schattendorf. The schism in the body politic had long been in the making. If one side of the country had come to feel acutely the futility and mediocrity of parliamentarianism and become increasingly conscious of a Marxist danger, the other side had come to see the revolution betrayed by corruption, and worse, by a counterrevolutionary conspiracy shrewdly held together and directed by a sinister priest.

The headlines of the late spring of 1927 increasingly brought news of an emotional kind. It was the time of the first transatlantic flights by men whose achievements the Austrians could share vicariously. The popular excitement over the flyers was easily matched by the attention paid to gory murders such as that of the opera singer Trajan Grosavescu by his wife Nelly, whose sensational trial ended, to the satisfaction of the good-natured Viennese, in acquittal.

But there were events that were more directly indicative of a new political mood. Pan-German students battled Social Democrats and Jews at the university in the name of the Unity Front, shouting "Out with the Jews." The mounting hostility between the right-wing *Heimwehr* movement and the Socialists prompted the ever watchful *Neue Freie Presse* to complain of "terror and counterterror" in Austria.[126]

When the news came out on July 15 that the jury of the criminal court on the Alserstrasse, deliberating over the Schattendorf

[125] Ibid., p. 22.
[126] "Terror und Gegenterror," *Neue Freie Presse*, July 6, 1927, evening ed.

incident, had acquitted the defendants, some public reaction was inevitable. But whether or not the court verdict was the occasion for the outbreak of July 15, the rousing editorial which appeared that morning in the *Arbeiter-Zeitung*, written by Friedrich Austerlitz, made it so. It translated the verdict as a capitalist refusal to do justice to the workingman. "The bourgeois world always warns against civil war. But is not this unconditional, agitating acquittal of men who killed workers itself civil war? We warn them all! For from the seeds of injustice nothing can arise but grave disaster."[127]

Here was the language of the Linz Program put to the test; in the charged atmosphere of that summer day, the "radical phrase" was to serve as a "substitute for action" on the part of the workers, as a "valve" for the workers' passions.[128] But had not Austerlitz, like Otto Bauer in Linz, confounded dialectics with politics, and thus incited the workers, however unwittingly, to rise up?[129]

The Palace of Justice on the Schmerlingplatz thus became the "symbol of class justice,"[130] and the flames lighting the skies of the troubled capital the sign of a civil war which cost eighty-five dead and hundreds wounded. Seipel called it a "revolution" on a scale such as Vienna had not experienced since the year 1848.[131] But he omitted any reference to 1918-1919. It was Otto Bauer who in Parliament reminded the country of those years, "incomparably more difficult than today," adding, to the applause of the House, that it had been the pride of all Austrians that this "enor-

[127] *Arbeiter-Zeitung*, July 15, 1927, quoted in Gulick, *Austria*, I, 734.

[128] Cf. Gulick, *Austria*, I, 734; Jacques Hannak, *Im Sturm eines Jahrhunderts* (Vienna, 1952), p. 343.

[129] Julius Deutsch recollects that at the time he feared precisely such consequences from his reading of Austerlitz's editorial; Deutsch, *Ein weiter Weg*, p. 166.

[130] Hannak, *Im Sturm*, p. 343.

[131] Seipel to Marga Lammasch, Vienna, July 17, 1927; in the possession of Marga Lammasch.

mous revolution [*Umwälzung*]" had been mastered with a minimum of bloodshed.[132] At the time as much credit went to the Social Democratic leadership for its efforts to restrain the workers from violence as to Seipel personally for preventing counter-revolution.

The situation now was utterly changed. The consensus had gone and given way to conflict along all lines, political, ideological, social. Once too often had the Social Democrats threatened a civil war; they were now unable to prevent it or to hold back the masses. Since 1918 it had been their policy—namely Otto Bauer's policy—to talk tough and act gently, to incite the masses and at the same time to appease them. But while this policy had worked between 1918 and 1920, it now collapsed under the weight of its own contradictions. Imperceptibly, at least to themselves, they had moved over to the method of violence.

The chief problem of Otto Bauer, however, in the uprising of 1927 was his own weakness and Seipel's strength. He was neither prepared nor able to exploit what was an almost perfect revolutionary situation. When the chips were down he was a paper tiger—Seipel and Redlich both talked about his *Papierform*[133]—and not sufficiently tough to see the revolution through. His course proved to be pure theory. It had spoilt any cooperation in Parliament and thus ruined the workings of democracy, and it now spoiled revolution. Seipel is supposed to have said of Otto Bauer that he was "the man with two left hands";[134] indeed, by 1927 Bauer had led his party straight into defeat. And the very fact that the opposition leader had to be lectured by the Chancellor to make the revolution properly, if at all, and face the consequences,[135] was a measure of the depth of the former's defeat and the latter's triumph.

[132] *Sten. Prot.*, 7. *Sitzung*, III.G.P., July 26, 1927, p. 138.
[133] Redlich diary, August 6, 1927, "Politische Tagebuchnotizen."
[134] *Wiener Politische Blätter*, I, June 18, 1933, 59.
[135] "Sie müssen wirklich eine Revolution machen!"; Redlich diary, August 6, 1927, "Politische Tagebuchnotizen."

The Chancellor kept his composure in the midst of the turmoil. Unlike Bauer, Seipel did not let his otherworldliness stand in the way of his political sense. He watched, like a spider, while his antagonist made his mistakes. When Bauer and Seitz appeared helplessly on the Ballhausplatz on the afternoon of July 15 and asked the Chancellor to make concessions to appease the workers, Seipel calmly refused. To their demand for his resignation he responded with cutting irony that while in the days of the Monarchy this would have been possible, now he could only resign constitutionally, on the basis of a vote of nonconfidence on the part of Parliament.[136] In his calm and sovereign fashion and not without a certain malice he escorted his visitors to an antechamber where they were to await the arrival of his Minister of the Interior.[137] After the angry crowd had been silenced by the interference of Schober's armed police, the traffic strike, which followed a one-day general strike, broke down over Seipel's refusal to negotiate while it lasted. Seipel was a "too experienced statesman," *Le Temps* commented, not to know that a government which compromised with rebellion was a lost government.[138] His concern lest the Communists take advantage of the situation made him as adamant as his hold over the police, army, and self-defense organizations in the provinces made him confident. The uprising of July 15 ended in utter defeat for the Social Democrats.[139]

After the bloody Friday in July 1927 Seipel stood at the height of his power. His triumph over the Vienna riot, remarked Clar-

[136] Redlich diary, August 6, 1927, "Politische Tagebuchnotizen"; cf. also the slightly different version of Alexander Spitzmüller . . . *Und hat auch Ursach* (Vienna, 1955), p. 416.

[137] Memorandum by Karl Hartleb, then Minister of the Interior, November 23, 1964, in Jacques Hannak, *Johannes Schober* (Vienna, 1966), p. 84. Hartleb stressed that Seipel kept "his humoristic way" throughout the crisis days of July 1927.

[138] *Le Temps*, editorial, July 17, 1927.

[139] Otto Bauer used the word *Schlappe* at a meeting of metal workers; *Neue Freie Presse*, September 30, 1927, morning ed.

ence K. Streit in the *New York Times*, illustrated "anew his genius for composing difficult situations."[140] His procedure, *Le Temps* found worth stressing, kept strictly within the limits of constitutionality.[141] The emphasis on Seipel's constitutional role here is important. The Chancellor refused to let it come to a final showdown with the Socialists, a demand which must have come to him from the Heimwehr,[142] increasingly the militant focus of anti-Marxism and in close touch with him.[143] Such a step, Seipel protested, would have meant a "violation of the democratic idea" and, moreover, would have helped to consolidate anew the defeated and disoriented Socialist camp.[144]

But the Chancellor, it can be argued, did not go all the way toward conciliation. He had little of the Churchillian magnanimity in victory that one might have expected from a churchman. In the account before Parliament, which was a strong one, elegant and sober, Seipel addressed himself primarily to the problems and interests of the state. He reminded the House that among the wounded there was the Austrian Republic which required attention. In the name of the "wounded Republic" he appealed to the Social Democratic party to dissociate itself from its extremists, and he concluded on this moving and stern note:

> Demand nothing from Parliament or the government which may seem merciful toward the victims and the guilty of the catastrophic days, but which would be cruel toward the

[140] Clarence K. Streit, "A Priest Who Is Austria's Strong Man," *New York Times Magazine*, July 31, 1927, p. 10.

[141] *Le Temps*, July 21, 1927.

[142] Cf. Lajos Kerekes, *Abenddämmerung einer Demokratie* (Vienna, 1966), p. 13.

[143] Seipel diary entries registered during this critical time three visits by the Tyrolean Heimwehr leader Richard Steidle to Seipel on June 28, July 26, and August 2, 1927.

[144] Clemens Wildner, *Von Wien nach Wien: Erinnerungen eines Diplomaten* (Vienna and Munich, 1961), p. 156.

wounded Republic. Demand nothing which might give the impression of an acquittal for those who rose up. . . . Nothing is further from us than to be hard, but we want to be firm. To be firm means as little to be hard as to be gentle must mean to be weak. But for both the right day and hour must be chosen.[145]

These were unbending words from a Christian statesman of the school of a Richelieu. They addressed themselves explicitly to the *raison d'état* and not to the human suffering left in the wake of the riots; to justice, but not to clemency. It was this speech which earned Seipel from the Left the not wholly unjustified and all the more effective name of the "Prelate without mercy." Why was there no government representative at the funeral of the fifty-seven workers on July 20, while on the following day, when the four policemen were buried, the government was present in full force? Had not the hour of reconciliation come now, if ever? Seipel's old friend and admirer, Hermann Bahr, was wrong after all, when he advertised the "victory of the politician Seipel as well as of the man."[146] Seipel's antagonist Bauer was in this instance closer to the truth when he said: "Dr. Seipel is very clever, but had he been a bit more clever, he would have said over the graves of the shot proletarians: . . . 'now the moment for conciliation of all parties has come.' . . . 99 percent of the Austrian population would have seen in Dr. Seipel a great and farsighted statesman." Bauer continued his argument, visibly unregenerate: "But Dr. Seipel wants to manure with the corpses of our dead the vineyards of his party and his class."[147] This was sharp oratory. But it is true that Seipel thought of utilizing the bitterness in the population caused by the uprising for the pur-

[145] *Sten. Prot., 7. Sitzung, III.G.P.*, July 26, 1927, p. 133.

[146] *Deutsche Allgemeine Zeitung*, July 21, 1927, quoted in *Neue Freie Presse*, July 21, 1927, evening ed.

[147] *Neue Freie Presse*, September 30, 1927, morning ed.

poses of his policies. The man who for the greater part of his life had been a conciliator and a healer now thought only of keeping the human wounds open.[148]

He neither "settled accounts" with the opposition nor did he forgive. In other words, he did not take the risk of going far enough in either direction, and he might well have explored the second one and thus altered the political climate and perhaps also the course of the Social Democracy. Instead Seipel, evading decisive action and choosing the middle course, assumed the burden of a two-front war against both the recovered Left and a newly constituted extreme Right.

Personally the July days of 1927 left the statesman-priest at war with himself. The statesman had become the symbol of divisiveness in the country, and the priest did not heal. The whole tone of Seipel's diary from this time on changed.

Was the priest during his retreat early in August in Lainz, at the outskirts of Vienna, fully aware of what he did, when twice he compared himself to the "rider over Lake Constance"?[149] This legendary figure, after braving the frozen lake, heard what dangers he had escaped and is said to have dropped dead from the horse which had carried him across. Quite clearly Seipel took those August days to review his "crossing," indeed his whole life. Quite likely also, he may have entered at this point into a conscious preparation for death. Redlich, who visited him two days before the retreat began, found the Chancellor thinner than in the previous year.[150]

Concretely, a review of the past months confronted him with the degree to which his life had "developed away from the minis-

[148] In a letter to his friend Mataja he wrote that compensation to businessmen for damages incurred by the events of July 15 would, among other things, have the "dangerous" effect of "weakening every bit of bitterness against those, who through their agitation, incite to excesses"; Seipel to Mataja, Vienna, March 13, 1928.

[149] Seipel diary, August 9 and 10, 1927.

[150] Redlich diary, August 6, 1927, "Politische Tagebuchnotizen."

try of God."[151] Was he not guilty of yielding to the temptations of power and vanity? He was most burdened by the stepped up Socialist campaign advocating defection from the Church which, between August 1 and 10 alone, made 2,734 Viennese leave the Church in protest against his policies. Hardly less upsetting to Seipel was the criticism directed at him from Catholic groups and thinkers for his involvement in politics and his sharp anti-socialist course.[152] Seipel was troubled. But short of yielding to the longing, which he repeatedly expressed, to "leave politics"[153] he could not resolve the basic conflict within himself. Serenity and composure, which had distinguished the Salzburg theologian when he first appeared on the political scene in Vienna, had given way more and more to barely controlled impatience and irritability.[154] The man who had set out with an infinite store of faith and optimism to sanctify the world emerged disillusioned over the adversity and hostility which he had found, and disillusioned above all in himself, in his new role as a fighter.

The Aftermath: Collision Course

Immediately after the bloody Friday of July 1927 the question of great coalition, so vital to the fate of the divided Republic, came

[151] Seipel diary, August 8, 1927.

[152] Seipel diary, August 12, 30, and October 29, 1927.

[153] Seipel diary, October 29, 1927; in a letter to Princess Starhemberg he admitted that he was "personally quite tired, and particularly tired of politics"; Seipel to Princess Fanny Starhemberg, October 21, 1928, in Erwin Rieger, *Fürstin Fanny Starhemberg: Ein Lebensbild einer österreichischen Frau* (Vienna, 1935), p. 147.

[154] Cf. Seipel diary entries, passim. "The party is more solid and unified than ever," he wrote late in 1928 to Fanny Starhemberg. "I myself become harder, sharper, but also more nervous and self-righteous. My friends are frequently shocked about my appearance, which on bad days too visibly indicates my decline. I believe the good God would do well to remove me from the Ballhausplatz, but he alone knows what really is right"; Seipel to Princess Fanny Starhemberg, December 1928, in Rieger, *Fürstin Fanny Starhemberg*, p. 148.

July 27, 1927: Seipel before the Nationalrat. Courtesy of Österreichische Nationalbibliothek, Vienna

up once again. The Republic's almost ten-year history had made it more than clear that its best years had been the first two under coalition rule, and that since the breakup of the coalition in 1920 things had been going steadily down hill. From as well-informed an observer of the political conditions in Austria as Beneš came the well-timed and cautiously phrased advice that not only Austria but the Central European countries with their lack of parliamentary tradition needed coalition governments. He made this excellent point, particularly applicable to Austria, that public opinion was not independent and alert enough to educate the political parties and switch from one party to another. Only minute shifts, in the direction of the Social Democrats, had taken place during the elections. Under these circumstances, he argued, a coalition cabinet was necessary to give a basic stability to Central European governments.[155] It seems also that similar advice in favor of coalition, though less direct and indeed carefully disclaimed, came from the German Chancellor Wilhelm Marx.[156]

In Austria itself the idea was brought up once again by Karl Renner. Since he had left the government in 1920, he had been somewhat out of the spotlight of party affairs, and had little influence on major planning and decisions. Now, however, the man whose official career had been identified with coalition, saw the need to speak up on the issue and urged disarmament of paramilitary formations on both sides.[157] But the Chancellor dashed all hopes for coalition in one of the fiercest speeches he ever made, delivered not inappropriately at the occasion of the celebration of the counterreformatory saint, Peter Canisius (1521-1597). "If men divide into the army camp of Christ and the army camp of the enemies of Christ, there will be a fight."[158] And he

---

[155] Beneš interview with the Berlin correspondent of the *Echo de Paris*; *Neue Freie Presse*, August 5, 1927, morning ed.

[156] Minister of Commerce Dr. Hans Schürff reporting to Pan-German parliamentarians; A.V.A. 29. Sitzung V.A.G.V., November 22, 1927.

[157] *Neue Freie Presse*, October 7, 1927, evening ed.

[158] *Neue Freie Presse*, October 18, 1927, morning ed.; cf. Seipel's diary entry of August 8, 1928, about his "task after the first ten years in politics":

warned against "false compromises," coalition and disarmament, and proposed to "carry Christ the Lord into the people." His crusading tone merely encouraged the irreconcilables among the Social Democrats to get the upper hand, and thus the civil war atmosphere to continue unabated.

The Socialist party convention, lasting from October 29 to November 1, 1927, met in a militant mood. The debate, revolving around the coalition issue, featured Bauer and Renner as chief antagonists. In effect Renner's brief, following upon Bauer's usual theoretical diatribe, was an impressive summation of the country's political course during the past nine years and an eloquent indictment of both Seipel's and Bauer's positions. It was a truly great speech, a last warning against "the street," against the polarization of political forces and an overemphasis on the ideological moment, which seized Austria as it did most countries on the Continent, and a last plea for practical reform, practical cooperation among the parties, and political sanity. Doctrinairism had bred doctrinairism, class war had bred class war, civic armament had bred civil war. If now, according to Renner, the Socialists were to enter as junior partners into a coalition, it was to avert the threatening "abuse of power" of the majority, in short, "the threat of fascism." The coalition will have to be made, he urged, if not in the name of the parties, in the name of the people.[159]

Renner's speech heavily underscored the tragedy which had befallen his country. When in the years past Seipel had urged, perhaps too readily, the substitution of *Staatspolitik* for *Parteipolitik*, he was rebuked by the Left. Now that Renner spoke up, the tables were turned. Now it was Renner who urged the overcoming of *Parteipolitik* in the interest of the people. Now, how-

---

"Counter-Reformation in view of all the events and tendencies of the time, etc., leading away from religion and the Church."

[159] Hannak, *Karl Renner*, p. 495ff.

ever, Seipel's position had stiffened, and he firmly rejected any concession to the Social Democrats, as well as any thought of coalition.[160] He was no longer concerned with the persuasion of an opposition that had proved a threat to the best interests of Church and state. He was indeed launched upon the much-heralded policy of the "strong hand," of seeking an effective "secular arm,"[161] outside Parliament if necessary, to protect the Catholic Church and strengthen the authority of the state.

What Renner said at the Socialist party convention made little difference politically. It reached neither Seipel nor the majority of the Socialists who were set upon opposing toughness on the Right with toughness on the Left. Thus by 1927 the two parties which had set up the Republic together had unalterably decided upon a collision course. Renner was quite right in suggesting in his analysis that whereas between 1918 and 1920 the purpose of coalition had been restraint of the Left by the Right, now it would have meant restraint of the Right by the Left.[162] Instead the "dialectics of the civil war psychosis,"[163] as Renner once aptly put it, were allowed to take their course, and both sides contributed to bringing the Republic closer to fascism and to the final showdown between Right and Left in February 1934 which the country itself was not to survive much longer.

[160] On the coalition question Seipel had been constantly negative since his return from Geneva in October 1922; see Johann Auer, "Seipels Verhältnis zu Demokratie und autoritärer Staatsführung" (diss., Vienna, 1963), p. 55. Cf. Franz Dinghofer: "As long as Seipel leads the Christian Socialists, no coalition with the Social Democrats will come about," A.V.A., 189. Sitzung V.A.G.V., March 21, 1923. Cf. also Seipel: "With the Social Democrats I shall, as long as I am in politics, make no coalition," ibid., 3. Sitzung, May 12, 1927. And see Franz Dinghofer: "Seipel declares now as before that he will make no Black-Red coalition. Once the day for such a coalition comes it will be done without Seipel." Ibid., 28. Sitzung, November 4, 1927.

[161] Cf. Wandruszka in Benedikt, *Geschichte*, p. 327.

[162] Hannak, *Karl Renner*, p. 496.

[163] *Sten. Prot.*, 56. *Sitzung, III.G.P.*, October 3, 1928, p. 1624.

The Crisis of Austrian Democracy

In Search of "True Democracy"

Starting in the autumn of 1927, the search for alternatives to parliamentary democracy commanded more and more attention. While Seipel's part in this search was increasingly active, his direction was ambiguous. No statement was more indicative of his uncertain position than the one which he made early in the critical year of 1927, when he characterized the situation in Austria and elsewhere as a "time of transition toward something new."[164] His vision of that "something new" remained blurred, though, to be sure, he was more explicit when he stated flatly after the July 15 catastrophe: "The government, in order not to lose the people's confidence, is almost forced to make itself more or less independent of Parliament."[165] He was not the kind of man to stage a frontal attack against the Republic and its institutions. He was committed to a mode of political thought and action whose dominant note was a Christian latitudinarianism. Even now, when there was good reason to look upon his "accommodative" course as a failure, he did not fall back on an ideological position which indiscriminately dismissed the whole tradition of modern secularism. A pragmatist, he was primarily concerned not with destroying modern institutions but rather with improving and correcting them.

In the budget debate of the Nationalrat's Finance Committee in November 1927 he outlined his position by reiterating his aversion to "dogmas"; he said that he was guided merely by "principles." And then the *Fiaker's* son went on to compare the state to a coach: "But if in a curve the coach threatens to turn over, then one leans toward the side that counterbalances the carriage's tilt. . . . If our state coach now threatens to turn over to the left, we naturally incline very far to the right. This does not mean that this inclination will have to be maintained forever. If we are in a position once again to sit straight . . . we shall perhaps

[164] *Neue Freie Presse*, January 27, 1927, morning ed.
[165] *Neue Freie Presse*, November 10, 1927, morning ed.

274

be able to conduct our state coach according to clearly established principles."[166] This statement may be taken as a reaffirmation of Seipel's accommodative course. Though he now stressed his counterbalancing rather than his adjusting function, he still subscribed to a flexible concept of politics. Politics was not a matter of maintaining fixed dogmas, but of maneuvering according to certain "principles," within the realm of the advisable and possible.

A vital question of which Seipel seems to have been unaware at the time, however, was whether after the events of July 1927 he was still the "coachman" in control of the "state coach," free to throw his weight as he saw fit. He himself had hardened—perhaps for good reasons—against the Left. While he remained somehow committed to his own past policies, Seipel could not escape the existence, indeed cogency, under the impact of the political crisis, of pressures that favored a drastic break with the democratic experiment.

These pressures were not altogether a new phenomenon in Austria. While following Seipel's career, we have perhaps lost sight of the tradition of Austrian integralism, supported by the various groups and individuals who, quite unlike Seipel, maintained an intransigent conservatism in the face of modern society and the secular state. The integralists were the romantics among the Catholics. And though in the 1920s they were no longer in the mainstream of Catholic thought and politics, they were vociferous and determined opponents of capitalism as well as of democracy. Their criticism of revolution, of the Republic, of parliamentarianism, and of the party state was a fundamental one. As Platonists or even Wagnerians, as loyal disciples of Karl von Vogelsang, they saw in the Thomistic-Leonine practice of accommodation the surrender of an essentially religious position to the forces of relativism. These two positions remained incompatible To someone like Anton Orel, therefore, the Republic was the ex-

[166] *Neue Freie Presse*, November 10, 1927, morning ed.

pression of the spirit of modern secularism which was destroying religion, the ultimate source of authority; it was in the last analysis a tool of the Jews, a "miserable Jew Republic" aiming at overthrowing the rule of the Lord.[167] In the columns of Joseph Eberle's *Das Neue Reich*, the forces of democracy were represented as the "rule of Satan," challenging the Christian state and theocracy.[168] Even though Eberle refrained from public and direct attacks on the policies of the Christian Socialist party and particularly of Seipel, he left no doubt that he saw in Seipel's accommodative course since November 1918 a dangerous departure from the right road.[169]

Unique and most influential in his criticism of democracy was Othmar Spann, who occupied one of the chairs of economics and sociology at the University of Vienna. Far from confining himself to strict scholarship, he developed a neo-Romantic philosophy. He preached death to individualism, and saw himself as spokesman of a "counter-Renaissance" which heralded the coming of a new organic, universalist social order as expressed in the corporative state. Spann was a fiery ideologist and throughout the twenties he attracted a growing flock of Austria's academic youth[170] and exercised a strong influence on antidemocratic theories and movements in Austria as well as in Germany.[171] While

[167] Quoted in A. Diamant, *Austrian Catholics and the First Republic* (Princeton, 1960), p. 144.

[168] Quoted in ibid., p. 147.

[169] Cf. Joseph Eberle to Seipel, Vienna, October 22, 1922, A.V.A., Bundeskanzleramt Inneres, Korrespondenz Seipel, K.79; cf. also Joseph Eberle, "Klerus und Sozialdemokratie in Österreich," *Schönere Zukunft*, III, October 23, 1927, 69f.

[170] His lectures were published in book form as *Othmar Spann, Der wahre Staat: Vorlesungen über Abbruch und Neubau der Gesellschaft* (Leipzig, 1921).

[171] Cf. Kurt Sontheimer, *Antidemokratisches Denken in der Weimarer Republik: Die politischen Ideen des deutschen Nationalismus zwischen 1918 und 1933*, 2nd ed. (Munich, 1964), passim, esp. pp. 249ff.; Diamant, *Austrian Catholics*, pp. 131ff.

appreciating Spann's "richness of thought," Seipel was critical of his academic and political romanticism. The "obscurity" of Spann's affected and contrived language irritated him and reminded him unpleasantly of the German mystic, Johann Georg Hamann (1730-1788), the "magus of the North."[172] But Seipel's increasing rigidity against the Left made him also susceptible to the influences of antidemocratic thought, and in particular, as we shall see, to Othmar Spann.

But the most vociferous, dynamic, and politically effective force on the Right was the Heimwehr movement. It had its beginnings in the home-guard units which originated in the various Länder in the period immediately after the war to defend the country against foreign enemies as well as against the Red threat at home. A paramilitary formation of a staunchly anti-Marxist and even antidemocratic orientation, it was marked by loyalties to local traditions and leaders that gave it a somewhat feudal character. Partly because of its lack of unity and also its lack of a coherent ideology, it had not figured before 1927 as a serious political force in Austria. Since the July crisis of that year, however, it had assumed a distinctly political character, rallying around it the more militant elements of bourgeois Austria. Wealthy aristocrats as well as industrialists and financiers and disinherited *Bürger*, Austrian patriots and Germany-oriented nationalists, Catholics and Pan-German anticlericals, aggressive anti-Semites along with frightened Jews joined forces to form what appeared as an almost irresistible popular movement of the Right.

It was the Heimwehr movement which emerged, as even one of its most determined foes conceded, as the "real victor" from the events of July 1927.[173] While before the summer of that year the *Neue Freie Presse* had dismissed the mere thought that "any federal chancellor in the foreseeable future" would lend his sup-

---

[172] Seipel to Eduard von Poppy (Austrian Legation, Berne), Vienna, June 18, 1925; Schmitz Archive.

[173] Cf. Deutsch, *Ein weiter Weg*, p. 172.

port to a few ultras of the Right and their fantastic dreams,[174] the situation then had changed. In the flush of victory, the "ultras," bolstered by generous financial support from banks, industry, and large landowners, now saw themselves in a position to put pressure on the Christian Socialist Chancellor. Immediately after the "bloody Friday," the Tyrolean Heimwehr leader, Richard Steidle,[175] warned Seipel "in the name of all Heimwehr organizations in the Alpine provinces . . . to oppose unwaveringly all attempts to take into the government those responsible for the events of July 15." "Otherwise," he threatened, "the Heimwehr would be obliged to undertake steps of gravest consequence."[176]

When the Styrian Heimatschutz, one of the more radical branches of the Heimwehr under the leadership of Walter Pfrimer, scheduled a parade for October 7, 1928, in Wiener Neustadt, an industrial city some thirty miles to the south of Vienna, this meant a challenge not only to the Social Democrats, who were in solid political control of the city, but also to Seipel. When the Socialists, in turn, defying intimidation and trying to forestall an Austrian "march on Rome," announced a counterdemonstration of their own, the country was confronted with a repetition of July 15, 1927, on a grand scale. Latent civil war once again threatened to turn into an open, bloody confrontation. Since the Socialists did not back down before an obvious challenge, Seipel had little choice, short of risking the collapse of his anti-Marxist front,[177] but to defend the Heimwehr's "legal right"[178] to "the

[174] *Neue Freie Presse*, March 7, 1927, evening ed.

[175] In the summer of 1928 the Heimwehr even managed, for the time being at least, to compose its leadership problems; Steidle became the allover leader, with the Styrian Walter Pfrimer as his deputy.

[176] *Neue Freie Presse*, July 23, 1927, morning ed., quoted in Gulick, *Austria*, I, 758.

[177] In the days preceding October 7 Seipel had a number of sessions with the Heimwehr leadership; Seipel diary entries, September 25, October 3, 4, 1928.

[178] *Sten. Prot., 56. Sitzung, III.G.P.*, October 3, 1928, p. 1627. In answer to an "urgent inquiry" by Renner before Parliament, he saw fit not

street." He took a momentous chance by letting both parades proceed through the city which, carefully divided into two by police and army and barbed wire, became a symbol of a divided country. Even though his calculation turned out to be right and nothing occurred on that much-dreaded but fortunately rainy day of October 7, even though Seipel had once again kept his "nerves," asserted the authority of state and thus emerged once again victorious, his victory was Pyrrhic. The Wiener Neustadt challenge on the part of the Heimwehr was one of the most spectacular of its kind. It was part of a plan of the fascists to demonstrate their presence and to drive the "hesitant government, and above all Dr. Seipel, into . . . some kind of *Putsch* or *coup d'état.*"[179]

Wiener Neustadt 1928, like Vienna 1927, marked the ascendancy of the Heimwehr and not of Seipel. He had shown strength and shrewdness toward his Socialist foes, but for his "friends," whom he once called the "lesser evil,"[180] he was no match. He was a priest after all, averse to violence and on the defensive against a movement that was recklessly charting its way to power. He was an impressive chancellor, parliamentarian, party man, but somehow he was not cut out to dominate the "street," much as he

---

only to defend the Heimwehr against the charge of "aiming at overthrowing the republican constitution," but to stage a full-scale defense of the Heimwehr's chief of staff, the notorious German putchist Major Waldemar Pabst, whose activities were followed with apprehension not only by the Socialists but by everyone concerned with democracy in Austria; *Sten. Prot., 56. Sitzung, III.G.P.*, October 3, 1928, pp. 1625f. Only after his public defense of Pabst did Seipel bother to check with Gustav Noske, at the time *Oberpräsident* of Hanover, on Pabst's political past; copies of letters Z.24696-13, Seipel to Noske, Vienna, October 12, 1928, and Noske to Seipel, Hanover, October 18, 1928; St.A., Personalia K.481.

[179] Ludwig Jedlicka, "The Austrian Heimwehr," *Journal of Contemporary History*, I (1966), 136.

[180] Copy of letter from Seipel to "Herr Mertens," Davos-Platz, February 21, 1931, from autograph collection of Professor Iring Fetscher, courtesy of the late Professor Klaus Epstein.

tried to do so. He figured that he could gain control over the Heimwehr and perhaps over the more constructive elements of the National Socialists,[181] prevent it from moving into party politics by itself, and channel its energies toward the postive purpose of constitutional reform.[182]

But Seipel's Heimwehr policy cannot wholly be explained in terms of a calculated risk, as an effort of the Chancellor to gain control over the increasingly restive militant movement. It was a necessity for him in view of the cracks that had become increasingly visible in his governmental coalition. In a number of motions that came before Parliament in the winter of 1928-29 pertaining to questions of marriage and school legislation, including the still open question of Salzburg University which was so close to Seipel's heart, the Christian Socialists found themselves confronted by a Pan-German–Social Democrat majority.[183]

To Seipel in his position all these votes were crucial, since they touched upon some essential concerns of the Church. The "religious and moral ideals" of the Church, first threatened by the Kulturkampf position of the Social Democrats, now appeared threatened by the partners in the Unity Front. The combination of anticlerical elements in the country, which Seipel so much feared and which he had successfully prevented throughout the twenties, now moved into the realm of possibility.

The gradual alienation from his coalition partners may well have encouraged Seipel to seek closer ties with the Heimwehr. The latter may then have appeared to him as the lesser evil compared with the unreliable Unity Front which was no "front" after all. In short, Seipel was actually in need of support from outside Parliament. All in all it was fear of the Socialists, fear of the

---

[181] Ibid.

[182] Cf. Spectator Noricus (pseud. for Richard Schmitz), "Von Seipel zu Schober," *Volkswohl*, xxii (April 1931), 247.

[183] Cf. *Neue Freie Presse*, November 26, 1928, and December 13, 1928, morning eds.; *Salzburger Nachrichten*, December 13, 1928, *Sten. Prot.*, 77./78. *Sitzungen*, III.G.P., January 22-23, 1929, pp. 2220, 2284ff.

Heimwehr itself, fear of the unreliable coalition partners that drove the Chancellor into the arms of the fascists. This meant that he lost the initiative in the conduct of affairs and was driven into statements and actions which tended to disavow his whole previous political course.

Seipel's "critique of democracy" and search for alternatives was necessarily ambiguous, prompted as it was by divided counsels. His central theme of "true democracy," which he launched about the time of the Wiener Neustadt scare and with which he sought to prepare the ground for a comprehensive change in the political climate, was accordingly so ambiguous as to be misleading.

Much ink has been spilled in the evaluation of Seipel's "true democracy." Gulick's equation that "true democracy equals estates state [the corporative state] equals fascism"[184] disposes too sweepingly of an extremely complex matter. On the other hand, the theory presented by the Viennese political scientist Adolf Merkl that "Seipel has more and more criticized the *reality* of democracy, but has consistently opposed to it the genuine *idea* of democracy as his political ideal"[185] takes too little account of Seipel's semantic deception. There is no doubt that in the course of his public career the "autocratic component," as E. K. Winter aptly put it,[186] had gradually gained the upper hand over the "democratic" one, and that he responded to the political chaos in his country with an increased scepticism, and even hostility, toward democracy.[187]

Semantic deception was inherent in Seipel's usage of the dis-

[184] Gulick, *Austria*, II, 835.

[185] Adolf Merkl, "Seipel und die Demokratie," *Der österreichische Volkswirt*, xxv, August 12, 1933, 1107; italics in original.

[186] Winter, *Seipel*, p. 110.

[187] Cf. A. M. Knoll's somewhat mechanical distinction between a "leftist" course of Seipel's (since 1918), a "capitalistic" one (since 1922), and a "rightist" one (since 1927), in August Maria Knoll, "Ignaz Seipel," *Neue Österreichische Biographie ab 1815*, IX (Zurich, Leipzig, and Vienna, 1956), 113ff., passim.

tinction between the "true" or "ideal" and the "real," a distinction that had always directed his thinking. In fact, Seipel had always used the term "true democracy." It was the awareness that the "perfect democracy" existed only "in heaven"[188] that had allowed Seipel to follow the liberating path prescribed by Leo XIII and to "accommodate" himself to an imperfect world. Now, however, under pressure of the political crisis, the tenuous relationship between the "ideal" and the "real" threatened to break down, and the Leonine experiment seemed compromised. In his mind the discredited reality gave way more and more to a vision of a perfect democracy which, brought down from heaven so to speak, threatened to substitute for democracy a model that was wholly alien to it.

It must be recalled that the two major public addresses which Seipel dedicated to the "critique of democracy" were delivered in Germany in 1929[189] at a time when Germany itself was in the midst of its own crisis of parliamentarianism. In view of this, they are sober and restrained. Seipel's "affirmation of democracy"[190] is striking: "I for myself avow that there can and will be no better way of life in which man may conduct and administer public affairs than democracy, the true, properly understood democ-

[188] Ignaz Seipel, "Autorität Eigentun und Familie" (Vienna, March 9, 1924), *Im Dienste des Wortes*, p. 139.

[189] Ignaz Seipel, "Die Münchener Kritik der Demokratie" (address to the Catholic students of Munich, January 22, 1929), and "Die Tübinger Kritik der Demokratie" (address to the Catholic students of Tübingen, July 16, 1929), *Kampf*, pp. 167ff. Notice that at the time of the second address Seipel was no longer in office. The volume in which they were reprinted (Seipel, *Kampf*) was dedicated to the memory of Jodok Fink, "the great patriot and democrat."

[190] "Bekenntnis zur Demokratie," Seipel, *Kampf*, p. 178; compare the address delivered in the same auditorium in Munich some two years earlier by Seipel's compatriot Hugo von Hofmannsthal, whose poetic vision of a conservative revolution by contrast, encouraged the extremist tendencies among the students.

racy."[191] Much as he was impressed by the workings of democracy in the New World, he betrayed a justified skepticism concerning preparedness of his country for democracy. Austria had drifted into a parliamentary "sham democracy," or "pseudodemocracy,"[192] in which the role of the people was repressed by the role of party oligarchies and in which party loyalties had taken precedence over loyalty to the country. This situation he set out to remedy.

As a major implementation of his general ideas and in response to pressure from the Heimwehr, Seipel launched a campaign for constitutional reform. He had been one of the fathers of the constitution,[193] which, based on Kelsen's "pure theory of law," had furnished a mere formal framework to bind a pluralistic society, a framework that could work as long as there existed in the state of Austria a basic consensus and a general willingness to compromise. The consensus had eroded, and with it the will to compromise. The election of October 1920 had brought about a domestic "shift of power," as Kelsen himself later interpreted it,[194] with the executive, now in the hands of the non-Marxist parties, eager to expand its prerogatives at the expense of the cumbersome legislature.

The movement toward reform of the constitution, which had been spearheaded in 1922 by the Christian Socialist Wilhelm Miklas,[195] gained renewed momentum both within and outside

[191] Ibid., p. 168.

[192] "Scheindemokratie," *Reichspost*, November 28, 1928, ibid., p. 123; "Pseudodemokratie," Ignaz Seipel, "Die Zeit der Reformarbeit" (Graz, February 4, 1929), ibid., 151.

[193] For Seipel's original reservations, see Seipel, *Kampf*, pp. 95f.

[194] *Neue Freie Presse*, October 6, 1929, morning ed.

[195] Cf. Seipel, *Kampf*, pp. 264ff.; Brita Skottsberg, *Der österreichische Parlamentarismus* (Göteborg, 1940), pp. 351ff.; initially Seipel was skeptical towards Miklas's move, lest it be interpreted as a sign of weakness in the Christian Socialist party. It is hard to overlook the possibility that Seipel's reversal may have been motivated by immediate and very down-to-earth

Parliament after the July uprising. The Chancellor himself took the occasion of the tenth anniversary of the Republic to enter formally into the argument. At the official reception of the cabinet by President Hainisch on November 12, 1928, Seipel suggested, after a pointed reference to the sharp proliferation in the constitution of parliamentary democracy, the "necessity and advisability of future *constitutional reforms*."[196] He thus took a stand on which all political parties, including even the Socialists, could agree at that time.[197] All more or less accepted the fact that Parliament as it was set up was not workable. They were also more or less forced to agree, in view of the past years, that the gap between democratic ideal and reality could not be closed by means of the old constitution. Seipel's initiative was thus founded, at least, on a consensus of failure.

The immediate issue on Seipel's mind was the position of the president. This was a pressing matter, since President Hainisch's final term of office was almost over. But Seipel personally was not wholly disinterested on the issue. Since he was mentioned increasingly often as a candidate, he clearly could not see himself as a mere figurehead. Thus, when the party leaders met on November 13, Seipel seized the occasion to take concrete steps toward broadening the presidential powers "according to the example of the German constitution."[198] In accordance with the demands of the three coalition partners, he proposed election of the federal president by popular election rather than by the combined Chambers of Parliament (*Bundesversammlung*), and a

---

considerations. In January 1922, when Miklas first raised the issue of reform, Seipel may have hesitated to strengthen Schober's position. Seipel's backing of Miklas's motion goes back to the time (June 1922) when he had just assumed the chancellorship.

[196] Ignaz Seipel, "Zum zehnjährigen Bestand der Republik" (November 12, 1928), *Kampf*, p. 116; italics in original.

[197] Cf. Macdonald, *Austria*, pp. 49ff.

[198] *Reichspost*, November 14, 1928; Ignaz Seipel, "Der Vorschlag anlässlich der Bundespräsidentenwahl 1928," *Kampf*, p. 121.

strengthening of his prerogatives by conferring on him the right to appoint (and to dismiss)[199] the government and to dissolve the Nationalrat. The Chancellor added cautiously that the government would still have to be responsible to the Nationalrat.

But Seipel's plan was foiled by the Socialists. Popular election, they now argued with an almost self-incriminating irony, was bound to lead to "Caesarean policy."[200] In the course of the electioneering in the Bundesversammlung, with which the parties had to proceed after all, the Christian Socialist Wilhelm Miklas defeated Schober by a vote of 94 to 26. The Socialists, unwilling to back Schober for his role in the July days, abstained from voting in a surprise move designed chiefly to forestall an imminent Seipel candidature.[201] Naturally the outcome of the presidential election was a setback for Seipel both in terms of his long-range plans and his immediate ambitions.

All the other reform proposals outlined by Seipel were accompanied by cautionary notes. While he favored a plebiscitarian presidency, he advised against too precipitate a reduction of parliamentary democracy in favor of direct democracy. "The times are such that otherwise the people could get the taste for a much more radical reduction of pure parliamentarianism."[202] The po-

[199] Unsigned, undated draft, "Verfassungsreform," typewritten with handwritten annotations by Seipel; Seipel Archive. The date most likely goes back to the late months of 1927.

[200] Seipel, *Kampf*, p. 122.

[201] A.V.A. 92. Sitzung V.A.G.V., December 5, 1928; cf. 89. Sitzung, November 30, 1928.

[202] *Sten. Prot.*, 75. Sitzung, *III.G.P.*, January 18, 1929, p. 2131; cf. Seipel, *Kampf*, p. 140. This statement was made in reaction to Otto Bauer's defense of his party's motion for an extension of the constitutional provisions for the popular referendum (cf. *Sten. Prot.*, 74. Sitzung, *III.G.P.*, January 17, 1929, p. 2104). Seipel then combined his "great satisfaction" over the Socialists' interest in the extension of "direct democracy" with a distinct caution. Cf. also Seipel's warning against a too extensive use of the popular referendum and the dangers connected with the flight from indirect to direct democracy; Seipel, "Die Münchener Kritik der Demokratie," *Kampf*, pp. 171f.

litical parties, then, were not to dominate Parliament.[203] Nevertheless they remained "very necessary instruments of democracy" since they were the only means by which a "freely elected representation of the people could express themselves."[204]

Seipel resisted proposals circulating at the time to tamper with universal equal suffrage and to replace it by giving special weight to family heads or to academicians.[205] Since suffrage had been gradually expanded in Austria during the past fifty years, Seipel stressed in particular, "One would be mistaken to believe that the wheel could be turned back without danger." Thus rejecting the reactionary solution, he spoke the language of the conservative, urging that "mankind must be educated to become mature enough for the proper use of democracy."[206]

In a similar way Seipel was cautious, indeed reluctant, to inject the issue of the corporative state into the debate over constitutional reform. Corporative theories have always occupied a central place in Catholic social thought. But under the influence of Vogelsang they had come to serve as an argument against the modern secular state, which had deprived man of his organic ties with his "estate," and in which, through parliamentary institutions, the capitalist class held sway over an atomized, disinherited proletariat. Christian ethics then called for a restoration of the original, natural unity between the individual and the whole and between society and the state, and for replacement of the modern atomistic state by the organic state, of parliamentarianism by corporative organization, of capitalism and class warfare by a regained solidarity between capital and labor. With Vogelsang's corporatism feeding into integralism and into rejection of the modern society and the secular state, Seipel was bound to stay shy of it. If therefore he resorted to the corporative argument, he did so, initially at least, not to establish a rigid alterna-

---

[203] Seipel, "Verfassungsreform."
[204] Seipel, "Die Münchener Kritik," *Kampf*, p. 171.
[205] Seipel, "Die Tübinger Kritik," *Kampf*, p. 182.
[206] Seipel, "Die Münchener Kritik," *Kampf*, p. 172.

tive to modern democracy, but to improve upon it, bring it into line with Christian ethics, and facilitate the accommodation of the Church to a changing world that was no longer uniformly Christian.[207]

Seipel never quite overcame basic doubts concerning the "vagueness"[208] of the corporate idea, as he put it; it was the specific occasion of a debate in the Nationalrat[209] which precipitated

[207] For a systematic though not exhaustive treatment of Seipel and corporatism, see Emmerich Prettenhofer, "Der 'Ständestaat': Nach den Ideen des Altbundeskanzlers Seipel," *Soziale Revue*, xxx (June 1930), 301-308, and Prettenhofer, "Der Werdegang der Ständestaatsidee bei Seipel," *Der christliche Ständestaat*, I, January 14, 1934, 10-13; cf. also Diamant, *Austrian Catholics*, pp. 189ff. Already in Seipel's imperial reform plan of 1917 there were traces of corporative thinking (Ignaz Seipel, "Gedanken zur Reform der österreichischen Verfassung 1917," *Kampf*, p. 25). Immediately after the revolution, Seipel had stated in one of his *Reichspost* articles his preference for the "organic" over the "atomistic" concept of state and raised the issue of corporative representation alongside political representation; Ignaz Seipel, "Die demokratische Verfassung" (November 20, 1918), *Kampf*, p. 58ff. The first constitutional draft of the Christian Socialist party of May 19, 1919, had contained provisions for a corporate representation; Skottsberg, *Der österreichische Parlamentarismus*, pp. 189f., 204.

Throughout the twenties the issue of corporatism remained in abeyance. The Christian Socialist party under Seipel's leadership had become committed to parliamentarianism. In the course of a parliamentary debate in December 1926 Seipel maintained that, compared with parliamentarism, corporative representation could make it much more difficult for the representatives to transcend special interests and act in the interest of the whole (*Sten. Prot., 168. Sitzung, II.G.P.*, December 10, 1926, p. 4050). The Christian Socialist program of 1926, apart from a general reference to all estates as "equal members of the *Volksgemeinschaft*," omitted direct references to a corporative order. Richard Schmitz in his commentary dismissed the concept of the corporative state as misleading; *Das christlichsoziale Programm*, pp. 7, 30.

[208] Seipel, *Kampf*, p. 142, n. 1.

[209] Following Bauer's attacks on the government's policy of "conventicles," according to which decisions were made outside Parliament in secret negotiations between ministers, parties, and interest groups (*Sten. Prot., 74. Sitzung, III.G.P.*, January 17, 1929, p. 2105), Seipel was prompted to re-

287

his change of opinion and made him seek actively to realize corporatism, but he never became doctrinaire on the matter. He was much too sober and realistic a man not to envisage the possibility that party struggles would originate within the estates or that the estates themselves would become parties.[210] Shortly after his resignation, Seipel presented the issue of corporatism to his countrymen in an anonymous *Reichspost* article,[211] proposing a Federal Council (*Bundesrat*), which was to be transformed into a Council of Länder and Estates (*Länder-und-Ständerat*) and to work alongside the existing Nationalrat. The survival of parliamentarianism, in the last analysis, was imperative in Seipel's view as a protection against an excess of presidential power as well as against mass rule, and also as a means of keeping political and class conflict out of the new Chamber.

Once all this has been said, it must be added that Seipel carried his share of responsibility for undermining his own carefully balanced structure. It was somewhat alarming that in 1929 he alluded repeatedly to "dictatorship" as a way out of crisis. He referred elsewhere to the "crises of democracy," in which democracy had to be "put aside" at least for restricted periods, and to the possibility, if not the necessity, for a dictator who would take over "without mandate," and safeguard the interests of the *res publica* relying on his "authority."[212] In itself a call for dictatorship was not necessarily antidemocratic in tendency. Emergency dictatorship, such as the one provided for in Germany's Article 48, has at all times been accepted as a legitimate temporary expedient of democratic polity, and in the case of Austria the absence of such an expedient made the call for it all the more vociferous. However, the political impact of Seipel's references

---

consider his own position on corporate institutions and actively explore their introduction (Seipel, *Kampf*, p. 142).

[210] Seipel, "Die Tübinger Kritik," *Kampf*, p. 184.

[211] "Von akademischer Seite," "Was sind 'Stände'?" *Reichspost*, October 19, 1929, *Kampf*, pp. 199ff.

[212] Ibid., pp. 174, 179.

to dictatorship was inevitably more far-reaching. In the context of the breakdown of democratic systems all over eastern[213] and southern Europe and the internal argument that raged in Germany over the issue of dictatorship and democracy, they inevitably gave encouragement in Austria to those forces, in particular the Heimwehr, for which dictatorship was not a merely temporary expedient.

But the most clear-cut indication of Seipel's break with his own past finally came neither from a single political move nor from an occasional policy statement but from the perfection of his "semantic deception," which allowed him to identify the Heimwehr with his cherished "true democracy" and his own domestic struggle with "true peace."[214] In his Tübingen "Critique of Democracy" he finally came out with his most sweeping public endorsement of the Heimwehr as a "people's movement" intent upon liberating democracy from party rule. He defended its militancy as serving not militarism but discipline, and its unruliness as being defensive against "undemocratic party rule." On these premises, then, Seipel based his altogether misleading conclusion: "I believe in the future of democracy in Austria, as long as it wants to be and will be a true democracy."[215]

The increasing emphasis which Seipel gave after the July events of 1927 to the concept of "true democracy" suggests how far he had moved away from his initial casual and accommodative position. Previously he had, in a more or less offhand way, given expression to his vision of a "true," "perfect," "higher" order of things. But the dominant note of his political thought and action had been not a Christian perfectionism precisely, but

[213] Even Bolshevik Russia appeared to Seipel as part of the wave of the future. It represented, as Seipel once put it, an attempt to overcome democracy ("um aus der Demokratie und über die Demokratie hinauszukommen"); Ignaz Seipel, "Die grosse Linie der geistigen Entwicklung unserer Zeit" (January 5, 1924), Gessl, *Reden*, p. 91.

[214] Cf. Ignaz Seipel, "Der Ruf nach echter Demokratie" (Graz, December 18, 1928), *Kampf*, pp. 133, 135.

[215] Seipel, "Die Tübinger Kritik der Demokratie," *Kampf*, p. 188.

a Christian latitudinarianism; not defensiveness and rigidity, but a confident and bold venture into a society which was no longer predominantly Christian; not fanaticism but moderation. His whole scholarly career had served as a preparation for the conciliatory and accommodative course which he had followed at the time of his striking entry into politics during the last phase of the Monarchy and the early years of the Republic. If he had drifted increasingly to the Right since the breakup of the coalition in 1920 and after the futile parliamentary debates in 1922, this was merely another form of the same policy. Accommodation to the Left gave way to accommodation to the Right; a socialist course gave way to a capitalistic one. In both phases, though, Seipel was in search of a policy which would allow the country to govern itself effectively, while protecting the essential interests of the Church. Even after 1927, when Seipel had become convinced of the fact that no *modus vivendi* with the opposition could be found within the framework of parliamentary rule such as it existed in Austria, even after he had turned fiercely against the Socialists, he remained strikingly explorative, open-minded, and flexible in formulating alternatives for parliamentary rule. He was, after all, carried by a general agreement, which even extended into the ranks of the Social Democrats, that some change in the constitutional structure of the country was imperative. In many ways the proposals which he launched in 1928 and 1929 were marked, as we have seen, by caution, moderation, and a distinct emphasis on the need for checks and balances, and furthermore in most instances they were guided by the example of the Weimar Constitution. Even Seipel's concept of dictatorship can be defended on the grounds that it was not meant to burst the confines of democracy. Seipel's "critique of democracy" was in many ways explorative and constructive.

Paradoxically, it was Seipel's concentration on "true democracy" that led him away from his earlier explorative path. It spelled the end of his accommodative position. The Aristotelian element in Seipel disappeared behind the Platonic one, the

290

Thomistic behind the Augustinian one. The Leonine tradition had after all not proven feasible in Austria.

Bitter, disillusioned, unwilling to function any longer within the confines of the secular state, Seipel retreated more and more to his ideal world. But what the priest should have known, the statesman in this instance chose to ignore, namely that there is no perfect society on earth, that any perfect society, by its very nature, is worse than the imperfect one, that the perfect society is potentially total, whereas the imperfect one, through trial and error, is potentially improvable and bearable. It was by ignoring these realities that Seipel was able to bring himself to settle for the Heimwehr, an "ideal order" that was blatantly fascist in character.[216] Strange it was to hear now from the democratic churchman accusations against the "system" which he himself had helped to found, from the pacifist an apology for "paramilitary discipline."[217] This was the terminology of antidemocrats. How far had Seipel traveled since he entered politics in 1918! When he now said democracy he meant, indeed, fascism; when he now said peace he meant war. This casuistry was not simple jesuitry, as Seipel's foes had always maintained. It was despair over his imperfect world—a very imperfect one indeed—which drove Seipel to retreat to an even worse alternative. About the time when Seipel handed in his resignation as Chancellor in April 1929, of which more will be said at the end of the next chapter, Josef Redlich, after a visit with his old friend, wrote the following

[216] Cf. E. K. Winter's suggestion that Seipel parted company with Kelsen and his "pure theory of law" to move closer toward the German political theorist Carl Schmitt, who, in reaction against legal positivism and its pluralistic tendencies, turned toward a value system that was primarily derived from responsibility of the leader, and also toward Rudolf Smend and his theory of integration; Winter, *Seipel*, pp. 115, 119f. Winter's question whether Seipel was familiar with Schmitt's work can be answered in the affirmative; at least in his notes for a second edition of *Nation und Staat* there is a reference to Carl Schmitt's work as "one-sided but deep"; Kurt Adamus, "Die Theorie Ignaz Seipels" (diss., Graz, 1952), p. 65.

[217] Seipel, *Kampf*, p. 188.

notation into his diary: "The days until June 20 went by quickly. I had a talk with Seipel, who for the moment was wholly taken up with his plans to force the bourgeois parties to an act of aggression [?] against the Social Democracy. But I found him just as ambiguous as he has always been on his objective. On the whole he made a disagreeable impression on me."[218]

[218] Redlich diary, September 14, 1929, "Politische Tagebuchnotizen." There is some doubt about the word "aggression.'" The diary entry is the first one since August 6, 1927.

IN SEARCH OF A DIPLOMACY FOR CENTRAL EUROPE: 1923-1929

After Geneva

FOR SEIPEL, politics, foreign as well as domestic, meant maintaining a careful balance between long-range objectives and concessions to the needs of the moment, between ideas and expedience, between the heart and the head. *Hic Rhodus, hic salta* was the device not of a Machiavellian, nor of an unprincipled opportunist, but of a statesman securely rooted in his faith; it allowed him to adjust to what he called the facts, or a broad range of realities which were all part of a divine pattern and could, at least, be made serviceable to it. Theory and action, principle and flexibility thus went hand in hand with Seipel, the priestly statesman.

In foreign as in domestic affairs Seipel followed a course of accommodation to the realities of the postwar situation. To describe him as "in his inner heart a man of the *ancien régime*" may have been accurate,[1] but it was somewhat misleading to suggest that the reconstruction of the old order was the Austrian Chancellor's "ultimate political ideal." In no way was he committed to a narrow understanding of legitimacy. While Seipel himself liked to distinguish between his emotional attachment and his realistic assessment of politics as the art of the possible,[2] he did not allow the "heart" to get the better of the demands of expedience. In fact

[1] Report by the German Minister to Budapest Prince Viktor zu Wied, Budapest, February 25, 1923; A.A., Abt.II, Geheim, Ö.: Po.2, Bd.1.

[2] Cf. Seipel, "Die zweite Regierungserklärung," in Josef Gessl, *Seipels Reden in Österreich und anderwärts* (Vienna, 1926), p. 78; also Seipel to Bishop Wenzel Frind, August 16, 1928, Franz Lorenz, "Weihbischof Dr. W. Frind und Prälat Dr. I. Seipel," *Schönere Zukunft*, VIII, January 29, 1933, 399f.

A Diplomacy for Central Europe

Seipel's feeling that the Austrian Germans may have "gambled away" their "mission" in Central Europe[3] goes back to his critical assessment of the last half century of monarchic policies. His ideal model was not strictly speaking the old Monarchy, but the sort of Central European order he had outlined in *Nation und Staat*, which allowed the different nationalities to share the benefits of a common political and economic unit. The tension within Seipel between the heart and expediency was defined by his vision of a Central European commonwealth and the order dictated by the Treaty of St. Germain. The former, while not excluding the possibility of a "resurrected Monarchy" or some "Central European empire," as Seipel once admitted to one of his trusted lieutenants,[4] allowed for a whole range of alternatives. Among these Seipel doubtlessly would have preferred a Greater Austria in the tradition of Prince Schwarzenberg, or some variation in the form of a Greater Germany with a strong Austrian and Catholic accent. On the other hand, the close ties which he kept with the neighboring Succession States, in particular Czechoslovakia, demonstrated his keen vigilance over new approaches to Central European unity. If political reintegration seemed out of the question, Seipel spoke of some form of economic union. Furthermore, he thought that he could advance his plan for Central European cooperation through a League policy as well as by actively supporting Count Richard Coudenhove-Kalergi's Pan-European movement.

Seipel's accommodation, on the other hand, meant accepting Austria's smallness, insignificance, and *de facto* neutrality; he had little choice, as he demonstrated in the late summer months of 1922, but to follow a policy of fulfillment. In an ironical and al-

[3] Seipel to Frind, August 16, 1928; cf. Paul Sweet, "Seipel's Views on Anschluss," *Journal of Modern History*, xix (December 1947), 322.

[4] Seipel to the Austrian Minister to the League of Nations, Emmerich von Pflügl, December 26, 1927, St.A., Völkerbund, Innere Organisation, K.162, Fs. 208-211.

most absurd sense even the dismembered Austria could be fitted into the framework of Seipel's premises as laid down in *Nation und Staat*. While he still believed in the ideal of various nationalities under one political roof, he was now confronted with the very different fact of a New Europe, which turned out to be a *Europa irredenta* with troublesome minority problems. But there was a certain resemblance between prewar and postwar Central Europe: the old Monarchy had at its best been a Christian commonwealth; the whole new order established by the Treaties, from the very day of its inception, called for some comparable supranational bond. The new Central European order was faced, Seipel saw, with the same need as the old one. Thus the new order, largely through its inadequacies, reaffirmed his belief in Central Europe as a "living unit in the consciousness of the European peoples" and spelled out the "justification" and the "necessity" of "coping with the Central European problem."[5] Accommodation was Seipel's way of overcoming an unwelcome situation in foreign affairs:

It is imperative that we be concerned with the reorganization of Europe, the past one as well as the coming one. We must at some point acknowledge the past reorganization of Europe and assess its whole import. Only thus can we make *Realpolitik*. . . . It would be sheer illusionism if we remained committed to an outdated past at a time when the world has changed, or if we followed a policy based on the assumption that the desired aim for the future had already been reached. It is a different matter, though, to examine the changes brought about by the World War for their durability and to envisage the possibility of new changes in order to proceed at the proper moment from a passive policy of accommodation to the realities to an active political involve-

[5] Ignaz Seipel's speech at the Mitteleuropäische Verkehrstagung, *Neue Freie Presse*, October 2, 1926, evening ed.

ment—largely by the means of ideas—in the reorganization of Europe[6]

Geneva was a fruit of *Realpolitik* as Seipel defined it, superseding the two alternatives, Anschluss or Danubian confederation, which, Seipel knew, were blocked.[7] But in Seipel's mind the Geneva Protocol did not permanently settle the question of Austria's independence. Independence as such was not his ultimate objective. Austrians, he emphasized, are "big-state people,"[8] unwilling to cultivate a narrow Austrian national consciousness. "To cultivate our own little garden and to show it to foreigners in order to make money out of it are no proper tasks for the inhabitants of the Carolingian Ostmark and the heirs to the conquerors of the Turks."[9] Geneva, with its guaranty of Austrian independence, merely substituted a policy of realism for a policy of illusion. It prevented the immediate danger of Austria's being partitioned; it allowed Austria to assert, as Seipel once put it, that it was "here to stay."[10] For the rest, however, it was only a begin-

[6] Ignaz Seipel, "Die Neugestaltung Europas," Cologne, March 2, 1925, Gessl, *Reden,* p. 178.

[7] *Verrammelt;* Strictly Confidential "Darstellung der ersten Besprechung des Herrn Bundeskanzlers in meiner Anwesenheit [Grünberger] mit dem Herrn ungarischen Ministerpräsidenten Grafen Bethlen und dem Minister des Äusseren [von] Daruváry in Budapest am 7. Jänner 1923," St.A., Liasse Ungarn I/III, K.879, F.243; cf. "Aufzeichnung des Bundesministers Grünberger über die in seiner Gegenwart erfolgte politische Aussprache des Bundeskanzlers Seipel und des Grafen Bethlen," n.d., A.A., Abt.II Geheim-Ö.: Po.2, Bd.1.

[8] Seipel to Dr. W. Bauer, July 30, 1928, Sweet "Seipel's Views on Anschluss," *Journal of Modern History,* xix (December 1947), 323. The German copy of Seipel's letter to Dr. Bauer (ad Z.23808/13) is in St.A., Liasse Deutschland I/1, Geheim, K.465. It undoubtedly represents one of the most authoritative statements by Seipel on the Anschluss. Seipel's letter on the same subject to Professor Blümelhuber (cf. below p. 299n.), by contrast, has been conceptualized for him by Norbert Bischoff.

[9] Ibid.

[10] "Immer weider betonen, dass man auf der Welt ist," Strictly Confidential "Darstellung der ersten Besprechung."

ning. Independence was not, as the Chancellor once privately explained, a device of "slamming a door through which some day could lead the road to a freer and greater future."[11] It would enable Seipel to step from the role of Chancellor of defeat into that of guide into this future.

The course of Seipel's foreign policy after Geneva was hardly less intricate than it had been before. It has been described as a "policy of nonpolicy,"[12] which amounted to no foreign policy at all.[13] Naturally Austria's continued impotence and confirmed dependence upon the powers made it imperative for her to follow a pacific path, to build up economic ties and to cultivate friendly relations with all other powers. Seipel thus committed his little country to active support of the League, which he visualized as a substitute for all power groups and alliance systems,[14] and to an elaborate network of arbitration treaties and trade agreements.

If beyond this policy Seipel did not immediately take the initiative with a broadly outlined Central European offensive, it was not because he lacked distinct vision, but simply because the time was not ripe. What was needed was not a blueprint emanating from defeated Austria but a cautious vigilance over the new post–St. Germain policentric international scene. In the midst of the pressures exerted from Paris and Prague, from Berlin, Rome, and Budapest and, last but not the least, from the Socialist opposition as well as the Pan-German coalition partners at home, Seipel's studied noncommitment was a policy in itself. He kept puzzling and confusing the foreign offices and public opinion generally about his intentions. The tactics which he employed on

[11] Copy of letter Z.21953/13, Seipel to Professor Blümelhuber, Vienna, May 1929, St.A., Liasse Deutschland I/1, Geheim, K.465.

[12] "Politik der Politiklosigkeit," Report by German Minister to Budapest, Budapest, February 25, 1923, A.A., Abt.II Geheim-Ö.: Po.2, Bd.1.

[13] Cf. Walter Goldinger in Heinrich Benedikt, ed., *Geschichte der Republik Österreich* (Vienna, 1954), p. 167.

[14] Cf. Seipel "Die Neugestaltung Europas," Gessl, *Reden*, p. 183.

the way to victory in Geneva now became his all-embracing strategy. Carefully placed interviews with the international press—always eager to decipher his thoughts—carefully phrased and often deliberately ambiguous professorial lectures in Austria and abroad, carefully planned trips to foreign capitals, all were designed to augment the stature of Austria and at the same time to sow confusion and mutual distrust abroad. While Seipel's "political tourism"[15] in the year following Geneva, which took him to Budapest, Belgrade, Rome, and Warsaw, served to foster good political and economic relations, it also had its disquieting purpose. In a masterful analysis of Seipel's intentions, the semiofficial Czechoslovak journal *Zahraniční Politika*, following Seipel's Warsaw visit, paid tribute to the Chancellor's unusual "agility, initiative, and activity." "The clever Seipel belongs to those who know how to seize the right psychological moment in order to reap the most gain." But the journal could not help voicing fears lest Austria enter unilateral agreements designed to upset the tenuous Central European balance. "Seipel in a masterful way knows how to take advantage of those fears and to add to the desirability of Austria; he has created out of a minor state a political and economic force of great significance in Central Europe."[16] It may not be quite fair to characterize Seipel's foreign policy as "typically scholastic" in its duplicity and indecision, parallel to the Leonine "pastoral accommodation."[17] Still, he did play a sphinx-like role in his conduct of foreign affairs. A "calculated indifference" toward the "various alternatives"[18] allowed Austria to withstand pressures from its neighbors, to "keep itself free" for a future in

[15] Term is taken from Rudolf Olden, "Österreichische Köpfe; Ignaz Seipel," *Die Weltbühne*, XXI, February 3, 1925, 163.

[16] Eduard Parma, "Rakousko [Viděn-Varšav] *Zahraniční Politika*, September 25, 1923, pp. 1205ff.

[17] "Dieses echt scholastische Sowohl-als-auch"; E. K. Winter, *Ignaz Seipel als dialektisches Problem* (Vienna, Frankfurt, and Zurich, 1966), p. 152; cf. p. 65.

[18] Seipel, "Das wahre Antlitz Österreichs," Vienna, February 11, 1926, Gessl, *Reden*, p. 296.

which it could with renewed vigor actively shape Central European affairs. While no one in the European foreign offices who watched Austria's course could really understand Seipel or trust him, there was general agreement that he was one of the most capable statesmen in Europe and that his importance was much greater than his country's modest size would seem to warrant.

Seipel and the Anschluss Question

In spite of St. Germain, in spite of the Geneva accords, the Anschluss question was Austria's chief preoccupation. Affecting the relationship between the two German states, it was an emotion-filled issue which pervaded all aspects of Austrian life—cultural, economic, political—and which dictated almost every move in domestic as well as in foreign policy. Its supporters, who were by far the majority in Austria, maintained that it should receive nothing less than wholehearted endorsement; its foes, particularly those in the Quai d'Orsay and its satellite foreign offices, would accept nothing less than an unreserved rejection. To the former it appeared as the only road to salvation for the Austrian Republic, which was not viable alone and therefore destined to merge with the German Reich; to the latter it conjured up a specter of Pan-German annexation, destruction of the Austrian identity, and a threat to the European balance of power as established by the Paris Treaties.

Toward this question, which provoked so much partisan passion in all quarters, Chancellor Seipel's attitude remained complex and enigmatic. The man who had signed the Geneva Protocols talked a great deal and compulsively about the Anschluss, without speaking either for it or against it. This question was the first and chief issue to which Seipel applied his studied "one never knows" approach.[19]

It is not surprising, then, that Seipel's Anschluss policy should have invited the most diverse interpretations, and also distrust,

[19] Seipel, "Das wahre Antlitz Österreichs," Gessl, *Reden*, p. 296.

from almost all quarters. While many saw in his policies a design to avert an Anschluss[20] and others thought they could detect a complicated scheme leading toward it,[21] nearly all agreed that, whatever the Chancellor's intentions, he was dark and ambiguous and impenetrable. His Anschluss policy, though often praised for its caution, was suspected both in the Wilhelmstrasse and at the Quai d'Orsay, to be a *double jeu*.

Anyone taking the trouble to study *Nation und Staat* and Seipel's major addresses on the subject[22] could detect a distinct line, even though not a straight one, in his Anschluss policy, and find much less mystery and ambiguity than some thought. Even though some of the reservations about union with Germany voiced by Seipel in the period immediately following the war had lost substance, since Germany had not succumbed to a "socialist dictatorship," there were deeper reasons, indeed reasons of prin-

[20] In this interpretation of Seipel's course the Social Democrats were vigorously seconded by *Der österreichische Volkswirt* (cf. Franz Klein, "Wohin," *Der österreichische Volkswirt*, XXI, August 10, 1929, 1205-1207, and by the same author, "Ignaz Seipel," ibid., XXIV, August 6, 1932, 1085-1086). They were also seconded by the standard pro-Anschluss publications in Germany (cf. Willy Andreas's comment on Seipel's "declared hostility to the Anschluss," "Österreich und der Anschluss," *Archiv für Politik und Geschichte*, VIII [1927], 590), and by National Socialist authors (such as Wilhelm Deutsch, "Die Anschlussbewegung 1918-1938," *Berliner Monatshafte*, XVI [October 1938], 916-927). A divergent Nazi view of Seipel is represented by Franz Riedl, who himself belonged to the nationalist, Germany-oriented group of Austrian Catholics, in *Kanzler Seipel: Ein Vorkämpfer volksdeutschen Denkens* (Saarbrücken, 1935); as the title of his work indicates, Riedl saw in Seipel a pioneer of *völkisch* thinking.

[21] Cf. the fine article by Barbara Ward, "Ignaz Seipel and the Anschluss," *Dublin Review*, CCIII (July–September 1938), 33-50, in particular 45f., which, however, is somewhat too heavily based in its conclusion on Riedl's work and Verax, "Monseigneur Seipel," *Revue des Deux Mondes*, XCIX (March 1929), 54-87, esp. 83-87.

[22] Cf., in particular, "Probleme des deutschen Staates" (Berlin 1926), "Das wahre Antlitz Österreichs" (Vienna 1926), "Österreich, wie es wirklich ist" (Paris 1926), in Gessl, *Reden*, pp. 286ff., 290ff., 312ff.

ciple, which impelled him to pursue a cautious and intricate course.

Like the Balkanization of Central Europe at large, the existence of the small Austrian state, totally different from the old supranational Empire, confirmed in an ironic way the continued relevance of Seipel's *Nation und Staat*. The new Austria, separated from the bulk of Germany as well as from the South Tyrol and Sudeten Germany, was in effect an "infranational state"[23] being part only of a greater national, that is German, unit. The nation and the state were just as distinct now as they had been in the old Monarchy. Austria could hardly allow the state boundaries, drawn up by the Treaty system, to become at the same time cultural boundaries. She had, Seipel emphasized, all the more reason to uphold the German concept of "nation" as opposed to state, in contradistinction to the French one.[24]

Seipel was able, then, to invoke Austria's ethnic and cultural kinship with Germany and at the same time to play down the desirability of the Anschluss. The more the Germans could communicate with each other across political borders, he argued, the less would they need political union. Indeed, in view of the fact that Seipel's ultimate goal was a supranational organization, political union was not even desirable.[25] The Wilsonian principle of political self-determination, which the German world in its postwar diaspora claimed for itself, was not, for Seipel, the highest principle of political association, since it led to nationalism. He therefore held out for higher alternatives, and the settlement at St. Germain, restrictive as it was, forced the Germans to seek ties with each other that were "much higher," as he once put it, than merely political ones.[26] At the same time it allowed the Austrian Germans to keep themselves free for their higher calling.

[23] Ward, "Ignaz Seipel," 42.
[24] Cf. Seipel, "Österreich, wie es wirklich ist," p. 323.
[25] Seipel, "Das wahre Antlitz Österreichs," p. 296.
[26] Ignaz Seipel, Österreich und Deutschland," *Neue Freie Presse*, June 9, 1928, evening ed.

A Diplomacy for Central Europe

When Seipel himself raised the issue of the Anschluss, as he did frequently, it was for carefully calculated reasons. First and foremost he did so to impress upon the Germans as well as upon his Pan-German coalition partners the distinction between Anschluss and "annexationism."[27] Austria, he argued, was not to serve as a substitute for Germany's lost provinces nor did it want to be an object of the Germans' "patronizing" pity.[28] Reasonable though he was in hoping that Austria would someday make her own decisions from a position of strength, avoiding the predominance of Berlin over Vienna, he was quixotic in letting it be understood that, in his books, Anschluss meant ideally a union of Germans around Catholic Austria.

While he missed no opportunity to warn against a policy of threats, as he identified Renner's past policies,[29] as well as against a futile "policy of demonstration" for union with Germany,[30] he reserved the right to use the threat at his own discretion. When he was out of office in 1925 and on a Swiss lecture trip, he dropped hints to the foreign press, designed for consumption by the Quai d'Orsay, to the effect that more than 90 percent of the Austrian populace would, if asked, vote for an Anschluss; and at carefully calculated moments he launched releases to the press which kept the Anschluss possibility alive at least through the machinery of the League of Nations. Stretching the terms of

[27] Ignaz Seipel, "Das wahre Antlitz Österreichs," p. 293; cf. also "Dr. Seipel über die Anschlussfrage," *Neue Freie Presse*, February 5, 1926, morning ed.

[28] "Dr. Seipel über die Anschlussfrage."

[29] Seipel's statement as reported by Leopold Waber, A.V.A., 4. Sitzung V.A.G.V., May 17, 1927.

[30] *Neue Freie Presse*, February 5, 1926, morning ed. Cf. "Dr. Seipel über den Anschluss," *Reichspost*, July 5, 1925; Seipel before the budget committee of the Nationalrat, *Reichspost*, December 2, 1926; and Seipel to Dr. Wilhelm Bauer, Sweet, "Seipel's Views on Anschluss," *Journal of Modern History*, xix (December 1947), 322.

Article 80 of the Versailles treaty and Article 88 of the Treaty of St. Germain, he suggested that the treaties had actually provided for a peaceful procedure for realizing the union between the two German peoples.[31] One might say that by raising the Anschluss question in this peculiarly roundabout fashion Seipel merely introduced another element into his intricate policy of flexibility. At the same time, however, his public identification with the Anschluss issue, so clearly alien to his basic position, was a measure of his increasing despair over the future of Central Europe. Only when the search for all other alternatives was exhausted and Austria's higher calling was clearly lost, only when it had become evident that the European powers were unwilling or un-

---

[31] Seipel's interview to the Berlin *8-Uhr-Abendblatt*, February 4, 1926, as reproduced in *Le Temps*, February 6, 1926, caused, according to Austria's Minister in Paris, Alfred Grünberger, a "minor storm"; Report Z.7/P. (910) Grünberger to Generalsekretär (Franz Peter), Paris, February 18, 1926, St.A., Fasz 144, Deutschland I/III; cf. also "L'Autriche et l' 'Anschluss' " and "L'Ancien chancelier Seipel à Berlin," *Le Temps*, February 6, 1926. Seipel caused even more of a stir during the time when he represented Austria at the Assembly of the League of Nations in the late summer of 1928. He launched an inspired article, "L'Anschluss," in the *Journal de Genève* of September 18, 1928, signed W(illiam) M(artin), which was followed the next day by a lengthy article in the same newspaper by himself on the same subject under the column "La discussion générale." Paris reacted sharply. The Quai d'Orsay's Political Director Charles Corbin, who recognized in Seipel a "statesman of the first order," saw himself suddenly confronted by the full seriousness of the Anschluss; Grünberger to Seipel, 15/Pol. Z.7281, Paris, October 25, 1928, St.A., Fasz. 148, Deutschland I/1. *Le Temps*, commenting elaborately on Seipel's arguments, warned in conclusion that the Anschluss in any form "would mean war for all powers interested in the maintenance of the *status quo* in Central Europe"; "Les Idées de Mgr. Seipel," *Le Temps*, September 20, 1928. Cf. also the summary article, "La France et l'Anschluss," *Journal de Genève*, September 20, 1928. On the other side of the Atlantic, the *New York Times* mused in an editorial: "This was one of the few cases in history when the head of one state has publicly looked forward to the demise of its own government and its absorption by another power. Something of this sort happened to the Texas Republic"; *New York Times*, October 2, 1928.

able to grant satisfactory guarantees to the European minorities, including of course the Austrian minorities under foreign rule, was he prepared to scrap the premises of *Nation und Staat* and fall back on the unitary state as a political objective. The Anschluss, in short, was in Seipel's political strategy a "last resort."[32]

[32] The connection between the failure of other alternatives and the Anschluss had been frequently stated by Seipel, most explicitly in his already quoted Viennese address of 1926, "Das wahre Antlitz Österreichs":

> For us Germans the nation . . . , the great cultural community, is higher than the state. . . . Specifically this difference in our assessment of the conception of nation and state . . . gives us the opportunity to find our own way in the so much discussed question of the Anschluss of Austria to Germany. If we do not consider our life fulfilled in the creation of the unitary state, then we can somehow reconcile ourselves with living in a German state which is not part of the German Reich. That there is an advantage to having such a German state we recognize, especially in these times when we must witness that the other Germans, who belong to the Reich as little as we but live under other sovereignties, do not have the same national liberties as we do. If, however, only the Western concepts of nation and state are to prevail, then the German nation cannot help but aim at the German unitary state, the German national state. (Gessl, *Reden*, p. 295.)

Cf. also the memorandum sent out by the Secretary General of the Ballhausplatz Franz Peter to all Austrian chiefs of mission concerning the Chancellor's view on the Anschluss question at the time of the Schubert Festival (July 19-22, 1928), which turned out to be an impressive Anschluss demonstration. It stressed the importance of keeping apart the cultural and political union of Germans; the failure of the Treaty system to allow for a "larger unit" as an alternative to the Anschluss (though the sentence "in fact every counterweight is missing against the desire of the Austrians to be united with the Reich" was subsequently crossed out); the Peace Treaties as a device to bring about the Anschluss; and finally the boost which the "will toward the Anschluss" was getting from the unsatisfactory solution of the minority question in Central Europe, Z.23805/13, "Äusserungen des Bundeskanzlers gegenüber dem deutschen Gesandten über die Anschlussfrage. An alle Missionschefs und Genf," Vienna, August 13, 1928, St.A., Liasse Deutschland I/1, K.465.

Sibling Rivalry: Seipel and Stresemann

It stands to reason, then, that among Seipel's encounters with Central European statesmen the ones with his German counterparts should have been most difficult, for they were overshadowed by the clash between cultural ties and political calculations, between considerations of the heart and expediency. This condition indeed prevailed on both sides. It had, after all, affected the hurried and unsatisfactory meeting between Chancellors Wirth and Seipel in Berlin in August 1922. But each man had learned to understand the other's predicament and also to trust him. The Catholicism common to both had established a bond which did not again exist between Seipel and any other German statesman, whether Protestant or Catholic.[33] In fact, as relations visibly cooled between Vienna and Berlin during the twenties and early thirties, Wirth was repeatedly used as a go-between by the German Foreign Office and served as a sympathetic interpreter of Seipel's position.[34]

[33] It might be of interest to note at this point that Seipel had met Konrad Adenauer, then Lord Mayor of Cologne, while visiting the city in 1925 (Seipel diary, March 3, 1925) and had come away with a high opinion of the man who was later to be the German chancellor. During the following year, when rumors connecting Adenauer and Seipel in a separatist venture reached the Ballhausplatz, Seipel, not even bothering to defend himself, wrote the following striking lines about Adenauer: "I urge that Consul General [Clemens] Wildner [who had reported on this matter from Cologne] not meddle in these affairs. He should be very guarded and clever in his statements to the Lord Mayor Dr. Adenauer. *Dr. Adenauer is a very great man, and the future belongs to him.* Not for a long time will he commit himself to a definite formula. Whatever he does will be in the German interest. He will certainly not reveal to the Consul General his position on the question 'Prussia and the Rhineland' "; Letter Z.12147/13, Seipel to Secretary General Peter, Vienna, April 28, 1926; St.A., Liasse Österreich 19/48, K.402; italics mine.

[34] Wirth called on Seipel four times in Vienna, in May 1928 (cf. the elaborate report June 13, 1928, by Wirth, G.F.O., 2347/4576/E173471-173483; cf. A.A., St. S. [alt], "SO," Bd.8), late in November 1928 (op. cit., Bd.9), late in March or early in April 1929, shortly before Seipel's final

307

A Diplomacy for Central Europe

Between the Austrian Chancellor and the chief architect of Germany's postwar foreign policy, Gustav Stresemann, relations were more strained. It would not suffice to say that Stresemann, a product of the Protestant heart of Germany, had no understanding of the Austrian and his Catholic mentality. Stresemann shared the feelings of many Protestant Germans who looked at everything Austrian with mixed feelings, with both exasperation and affection. And while he was well aware of the unwelcome change in the religious balance which an addition of more than six million Catholic Austrians would bring to Germany, he also felt that Germany had become too "Americanized," that it had lost part of its "soul," which, he felt, might have been regained in Austria.[35] Actually, like Seipel, Stresemann was eminently conscious of the conflict within himself between what he called "political reality" and "emotional values."[36] He was a romanticist as well as a realist. Moreover, like Seipel, Stresemann was an exponent of the fulfillment policy who accepted the hard-and-fast realities created by war and defeat and aimed at overcoming them through a constructive policy of cooperation within the framework of the League. But there were other problems of German foreign policy that took priority over her relations with Austria, the most important being the evacuation of the Rhineland, a renegotiation of the Dawes Plan, the settlement (*Bereinigung*) of Germany's eastern problems, and finally the colonial issue. "Once these questions are taken care of, the time will have come to tackle the German-Austrian question."[37]

---

resignation as chancellor (ibid.), and finally early in April 1931 (cf. the elaborate report by Wirth, Rome, April 9, 1931, G.F.O., 1485/3086/D61532-615318).

[35] Gustav Stresemann, *His Diaries, Letters and Papers*, ed. and trans. Eric Sutton (London, 1940), III, 386.

[36] Ibid.

[37] Report Z.3/P., Felix Frank (Austrian Minister to Berlin) to Generalsekretär Franz Peter, Bundeskanzleramt, Ausw. Angel., Berlin, January 6, 1927, annotated: "Read by Federal Chancellor"; St.A., Fasz. 13.

The German and the Austrian statesmen found themselves in a similar predicament. Both wanted the Anschluss and at the same time did not want it. Both were subject to domestic pressures that forced them to appear as champions of a Greater German unity; both had compelling reasons, Seipel's of a predominantly idealistic nature, Stresemann's of a predominantly political nature, for dealing cautiously with the Anschluss movement. But without much personal understanding of one another, their mutual relations were reduced to a great deal of maneuvering that deteriorated into a misunderstanding which caused much ill-feeling. While Stresemann had a tendency to be condescending towards Austria, Seipel rarely shed his "frosty" ways.[38] Austria, he insisted, was not to play the role of Germany's junior partner; its freedom to maneuver was not to be cramped even by its brethren across the border.[39]

Finally, in the spring of 1924, Stresemann set out for Vienna in the company of Chancellor Marx. Thus the first visit of state made after the war by a German chancellor and foreign minister took them to the Austrian capital. The visit was more a ceremonial affair than a working meeting. The one piece of business transacted was the initiation of negotiations for a German-Austrian trade agreement, which turned out to be lengthy and arduous and in subsequent years added more to tensions than to

[38] Julius Curtius, *Bemühung um Österreich. Das Scheitern des Zollunionplans von 1931* (Heidelberg, 1931), p. 13.

[39] Indeed during Germany's time of troubles before 1924 the wily Seipel never bypassed a chance of scoring. His image of Austria as a safe island compared with battered Germany (Ignaz Seipel, "Österreichs Stellung zur Weltpolitik," address to Catholic students February 15, 1923, *Reichspost*, February 18, 1923) confirmed the rightness of the reconstruction policy of 1922. At the height of the Ruhr struggle during Easter of 1923, when visiting Rome, he was in a position to play the mediator, which gave him no little satisfaction. Mussolini's response to Seipel's probing was as stern as the Pope's was cautiously negative; "Reise des Herrn Bundeskanzlers nach Mailand und Rom, 28. III-4. IV. 1923," St.A., Liasse Österreich 7/1, Geheim, K.470, Fs.132-149, and Top Secret letter Cuno to von Bergen, Berlin, March 19, 1923, G.F.O., 1736/3398/D739592-739595.

a rapprochement between the two countries. No doubt the Viennese appreciated the German gesture, and even the otherwise reticent Dr. Funder was moved to admit, in an editorial entitled "Two Chancellors," that "possibly this sick world will after all be cured by the German spirit, renewed and rededicated to Christianity."[40] Stresemann evidently emerged impressed by Seipel's stature.[41] Upon his departure, he is quoted as having said: "Two more days of this, and our gravestones would have read: 'Died of Austrian hospitality.' "[42]

The Austrians' return visit to Berlin took place in March 1926, during the very time when Seipel was out of office. It was Ramek, interim Chancellor by the grace of Seipel, who took the trip, which was distinguished in every respect by its routine character. In fact while Ramek held the fort for Seipel, Europe's foreign offices kept their eyes focused on the traveling Prelate. For him it was the time of the "great speeches" abroad as well as behind-the-scene activities at home. "How does it happen," asked the liberal Viennese *Der Morgen* in exasperation, "that this man alone has established the position of political representative of our country, that his influence reaches much farther than the power of any other personality?"[43] His speeches in Holland during the spring of 1925, while admittedly "by far exceeding the normal scope of such occasions" and representing a "great personal success for Seipel,"[44] kept the Germans puzzled. In their uncertainty they filed side by side a report from their Vienna Legation, according to which Seipel was a "friend, after all of the Anschluss"

[40] Dr. Friedrich Funder, "Zwei Kanzler," *Reichspost*, March 20, 1924.

[41] *Neue Freie Presse*, March 26, 1924, morning ed.

[42] Max von Stockhausen, *Sechs Jahre Reichskanzlei: Von Rapallo bis Locarno. Erinnerungen und Tagebuchnotizen 1922-1927* (Bonn, 1954), p. 113.

[43] *Der Morgen*, June 7, 1926; this clipping was kept in the files of the German Foreign Office; A.A., Abt. II.-Ö.: Po.11 Nr.3, Bd.1.

[44] Report Freiherr Lucius von Stoedten (German Legation, The Hague), April 24, 1925, A.A., Abt. II-Ö.: Po.2, Bd.10; Report Lucius, May 8, 1925, A.A., Abt. II-Ö.: Po.11 Nr.3, Bd.1.

and trying to demonstrate the absurdity of all other alternatives, and a report from their Hague Legation according to which he was a "not . . . unqualified" friend of Germany who, lacking a "deeper German sensitivity," was about to steer Austrian policy in the direction of the Little Entente.[45] The two legations agreed only about Seipel's "great reticence" and "ambiguous expression." His journey to Switzerland in June 1925 in turn had the effect of disquieting Paris.[46]

The year 1926 took Seipel directly to the German and French capitals. The Berlin visit, preceding Ramek's official one by one month, was called by the *Neue Freie Presse* "a milestone of Austrian as well as German policy."[47] Besides lecturing to the conservative *Volksdeutscher Klub* on the differences between "nation" and "state," as well as between "state" and "Reich,"[48] Seipel had separate talks with Stresemann and Chancellor Luther. In Paris he spoke at the Sorbonne to a crowd of almost a thousand people.[49] The "vacationing Chancellor," far from being idle, lost no chance of mystifying the European capitals about his aims; in this way he hoped to make the Powers take more interest in the little Austrian Republic and also to increase his country's maneuverability.[50]

[45] Memorandum "Beurteilung der politischen Ziele des Bundeskanzlers a.D. Seipel. Durch die Deutsche Gesandtschaft in Wien (Ber. vom 18.4.25); Durch die Deutsche Gesandtschaft im Haag (Ber. vom 8.5.25)"; A.A., Abt. II-Ö.: Po.11 Nr.3, Bd.1.

[46] Cf. above, p. 305n.

[47] *Neue Freie Presse*, February 4, 1926, morning ed.

[48] Ignaz Seipel, "Probleme des deutschen Staates," Berlin, February 5, 1926, Gessl, *Reden*, pp. 286-289.

[49] Ignaz Seipel, "Österreich, wie es wirklich ist," Paris, June 3, 1926, Gessl, *Reden*, pp. 312-324. Cf. also *Neue Freie Presse*, June 4, 1926, morning ed. and report by Leopold von Hoesch (German Embassy, Paris), June 4, 1926, A.A., Abt. II-Ö.: Po.11 Nr.3, Bd.1.

[50] In this period Seipel also decisively affected a number of specific issues bearing on German-Austrian relations. It was due to his interference in the spring of 1926 that a projected acquisition of the *Neue Freie Presse* by the Gäa, an organization backed by German industry (Gutehoffnungshütte,

A Diplomacy for Central Europe

Seipel's studied ambiguity on the Anschluss question was reinforced in 1927, when he was back in office, by two conflicting
developments. On the one hand the civil-war condition at home
had left the bourgeoisie with a distinct sense of frustration and
had thus encouraged pro-Anschluss sentiment.[51] On the other, a
reverse development had taken place in the Socialist camp. The
Austrian Social Democrats had, since the revolution, become the
standard-bearers for the Anschluss with Germany. Now, partly
in response to political trends among the bourgeoisie, Otto Bauer
came out with a spectacular article in the Socialist monthly *Der
Kampf* in which he lamented the fact that the Anschluss movement had been taken over in the name of the bourgeoisie by leaders of Austrian industry and agriculture.[52] "Now that the bourgeoisie has turned towards the Anschluss, we Social Democrats

---

Paul Reusch), was prevented. I owe this information to Professor Karl
Otmar Freiherr von Aretin.

Moreover, we are told by Seipel that he intervened in person with Chancellor Marx in the matter of the choice of the new German Minister to Vienna after the sudden death in the spring of 1926 of Maximilian Pfeiffer,
who had headed the Legation since 1922. His successor, Count Hugo
Lerchenfeld, a Bavarian nobleman, was less closely identified than his
predecessor with an Anschluss policy and was, for this very reason, much
more acceptable to Seipel as well as to the Ballhausplatz (Seipel to Mataja,
May 29, 1926).

By mid-1926, when Seipel celebrated his fiftieth birthday, his policies
had so irritated the Wilhelmstrasse as to make it seem inadvisable to send
a congratulatory telegram, "since Seipel is . . . not especially pro-German
in his orientation," "Gehorsamste Aufzeichung," Gesandter Ernst Lothar
Julius Graf von Zech-Burckersroda, Berlin, July 19, 1926, A.A., Abt. II-Ö.:
Po.11, Nr.3, Bd.1.

[51] Cf. Hugo Lerchenfeld, "Das Verhältnis zwischen dem Deutschen
Reiche und Österreich: politischer Bericht," Vienna, August 1927, p. 19;
A.A., Abt. II-Ö.: Po.2, Bd.16. For the endorsement of the Anschluss by
the Austrian mining industry cf. M. Margaret Ball, *Post-War German-
Austrian Relations: The Anschluss Movement, 1918-1936* (Stanford, 1937),
p. 87.

[52] Otto Bauer, "Wandlungen und Probleme der Anschlusspolitik," *Der
Kampf*, xx (July 1927), 297-302.

312

need to remain aware . . . of the fact that the Anschluss can be realized only in the course of revolutionary upsets in Europe, only in company with social revolutions."

While Bauer's article was written to salvage rather than to reject the Anschluss idea, and to encourage and keep alive rather than dampen pro-Anschluss sentiment in the Austrian proletariat, it stands to reason that it was read differently by those outside the Socialist camp, particularly in circles which were skeptical toward the Anschluss. Did it constitute a refusal to join "Hindenburg's Germany"? Indeed Seipel recognized the irony of the fact that his chief political antagonist in Austria, at the very time when things were coming to a head in Vienna, was moving closer to his own position on the Anschluss issue. In the course of a lengthy discussion with Count Lerchenfeld, he conceded that Bauer's article had brought "significant foreign political relief" to the Austrian government, though he added shrewdly that Otto Bauer certainly had not intended to give him support.[53] In view of the close connections between the Czechoslovak government and the European Social Democracy, a dispatch from Prague concluded that the "Hradschin" had "succeeded in alerting against the Anschluss the whole Second International and in making the latter serve its own policies." From the Czech perspective, then, Bauer's article ranked as "the greatest Central European sensation."[54] In any case Lerchenfeld was no doubt right in saying that Bauer's article had done "considerable damage" to the movement towards union with Germany.[55]

When Chancellor Marx and Foreign Minister Stresemann visited Vienna in November 1927 to review German–Austrian relations, neither Stresemann nor Seipel was actually ready for

[53] Report Lerchenfeld, Vienna, July 5, 1927; A.A., Abt. II-Ö.: Po.2, Bd.15.

[54] Strictly Secret Report Z.94/P., "Die Anschlussfrage und die II. Internationale," Marek (Austrian Minister to Prague) to Seipel, Prague, July 14, 1927; St.A., Fasz.148, Deutschland I/1.

[55] "Das Verhältnis zwischen dem Deutschen Reiche und Österreich: politischer Bericht," Vienna, August 1927, p. 25.

anything more than polite speaking. But polite speaking among siblings makes for hurt feelings. It is for these hurts rather than for any positive results that the state visit was memorable. The meeting was fraught with irony, for while Stresemann and Seipel both actually believed that Austria had no choice, for the moment at least, but to maintain its independence, neither was willing to reveal his position to the other.

To begin with, the entire occasion was ill-starred. Seipel's carefully worded and deliberately distant draft of his welcome address, which as a matter of protocol had been shown to the Germans ahead of time, hurt their sensitivities and almost precipitated a major *crise diplomatique*. On November 12 the following telegram went out from Erwin Wasserbäck, the Austrian press attaché in Berlin, to Seipel:

> My relatives here, according to confidential information, dissatisfied with today's missive. See in it equation with other cousins abroad. Since more beautiful return present is intended, better trimming is expected. In case no improvement occurs, return present also will have to be more modest, which would be noticed by all relatives. . . . Recommend for present possibly more attractive wrapping without other contents. . . . Signed Cousin Erwin Wasserbäck.[56]

Wasserbäck, unable to reach anyone in the Ballhausplatz during the weekend of November 12, sent this telegram through the normal postal channels to Seipel's monastery, which accounts for its protective and oblique wording. He felt a sense of urgency about the matter since he was given to understand that "possibly someone might become sick," that certainly the German Chancellor's speech would be "toned down."[57]

There is no doubt about Seipel's deliberate coolness. He knew

[56] Telegram Wasserbäck to Seipel, November 12, 1927, St.A., Liasse Deutschland I/III, Geheim, K.464, Fs. 1-2.

[57] Wasserbäck to Seipel, Berlin, November 15, 1927, ibid., Fs. 114-115.

very well what he was doing when in the typewritten draft of his controversial speech he replaced with his own fine hand the reference to "the German people" in Germany and Austria by one to "our people" in Germany and Austria. Such innuendos matter among diplomats. Indeed, when the Germans finally arrived, the host's talk at the official dinner of November 14 was infinitely more guarded than the visitors'. While Seipel stressed the importance of the spirit of Locarno and international peace and cooperation, Chancellor Marx addressed himself more directly to the German–Austrian bonds of friendship.[58] The *New York Times* commented the following day that the Germans' speeches "smacked more of hands across the frontier and blood ties."[59]

During the morning session between the German and Austrian statesmen on November 14,[60] which was held at the Ballhaus-

[58] *Neue Freie Presse*, November 15, 1927, morning ed.

[59] *New York Times*, November 15, 1927.

[60] Present were Marx, Stresemann, Lerchenfeld, and Hermann Pünder (State Secretary in the Chancellery), Seipel, Peter, and, for the afternoon meeting, Schüller.
There are no less than five extant official versions of varying length, detail, and emphasis, four Austrian and one German. Among the Austrian ones the most inclusive, which I have used as the basic reference, is Z.25299/13, "Niederschrift über die politischen Besprechungen anlässlich der Anwesenheit des Herrn deutschen Reichskanzlers Dr. Marx und des Herrn Reichministers für Auswärtiges Dr. Stresemann in Wien," Vienna, November 14, 1927, signed Peter (from here on cited as Version I), St.A., Liasse Deutschland I/III, Geheim, K.464. Compared with Version I, Confidential Z.25299/13, "Niederschrift über die politische Aussprache in Wien am 14. November 1927" (Version II), ibid., has some minor additions but major omissions. It has the distinct advantage over Version I, however, of a handwritten clarification by Seipel on the Anschluss question. Z.25627/13, "Resumé über die politischen Besprechungen anlässlich der Anwesenheit des Herrn deutschen Reichskanzlers Dr. Marx und des Herrn deutschen Aussenministers Dr. Stresemann in Wien, am 14. November 1927" (Version III), ibid., somewhat shorter than the above versions, written by Peter, Secretary General of the Ballhausplatz, and approved by Lerchenfeld and Seipel, was sent out to Austrian missions abroad. Z.25299/13, "Kurze Übersicht über die Themen und die Ergebnisse der Besprechungen des

platz, there was a good deal of fencing over the issue of political stability in Austria. After a lengthy and on the whole harmonious exchange of opinion between Stresemann and Seipel on the South Tyrolean issue,[61] it was the Austrian Chancellor who brought up what was perhaps the touchiest issue of all, "the Central European question"[62]—which meant, first of all, the Anschluss. This he did not do without calculation. Taking the initiative in this matter allowed him to appear concerned about the Anschluss and to put the Germans on the defensive. He practically charged into the issue of the German list of foreign political priorities.[63] "It would be unbearable for Austria if on any occasion an official German program of action was publicized in which Austria and the Anschluss were explicitly placed in order *after* other problems. Naturally it would be still more unbearable if in such an official program there were no mention at all of the Austrian question."[64] Would the establishment of priorities not spell defeat

---

Bundeskanzlers mit dem deutschen Reichskanzler und dem deutschen Reichsaussenminister in Wien am 14. November 1927" (Version IV), ibid., is an admirably concise summary. The German version, "Vertrauliche Aufzeichnungen über die politischen Besprechungen in Wien anlässlich des Besuches des Herrn Reichskanzlers und des Herrn Reichsaussenministers, Berlin," November 23, 1927 (Version V), G.F.O. 1483/3086/D614238-614260, written by Dr. Pünder, differs from Version I especially in the passages on the Anschluss question, rendering more fully Seipel's irritation at the German position. Cf. also handwritten commentary by Seipel on Version V in St.A., Liasse Deutschland I/III, Geheim, K.464, Fs. 88-91.

[61] According to Version V, Seipel compared Italy with an "overheated boiler" (D614249) likely to burst, thus enabling Austria to demand the return of the South Tyrol. However in his commentary to Version V he interpreted his "boiler" metaphor to have referred to the excess energies of Italy. The boiler, far from being in danger of bursting, needed "valves," namely colonies or mandates. In that case, Seipel speculated, something might be achieved in the South Tyrolean issue; handwritten commentary by Seipel in Version V, loc. cit., Fs. 89f.

[62] Version III.

[63] Cf. above, p. 308.

[64] Version I: italics in original.

316

for the Austrian government and postpone the Anschluss question *ad calendas graecas?*[65]

After Chancellor Marx had jumped into the breach and allayed Seipel's fears, Stresemann finally, perhaps in irritation, came out with the statement that, in any case, the Anschluss question was not pressing; it would be best "to let the matter rest." For the moment the Anschluss was "a *cauchemar* for the others."[66] But this was what Seipel had been waiting for. In fact he had maneuvered his German counterpart into saying what he had wanted him to say without having had to say it himself. The Austrian had outwitted his German guests.

The turn which the conversations had taken put Seipel in the position of impressing his coalition partners at home with his own forthrightness about the Anschluss question;[67] in turn he was not above letting the friends of the Anschluss feel, as one source put it, "the coolness of the German pseudo-Bismarck."[68]

The agenda for the afternoon session of November 14, which was moved to the German Legation, promised an exchange of information rather than of views, and the very fact that Dr. Schüller joined the Austrian party indicated that matters of economic import were to be discussed. But after Stresemann, upon Seipel's

[65] Version V shows Seipel in a more bellicose posture, suggesting that a German action program would give to the Austrians "a renewed impression of being defeated, as also the awareness that Germany dealt with this . . . question without consultation with the fraternal people (*Stammesbruder*) and without the necessary discrimination. This could do harm to the cause and precipitate despair and bitterness in Austria. It would be particularly pernicious if the Germans in the course of negotiations with the former enemies came to shelve the Anschluss question, using it as an object of compensation." Version V, 1483/3086/D614251; the last sentence is also included in Version II.

[66] Version I.

[67] Cf. A.V.A., 29. Sitzung V.A.G.V., November 22, 1927.

[68] Strictly Confidential, unsigned copy of a letter by Hermann Kandl (formerly chairman of the Pan-German party) to "Lieber Freund" (a friend in Berlin), Vienna, November 22, 1927, St.A., Liasse Deutschland I/III, Geheim, K.464, F.117.

prompting, had opened up the subject of a customs union between the two countries, tempers flared up again, ignited by a perfectly innocuous statement by the German Foreign Minister, but one that Seipel found condescending: "Certainly Austria cannot live by itself; something should be done for Austria, and it should be Germany's aim to interfere, lest Austria be forced to turn in another direction."[69] At this point Seipel's irritation burst out. Whereas he had scored earlier by virtue of his restraint, he now came close to losing his temper, he talked about a "theory of pauperism" which seemed to be prevalent in Germany.[70] There was, he said, a circle of people who were still not happy about the fact that things in Austria were improving. He could once again emphasize that the opinion that Austria was already so destitute as to require immediate rescue action was wholly erroneous. Austria had every reason to face the future with confidence.[71] In response the expert Dr. Schüller brought the discussion down from the dangerous level of sibling rivalry to the hard-and-fast facts of economics.

The following day was reserved for social functions. Since November 15 was the day of St. Leopold, the patron saint of Lower Austria who was buried in Klosterneuburg, the party took a luncheon trip out to that magnificent abbey northwest of Vienna. In the evening everyone attended a gala performance at the opera. Outwardly the state visit ended on a pleasant note and Chancellor Marx at least, so we are told, returned from Vienna "highly satisfied," except that he thought the motorcade's speed, dictated by Seipel, "suicidal."[72] But there is reason to believe that Stresemann emerged with his deep suspicions of the inscrutable

[69] Version I; it is interesting that this argument of Stresemann's and the following rejoinder on the part of Seipel are altogether omitted from Version V.

[70] The term (*Verelendungstheorie*) is to be found only in Version III.

[71] Version I.

[72] Wasserbäck to Seipel, Berlin, December 1, 1927, St.A., Liasse Deutschland I/III, Geheim, K.464, Fs. 129-130.

Prelate reinforced.[73] Seipel, as he saw it, had chosen to remain the sphinx.[74] Things were somehow patched up when the Germans accepted the Austrian version[75] of the Vienna meeting over their own "for foreign political reasons," since in the latter the crucial passages on the Anschluss had too sharply profiled Seipel's brusque statement.[76] Substantially there had been a consensus only on one point; the need to embark upon preparations for a German-Austrian customs union. In this respect the meeting of November 1927 in Vienna had a positive and decisive effect upon later developments. It set the switches for a course that seemed at the time more feasible than the Anschluss itself.

Seipel, the Question of the Move of the League to Vienna, and the Interview with Beneš in 1928

In the winter of 1927-28 the question of the League of Nations' move to Vienna almost developed into a major diplomatic issue. Interest in making Vienna the seat of the world organization actually went back to the early days of the League, but it had remained sporadic. This time, however, it moved into the headlines of the world's newspapers and preempted the wires of the foreign offices. In the end, the diplomatic maneuvers of that winter proved to be little more than a storm in a teapot, which in subsiding left hardly a trace on the *grosse Politik*. They are worth recounting, nevertheless. They throw an interesting light on the European power structure of the late twenties, especially on the interests of the Great Powers in Central Europe and on

[73] According to Curtius, Stresemann returned from Vienna "disappointed and disgruntled"; Curtius, *Bemühung*, p. 14; according to Wasserbäck, Stresemann, was impressed by the "unharmonious" outcome of the meeting; Wasserbäck to Seipel, Berlin, December 1, 1927. According to Stresemann himself, he "had received a not very good impression of Herr Seipel"; Secret Memorandum by von Schubert, Berlin, May 22, 1928, G.F.O., 2346/4576/E173431.

[74] Wasserbäck to Seipel, Berlin, December 1, 1927.

[75] Version I.   [76] Version V, 1483/3086/D614239.

the range within which the small powers, including Austria itself, were able to operate. Furthermore, Chancellor Seipel's quixotic handling of the case made the possibilities and limits of small-power policy singularly evident.

It all started with a whimper—literally a whimper—on the part of the League's staff. Continuous complaints about Geneva had been emanating from the Secretariat: the city was not central enough, the climate was unbearable, and the atmosphere was altogether stuffy and constricting. It was said that life in Geneva resembled a state of siege.[77] The Berlin *Vossische Zeitung* observed caustically that in Geneva "everybody is in bed" at 11 P.M. "Is there no other city where one can dance?"[78] No doubt the issue between Geneva and Vienna lay, in part at least, between what Stresemann sarcastically called the "Calvinistic passions" of Geneva and the less austere passions of baroque Vienna. However, as the Austrian Minister to Geneva said somberly, there were more serious *gravamina* against Geneva, which were connected with the nature of a Swiss neutrality. What if the League were to become involved in a military punitive action against one of its delinquent members? The Swiss authorities had all along declared that they could not be party to it and allow transit of troops or arms. The League, in short, was to be a guest in Geneva, not a sovereign.

All the latent grumblings were finally brought into the open in a resounding article by the Geneva correspondent of the *New York Times*, Wythe Williams, headed "Vienna Moving to Get League Seat."[79] This article was well timed, since no solution had yet been reached concerning the construction of a new League palace in Geneva. Vienna, the city of empty palaces, seemed a

[77] Dispatch Z.49/P.2017, Johann Andreas Eichhoff (Austrian Minister, Paris), Paris, May 1, 1922, St.A., Liasse, Völkerbund, Innere Organisation, K.162.

[78] Karl Lahm, "Der Völkerbund in Wien," *Vossische Zeitung*, November 23, 1927.

[79] *New York Times*, October 24, 1927.

peculiarly appropriate alternative that might save the League some 20 million Swiss francs. A second article by Williams suggested that the diplomatic corps and citizenry of Vienna were ready to play an active role in moving the League to Vienna.[80] Little wonder that the news became a major topic of political speculation in Europe!

The great guessing game could now begin. Who was behind the *Times* articles? The Catholic *Kölnische Volkszeitung* wrote about a "trial baloon."[81] The Berlin *Vossische Zeitung*, more suspicious and bitingly sarcastic, hinted at a Pied Piper behind the flute.[82] There was also some talk about "a little blackmail" against Switzerland.[83]

Seipel moved into the battle cautiously but not without a plan. Unlike the Social Democrat Mayor of Vienna, he refused to see Williams. In answer to a top-secret report from his representative at the League,[84] Seipel summarized his strategy succinctly.[85] He made it quite clear that the issue of moving the League was "more than it may appear from Geneva, a question of highest politics" (*eine Frage der ganz grossen Politik*). Considering the active agitation for the move on the part of Count Charles de Chambrun and Hugo Vavrečka, the French and Czech representatives in Vienna, and considering the interest shown in it by Marquis Paulucci, the Italian Under-Secretary General of the League, the question was, so Seipel reasoned, "no longer to be viewed merely as a matter of the convenience and wishes of the League bureaucracy, of the poorer qualifications of Geneva for the seat of the League, of material benefits for Vienna and simi-

[80] *New York Times*, November 11, 1927.
[81] *Kölnische Volkszeitung*, February 12, 1928.
[82] *Vossische Zeitung*, November 23, 1927.
[83] Minister of Justice Dinghofer in A.V.A., 46. Sitzung V.A.G.V., February 21, 1928.
[84] Strictly Secret Dispatch Z.25941, "Verlegung des Völkerbundes," Österreichische Vertretung beim Völkerbund in Genf (Pflügl), December 17, 1927; St.A., Liasse Völkerbund, Innere Organisation, K.162.
[85] Seipel to Pflügl, December 26, 1927; ibid.

lar considerations." "Nothing less" was involved "than the question of the final reconstruction of Europe." On another occasion Seipel called the issue of the move "prejudicial." There was, to begin with, the tactical consideration of Swiss sensitivities, of which Seipel was very much aware.[86] More important still, Seipel saw clearly the connection between the League's move to Vienna and his long-range political objective, which was to keep Austria free for a broader Central European solution of one sort or another. The move of the League to Vienna would preclude Vienna's becoming the capital of a "reconstructed Austro-Hungarian Monarchy, a Central European empire" (undoubtedly Seipel's preference); it would also preclude the Anschluss (at best Seipel's second choice). It would lead to the much-discussed formal neutralization of Austria, which Seipel did not favor. Worse, the price for the move might be the neutralization of Vienna alone, with the city becoming a sort of District of Columbia for the whole League of Nations world. But this would mean that Austria would after all revert to the miserable position in which she had found herself before the financial reconstruction in 1922 at the time of the Anschluss plebiscites. Seipel's exposition concluded as follows:

> It would be a masterpiece of shrewd diplomacy if they [Paulucci and Vavrečka] could seduce us, blinded by possible material and other domestic advantages, to petition ourselves for the League of Nations to move to us. Because then everything else that followed could be forced upon us. . . .
>
> Do not read into this exposition a total rejection. Should I become convinced that there is no more time in the devel-

[86] Cf. Seipel to Eduard Beneš: "We are not in competition with Switzerland," Z.20779/13, Secret, "Aufzeichnungen über die Unterredungen zwischen dem Herrn Bundeskanzler Dr. Seipel und Herrn Aussenminister Dr. Beneš in Prag, 13. and 14. Februar 1928 in Anwesenheit des Gesandten Dr. Marek," Prague, February 17, 1928; St.A., Liasse Tschechoslowakei I/III, Geheim, K.479.

opment of Europe for a Greater Austria and for a Greater Germany, then it could be that I myself would raise the question of the construction of Europe. For this, however, a very good domestic and international preparation would be necessary. The League will not come to Vienna by the back door. We shall not fall back into a condition in which we are only objects of the policies of others, not subjects. Remember our showing in Geneva in 1922.

There is no need to become nervous. . . .

One wonders why he did not see fit to inform the German Legation about his position on the matter. Officially, of course, there was nothing to be said. Austria had not made a move; indeed nobody had, and why should the Ballhausplatz react to conjectures in the press? But keeping the German Legation informed would have done much to allay German suspicions and fears. Here we see Seipel at his worst—cagey, almost sinister, and in the long run his own worst enemy. The Germans, almost frantic for information, obtained it surreptitiously from the Austrian Minister to Berlin, Dr. Felix Frank, who was ill-informed and openly hostile to Seipel.

Actually an almost grotesque reversal of roles had taken place at that time in the diplomatic missions of the two German republics. The German Minister to Vienna, Graf Lerchenfeld, a Catholic nobleman from Bavaria, was by background and inclination much closer to the climate of Vienna than to that of Berlin. He was much too close to Seipel, too uncritical and unsuspecting, to be of much use to the Wilhelmstrasse, where his prestige was fairly low. Certainly his reporting on the question of the move of the League could not be regarded by any standards as either sharp or penetrating.

Still more absurd was the position of Frank. A Pan-German, he had been Vice-Chancellor in the two first Seipel governments from May 1922 to May 1924. In keeping with the stipulations of the coalition, the post of the Austrian Minister to Berlin was customarily occupied by a Pan-German. He was to be a visible bridge between the two German countries and to work for the Anschluss. That he might be caught in a conflict of interests between the two sovereign states had not been foreseen. Frank found himself involved in a real conflict over the question of the move of the League. His solution to his dilemma went far beyond that of Lerchenfeld, who was at best soft toward the country to which he was accredited and at worst inefficient. Frank chose what bordered on treason. He appeared early in February 1928 at the Wilhelmstrasse office of Ministerial Director Köpke and warned him "merely as a private person and friend"[87] that the question of the move of the League had proceeded further than was generally known. He proceeded to give an account of Seipel's position which was badly garbled and tendentious.[88] Needless to say, this was an altogether shocking performance on the part of the envoy, from the point of view of professional ethics as well as that of competence. He misled his German friends and served very poorly his chief purpose, that of an understanding between the two German republics.

Prague was no less concerned and suspicious than Berlin over the developments in Vienna. Where the Germans had always suspected that the Ballhausplatz, and Seipel in particular, would veer in the direction of some sort of Danubian confederation or

[87] Köpke noted: "This all the more since he [Frank] did not consider it impossible that soon the Legation would obtain direction from Vienna to hand us officially information which might be contradictory to what he was about to impart to me now." Strictly Confidential Memorandum by Köpke, February 6, 1928; G.F.O., 2346/4576/E173291-173293.

[88] Frank's prime source was, he claimed, Seipel's exposé at the secret meeting of the Nationalrat's steering committee of January 12, 1928. No minutes of the important session are available, but a highly reliable source (the report by the chairman of the Pan-German party, August Wotawa, about Seipel's exposé, A.V.A., 36. Sitzung V.A.G.V., January 17, 1928) relates that the Chancellor's position on the move of the League was guarded, while basically receptive. According to Frank, Seipel favored an internationalization of Vienna, and projected for the rest of Austria an Anschluss to neighboring countries, for example the Tyrol and Styria [sic!] to Bavaria.

connection with the Little Entente, the Czechs feared the Anschluss. Oddly enough, in spite of the Austrian Pan-Germans' elaborate agitation for Anschluss during the late twenties, German–Austrian relations were at a low ebb in 1927 and 1928, partly because of the German failure to conclude a satisfactory trade agreement with the Austrians, and partly because of the mutual distrust between their foreign offices. By contrast, relations between the Austrian and the Czech foreign offices were highly satisfactory, though on the whole not reflected in public opinion in either country. In fact, Austro-Czech diplomatic relations had steadily improved since the days of the Treaty of Lana of December 1921. Beneš himself, the architect of Czech foreign policy between the two wars, had quickly learned that Austria was no *quantité négligeable*; he had to admit that "Austrian foreign policy in all directions was very ably conducted."[89] In other words, Seipel deserves much credit for having established a balance between the two countries. Moreover, Austria was represented in Prague by an excellent foreign servant of the old school, Dr. Ferdinand Marek, a thoughtful, imaginative, vigorous, and honest diplomat who had the ear of both Seipel and Beneš.

All this meant, of course, that Beneš, insofar as his plans for making Prague the center of Central Europe were concerned, had to be more patient, more subtle, and more ingenious than he had been in the period immediately following the First World War. Certainly he would no longer advocate Austria's joining the Little Entente or, by name at least, the forming of a Danubian confederation. Thus in 1927 and 1928 he launched, in a number of talks with Marek, the concept of a Central European Locarno,[90] to be concluded by the former members of the Austro-Hungarian Monarchy, and first of all by Czechoslovakia, Austria, and Yugoslavia. In return for neutralizing Austria, Beneš im-

[89] Strictly Confidential Dispatch Z.40/P., Marek to Seipel, Prague, January 20, 1928; St.A., Fasz. 84.
[90] Ibid., cf. also Strictly Confidential Dispatch Z.73/P., Marek to Seipel, Prague, May 17, 1927; St.A., Fasz. 84.

plied, Vienna [*sic!*] would be made the "point of crystallization" of a Central European system.[91] Beneš was so much taken by his latest euphemism for his cherished Danubian confederation that he let Seipel know that he would welcome a visit from the Chancellor to talk over this matter. Meanwhile Marek had already reported to the Ballhausplatz on Beneš's interest in the move of the League to Vienna; indeed he made allusions to a "systematic action . . . from which even the Prague Foreign Office seemed not too far removed."[92]

It was characteristic of the relations between Austria and Germany and Austria and Czechoslovakia that the Austrian Chancellor, who had not even bothered to inform the Germans about the move, should have boarded the train at the slightest hint from Prague. He softened the blow for the Germans by arranging to give a public lecture in Prague which would provide an official pretext for his trip.

For tactical reasons, this was an opportune time for Seipel to set out on his journey. Aside from chronic fears of a German role in Central Europe and of the Anschluss, there prevailed in Prague an increasing uneasiness over the penetration of this area by other powers, in particular by Italy. This made Seipel's relationship with Beneš all the stronger. Furthermore there was disagreement in ruling circles in Prague, even between Masaryk and Beneš, on the matter of the future of Central Europe, and more and more voices were heard in influential Czech circles to the effect that the Anschluss might after all be inevitable. This certainly weakened Beneš's position toward Seipel. The Chancellor certainly did not travel to Canossa. Beneš did not speak to his partner of a Danubian confederation, nor did Seipel mention to Beneš his dream of the restoration of the Austro-Hungarian Monarchy. The confrontation between the two statesmen took place

[91] Strictly Confidential Dispatch Z.9/P., Marek to Seipel, Prague, February 9, 1928; St.A., Fasz. 84.

[92] Ibid.

in the best of styles, like a fencing match with elaborate rules. They were extremely polite. Compared with the encounter between Seipel and Stresemann this was a meeting of two statesmen who shared a basic understanding of Central Europe and its problems. Stresemann was after all the latter-day Bismarck, interested in maneuvering Germany out of defeat and back into a position of power. But Germany's power interests were not fully absorbed by either a German-Austrian Anschluss policy or a Central European policy. Seipel and Beneš were, strictly speaking, Central European statesmen. Seipel's whole approach to foreign policy was dedicated to the reconstruction of a Central European order. Beneš was a more recent convert to the cause of general Central European order: it gradually dawned on him that the Little Entente, born out of fear of a Habsburg revival, had a divisive effect on Central Europe. The Little Entente was a regional treaty "of the old style," he admitted to Seipel,[93] and he now aimed at constructing "new types of regional treaties with no barbs against third states" and within the framework of the League. Such treaties—here Seipel enlarged on Beneš's thought, to the latter's satisfaction—were to be concluded, like Locarno and Thoiry, "metaphorically" speaking "near Geneva."

To the transfer of the League the Czechs proved to have no basic objection, provided that Austria was to be neutralized, while Seipel made sure that Beneš did not mean that Vienna alone should be neutralized. Seipel was quite frank in stating that he saw definite advantages in moving the League or perhaps some of its institutes to Vienna.[94] However, on the question of guarantees against the Anschluss, Seipel said quite clearly, "We would not tolerate any settlement that would force us once again

[93] "Aufzeichnungen über die Unterredungen Seipel-Beneš."

[94] Seipel specifically mentioned the Secretariat's Minorities Section; one of his main interests, deriving from his work on the nationality problem in the Monarchy, was the minority problem. He shared this interest with Bishop Frind of Prague, with whom he stayed during his visit.

327

to sign any article disagreeable to us."[95] The Seipel of 1928 had clearly outgrown the shoes of the Seipel of 1922. Indeed in his later conversation with Wirth he said that the talk with Beneš had had no immediate results because of the issue of guarantees against the Anschluss. "Herr Wirth, this joke is over now." After all, Chancellor Seipel, by going to Prague, must have appeared to Beneš much as he had appeared to Stresemann by not going to Berlin: domineering, haughty, inscrutable.

The following notice of March 10, 1928, appears in the files of the Ballhausplatz:

> From an enclosed report of the Austrian representation at the League of Nations . . . and from the minutes of the League Council of March 6, 1928, it is evident that the League of Nations has finally decided to build the new League palace in Geneva. . . . *Thus the question of the move of the League of Nations is for all practical purposes to be considered closed.*[96]

A sober ending indeed for a fairly explosive issue. Was Vienna after all, as one Viennese newspaper had initially put it, "too full of *joie de vivre,* politically unsuited and too close to the Balkans"?[97] All indications of the reason for this fairly abrupt ending point in the direction of the Quai d'Orsay, which in turn swayed Beneš.[98] In fact it is not at all impossible that the whole issue started in Paris, as Seipel once claimed, with Philippe

[95] "Aufzeichnungen über die Unterredungen Seipel-Beneš."

[96] Office Memorandum, Z.21173/15, March 10, 1928; St.A., Liasse Völkerbund, Innere Organisation, K.162.

[97] *Welt am Morgen,* December 9, 1927.

[98] Z.20985, "Unterredung der Herrn Bundeskanzlers mit dem Herrn tschechoslowakischen Gesandten anlässlich des Diplomatenempfanges am 27. Februar 1928," Vienna, February 29, 1928, St.A., Liasse Italien 2/8, K.668; also Memorandum by Stresemann on report by Wirth, April 12, 1928; G.F.O., 1483/3086/D614378.

Berthelot, the Secretary General of the Quai d'Orsay,[99] and ended there too. The Quai d'Orsay at that time was still master of Europe.

Lerchenfeld may have been right in reporting that Seipel's reaction to the proposal that the League should be moved showed his desire to "improve the range of Austrian statecraft."[100] No doubt the Austrian Chancellor played his hand shrewdly, almost too shrewdly. He played the game as if the "revenge for Sadowa" were still within Austria's reach, as if Austria were still, or once again, a great power. He harvested the distrust of his German colleagues without allaying Czech and French suspicions concerning an Anschluss policy; but no statecraft, however shrewd, could overcome the fact that Austria after 1918 was a small power. Seipel, with all his broad horizons, with all his abilities, had after all failed to abide by his own *hic Rhodus, hic salta* formula. In the final analysis he overreached himself. By so doing he explored daringly, quixotically, both the possibilities and the limits of the role of a small power in big diplomacy.

Seipel—Mussolini—Bethlen

For the Ballhausplatz 1928 was a busy year. While the fencing with Stresemann over the Anschluss question and with Beneš over a new Central European order and the possibility of moving the League was carried on in an atmosphere of unreality, with the issues at stake somewhat hypothetical and remote, the controversy with Italy which broke out a few days after Seipel's return from Prague did have an air of immediacy. The South Tyrolean question was an insistent issue in Austrian politics. Of the many wounds going back to the Treaty of St. Germain, it was

[99] Memorandum by Lerchenfeld, March 27, 1928; G.F.O., 2491/4938/E265855; also Memorandum by Stresemann on report by Wirth, April 12, 1928.

[100] Dispatch Lerchenfeld, Vienna, February 17, 1928; G.F.O., 2491/4938/E265872.

the one that hurt most and that seemed most to resist Seipel's formula of *hic Rhodus, hic salta.* The fate of the two hundred and fifty thousand peasants under Fascist rule stirred up strong feelings among Austrians from all the different Länder and of all political persuasions. The South Tyrol was very much a matter of the heart—even, said his envoy to Berlin, to Seipel himself, although he usually had a "rather cold character."[101]

Austro-Italian relations, especially since Mussolini's take-over in 1922, were strained by the South Tyrolean question. For the Fascists, said Mussolini, a minority problem existed "neither *de jure* nor *de facto.*" He boasted that Italy was "the most homogeneous country of the Occident."[102] Under these circumstances it was hard for the makers of Austrian foreign policy to steer a course that was friendly to Italy. "You complicate my policy, which often has been criticized for its Italophilism," Seipel once reproached the Italian envoy.[103] Seipel repeatedly exercised a moderating influence on Austrian patriots and nationalists who advocated a more aggressive policy toward Italy.[104] Indeed in a gesture toward Italy in 1924 Seipel had gone so far as to give, through Lothar Egger, his Minister at the Quirinal, a one-sided declaration to Mussolini to the effect that Austria, without entering into any commitments beyond the terms of the Treaty of St. Germain, would refrain "now and in the future" from fortifying

[101] Strictly Confidential Memorandum by Köpke about visit of Frank on July 6, 1928, Berlin, July 6, 1928, A.A., St.S. (alt) "SO," Bd. 8.

[102] Ad Z.22481/13 Message Mussolini to Seipel, Rome, May 21, 1928, St.A., Liasse Italien, Geheim, K.476.

[103] "Amtsnotiz" Z.3293/17 Präs, Vienna, November 5, 1923, St.A., Liasse Italien, 2/8, K.664. According to the Memorandum, the Italian Minister, Luca Orsini Baroni, appeared crushed by Seipel's revelations and offered his services to improve things. But when Orsini asked what he should telegraph to Rome, the Austrian Chancellor answered imperiously, "He may write or telegraph, whatever he may wish to."

[104] Cf. copy of letter Z.11106-17, Seipel to Stumpf, Governor of the Tyrol, Vienna, January 2, 1924, St.A., ibid., and copy of letter Z.21268, Seipel to Dr. Eduard Reut-Nicolussi, Vienna, March 10, 1928, St.A., Liasse Italien 2/8, K.668.

the Brenner frontier.[105] But Mussolini had also meant to have the Brenner frontier guaranteed in Locarno. The failure to achieve this objective left him deeply disappointed and embittered.

Caught between the insatiable Mussolini and increasing domestic pressure, which came particularly from the Tyrol, the Austrian governments of Ramek and Seipel remained impressively restrained. When, in an address to the Italian Chamber on February 6, 1926, Mussolini bragged that Fascist Italy could, if necessary, carry its tricolore "even beyond the Brenner,"[106] it was Stresemann, not Ramek, who answered in the Reichstag. Seipel, criticized in October 1926 for having sent his volume of speeches to Mussolini, the "renewer of Italy,"[107] told the budget committee of the Nationalrat that a foreign political gesture ought not to be judged by domestic standards.[108] His Declaration of Policy of May 1927 was singularly restrained on the South Tyrolean problem, which, he stressed, affected, if not Austria's foreign policy, at any rate the "tone of the public controversy."[109]

"Dr. Seipel is under no suspicion of nationalistic vehemence. God knows, he is no politician who lets himself be guided by the bubbling of the blood, by the desire to arouse the masses."[110] This was the comment of the *Neue Freie Presse* on the events of February 17, 1928, when Seipel finally spoke up in the Nationalrat in response to an interpellation by Tyrolean parliamentarians from the Christian Socialist and Pan-German parties. In short, Seipel was forced, much against his better judgment,[111] to make a public

[105] For the background see Letter Z.2821/17, Bischoff to Egger (Rome), "Verhandlungen über die Contarini Note," Vienna, December 10, 1923; for the text Z.13052/17, July 1924, St.A., Liasse Italien I/II, K.654. Mussolini confirmed the declaration in a personal message to Egger; letter Mussolini to Egger, Rome, July 16, 1924, ibid.

[106] *New York Times*, February 7, 1926.

[107] Johann Auer, "Seipels Verhältnis zu Demokratie" (diss., Vienna, 1963), p. 80.

[108] *Wiener Zeitung*, December 2, 1926.

[109] *Sten. Prot.*, 2. *Sitzung*, III. *G.P.*, May 19, 1927, p. 10.

[110] *Neue Freie Presse*, February 18, 1928, morning ed.

[111] Cf. A.V.A., 64. Sitzung V.A.G.V., July 12, 1928.

statement on the question of the South Tyrol. For once he had to give the heart precedence over reason, domestic pressure precedence over the exigencies of foreign affairs. As a matter of fact, Seipel's statement in Parliament was tempered and explorative; it admitted that Austria had no alternative but to appeal to Italy for better treatment of its brethren across the frontier.[112] "The result . . . is nil," concluded the *Neue Freie Presse*,[113] thus expressing what for once amounted to a general consensus of public opinion. Therefore, in the next round in Parliament the critics of Seipel's all too cautious foreign policy were joined by speakers from the opposition,[114] and the Chancellor, taking the floor again, spoke of the South Tyrol as a "matter of the heart" in which Austria could not after all remain silent.[115] While emphasizing that Austria had no intention of interfering in Italy's domestic affairs, he stated with dignity his country's claim to be heard: "We cannot accept the view that the highest law is the written law . . . we believe in a higher justice, just as we believe that there are international morals which stand above international law."[116] Seipel achieved nothing tangible vis-à-vis Italy. The Italian envoy to Vienna, Giacinto Auriti, was demonstratively recalled to Rome for consultation. Furthermore on March 3 Mussolini, addressing his Chamber in the presence of most of the diplomatic corps, chose to respond dramatically: "Hannibal is not *ante portas*, and neither is Monsignor Seipel."[117] And he added his own variation on Clemenceau's oft-quoted and much-resented verdict that "Austria is what is left over": "Austria is what it is." However, it can be argued that Seipel at least forestalled more fireworks on

[112] Cf. Schulthess, *1928*, pp. 221f.; cf. also the manuscript of Seipel's statement, edited by himself, Z.11601, St.A., Liasse Italien 2/8, K.667.

[113] *Neue Freie Presse*, February 18, 1928, morning ed.

[114] Cf. Schulthess, *1928*, pp. 222ff.

[115] *Sten. Prot., 33. Sitzung, III. G.P.*, February 23, 1928, p. 956.

[116] Ibid., p. 958.

[117] *Neue Freie Presse*, March 4, 1928, morning ed.

the part of his compatriots—specifically, a mass demonstration originally planned for February 27. It must be stated, wrote Secretary General Peter to the Austrian foreign missions confidentially, "that the leadership in the South Tyrolean question now resides wholly in the hands of the federal government."[118]

Once again Seipel brought all his ingenuity to bear on this particularly hopeless diplomatic situation. Cardinal Piffl of Vienna, though not in the best of health, set out for Rome to ask for papal mediation in the conflict. The Pope took the occasion to state his unhappiness with the Austrians and Germans for their criticism of his inactivity in the matter without considering his own "unfree position." At the same time he stressed that the "all too loud complaints about the South Tyrol would merely do harm to the Germans there."[119] This was a terse, noncommittal statement, a "cold shower" according to the Austrian press attaché at the Quirinal, who took the credit for having inserted in the papal communiqué the mollifying passage: "We shall do whatever possible and pray."[120]

Seipel's reaction to his lieutenant's meddling was immediate and fierce. He argued that the Holy Father's declaration, far from being a "cold shower," should be considered a "sensation,"[121] inasmuch as it acknowledged, if only by inference, the unsatisfactory condition in the South Tyrol. Besides, the Pope's argument that activity on behalf of the minority would have been

[118] Memorandum Z.20913/13, Generalsekretär Peter to Foreign Missions of Austria, February 26, 1928, St.A., Liasse Italien 2/8 K.668.

[119] Strictly Confidential Report Z.33/Pol, Pastor "Kardinal Piffl in Rom," Rome, March 21, 1928; cf. Z.21552/13 "Briefwechsel zwischen dem Herrn Bundeskanzler [Seipel] und dem Presseattaché Dr. Jorda in Rom (Q) betreffend die Erklärung des hl. Vaters über die Südtiroler Frage," Ivo Jorda to Seipel, Rome, March 21, 1928, St.A., Liasse Päpstlicher Stuhl, K.710; cf. *Reichspost*, March 24, 25, 1928.

[120] Letter Jorda to Seipel, Rome, March 21, 1928, ibid., F. 240.

[121] Copy of letter Seipel to Jorda, Vienna, March 26, 1928, ibid., Fs. 241-242.

more harmful than useful was taken by Seipel as a justification of his own past policies. By alluding to his "unfree position" as a prisoner in the Vatican, the Pope declared himself a "prisoner . . . and thus a fellow sufferer, so to speak, with the equally subjugated South Tyroleans," and this identification with the South Tyroleans the all too imaginative Chancellor saw as a "gesture of world historical significance," far exceeding the South Tyrolean question itself. "This is my interpretation,"[122] wrote Seipel in his magisterial way. He had already in a similar way overestimated the significance of the proposal that the League be moved to Vienna. Seipel's visions, his broad horizons, turned out to be mirages.

The Chancellor went so far as to call Jorda, the press attaché, to task for inserting the passage on the Pope's praying for the South Tyroleans, arguing that it sentimentalized and therefore spoiled the basic tenor of the declaration, which was essentially political; Jorda, holier than thou, got himself a severe tongue-lashing from his priestly chief. "To me it is interesting that the Holy Father (or at least the reporting Cardinal) was less 'pious' than you and did not speak of praying." There was another feature of this reporting to which Seipel took vigorous exception. Jorda, relating to the Chancellor the circumstances of the Cardinal's meeting with the Pope, thought it necessary to report that the Cardinal, ailing and nervous, had thrown up during the audience. He had emerged terrified and, when departing from Rome, had commented to a group of shocked prelates that it had been "probably the first time that a Cardinal had puked at a Pope."[123] However, Seipel retorted that the Cardinal's ill-health was indeed a pity, but that his ill-fortune had been a blessing in disguise, because it made quite clear that the initiative for the political declaration came from the Holy Father himself, and not from the ailing Cardinal.[124] The instruction which the Ballhaus-

[122] Ibid.
[123] Jorda to Seipel, Rome, March 21, 1928.
[124] Copy of letter Seipel to Jorda, Vienna, March 26, 1928.

334

platz then sent out to its chiefs of mission reflected point by point Seipel's interpretation of Cardinal Piffl's mission.[125]

Meanwhile the cards were hopelessly stacked against Seipel. He clearly had no legal or political recourse for helping the South Tyroleans and he had let himself be pushed into unleashing precisely the kind of "demonstration policy" that he had always rejected and that was bound to boomerang.

The captive of the Austrian chauvinists was at the same time the victim of Mussolini's bullying. Finally there was nothing left for Seipel but to surrender. Short of entering into a discussion as to whether Italy faced any minority problems at all, he conceded that the Germans of the "Alto Adige" should turn to Rome as Italian citizens with their complaints, and promised that neither Innsbruck nor Vienna would interfere in the domestic affairs of Italy and that responsible Austrians would neither join nor encourage anti-Italian or anti-Fascist agitation.[126] Since Fascist magnaminity is never unaccompanied by total humiliation of the recipient, the Agenzia Stefani issued a communiqué on the evening of July 2 announcing the satisfactory settlement of the differences between Italy and Austria, adding that according to the exchange of messages between Mussolini and Seipel the South Tyroleans were to turn "only"[127] to Rome with their complaints and that Auriti would return to Vienna. Seipel refrained from any countercommuniqué of his own, and even managed, for the sake of peace, to prevent renewed discussion of the issue on the floor of Parliament. He merely reported, in secret session, to the Nationalrat's steering committee, which upheld his policies, with

[125] One of the salient points in Seipel's assessment of Cardinal Piffl's audience was that the Pope's mention of his "captivity" reflected upon his hostile view towards Fascist Italy, which, in spite of all appearances to the contrary, was not different from the "liberal and freemasonic" Italy of 1870.

[126] "Rückantwort-Message" Z.22654/13, Seipel to Mussolini, Vienna, June 5, 1928, St.A., Liasse Italien, Geheim, K.476.

[127] *Le Temps*, July 4, 1928; cf. Strictly Confidential "Aufzeichnung von Schubert 21. Juli 1928, von Frank übergeben (von Herrn Junkar verfasst)," G.F.O., 2347/4576/E173559.

only the Socialist members dissenting. The whole affair added up to a fiasco.

Seipel's hope of keeping a "free hand" with Mussolini, as he thought he had done in his negotiations with Beneš, had proved a false one. This time the proud and ingenious Chancellor had to go to Canossa, and this weighed heavily on him. The unequal duel with the Fascist dictator brought him, for the first time, to face the unarguable reality of Austria's weakness and impotence.

It should be registered, though, that Italy's harsh anti-Austrian course did not fit into the long-range plans of Italian foreign policy. Since the mid-twenties Italy had given distinct indications that she was embarking on an active Central European policy, whose immediate objective was to counteract the French-Czechoslovak and neutralize the German influence in Hungary and Austria and to affect some Italian-German-Hungarian-Austrian combination.

We now know, however, that the Hungarians did not relent. Their effort to bring about an anti-French-Czechoslovak bloc in Central Europe got actively under way in the spring of 1928 when the Hungarian Prime Minister Count István Bethlen secretly visited Rome and succeeded in talking the Duce into giving financial support to the amount of one million lira, and weapons as well, to the Austrian rightist organizations.[128] The aim was to bring about an Austrian rightist regime which would, it was hoped, be less insistent on pursuing the South Tyrolean question, delay the Anschluss with a democratic Germany, and facilitate the weapons traffic between Italy and Hungary.[129] The pattern envisaged by Bethlen then called for a reversal of Mussolini's policies toward Austria. It relegated border conflicts, such as the one on the Brenner Pass, to the past and pointed toward a re-

---

[128] Cf. Lajos Kerekes, *Abenddämmerung einer Demokratie: Mussolini, Gömbös und die Heimwehr* (Vienna, 1966), p. 10, and D. Nemes, "Die 'österreichische Aktion' der Bethlen Regierung," *Acta Historica, Journal of the Hungarian Academy of Sciences* (Budapest), XI (1965), 199.

[129] Kerekes, *Abenddämmerung*, p. 10.

alignment of "revisionist" powers and a front of right-wing, fascist states against the democratic West. Count Bethlen emerged as the chief architect of this policy, with Mussolini willing to play the game and also to finance it, even though his own Foreign Minister Grandi was by no means in agreement with it, calling it "romantic" and "dangerous" and stressing its incompatibility with Italy's actual South Tyrolean policy.

Bethlen's foreign policy throughout the 1920s had been nothing short of fantastic and erratic. Now, in order to live up to his newest scheme, he had to straighten out Hungary's relations with Austria. Although the two countries after 1918 were in similar positions as vanquished states, and although they were disposed to be friendly to each other, the Burgenland issue still came between them. It was their "South Tyrol," so to speak. But Bethlen, so keen on cementing the relations between the two countries, never let the Austrians forget Hungary's claims to its former territory.

Altogether Bethlen's "Austrian Action" was a bubble and he himself had neither the old-world shrewdness nor the revolutionary *élan* to get his daring project off the ground. Mussolini, who alone could have given the plan the necessary revolutionary persuasiveness, was still hampered by the recent memories of his anti-Austrian harangues. The Heimwehr leaders, who were the Austrian accomplices in the scheme, were plagued by feuds and dissension and were hardly reliable as Mussolini's and Bethlen's sole "trump card" in Austria.[130] As for Seipel, he was too suspicious of Mussolini and too unimpressed by Bethlen's wisdom in international affairs to take part in any project which Bethlen was promoting. The fact was that Count Bethlen was not in any way equal to Seipel. The former was indeed a wild schemer; the latter kept his dreams under control by his grasp on the hard-and-fast realities of foreign policy. Seipel's setbacks in foreign affairs, such as those suffered in his encounter with Mussolini, the mistakes he made, such as those in the Marinković episode, which

130 Nemes, "Die 'österreichische Aktion,' " p. 255.

will be related in the following pages, were but the results of
frustrations arising from the disproportion of his imperial memories, the actual impotence of his small Republic, and his undaunted vision of a future for Austria.

The Marinković Incident

All this does not mean that Seipel closed the doors on an Italo-
Hungarian-Austrian combination. His strange performance in
Parliament on June 27, 1928, certainly could have been interpreted as lending support to it. This took place in the course of
a rare duel over foreign affairs in Parliament between Otto Bauer
and Seipel. Bauer, to say the least, was no expert on foreign affairs, which lend themselves even less than domestic ones to a
rigorous doctrinaire frame. But he saw himself called upon to
challenge the Chancellor in the Nationalrat about a press interview which the Yugoslav Foreign Minister Voyislav Marinković
had given at the tail end of the Little Entente Conference of
June 20-22 in Bucharest, suggesting, after some pointed remarks
against the Anschluss, that the Little Entente considered Austria
as part of its economic system. Seipel knew that Parliament was
not the best forum for a discussion of sensitive matters pertaining
to foreign affairs, and even less for a response to an interview
with a foreign statesman. But he took occasion to strike out
against both his old foe Bauer and the Yugoslav as well. Bauer
had asked for a lashing, and he got it. Might one not have learned
from the anti-Anschluss statements, such as the one made by
Marinković, that the time for public support of the Anschluss was
not ripe? And he lectured to Bauer that it would elicit merely a
"no."

However, in the rest of his speech he addressed himself to the
essence of Marinković's statement. Did it not amount to confirma-
tion, however late, of Seipel's persistent urging that the economic
structure of Central Europe, as derived from the Peace Treaties,
needed basic revision and a liberalization beyond mere improve-

ments in commercial treaties?[131] All the adversities and disappointments which Seipel had recently suffered in the foreign field once again seemed to confirm his basic assumptions. Once again, he used the occasion to recall the need for his "third act," whether it be negotiations within the frame of the League, a world economic conference, or a Central European conference.[132]

Subsequently, Seipel made an unnecessarily vitriolic attack against the Yugoslav statesman. Austria wanted to be neither a full member nor a second-class member of the Little Entente.[133] He concluded his speech with a grand policy statement on the need to step out of the "narrowness of the borders"—and he meant economic borders—which had been drawn by the Treaties. Until this aim had been achieved, however, Austria's obligation was to "keep itself free [*freihalten*] to enter into a larger or smaller, a European, Central European, German solution, as soon as the door opens up for us into this or that larger economic unit. But we shall never consider the Central European question solved if the great state which constitutes Central Europe properly speaking, namely the German Reich, should not be included in this solution."[134]

For once Seipel had made an unequivocal public statement on the Anschluss. All this verbiage, and the somewhat unwonted tone of his eloquence, was but an indication of a deep resignation on his part. Seipel's speech did indeed irritate Beneš and cheer the Italians;[135] in the latter's eyes it gave added impetus to speculations about an Italo-German-Hungarian-Austrian combination. But it was with a marked irony that the *Popolo d'Italia* of June 29 characterized Seipel's address as "Il 'non possumus' di

[131] *Sten. Prot., 46. Sitzung, III. G.P.*, June 27, 1928, p. 1362.
[132] *Sten. Prot., 46. Sitzung, III. G.P.*, June 27, 1928, p. 1363.
[133] Ibid., p. 1364.
[134] Ibid., pp. 1364f.
[135] Cf. Strictly Confidential Dispatch Z.98/P, Marek to Seipel, Prague, July 11, 1928, St.A., Fasz. 84, and Dispatch Z.81/P, Egger to Seipel, Rome, July 2, 1928, St.A., Fasz. 108.

A Diplomacy for Central Europe

Seipel."[136] With the same words—"non possumus"—one of the speakers in the Austrian Nationalrat, in a rare atmosphere of general consensus, had appealed to the Vatican for support.[137] The fact was that Seipel came closer and closer all the time to the "non possumus."

Between Vision and Despair

Of all his contemporaries in the European foreign offices concerned with Central Europe, Seipel was the closest to Beneš, his Czechoslovak counterpart. By the mid-twenties the latter had come around to an understanding that a Central European order could be based neither entirely on France's remote control nor on a perpetuated division among the Central European states themselves. But Beneš's former self, narrow and vindictive, cast a shadow over his present effort to come to an understanding with the Austrians, a shadow that deeply disturbed and swayed Austrian public opinion. Seipel could not entirely free himself of a lingering suspicion of Beneš as an agent of French-Czecho-slovak hegemonial policies in Central Europe. Between Stresemann and Seipel, as we have seen, there had come tensions and suspicions that made them talk past each other. But the very reticence which both observed on the Anschluss question at the time, their common absence of chauvinism, should have brought them together to outline some broader supranational Central European order. The three statesmen, Stresemann, Seipel, Beneš, represented a residue of sanity and rationality which distinguished them both from Mussolini and from Bethlen; and a German-Czech-Austrian nucleus for a new Central Europe might have been a viable alternative to the chaos which Seipel had hoped to overcome. It might have led to the sort of "Central European Locarno," discussed by Seipel and Beneš, that was so much

[136] *Popolo d'Italia*, June 29, 1928, quoted in Dispatch Z.81/P, Egger to Seipel, Rome, July 2, 1928, St.A., Fasz. 108.
[137] Schulthess, *1928*, p. 223.

needed for peace in Central Europe and in Europe at large. But this alternative was not sufficiently explored. Neither public opinion nor the foreign offices were ready for it. It was elaborately discussed in the November 1927 meeting between Stresemann and Seipel as the favorite Central European idea of the Czechoslovak Prime Minister, Antonín Švehla, and supported by the historian Kamil Krofta and the Berlin envoy František Chvalkovský.[138] This group of Czech politicians was convinced that France merely used Czechoslovakia and was economically of less importance to her than Germany and Austria. As for Seipel, he made no serious effort to follow up Švehla's plan. In general, it is fair to say that his excessive emphasis on Austria's need to keep herself free for an ideal solution, that is, a "sort of Holy Roman Empire of the German Nation," as the *Neue Freie Presse* once put it,[139] kept him from exploring vigorously the more pragmatic and feasible solution.

Compared with a German-Czech-Austrian combination, a revisionist policy was no more than a disruptive alternative, replacing one form of chaos with another and probably worse one. Revisionism was never Seipel's course. It was simply in conflict with his "acute policy" (*aktuelle Politik*), as he explained to the Nationalrat—not without adding grandiloquently that if ever he came to consider a revisionist policy feasible, it would not be a matter of the revision of one frontier only.[140] The scheme for a fascist organization of Central Europe, Mussolini's and Bethlen's inspiration, grew out of a policy of resentment and irrationality that was alien to Seipel. Its soil was the chaos out of which he had, during his chancellorship, tried in vain to make a reasonable order.

Seipel's trip in September to the Ninth Assembly of the League

---

[138] Version I. Cf. also Strictly Confidential Dispatch Z.172/P., Marek to Seipel "Die mitteleuropäischen Konzeptionen," Prague, December 10, 1927, St.A., Fasz. 84.

[139] *Neue Freie Presse*, June 9, 1928, evening ed.

[140] *Sten. Prot., 62. Sitzung, III. G.P.*, October 18, 1928, p. 1859.

was in many ways a crowning of his statesmanship. It was a tribute and a surprise to him that he was elected one of the vice-presidents.[141] His priestly figure was much in evidence and his "great speech," as the *Neue Freie Presse* called it, not without a certain pride,[142] was remarkable, though admittedly somewhat theoretical.[143] But it was precisely this dimension that allowed him to lift himself above special pleading when he came to his main topic, the minority question,[144] and to bring his life's thought and experience into focus. His argument in *Nation und Staat* concerning different concepts of the nation[145] was still a pertinent one—all the more so since the record of minorities' treatment after the war was unquestionably unsatisfactory. His address, the *New York Times* commented with tongue in cheek, "if billed as a sermon, might have been from the text 'Let us not deceive ourselves!' "[146] The failure of the Treaty system to provide for the protection of minorities, which he called a "holy, natural, inalienable right,"[147] was one of the main threats to international peace.

While Seipel characterized himself as an incorrigible optimist,[148] the *New York Times* perceptively detected a note of "gloom" in his performance.[149] The emphasis on the urgency of

[141] *Neue Freie Presse*, September 4, 1928, evening ed.

[142] "Grosse Rede Dr. Seipels in Genf," *Neue Freie Presse*, September 8, 1928, evening ed.

[143] *Neue Freie Presse*, September 9, 1928, morning ed.

[144] Draft of Seipel's speech to League Assembly, September 8, 1928, with handwritten corrections by Seipel himself, deleting a direct reference to the plight of Germans forming minorities in fifteen European states and also the passage relating to Austrians as a "branch of the German people," St.A., Liasse Österreich 7/1, Geheim, K.470, Fs. 84-92. The final passages of the draft dealing with the minority question were written entirely in Seipel's own hand—an indication of his special concern for the problem.

[145] Inserted into draft with his own hand; ibid.

[146] *New York Times*, September 9, 1928.

[147] *Neue Freie Presse*, September 8, 1928, evening ed.

[148] *Neue Freie Presse*, September 9, 1928, morning ed.

[149] *New York Times*, September 9, 1928.

342

the minority problem included at least a hint, if not a threat, and this did not escape *Le Temps*, which was ever watchful of the Anschluss danger.[150] In fact in Seipel's conferences with his foreign colleagues the Anschluss note was sounded much more distinctly. With the new German Chancellor Hermann Müller, a Social Democrat, Seipel had reached an initial understanding on the conduct of their respective conferences with other statesmen.[151] To Aristide Briand he outlined the compatibility of the Peace Treaties with the Anschluss.[152] Vittorio Scialoja, Italy's representative at the League Council, was impatiently told: "We prefer being pushed around by the Prussians than by others."[153]

Seipel had become a "doubter," after all, concerning Austria's "special mission" in Central Europe, as he confided to the one man who, aside from Lammasch, had more than anyone else been his companion in thought on the nationality and minority questions. This was the Prague Suffragan Bishop Frind,[154] the leader of the German Catholics in Czechoslovakia. If the Austrians' "calling," the organization of a multinational area, had clearly come to an end, there was nothing left for them, Seipel concluded with a heavy heart, but "simply to be sent home to the Reich and there to be a province among provinces under the rule of Prussia."[155] Neither courage nor illusions could any longer conceal the record of diplomatic failures and frustrations that had accompanied Seipel since his return to the chancellorship. If Central Europe was dead, Seipel's alternative was "to serve the fatherland."[156] But this would be his last resort; it would mean accept-

---

[150] *Le Temps*, September 10, 1928; cf. also "L'Anschluss," *Le Temps*, September 5, 1928.

[151] "Aufzeichungen über die Sitzung des Hauptausschusses vom 26. September 1928," signed Peter, St.A., Liasse Österreich K.342, Fs. 338-343.

[152] Ibid.

[153] Ibid.

[154] Seipel to Bishop Wenzel Frind, Vienna, August 16, 1928, Franz Lorenz, "Weihbischof Dr. W. Frind and Prälat Dr. I. Seipel," *Schönere Zukunft*, viii, January 29, 1933, 399f.

[155] Ibid.　　　　　[156] Ibid.

ing God's "penalty"[157] for not having lived up to the "divine ideal of Austria."[158]

Exit Seipel

In the early days of April 1929 the public was startled by the news that Seipel, and after him his government, had resigned. More than in November 1924, the decision was a sudden one, particularly since no immediate crisis had preceded it. It was like "lightning . . . out of a blue sky." But once again, as in November 1924, Seipel himself had chosen the time of his resignation.[159]

The suddenness of Seipel's decision should not obscure the complexity of the causes leading up to it, which included a long internal struggle. After the July events of 1927 he registered a

[157] Ibid.

[158] Ignaz Seipel, "Die österreichische Idee," *Schönere Zukunft*, IV, July 21, 1929, 884-886. It would be too much, however, to deduce from this mood of Seipel's that he had arrived at a definite position favoring the Anschluss (cf. Barbara Ward, "Ignaz Seipel and the Anschluss," *Dublin Review*, CCIII [July–September 1938], 46). Political realities notwithstanding, the vision of the Austrian mission remained before Seipel's eyes. He therefore continued to hedge on the subject of the Anschluss. Thus on his much-criticized Munich lecture, "Der Föderalismus in Österreich" (January 21, 1929; Seipel, *Kampf*, pp. 156-167) the only agreement was that it was ambiguous. While Lerchenfeld from Vienna and von Neurath from Rome assessed the speech positively, Edgar von Haniel, the representative of the Reich Government in Munich saw it as a rejection of the Anschluss (Dispatches Lerchenfeld, "Die Münchener Rede des Bundeskanzlers Dr. Seipel," Vienna, January 30, 1929; von Neurath, "Italien und die Münchener Rede Seipels," Rome, January 31, 1929; von Haniel, "Seipel Besuch in München," Munich, February 2, 1929, A.A., Abt. II-Ö.: Po.2, Bd.20). Haniel also reports the very interesting and otherwise unnoticed fact that the key passage—that Austria because of its complex federalism, which was hard to fit properly into the structure of the Reich, was "destined forever to an independent position after the model of Switzerland, its only and real example" (Seipel, *Kampf*, p. 158)—was distributed in advance to the press, but left out in the delivery; von Haniel, "Seipel Besuch in München."

[159] Cf. *Neue Freie Presse*, April 4, 1929, morning ed.

"longing to leave politics," a "fear of defeats," and "tiredness," personal as well as political; and he felt that he was a burden to his party. He had even anticipated a "theatrical resignation."[160] He explained his step to his assembled cabinet on April 3, when he cited "inner tensions" which had reached a "high degree." But while he saw fit to assess these tensions positively as an "expression of strong, vigorous forces" effective in the Austrian people, he conceded that they had prevented urgent domestic reforms from being achieved. The solution of economic and political issues, which from a "purely pragmatic perspective" had been within the realm of possibility, had been prevented by a harmful "party rigidity." Seipel did not spell out as factors leading to his decision "a certain laxity in some circles of the majority,"[161] as the *Neue Freie Presse* put it, nor indeed the frictions within his own party between the interests of the central authority and of the Länder.[162] Neither did he dwell on how much he had been hurt by the fact that the Socialist agitation against him and his priesthood had been extended to the Church,[163] and that he had increasingly felt himself a liability to his Church as well as to his party. Also somewhat underplayed in Seipel's account was the matter of foreign affairs. But the disproportion between his commitment to the rebuilding of Central Europe and the little he had achieved must have weighed heavily on him. His sequence of failures in foreign political matters could not be denied,[164] and, since the Italian fiasco in particular, the question of his res-

[160] Seipel diary, October 29, 1927; Seipel to Princess Fanny Starhemberg, Vienna, October 21, 1928, in Erwin Rieger, *Fürstin Fanny Starhemberg: Ein Lebensbild einer österreichischen Frau* (Vienna, 1935), p. 147.

[161] *Neue Freie Presse*, April 4, 1929, morning ed.

[162] Cf. Karl Renner, "Die Wendung in Österreich," *Sozialistische Monatshefte*, LXVIII (May 21, 1929), p. 378.

[163] This reason for his resignation he confided to his friend, Dr. Funder; Friedrich Funder, *Als Österreich den Sturm bestand: Aus der Ersten in die Zweite Republik* (Vienna and Munich, 1957), p. 24; cf. *Neue Freie Presse*, April 4, 1929, morning ed.

[164] Cf. Otto Bauer in the budget committee of the Nationalrat, November 19, 1928; *Neue Freie Presse*, November 20, 1928, evening ed.

ignation had become inescapable.[165] Indeed, Seipel took the occasion of his conflict with Mussolini to communicate to the Duce, somewhat melodramatically, his intention to "retire from the affairs of state and shift over to a pure Church career."[166]

From a domestic as well as a foreign point of view, then, Seipel's position had become increasingly vulnerable, and his resignation, as he concluded in his address to his cabinet, was designed to enable the political parties to "secure the future in a different way" than had been possible under his leadership.[167]

Dr. Seipel, the *Neue Freie Presse* commented perceptively, well knew "in what direction he would fall."[168] But there was no doubt that a titan had fallen. For better or worse his policies and reactions to his policies had brought his country back into the headlines of the European press. Dr. Seipel's Austria had become a test case of the struggle between democracy, autocracy, and fascism in Central Europe, as well as a prime mover in the struggle for a Central European reorganization after the New Europe of 1918 had proved wanting. However, Seipel's towering personality, while it had restored the self-consciousness of his countrymen, had also led them almost to fratricide; the phenomenon of an Ignaz Seipel had called for an Otto Bauer. Seipel's successor was bound to be a less dominant man, but the *Prager Tagblatt* suggested that this was just as well.[169] Austria for the moment needed not titans but more pragmatic leadership. In his *tête-à-tête* with Funder, Seipel conceded that he envisaged, after his departure from the scene, a reconciliation of the Social Democrats with the state,[170] which implied the possibility of a Black-

---

[165] Cf. *Neue Freie Presse*, July 12, 1928, evening ed.; Cf. also *Germania*, July 13, 1928; *Vossische Zeitung*, July 13, 1928.

[166] Strictly Confidential Dispatch Z.22105/13 Seipel to Egger, Vienna, May 3, 1928.

[167] *Neue Freie Presse*, April 4, 1929, morning ed.

[168] *Neue Freie Presse*, April 3, 1929, evening ed.

[169] *Prager Tagblatt*, April 4, 1929, quoted in *Neue Freie Presse*, April 4, 1929, evening ed.

[170] Cf. Funder, *Als Österreich*, p. 24.

Red coalition[171]—or, failing this, controversies of a kind in which a priest as a federal chancellor would be out of place.[172] By these "controversies" Seipel evidently meant civil war.

Austria without Seipel, the *Neue Freie Presse* remarked, had suffered a "loss of its European horizon."[173] Seipel, who had insisted that the Austrians play the role of "heirs to the conquerors of the Turks,"[174] had been rebuffed and told that "Austria is what it is." In the early months of 1929 he himself came to the conclusion, for the moment at least, that neutral, happy, unheroic Switzerland could after all serve as an example for his country.[175] From every point of view then, Seipel's resignation speaks of self-restraint and of a glimpse into a society that was less heroic but happier than the one with which he had been identified.

To de-dramatize the political climate Seipel chose a dramatic step. No doubt his exit was in the nature of a personal sacrifice. Seipel's intentions were blatantly misrepresented when Otto Bauer put his "patriotic sacrifice" in quotation marks and called it a "speculation with chaos."[176] Bauer chose not to second his colleague Renner's fairer and more sober expression of "respect" for Seipel's "swift" resignation which, as Renner saw it, demonstrated Seipel's ultimate rejection of violence.[177] To avert chaos, and in particular to steer the ship of state away from imminent civil war, Seipel handed back his mandate. The chances were that another government, under a chancellor less controversial than he, might succeed where he had failed.

[171] Cf. Josef A. Tzöbl, "Ignaz Seipel," in Hugo Hantsch, ed., *Gestalter der Geschicke Österreichs* (Innsbruck, Vienna, and Munich, 1962), p. 599.

[172] Funder, *Als Österreich*, p. 24.

[173] *Neue Freie Presse*, April 21, 1929, morning ed.

[174] Cf. above, p. 298.

[175] See the passage in his lecture on "Federalism in Austria," Seipel, *Kampf*, p. 156; cf. above, p. 344n.

[176] "Spekulation auf Chaos" *Arbeiter-Zeitung*, August 28, 1929.

[177] "Bürgerblock ja, aber Bürgerkrieg nein"; Karl Renner, "Die Wendung in Österreich," *Sozialistische Monatshefte*, LXVIII (May 21, 1929), 376.

Seven

ELDER STATESMAN OR GRAY EMINENCE? 1929-1932

After Seipel: Détente

PARADOXICALLY, the suddenness of his resignation gave a sense of finality to Seipel's departure from the helm of state. His ill-health had begun to tell, for in his wry and stubborn way he had for too long defied his doctors, ignoring his body for the sake of politics. He had "held out," he confided to Princess Fanny Star-hemberg, "to the last minute."[1] While his bearing remained as erect as ever, it became increasingly strained, and his stateliness finally gave way to frailty. It became clear that his strength was failing and that he needed at the very least a long convalescence.

Seipel then entered into a phase in which, by taking the neces-sary medical precautions and avoiding the exertions of public life, he might have played the role of Austria's elder statesman, had Austria been one of those stable democratic societies in which elder statesmen flourish and had he had the necessary temperament.

But much as Seipel was aware of what he called the "honorary row of former ministers" who formed a "first reserve"[2] in the modern democracies, he found it hard to live up to this elevated function. To begin with, as outgoing Chancellor he was still charged with the conduct of affairs, and in holding onto the party chairmanship he could not avoid being forced into renewed ac-tivity. Moreover, it is fair to ask whether any politician, even in a solidly democratic setting, would have wanted at the age of only fifty-two to play the role normally reserved for the aged.

[1] Erwin Rieger, *Fürstin Fanny Starhemberg: Ein Lebensbild einer österreichischen Frau* (Vienna, 1935), p. 149.
[2] Ignaz Seipel, "Der Fall Ahrer"; Schmitz Archive.

Elder Statesman or Gray Eminence?

Seipel was personally too much involved in politics, indeed too ambitious, to admit what would have meant final abdication and defeat. Under the prevailing circumstances, then, it was easiest for the ex-Chancellor to slip into the role of a gray eminence, never wholly detached from partisanship, and never wholly above suspicion.

Of course, the very agony of the struggling Austrian Republic made it seem imperative for Seipel, in spite of his ill-health, to keep his hands on things political. He repeatedly compared himself to the *triarii*, a last defensive line of the Roman legion. "Perhaps the *triarii* will be needed after all."[3] The always suspicious and often alarmist *Der österreichische Volkswirt* this time was not far off the mark in observing, not without malice, that Seipel had "stepped back as one who wanted to be recalled as a savior, that is a savior from chaos."[4] The political career of Ignaz Seipel, then, was after all not wholly ended on April 3, 1929. All in all his periodic reappearance on and compulsive interference in the political scene was as symptomatic of his own inability to stay away from politics as it was of the unstable and troubled political situation in Austria.

For the moment at least Seipel took a back seat in the sensitive and tedious negotiations preceding the appointment of a new chancellor, which not only resulted in a renewed understanding among the parties of his coalition, but also led to a basic agreement with the opposition on the question of rent control. Seipel's exit had, therefore, allowed the formation of a feasible working program for a new government; and, for the time being at least, it had produced a domestic *détente*. This in itself was a striking occurrence in the otherwise rocky history of the Austrian Republic.

[3] Seipel to Funder, Vienna, October 3, 1929, in Friedrich Funder, *Als Österreich den Sturm bestand: Aus der Ersten in die Zweite Republik* (Vienna and Munich, 1957), p. 30.
[4] Dr. Franz Klein, "Europa hat Seipel erkannt," *Der österreichische Volkswirt*, xxII, November 16, 1929, 181.

350

To see in this agreement between the coalition parties and the opposition "Seipel's shrewd plot"[5] does little justice to the glimmer of hope for a restoration of parliamentary life in the country which Seipel himself had shared with both political camps. In fact the Socialists did embark upon a policy of governmental toleration which meant neither participation in responsibility nor opposition. They saw their toleration course as a "lesser evil"[6] than allowing the radical Right to take over. A continued stalemate over rent control would have offered the Heimwehr a welcome pretext for taking action and doing away altogether with the unwanted Parliament. In abandoning their obstructionist policy the Socialists were acting on the chance—a realistically calculated one—that in doing so they would help normalize the political situation, or at last rally the parliamentary parties against the growing force of extra- and antiparliamentary pressures.

Seipel's successor, the Christian Socialist Ernst Streeruwitz, was a compromise candidate of the governmental coalition. A former imperial general staff officer, he was recommended because of his close ties with Austrian industry as well as with the Heimwehr; but he was not a politician. In a way he was the sort of person whom Seipel had intended to succeed him, and a man more conciliatory than himself. But there was no doubt that he was Seipel's tool and utterly dependent on his predecessor's dictates.

The new Chancellor's Declaration of Policy of May 7, which soberly outlined the tasks ahead, emphasized the need for a resuscitation of parliamentary work. There was none of the acrimony of previous years in the parliamentary session of that day.

[5] Charles A. Gulick, *Austria from Habsburg to Hitler*, 2 vols. (Berkeley and Los Angeles, 1948), II, 821.

[6] Cf. on the comparable developments in Germany after the September elections of 1930 Erich Matthias, "The Social Democratic Party and Government Power," in *The Path to Dictatorship 1918-1933* (New York, 1966), pp. 55ff.

351

Elder Statesman or Gray Eminence?

It was felt that the "secret" coalition between the Socialists and the government, as it has been called,[7] might bear fruit after all. Renner even thought that unless all signs proved misleading a "political turning point" had been reached, and the "era of intensified class and political party warfare" had given way to one of a "veritable God's Peace."[8] But this does not mean that the new government was not viewed quite differently from outside the walls of Parliament. Bluntly did Steidle, the Heimwehr leader, predict on the very day after Streeruwitz's accession: "The government will last only a few months and then Seipel will return";[9] and the word went around Vienna that the new Chancellor was destined to be the Austrian Facta.[10]

While both friendly and hostile augurs disagreed about the future of the new cabinet, Seipel embarked on a much deserved and even more needed four weeks' Mediterranean trip. "I shall stay away a good long time," he wrote to his political friend Heinrich Mataja, adding whimsically, "and I expect from my absence the best for the course of Austrian politics."[11] At some later date he hinted darkly that his Mediterranean journey had a *"distinctly political* purpose," indeed "more of a political purpose than any previous political trip," and he added even more darkly that "one can make politics by not making them for a while, but by letting a *political scheme complete itself, as it were, automatically,* that is to say, in reality, *by the work of others.*"[12] Such a statement speaks more of Seipel's political vanity and self-

[7] Jacques Hannak, *Karl Renner und seine Zeit* (Vienna, 1965), p. 515.

[8] Karl Renner, "Die Wendung in Österreich," *Sozialistische Monatshefte,* LXVIII (May 21, 1929), 375.

[9] Ernst Streer Ritter von Streeruwitz, *Springflut über Österreich: Erinnerungen, Erlebnisse und Gedanken aus bewegter Zeit 1914-1929* (Vienna and Leipzig, 1937), p. 398; Lajos Kerekes, *Abenddämmerung einer Demokrate* (Vienna, 1966), p. 35.

[10] Cf. Streeruwitz, *Springflut,* p. 400.

[11] Postcard Seipel to Mataja, Constantinople, May 28, 1929.

[12] *Neue Freie Presse,* June 22, 1929, morning ed.; italics in original. Cf. Gulick, *Austria,* II, 830.

352

esteem than of any sinister scheming on his part. As a matter of fact the ex-Chancellor had been away from Vienna barely ten days when, in view of Mount Athos, he speculated about his "return to politics, party, and government."[13] In one way or another even on this meditative cruise, the *homo politicus* came to the fore again, irrepressible, seeking some relation to affairs of state.

Actually the towering Prelate's absence from the political scene was quite beneficial to the immediate course of events, and the *détente* between the two camps bore fruit.[14] Seipel himself later conceded that in this respect the purpose of his resignation had been accomplished.[15] The Nationalrat, then, could go into summer recess on July 18 with considerable satisfaction. Its President, the Christian Socialist Alfred Gürtler, had good reason to label its recent achievements as "an honorable page in the history of the Austrian Parliament."[16]

A Disinterested Academician?

Upon returning from his journey Seipel seemed primarily concerned with resuming his university career after an interval of eleven years. For the fall term of 1929-30 he announced a lecture course on "Peace, a Moral and Social Problem,"[17] and these lectures were to crown his scholarly work. Independent and original in their argument, vigorous and at the same time measured, they tied in with Seipel's earlier theoretical works, notably with those on the Church fathers and *Nation und Staat*. Like property and nationality, they argued, peace in itself was neither good nor evil. There was a true and a false concept of peace, just as there was a true and a false pacifism. It was in his late work that Seipel

---

[13] Seipel diary, May 22, 1929.

[14] Cf. "Der Parlamentarismus hat gesiegt!" *Neue Freie Presse*, June 15, 1929, morning ed.; and Gulick, *Austria*, I, 495ff.

[15] Seipel to Mataja, Vienna, July 15, 1931.

[16] *Sten. Prot., 97. Sitzung, III. G.P.*, July 18, 1929, p. 2783.

[17] Ignaz Seipel, *Der Friede: Ein sittliches und gesellschaftliches Problem* (Innsbruck, Vienna, and Munich, 1937).

made most explicit the distinction, always implicit in his thinking, between the two levels—the true and the false. "True" peace, involving the order within a society as well as relations among nations, was "indivisible."[18] Moreover, "true" peace, in contrast to "banal" peace,[19] must be fitted into the context of Christian ethics. But Christian ethics were singularly ambiguous on this matter. The same Christ who had admonished his disciples to turn the other cheek had also said, "I came not to send peace but a sword." While the latter statement belonged, by Seipel's interpretation, to the world of the Ten Commandments, that is to the lower level and not the level of the "higher" ethics or the ethics of "evangelical counsels,"[20] it nevertheless reflected the inevitable reality of the human condition. No true peace could be achieved by an undivided concentration on the world of the higher level. Peace at all costs was the wrong formula; "true peace" had to be preceded by the *separatio,* namely decision and struggle.[21]

At best Seipel's argument showed the complexity of the peace problem. At worst, it evidenced a masterful sophistry[22] on the part of the pacific Prelate who, while pretending to advocate peace, in fact had come to justify the sword.

Seipel's Tübingen "Critique of Democracy," which identified the Heimwehr with "true democracy," was an expression of the same kind of thinking. It had been delivered when Streeruwitz was still in power, and even though Seipel had made a point of introducing himself to the students of Tübingen as a disinterested academician,[23] his political pronouncements had distinct repercussions which were not lost on those at home, where

---

[18] Ibid., p. 39.   [19] Ibid., p. 32.   [20] Ibid., p. 85.
[21] "Scheidung der Geister"; ibid., p. 66.
[22] "The reproach [of ambiguity] may be correct in part, because first neither in politics nor in lectures do I say everything I know, and secondly there is so much that all of us do not know"; Rudolf Blüml, *Prälat Dr. Ignaz Seipel* (Klagenfurt, 1933), p. 167.
[23] Seipel, "Die Tübinger Kritik," *Der Kampf um die österreichische Verfassung* (Vienna and Leipzig, 1930), p. 177.

Streeruwitz keenly sensed Seipel's encouragement of the Heimwehr as an "unfriendly act"[24] against himself.

The growing tension between the Chancellor, who insisted upon a constitutional solution of the country's ills, and the Heimwehr, which impatiently demanded action, made Seipel's interview with *Daily Telegraph* correspondent G.E.R. Gedye all the more sensational.[25] Maintaining an air of confidence in the future of his country, Seipel assured Gedye that there was no reason to fear civil war and bloodshed if the Heimwehr demands for thorough constitutional reform were honored. The constitution itself was the disease to be cured, and the armored formations of the Right and Left were merely symptoms of it. On the Heimwehr Seipel bestowed the epithet "irresistible," and he took pains to minimize its importance and compare it to the British Legion, whose members "liked to have an occasional parade, to wear their old uniforms and their old war medals."[26] Prodded by Gedye, however, he admitted that the Heimwehr, particularly its Styrian formations, had their own weapon depots, and that the weapons of the Vienna Heimwehr were "all deposited with the police."[27] This proved that Seipel was well informed about the situation of the Heimwehr, and he took the opportunity to discredit his rival Schober to the Socialists, with whom the latter had just recently resumed connections.[28] Moreover, Gedye was right in saying that Seipel used the occasion to remind the Heimwehr that "he was their master."[29]

There is little doubt also that Seipel was being kept fully informed about the triangular schemings between the Italians, the Hungarians, and the Heimwehr. Indeed on September 19, 1929, he received the Hungarian Foreign Minister Walkó, an talked

[24] Streeruwitz, *Springflut*, p. 415.

[25] *Daily Telegraph*, September 3, 1929; G.E.R. Gedye, *Fallen Bastions: The Central European Tragedy* (London, 1939), pp. 41ff.

[26] Ibid., p. 41.

[27] *Daily Telegraph*, September 3, 1929.

[28] Cf. Gedye, *Fallen Bastions*, p. 44, and Gulick, *Austria*, II, 841, 853.

[29] Ibid., p. 44.

freely with him of an impending governmental crisis. But he emphasized that it ought "somehow" to be arranged that the Heimwehr take over "the legal way," and to make the future government fully respectable he suggested either Rintelen or Vaugoin, both pronounced right-wingers within the Christian Socialist party, for the chancellorship.[30] In commenting on Seipel's Heimwehr course the German Minister was correct in saying that on the one hand he aimed at holding down the Social Democracy for good, but that on the other he hoped to encourage the "constructive" forces within the Heimwehr and to check its outright fascist elements.[31] But Lerchenfeld himself, referring to his "Bavarian experiences," warned against "illusions" about the possibilities of "personal influence" over "such movements." Today we see the futility of thinking that one can control fascism by working with it. But in the twenties and thirties many moderates hoped that they might appeal to the "constructive" elements among the fascists and encourage them to seek power by "legal" rather than revolutionary means. Legality, or the semblance of it, was essential to the rise of fascism because it helped to recruit the very elements in society, the threatened but order-loving middle classes, which came to constitute its social basis. Altogether, in Italy as well as in Germany, legality has furthered rather than arrested the consolidation of fascism. Ultimately it had the effect of victimizing the very "constructive" elements that Seipel wanted to encourage: they were duped by the deception of legality, and thus disarmed in the face of the revolutionary dynamics of fascism. Seipel's Heimwehr course, then, was fraught with self-deception. Plotting with people like Steidle, Pfrimer, and Major Pabst could lead only to fascism itself. For

[30] Kerekes, *Abenddämmerung*, pp. 44f. D. Nemes, "Die 'österreichische Aktion' der Bethlen Regierung," *Acta Historica*, XI (1965), 222; "Akten zu den geheimen Verbindungen zwischen der Bethlen-Regierung und der österreichischen Heimwehrbewegung," *Acta Historica*, XI (1965), 328f.

[31] Draft of letter Lerchenfeld to Dr. Arata (auditor of the Apolstolic Nunciature in Portugal), Vienna, August 15, 1929, G.F.O., 2491/4938/E266223-266224.

a nonfascist like Seipel, the Heimwehr course could not serve as a proper alternative to parliamentary democracy.

Whatever Seipel's role in the unmaking of his friend's short-lived cabinet—and there was little doubt that it was more than a minor one—it was understandable in view of the government's obvious weakness. But there is little doubt that the session between Seipel and the Heimwehr leadership on September 20 was decisive in toppling Streeruwitz.[32] In any case, since Seipel had made up his mind that Streeruwitz was not the man to give the country the necessary firm leadership, he dropped him without a wink, coldly and harshly,[33] and let the intrigues against the government run their course.

Exit Streeruwitz. He had resolved to be "neither Alba nor Facta."[34] He deserves credit for not playing Alba and not succumbing to Heimwehr pressures to join the grand attack against the Social Democrats. But he can hardly escape being ranked, by the verdict of history, among the Factas. An upright but limited man, he was able to find agreement with the opposition, but was unable to control the intrigues and pressures within his own camp. He gave way hurt and without fighting—though not without dignity. A man like this, too upright to be wicked, too timid and too indifferent to democratic institutions to prevail over his enemies, had nothing to fight for.

The Policy of Irresponsibility: Seipel versus Schober

It was a foregone conclusion that Johannes Schober, and not Seipel or any one of his protégés, would be the new Chancellor.

---

[32] On this day Steidle, Pfrimer, and Pabst visited Seipel; Seipel diary, September 20, 1929.

[33] Seipel to Streeruwitz, when asked what was to happen: "Resign! . . . You should have gone with the Heimwehr and renewed the constitution quicker"; Ernst Ritter von Streeruwitz, "Lebenserinnerungen eines alten Österreichers," p. 248, MS quoted in Werner Dallamassl, "Seipels Rücktritt und die Regierung Streeruwitz" (diss., Vienna, 1964), p. 232.

[34] Streeruwitz, *Springflut*, p. 227.

357

Next to Seipel he was the only politician of stature in the bourgeois camp. The relationship between the two men had never been a close one. Schober, all too thin-skinned, had never overcome the feeling of having been outmaneuvered by the wily Prelate in 1922 and deprived of the credit for having paved the way for Austria's reconstruction. In turn, though, as Chancellor, Seipel had liked the thought of being able to use Schober's services as Chief of Police of Vienna, he had always viewed Schober as a potentially dangerous rival, who apart from his efficiency, integrity, and political independence represented a secular position and was committed to a pro-German course. Seipel thought of him as "the independent with the cornflower."[35] But Schober's star had risen during the threatening and turbulent last weeks of the Streeruwitz government, when he took it upon himself to assure the public that "law and order" (*Ruhe und Ordnung*) would be maintained in Austria. A society faced with crisis and impending civil war tends at its eleventh hour to settle on the one figure whose sheer strength of personality might revive the old order and avert catastrophe. In the early autumn of 1929 Schober appeared as such a figure insofar as most of Austria was concerned, and he emerged, instead of Seipel, as the man of the hour. Essentially a well-meaning philistine, the master administrator behind the desk of the police *Präsidium*, he was upgraded by a public that was desperately seeking a strong man. To the lower bourgeoisie he appeared as one of their own; to financial and industrial interests he was the rampart against the Red danger. The Heimwehr, ill rewarding Seipel for his repeated public support, settled on Schober to carry through its militant demands for constitutional reform. Even the Socialists, while not forgetting Schober's role in July 1927, saw in him a lesser evil than Seipel. The latter therefore had little choice but to grin and bear it; according to his own account at a later date, it was he who "as-

[35] "Der Parteilose mit der Kornblume," the cornflower being the symbol of the Pan-Germans; Seipel to Mataja, Davos, March 15, 1931.

sumed once again the whole responsibility"[36] and, after obtaining the necessary agreement from the majority parties, urged the outgoing Chancellor to recommend Schober as his successor. Seipel may have done so "with great reluctance,"[37] but, as in June 1921 when he had first chosen Schober, he could comfort himself for having played the kingmaker, and hope to use his rival for his own purposes. The financial crisis indicated by the withdrawal of capital from the Austrian banks was now to become Schober's affair, as well as the political crisis accentuated by the Heimwehr demonstrations scheduled for September 29. He was made to take all the risks, in particular the one involved in presiding over the bankruptcy of a country threatened by civil war. At the year's end neither Seipel nor Schober could predict whether or not civil war would actually break out. No doubt Seipel did his best to steer the Heimwehr away from its course of violence and toward constitutional reform.[38] In fact it was upon his "signal" that the dreaded Heimwehr parades of September 29 came off peacefully.[39] But the chances were, Seipel conceded, that even the "legal" course would be accompanied with unrest. "Do not demand," he warned somewhat mysteriously in a New Year's Eve address to the Christian Socialist leaders of the Vienna municipal council, "that next year we have only peace and quiet,"[40] and he regaled them with the paradoxical conclusion of his university course, according to which "he who really wants peace must let himself be abused as enemy and disturber of peace; he must not be concerned by the commotion which will arise around him *in order that finally a true state of peace* may come."[41] Civil war,

[36] *Neue Freie Presse*, January 2, 1930, morning ed.

[37] Gulick, *Austria*, II, 879.

[38] "It was I . . . who induced the movement that initially seemed to stage a frontal attack against democracy and parliament to concentrate its force first upon the achievement of constitutional reform," *Neue Freie Presse*, January 2, 1930, morning ed.

[39] Kerekes, *Abenddämmerung*, p. 53.

[40] *Neue Freie Presse*, January 2, 1930, morning ed.

[41] Ibid.; italics in original.

then, was a distinct possibility, and Seipel had even found a formula to condone it. But Schober's being chosen for the post of chancellor allowed the churchman to pull the strings behind the scene, using the Chancellor as his "puppet."[42]

"In thy camp is Austria," wrote the *Neue Freie Presse* as it welcomed the new Chancellor by echoing the poet's famous ode to Marshal Radetzky.[43] While during his first chancellorship Schober had had to struggle with monetary inflation, now, so the liberal paper argued somewhat anxiously, he was confronted with the "inflation of political radicalism."[44] However, it was the very mood of urgency and anxiety accompanying the offer to Schober that in effect indicated a renewed trend away from parliamentary government. The profile of the new government was, then, to be a predominantly nonpolitical one. Politics and party rule had become sufficiently discredited to make it advisable to fall back once again on the politics of bureaucracy, or the politics of nonpolitics—as a way of establishing authority and of withstanding the intense political pressures that came from the militant Right.

There was a sad irony in the fact that Seipel's original achievement, parliamentary government, should have shown signs of crumbling so soon after his departure from the helm. Austrian politics, it has been pointed out, had thus come full cycle.[45] But the Seipel who had resigned in April 1929 was hardly the same as the Seipel of 1922. Then he had been hopeful, forward-looking, confident of his ability to control Parliament. Now he was disillusioned with parliamentary government, more devious, and toying increasingly with solutions outside the parliamentary realm and with forces like the Heimwehr which flatly opposed it. While Schober, the predictable nonpolitical administrator, had

---

[42] *Neue Freie Presse*, January 30, 1930, evening ed.
[43] *Neue Freie Presse*, September 26, 1929, morning ed.
[44] Ibid.
[45] Brita Skottsberg, *Der österreichische Parlamentarismus* (Göteborg, 1940), pp. 345f.

remained the same, Seipel had changed from the architect of parliamentary democracy to the disillusioned sympathizer with Austro-fascism. In 1922 Seipel's government, in replacing Schober's, had moved Austria a decisive step forward toward parliamentary government. Now Schober, by falling back on an essentially nonpolitical government to carry through constitutional reform, was attempting in a time of crisis to salvage constitutionality in the face of the schemes and policies of the outgoing Seipel of 1929.

Schober had hardly taken office when he was called upon to avert a financial disaster and deal with the collapse of the Boden-Creditanstalt.[46] The latter, one of the great banking institutions of the Monarchy and the bank of Emperor Francis Joseph, had badly overextended itself in the course of its adjustment to the conditions of 1918 and had become the creditor of more than a hundred and fifty industrial firms. Schober dealt resolutely with the situation by forcing the Creditanstalt, owned by the house of Rothschild, to swallow the bankrupt institution. He thus lived up to his reputation as a man of action, though in effect he merely pulled the chestnuts out of the fire for Seipel and prepared the ground for the crash of the Creditanstalt itself in 1931, which in turn undermined the very foundations of Austrian as well as of all Central European economic life.

Once the banking crisis had been patched up, the new government could devote itself to its primary task of constitutional reform. Schober's Declaration of Policy of September 27 had outlined this elaborately and at the same time, to the accompaniment of profuse bows to the Heimwehr as "representing the sentiments of broad circles of the population" and composed of "admirable men of all social strata,"[47] had almost frantically urged the "legal," which meant parliamentary,

[46] Cf. W.F., "Das Ende der Boden-Credit Anstalt," *Der österreichische Volkswirt*, XXII, October 12, 1929, 41-43.

[47] *Neue Freie Presse*, September 28, 1929, morning ed.; in fact Pfrimer sat in the gallery during Schober's address.

approach to constitutional reform. Schober then set himself the task, in which his predecessor had failed, of normalizing the domestic situation and of guiding the Heimwehr's putchism into constitutional channels. Naturally Schober's alliance with the Heimwehr was an uneasy one. But the Chancellor's real obstacle turned out to be Seipel. Constitutional reform was his brainchild, and accordingly he considered it his own preserve. But normalization was less and less his concern. A gnawing awareness that time was running out, his own as well as his country's, and a growing sense of irritation and failure drove him onto an adventurous course. In a bravado mood, unusual in a statesman once so cautious and level-headed, he had only recently confided to his friend Mataja that to him the demands of the Landbund and "even" the Heimwehr were "too little," adding, "Who at the time of advance would think of retreating?"[48] In turn the "grand master" had been assured by his disciple that he was the "source of all energy" among the bourgeois circles, and "singularly gifted in increasing tensions."[49]

Though the news item in the *Frankfurter Zeitung* reporting that Schober and Seipel had discussed the former's proposal previously in a lengthy session cannot be verified in the sources,[50] there is no doubt that its underlying principle, the "strengthening of the authority of state, was wholly in line with Seipel's ideas. The various forces pushing for constitutional reform were agreed on the need for firm governmental leadership.

Indeed even the Social Democrats had, throughout the year, given repeated indications of their readiness to talk about constitutional reform.[51] The constant danger that the country would collapse economically had the effect of "sobering" the opposition.[52] Moreover its extensive use of obstruction in the past years

[48] Seipel to Mataja, Hütteldorf, September 4, 1929.
[49] Mataja to Seipel, Vienna, September 5, 1929.
[50] Schulthess, *1929*, p. 245.
[51] Skottsberg, *Der österreichische Parlamentarismus*, pp. 361ff.
[52] Karl Renner, *Österreich von der Ersten zur Zweiten Republik* (Vienna, 1953), p. 85.

had clearly hindered the functions of Parliament and strengthened the forces of antiparliamentarianism. Oddly enough, the
pressure by the Heimwehr to use force if reforms failed actually
worked.[53] It had "improved the chances" of parliamentary discussion of the constitutional question. "The three majority parties
stood solidly behind the government and the opposition had
abandoned its intransigent attitude."[54]

The parliamentary atmosphere in the critical months after
Schober's accession benefited from Seipel's absence on a "parliamentary vacation." But once again seclusion did not mean inactivity for Seipel. In the autumn Seipel and Othmar Spann, the
latter-day "magus of the North," exchanged ideas in a series of
meetings whose intensity must have reminded Seipel of his prepolitical years in Salzburg. Seipel's formerly ambivalent feelings
toward Spann have been mentioned; the two men's paths had
hardly crossed before Seipel's retirement.[55] Seipel took it upon
himself to appear unannounced at the professor's house and to
propose to him an intellectual companionship which was to endure for the rest of his life.[56] It is tempting to guess at what was
discussed during these frequent meetings, but Seipel's diary,
apart from formal entries such as "in the morning at Spann's" or
"in the afternoon Spann with me," keeps its tantalizing secrets
from historians. Yet a glance back at Lammasch, the chief influence on the young Seipel in Salzburg, may indicate the transformation which Seipel had undergone. In Salzburg he had
learned most from Lammasch, the kindly, gentle, pacific man,
firm in his convictions but pragmatic in his thinking. Though
Lammasch had been drawn increasingly into the whirl of a

[53] Kerekes, *Abenddämmerung*, p. 51.

[54] Skottsberg, *Der österreichische Parlamentarismus*, p. 368.

[55] Seipel only once before 1929 registered in his diary a meeting with
Spann, namely on February 7, 1927: "Prof. Dr. Othmar Spann in the
chancellery." The first diary entry of 1929 concerning Spann is dated
October 2.

[56] For this information I am indebted to Dr. Raphael Spann; interview
with Dr. Raphael Spann, April 22, 1958.

crashing world, he had maintained his serenity and his faith; more than anyone else he set for the moral theologian a courageous example by dealing with disillusion and revolution in a calm and sovereign fashion. Spann who, by contrast, cast his spell upon the elder Seipel in the Vienna of 1929, was fierce and militant. Bitterness against his environment had made him a fanatic; and the deeper the shadows that fell over poor reduced Austria the more self-righteously and vaingloriously did he proclaim his doctrines. Spann was an incorrigible ideologist, and there is little doubt that he drew the disillusioned ex-Chancellor into his deceptive orbit.

It can be safely assumed that a major topic of the meetings between Spann and Seipel was corporatism, one of Spann's major concerns, which at this time moved increasingly into the center of Seipel's political thinking. Soon after the first encounters with the crusading professor he emerged converted to corporatism, thus moving into line with one of the basic political demands of the Heimwehr movement.

The constitutional draft, ready for presentation to Parliament on the afternoon of October 18, was a sweeping document. It went all the way in implementing the general guidelines, namely "the strengthening of the authority of the state, the reduction of the exaggerated parliamentarianism, the depoliticization of the administration and the judiciary, and the readjustment of the constitutional position of Vienna."[57] While the Heimwehr leaders had every reason to hail the proposal, and while the Socialists at least decided upon the path of negotiation, Seipel chose to strike from his seclusion. He launched in the *Reichspost* a series of anonymous and subtly but distinctly critical articles signed "from an academician." To begin with, the recent convert of Spann took issue with the projected corporate chamber, the council of

[57] Schulthess, *1929*, p. 249. Cf. also *Neue Freie Presse*, October 19, 1929, morning ed., and Nr. 382 der Beilagen zum stenographischen Protokoll des Nationalrates, III. G.P. in Seipel, *Kampf*, pp. 267ff.

Länder and Estates on a number of points,[58] but mainly on the question of estates. Chancellor Schober, by providing that detailed provisions for the new chamber were to be left to a future constitutional law, had, so Seipel put it, brought "no clarification" on the issue of corporatism—"quite to the contrary."[59] For the rest Professor Seipel lectured about the difference between a vertical organization of society into "estates" and a horizontal organization into "classes." The implication was that Schober's proposal had blurred this distinction.

In subsequent articles Seipel addressed himself to the question of the presidential election, underscoring the need for popular election[60] and maintaining that Schober's proposal in this matter only lived up to this standard *pro forma.*[61] In effect, he said emphatically, "the governmental draft on constitutional reform does *not* contain the election of the federal president by the people";[62] it would merely cover up the prolongation of party dictatorship. *"The aim of the presidential election is to bring the most representative man of the people to the head of the state."*[63] Thus Seipel stated the obvious, not without referring obliquely but distinctly to himself as "that bourgeois politician . . . who in the matter of fact is the most talked about and the best known man in Austria."[64]

[58] Ignaz Seipel, "Was sind 'Stände'?" (*Reichspost*, October 20, 1929), *Kampf*, pp. 199-204.

[59] Ibid., p. 202.

[60] Ignaz Seipel, "Die Wahl des Bundespräsidenten" (*Reichspost*, October 22, 1929), *Kampf*, pp. 204-209.

[61] Ignaz Seipel, "Die Stichwahl bei der Bundespräsidentenwahl" (*Reichspost*, October 24, 1929), *Kampf*, pp. 209-212; cf. also Seipel to Buresch, Vienna, November 21, 1929, ibid., pp. 212-215.

[62] Seipel, *Kampf*, p. 209; italics in original.

[63] Ibid., p. 208; italics in original.

[64] Ibid., p. 207. It is interesting that Seipel should have warned against tampering with the law in the matter of the official symbol of the Republic. While he left no doubt that Renner's original creation, the one-headed eagle with hammer (for the worker), sickle (for the peasant), and

Elder Statesman or Gray Eminence?

All in all, in mood and message this series of *Reichspost* articles was strikingly different from that of November 1918. While the earlier one had been designed to build bridges to an inevitable future, this one was defensive and in search of a retreat from an experiment that had failed. Earlier, Seipel had been heading toward a daring compromise between the old and the new; now "compromise" as such had become questionable. The only compromise acceptable was a "true compromise" distinct from "lighthearted horse deals" and tiresome "haggling" between government and Parliament.[65] But what Seipel meant by the epithet "true" was, as usual, misleading—all the more so since he chose to fight this rear guard action anonymously, with a blank shield.

There was, furthermore, a certain cynicism in his various hints, suggestions, and criticisms. He might have made more still, he suggested, had he not been more concerned with the "basic thought" than with the detail of the law;[66] as for the latter, he did

---

mural crown (for the middle class) was repugnant to him in its similarity to the Soviet Russian symbols, he suggested that a change could most likely be effected by agreement with the Socialists. The symbols of state, he urged, ought to be protected by constitutional law, lest Austria be plagued like the German Reich by a crippling *Flaggenstreit*; Ignaz Seipel, "Eine notwendige Ergänzung" (*Reichspost*, October 25, 1929), *Kampf*, p. 217. Arguing this way, Seipel may have remembered his own moderating influence in the early years of the Republic. As for the national colors, the red-white-red of the Babenbergs, he advised, should not be tampered with for the benefit of the black and yellow of the old Monarchy "since and as long as" (ibid.) the latter was defunct. The key words in this intricate argument undoubtedly were "as long as." Indeed this monarchistic hint was followed up by the demand for the reconsideration of the Law governing the Banishment and Property Confiscation of the House of Habsburg-Lorraine; ibid., pp. 217f. "His Excellency" in his retreat had clearly not discarded the vision of the double eagle, not even the one with the imperial crown over it.

[65] "Echten Kompromissen," "leichtfertigen Packeleien," "Feilschen"; Ignaz Seipel, "Die Aufgaben des Bundespräsidenten" (*Reichspost*, November 6, 1929), *Kampf*, pp. 243f.

[66] Seipel, *Kampf*, p. 268, n. 1, carrying over from p. 267.

not think it important in the least.[67] What may have seemed the height of wisdom coming from the pen of a common law practitioner like the American Chief Justice John Marshall,[68] was dubious and indeed dangerous advice coming from a man in Seipel's predicament. By rejecting "literal interpreters"[69] of the constitution in favor of those with a "higher" and "true" sense of the law, Seipel had worked out a rationale for arbitrariness.

The various articles by the ex-Chancellor indicated that he had decided to torpedo his rival's policy of normalization. It was at this point that Seipel vitiated the expected effects of his own resignation in April. After Streeruwitz's fiasco, the country had a Chancellor whose policy was firm as well as circumspect. Facing pressure from the streets, threats of a Heimwehr coup, and the continued danger of economic collapse, he followed a policy of hard parliamentary bargaining with the opposition. But Seipel seized on the Heimwehr leadership's mounting suspicions that Schober was selling out to the Social Democrats.[70] "The future government will, on the question of constitutional reform, cooperate openly with the Heimwehr."[71] The fact that Schober, like Streeruwitz before him, violated this assertion, cost him, not to Seipel's displeasure, the unrelenting hostility of the Heimwehr.

The constitutional reform, as it was passed by the two Houses on December 7 and 10, 1929, was indeed the result of hard bargaining between the Chancellor and the opposition.[72] The unani-

[67] Seipel to Funder, Vienna, October 3, 1929, in Funder, *Als Österreich*, p. 30.

[68] "We must never forget that it is a *constitution* we are expounding."

[69] "Buchstabenreiter," Seipel, *Kampf*, p. 148.

[70] Cf. Kerekes, *Abenddämmerung*, p. 57.

[71] Handwritten insertion by Seipel into an undated typewritten draft "Verfassungsreform"; Seipel Archive.

[72] The chief terms of the settlement were as follows: the extension of the presidential powers; popular election of the president for six years; another popular election, if no presidential candidate obtained the absolute majority, to decide between the two top candidates or substitutes for them; federal control of the police except on the local level; depoliticization of the ad-

mous acceptance of the bill constituted after all a singular vindication of parliamentary procedure and especially of Schober's statesmanship. Like the October constitution of 1920, the constitutional reform amounted to a compromise, but compromise then had left the bourgeois camp holding the shorter end of the stick, and now the situation was reversed. The new bill reflected the "shift of power"[73] which had taken place in Austria since 1920, and while presidential authority and power emerged augmented, the principle of separation of powers, as has been pointed out, was also validated.[74]

Even the perfect constitution cannot operate in a social and political setting that is not prepared to support it. The 1929 compromise was based upon even less of a consensus than that of 1920. The intervening years had left too many scars, and the focus of political life had shifted from Parliament to the street and from general agreement on legality to the threat of illegality, shifts for which the Socialists shared much of the responsibility. The Socialists themselves assessed the reform as, at best, a defensive victory, comparing themselves to the French in the first Battle of the Marne.[75] While the three representatives of the majority parties were all agreed on the need to work for further reforms, the Heimwehr, which had been the chief mover toward constitutional reform, was most conscious of defeat. Its Great Council, convening the night before the final vote in the Nationalrat, considered three alternatives: urging the overthrow of

---

ministration and the judiciary; the raising of active and passive franchise to twenty-one and twenty-nine years respectively; the replacement of the Federal Council by the Council of Länder and Estates, though the composition of the latter was to be left to a future constitutional amendment; Vienna to remain a *Land*, though its administration was to be subject to some federal controls, including the one by the federal auditor.

[73] Cf. Hans Kelsen, "Der Drang zur Verfassungsreform," *Neue Freie Presse*, October 6, 1929, morning ed.

[74] Skottsberg, *Der österreichische Parlamentarismus*, pp. 398ff.

[75] Cf. *Arbeiter-Zeitung*, December 12, 1929.

Schober on the floor, resisting with force, or accepting the fragmentary revision while continuing the struggle independently of the bourgeois parties.[76] During the same night of December 6, Steidle consulted the gray eminence in his monastic seclusion.[77] For the latter the reform work amounted to a compromise, but not a "true" one. Government and parliament had fallen far short of the desired objective; indeed Seipel maintained that "they will still have to be educated toward the true democracy."[78] But for the moment he cautioned Steidle against overthrowing Schober, since the situation was not yet ripe for the final "showdown."[79]

For the moment Schober had prepared the ground for the pressing problems of foreign policy. His January trip to the Second Hague Conference brought him the success for which the Ballhausplatz had vainly struggled for a decade. Austria was at last freed from reparation payments, the general mortgage as well as the interest on the relief credits, and the road was cleared for negotiations toward a new loan. Schober's visit to Rome early in February resulted in the conclusion of a Friendship and Arbitration Treaty (February 6) between Austria and Italy. In this case Schober scored where Seipel had so clearly failed in 1928. In April Schober finally achieved another success in foreign policy by concluding the long overdue German-Austrian trade agreement for which Seipel had struggled in vain.

But while Schober was fortifying Austria's position abroad, Seipel was preparing for his showdown at home with characteristic ambiguity. On December 24 he had the Christian Socialist News Agency announce both that he was resuming his political activity and that he had gone to give a lecture in Luxemburg. The press, understandably suspicious, ascertained that the Empress Zita had just arrived in Luxemburg. Had the scheming ex-Chancellor called on the scheming ex-Empress? Seipel disposed

[76] Kerekes, *Abenddämmerung*, p. 64.
[77] Ibid.
[78] Seipel, *Kampf*, x (preface, written on December 8, 1929).
[79] Kerekes, *Abenddämmerung*, p. 64.

of this question by stating simply that he had not seen "Her Majesty, the Empress"—a statement not exactly devised to lay the public's suspicions to rest.[80]

Otherwise the turn of the year was filled with visits between Seipel and Spann and between Seipel and the Heimwehr leaders Pabst and Steidle. It was undoubtedly under Spann's influence that Seipel launched a new trial balloon on the question of corporative representation that went way beyond the 1929 compromise, only to find himself rebuffed by his own party.

Between Seipel and the Heimwehr *condottieri* the topic of discussion was future tactics in the face of Schober's expected adherence to the compromise of December 1929. As it stood, the alliance between Seipel and the Heimwehr was an uneasy one. "Your Reverence," Pabst said to Seipel, "we trust you. But we have come to understand that a good stable-owner has been lost in you. You have two horses, the Heimwehr and the Christian Socialist party. One certainly will run through the goal as victor and the other one will merely set the pace; only we do not know which one you have marked to be the pacesetter and which one to be the victor."[81] Seipel, we are told, acknowledged this metaphor with a mere smile; but he did not answer.[82] There is good reason to believe that at this particular stage he did not himself know the answer.

When in April 1930 Seipel announced his resignation as party chief, for reasons of health,[83] his critics had little reason to be satisfied. While this "second resignation" may have been prompted by his increased sense of failure and frustration,[84] and while it also reflected the growing opposition by moderate elements within the party to Seipel's policy of harassment, it could

---

[80] *Reichspost*, December 30, 1929; *Neue Freie Presse*, December 30, 1929, evening ed.; cf. also *Neues Wiener Journal*, September 20, 1932.

[81] Kerekes, *Abenddämmerung*, p. 65.   [82] Ibid.

[83] *Neue Freie Presse*, April 12, 1930, morning ed.

[84] Dr. Franz Klein, "Seipels zweiter Rücktritt," *Der österreichische Volkswirt*, XXII, April 19, 1930, 789f.

not have been supposed that Seipel's "self-effacement" would in any way make the government's task easier.[85] Not only did the party eventually choose Seipel's lieutenant Vaugoin as his successor, upon his recommendation; but it was likely that the more the ex-Chancellor was pushed into the background, the more irresponsible he would become.

As before, the ailing Prelate shot his arrows from Germany. At a time when both the German and Austrian political scenes were crisis-ridden and in dire need of counsels of reason, he added his voice to the chorus of unreason. Addressing the Center party at Elberfeld, he chose a distinctly ambiguous title, "The Struggle over Democracy."[86] The speech was that of a man deeply disillusioned about the workings of the democratic process, which, he explained, had been oversold after the war and in Austria wrecked by Socialist obstruction.

The web of confusion and dishonesty which Seipel spun in pretending to defend democracy against the "nondemocratic" and "antidemocratic" influences could not conceal the fact that he had come a long way from his initial position on democracy. With a distinct slap at his one-time associate Hans Kelsen, he labeled the theory that the essence of democracy was compromise between majority and minority, "one of the most wrong-headed and pernicious theories that ever has been invented." "The compromise policy leads in all important matters to the prevention of all action."[87]

In many ways, this speech amounted to a blatant misrepresentation of the Austrian situation. If anything, compromise had had a salutary effect on the history of the Republic. And under

[85] "Mgr Seipel et la Politique Autrichienne," *Le Temps*, April 15, 1930.

[86] Ignaz Seipel, "Der Kampf um die Demokratie," typescript, Seipel Archive; cf. also *Neue Freie Presse*, April 24, 1930, morning ed.; *Der österreichische Volkswirt*, XXII, April 26, 1930, 809.

[87] Ignaz Seipel, "Der Kampf um die Demokratie." Indeed in the course of a lecture which Seipel gave subsequently in the Vienna Politische Gesellschaft, May 8, 1930, he referred to his Elberfeld address as his "polemic against Professor Kelsen"; *Neue Freie Presse*, May 9, 1930, morning ed.

Elder Statesman or Gray Eminence?

Streeruwitz's and in particular during Schober's chancellorship, the Austrian government had for once succeeded in obviating the Socialists' insistent complaint that the majority parties had run roughshod over a substantial popular minority represented by them.[88] The order of the day was no longer obstruction but, increasingly, parliamentary bargaining and compromise—if anything mild signs of a recovery in parliamentary life.

In fact, then, Seipel was now thundering not against parties but against parliamentary democracy itself; not against obstruction but against compromise itself; not against the Socialists but against the Schober government itself. One might say that his personal ambition and his rivalry with Schober had got the better of him. However, this was not all. Action was the key word in his Elberfeld address. This was what the Heimwehr demanded. By choosing to swallow his doubts concerning the activist Heimwehr, and by spelling out his doubts concerning democracy and parliamentarianism, Seipel came to lend his authority to the fascist position.[89]

Disillusionment had quite clearly driven him to a position that the *Neue Freie Presse* for once squarely characterized as "radicalism."[90] In any case, Seipel now wantonly undermined the very parliamentary coalition that he himself in earlier years had struggled to cement. In effect, the "struggle over democracy" in Austria had now become a struggle against democracy.

In the mid-twenties the workings of parliamentary democracy had been overshadowed and obstructed by the conflict between Seipel and Otto Bauer. They were now brought to a standstill by the conflict between Seipel and Schober. The former conflict had been a titanic one between two equals. Bauer, like Seipel, was a

[88] Cf. *Parteitag 1927* (Vienna, 1927), p. 87.

[89] Witness the following unusually positive statement on Italian fascism: "Italy saved itself by giving up altogether the democratic idea and replacing it by fascism, a wholly new system. The upswing which has since then taken place in Italy is unmistakable"; Seipel, "Der Kampf um die Demokratie."

[90] *Neue Freie Presse*, April 24, 1930, morning ed.

fighter; and he went down in battle in the summer of 1927 fighting valiantly. But Schober was not a fighter, not even a politician. He was a civil servant, and he administered his country as he was used to administering the Viennese police. He was doing his duty, and he never understood why he should have become involved in political controversy and attack, especially since these came from the bourgeois camp. But, while Schober had lost out against Seipel in the spring of 1922, he staged a comeback during his last chancellorship between the Septembers of 1929 and 1930. He not only held together the coalition which in the last months of Seipel's tenure had shown signs of crumbling, but also took steps toward healing the wounds of 1927. His patience and his dry bureaucratic pragmatism, his sense of fairness toward the Left, and his firmness toward the fascist Right had earned the confidence of the workers after all. But now he was all the more viciously attacked by a Seipel who had turned his back on parliamentary government and who was in search of a stronger secular arm for the Church. In the unequal fight between Seipel and Schober the last chance for parliamentary democracy in Austria was destroyed by Seipel.

When on May 18, 1930, the Heimwehr leadership took the occasion of a rally in Korneuburg to announce its program—the so-called Korneuburg Oath—Seipel was approaching a point of no return. Although the Heimwehr's membership was a strangely varied one representing all shades of anti-Marxism, and although it had continuously, particularly in the time of its greatest advance in 1928-1929, been plagued by dissension, the Korneuburg Oath left no doubt as to the character of this "people's movement." This oath was a synthesis of the Heimwehr's militant spirit and the corporative ideology of Othmar Spann. In its fierce *völkisch* nationalism, its blanket repudiation of Western parliamentary democracy and the party state, its declared anti-Marxism and also its hostility to the "liberal-capitalistic economy," its repeated identification with corporate organization, it was a distinctly fascist document. Grandiloquently it concluded:

Elder Statesman or Gray Eminence?

"Let every comrade realize and proclaim that he is the bearer of the German national outlook: let him be prepared to offer his possessions and his blood, and may he recognize the three forces: faith in God, his own unbending will, the command of his leaders."[91]

Although Renner's claim that Seipel had been shown the Korneuburg Oath by Spann's student Walter Heinrich cannot be verified,[92] it cannot be far from the truth. In any case, it can safely be assumed that Seipel was kept informed in this matter directly by Spann, whom he saw repeatedly during the time preceding May 18.[93]

The Korneuburg program in various ways aggravated the political climate of the country. Whether or not members of the coalition parties could reconcile swearing the oath with their party loyalties, and whether or not the private armies should disarm, became burning questions. In neither case did Seipel rally to the support of his rival in the interest of the embattled *res publica* which he had often previously invoked in public addresses. Indeed he persisted in his role of gray eminence. To speak on the issue of internal disarmament he chose the inappropriate occasion of an interview with the Budapest *Magyar Hirlap* on the strictly domestic Austrian matter: *"If it [the law] is seriously wanted, it will not pass; if however it should pass, it is not seriously wanted."*[94] It made little difference whether he was properly quoted or, as he subsequently stated, misquoted.[95]

[91] Ludwig Jedlicka, "Zur Vorgeschichte des Korneuburger Eides," *Österreich in Geschichte und Literatur*, vii (April 1963), 152f.; cf. also Ludwig Jedlicka, "The Austrian Heimwehr," *Journal of Contemporary History*, i, no. 1 (1966), 138f.

[92] Renner to Adolf Schärf, Mürzsteg, August 14, 1948, in Hannak, *Karl Renner*, pp. 699f.

[93] Seipel diary entries, February 11, 24, 28, April 30, May 15, 1930.

[94] *Neue Freie Presse*, May 21, 1930, morning ed.; italics in original.

[95] Upon request for elucidation, he said to a correspondent of the *Neue Freie Presse* that there had been a "misunderstanding" and that the published formulation had been "too pointed"; ibid.

In any case, he fell into line with the Heimwehr leadership which, following up the Korneuburg program, presented a memorandum to Schober categorically rejecting the proposition that it was on the same footing as the Socialist Schutzbund and demanding the unilateral disarmament—with Heimwehr help—of the Socialist organization.[96] The Chancellor, however, did not let himself be intimidated. Thus the day after the Nationalrat had passed a wholly ineffectual disarmament law, Schober proceeded against the Heimwehr by having Pabst banished as an undesirable alien for having instigated "the events connected with the Korneuburg Oath" as well as for his resistance to disarmament.[97] Schober did what neither Seipel nor Streeruwitz had dared to do. *Le Temps* rightly credited him with having shown "beaucoup de courage."[98]

There was one further issue which determined Seipel's stand against Schober. Just as his attitude toward the Social Democrats had been decisively affected by their stand on Church and state matters, so was his attitude toward Schober. It was Schober's attempt to deal with the sensitive issue of the reform of the marriage laws, and to enlist the cardinal's support, which aroused Seipel's particular wrath. Seipel, however, resenting such meddling in what he considered his own affairs, persisted in trying to solve the matter *via concordati*.[99] Schober, he wrote,

[96] *Neue Freie Presse*, May 22, 1930, morning ed.

[97] Information Peter to Austrian Missions Abroad, Z.27856, "Nach einem Diktat das Herrn Bundeskanzlers Schober," June 16, 1930; St.A., Personalia, K.481.

[98] *Le Temps*, June 19, 1930. By contrast Schober's excessively critical biographer does not even bother to enter into an assessment of his motivations and calculations. Cf. Jacques Hannak, *Johannes Schober* (Vienna, 1966), p. 139.

[99] Seipel to Mataja, Hütteldorf, August 18, 1930; cf. Seipel to Mataja, Vienna, April 28, 1930; cf. also Erika Weinzierl-Fischer, "Seipel und die Konkordatsfrage," *Mitteilungen des österreichischen Staatsarchivs*, XII (1949), 438, and Erika Weinzierl-Fischer, *Die österreichischen Konkordate von 1855 und 1933* (Vienna, 1960), pp. 179ff.

sought "the approval of all, the Social Democrats, and Liberals for the libertarian deed, the Church and the Christian Socialists for his piety and good behavior"; but he added firmly, "Precisely this he will not get."[100] At the same time Schober's overtures to the Socialists and to the Liberals conjured up in Seipel's mind the specter of an anticlerical bloc.[101]

All in all, working from behind the scenes, Seipel could confidently let things take their course. He had good reason to think that Schober's "kaleidescopically shifting dreams"[102] would eventually come to nought. He would leave it to others to throw bricks at him. "All we need, now more than ever," Seipel wrote cryptically to Mataja in April, "is to wait quietly and to be prepared,"[103] and a few months later he sent the same message, almost verbatim, across the Italian border to the exiled Pabst.[104] Then again he confided to Mataja in August: "I do not believe in a consolidation of his [Schober's] position. I see in a strange way many rats fleeing the Ballhausplatz."[105]

When the Schober government fell in September 1930, Seipel was on a Scandinavian trip. He had recently confided to Mataja: "Physically and politically the only right thing for me to do is neither to lead openly nor to conspire secretly, but to go my way *alone*, to speak here and abroad, possibly in a theoretical fashion, to mystify people and thus to assemble a possibly large congregation above and beyond, though entirely for the benefit of the party."[106] Absence could not serve Seipel as an alibi. *Le Temps* was correct in assuming that "Monsignor Seipel . . . despite his withdrawal has remained the veritable animator of Christian Socialist policies."[107] In saying that the charge that he had toppled Schober's government would give "too much credit" to the latter,

[100] Seipel to Mataja, Hütteldorf, August 18, 1930.
[101] Cf. in particular Seipel to Mataja, April 28, 1930.
[102] Ibid.   [103] Ibid.
[104] "Ruhig bleiben und die Entwicklung abwarten," Kerekes, *Abenddämmerung*, p. 78.
[105] Seipel to Mataja, Hütteldorf, August 18, 1930.
[106] Seipel to Mataja, Vienna, April 28, 1930; italics in original.
[107] *Le Temps*, September 30, 1930.

which lacked "the most essential power, namely the power of decision," and had collapsed by itself, Seipel was sarcastic but unconvincing.[108]

The more Schober lacked decisiveness and a sense of power, the more he needed the backing of Seipel and the Christian Socialists. The coalition, which constituted the only feasible and legitimately democratic basis of the government, was being systematically wrecked by Seipel, who no longer had his eyes on Parliament as the center of political decision-making. In any case, if Seipel in 1930 spoke of the "power of decision," he no longer meant the action growing out of the intricate process of advice and consent, but action as projected in the Elberfeld address—independent of advice and consent. It may well be that Schober lost out because he was unable to play the game of politics; his politics were the politics of bureaucracy, basically nonpartisan, neutral, concerned primarily with efficiency and rationality and unprepared for the trials of conflict. But a greater reason for his downfall was that his adversary, a highly political man, had himself decided against politics. Impatient of political dialogue, compromises, and coalitions, he cast about irresponsibly and indeed aimlessly for drastic formulas for breaking Austria's impasse, which had in part been precipitated by himself. Under the impact, then, of the encounter between nonpolitics and antipolitics the tender plant of Austrian parliamentary democracy was allowed to die.

Foreign Minister in the Vaugoin Cabinet

The fall of his rival's cabinet in Vienna made Seipel cut short his trip to return to the capital on September 28, and as negotiations toward the formation of a new government were dragging, Seipel once again moved into the center of political activity.

The new minority government of Vaugoin, Seipel, and Starhemberg, formed on September 30, left the country with the

[108] Seipel to Lothar Wimmer, Meran, December 18, 1930; courtesy the late Baron Lother Wimmer.

uneasy alternative of predated elections[109] or a Heimwehr *coup d'état*—or both. "From the very start" the government was considered a mere interim arrangement to administer the elections.[110] The new Chancellor Vaugoin was known as a man of action. Utterly lacking the stature and sophistication of Seipel, he beat the drum in the struggle against Marxism. As soon as he had assumed leadership of the party, he was rumored to be a potential Austrian MacMahon or Boulanger.[111] As for Ernst Rüdiger von Starhemberg, this young scion of one of Austria's oldest families had assumed the leadership of the Heimwehr early in September. While representing the more moderate elements in the movement, he entered the cabinet, as he later admitted, "with the object of bringing about a *coup d'état*."[112] In their first proclamation after the formation of the new government the Heimwehr leadership boasted that the anti-Marxist Unity Front had been "smashed." "If the Heimwehr today has put its hand on the rudder of government, it has done so not in order to support the Christian Socialist party, but to hold onto the rudder for our movement." "On the debris of the party-political parliament the new state, the Heimwehr state" was to be constructed.[113]

Seipel's return to the roster of ministers was designed to give legitimacy to the government. Indeed, *Le Temps*, closely watching developments in Austria, called his inclusion in the cabinet "the most weighty trump in the hands of the new federal Chan-

[109] In the normal course of events the mandate of the Nationalrat would have expired in April 1931, but on October 1 President Miklas, upon the recommendation of the new cabinet, dissolved it and scheduled new elections for November 9, 1930.

[110] "Wahlregierung"; Seipel to Wimmer, Meran, December 18, 1930; courtesy the late Baron Lothar Wimmer. Cf. *Neue Freie Presse*, September 24, 1930, morning ed.

[111] *Neue Freie Presse*, May 5, 1930, morning ed.

[112] Ernst Rüdiger Prince Starhemberg, *Between Hitler and Mussolini* (New York and London, 1942), p. 34.

[113] *Neue Freie Presse*, October 3, 1930, morning ed.; italics in original.

cellor."[114] But it hastened to observe that Seipel had been "less reticent" in his utterances since leaving the chancellery, and that his acting as "moral guarantor" on behalf of the Heimwehr was not helpful to his European prestige.[115]

Seipel's calculation that new elections could, even in an atmosphere of political and economic turmoil, bring about a stabilization of the political scene reflected his readiness to take real risks. The events in Germany in September 1930 should have been a warning to any Austrian statesman. Moreover, the Heimwehr could not be dissuaded from entering the elections separately;[116] shielded all too long by Seipel, it could now play the part of the sorcerer's apprentice with impunity. While Seipel thus kept hoping against hope for a two-thirds majority of the "bourgeois parties," to include the much-maligned former coalition partners, he himself did not dismiss the possibility of a *coup d'état*. To Lajos Ambrózy, the Hungarian Minister in Vienna, he said, cryptically as usual, "that in principle he did not consider a solution outside of parliament impossible."[117]

The result of the November election was a fiasco.[118] The Social

[114] *Le Temps*, October 3, 1930. During the first cabinet meeting Seipel elaborated that he had assumed the Foreign Ministry with the primary objective of reassuring the European Powers on Austria's unchanged foreign political course; A.V.A., M.R.652, October 1, 1930.

[115] *Le Temps*, October 3, 1930.   [116] As the so-called Heimatblock.

[117] Kerekes, *Abenddämmerung*, p. 87.

[118]

	Votes	Per- centage	Seats	(Compared with 1927 election)
Social Democrats	1,516,913	41.15	72	(71)
Christian Socialists	1,314,468	35.65	66	(73)
Schoberblock (combined Pan- Germans and Landbund)	424,962	11.52	19	(21)
Heimatblock	227,197	6.16	8	(0)
Others	203,542	5.52	0	(0)

Cf. Alfred Kasamas, *Österreichische Chronik* (Vienna, 1948), p. 503.

379

Democrats emerged as the strongest party. More decisive, the Christian Socialist–Heimatblock combination did not come close to obtaining the absolute majority. "Seipel's calculation," the *Berliner Tageblatt* commented, "has proven wrong to an even greater degree than his adversaries themselves had anticipated. He can now conclude that the weapon which he has hurled at Schober, against his constitutional reform plans and his parliamentary majority, has thoroughly boomeranged against himself."[119] The "flirting with the *coup d'état*," the *Neue Freie Presse* emphasized, had after all not found approval with the electorate.[120]

Seipel, marshaling the last reserves of his strength, took it upon himself to cover his party's retreat, ingeniously, but alas, vainly. As so often before, he put his fine scholastic mind to work in a futile attempt to translate a position of weakness into a position of strength. On November 25, the Vienna morning papers came out with an elaborate plan by Seipel, a "Statute for the Government and the Parliamentary Majority."[121] Advertised as a "purely personal plan," it pretended to aim at "removing or jumping barricades" which in times past had stood in the way of effective governmental and parliamentary work. Whereas in Germany Brüning, lacking a viable parliamentary majority, fell back on emergency legislation through Article 48 and thus initiated the authoritarian course of the Weimar Republic, Seipel in a similar situation fell back on extended powers of the presidency to outline the possibilities of "authoritarian government."[122] But whereas Brüning rightly or wrongly envisaged authoritarian rule as a

[119] *Berliner Tageblatt*, November 10, 1930, quoted in *Neue Freie Presse*, November 11, 1930, morning ed.

[120] *Neue Freie Presse*, November 11, 1930, morning ed.

[121] "Das Statut der Regierung und der Parlamentsmehrheit," *Reichspost*, November 25, 1930.

[122] Z.30508/13 Peter to Albert Mensdorff-Pouilly-Dietrichstein upon instructions of Seipel, Vienna, November 26, 1930, St.A., Liasse Österreich 2/3, Innere Lage, K.276.

last resort, and, hopefully, as a temporary one, Seipel saw it as a way of overcoming democracy. The word "democracy" in fact did not once appear in Seipel's elaborate draft.

A precondition of Seipel's scheme was the harnessing of the anti-Marxist parliamentary majority. It called for the formation of a joint parliamentary caucus, made up of Christian Socialists, Schoberblock and Heimatblock delegates, who would act as one party in the Nationalrat and so constitute its majority. The new superparty in turn would allow the formation of an "authoritarian government" and the assertion "along all lines" of the "authority of state."[123] In terms of the immediate situation a juggler's trick devised to transform defeat into victory, the statute amounted in long-range terms to a prescription for a cold transformation of the presidential democracy of 1929 into an authoritarian state.

The reaction to the statute, even in Seipel's own party, ranged from puzzlement to open hostility. The Schoberblock had good reason to see in Seipel's proposal for a two-party system an ill-disguised attempt to "eliminate every libertarian trend in Austria."[124] The Christian Socialists in Schober's view could not escape the choice between the Schoberblock and the Heimatblock.[125] In this position he found himself confirmed by both President Miklas and Otto Ender, the influential Governor of Vorarlberg.[126] Indeed it was largely because of the cooperation of these three "otherwise impeccable" men, so Seipel understood, that his scheme was spoiled[127] and drowned in the rash of negotiations for a new parliamentary cabinet.[128]

[123] *Reichspost*, November 25, 1930.
[124] Schober in A.V.A., 3, Sitzung V.A. des nationalen Wirtschaftsblocks, November 26, 1930; cf. also Sepp Straffner, ibid.
[125] Schober in A.V.A., 5. Sitzung V.A. n.W., November 29, 1930.
[126] Cf. A.V.A., 3., 5. Sitzung V.A. n.W., November 26 and 29, 1930.
[127] Seipel to Wimmer, Meran, December 18, 1930.
[128] Bowing to the inevitable, Seipel even made another gesture in the direction of a new Unity Front, condescendingly justifying it as a "minus malum"; Ignaz Seipel, "Grundsätzliches zur Reform des Wahlgesetzes,"

Elder Statesman or Gray Eminence?

Clearly Seipel was at the end of his road. He had so far pointed out every conceivable way in which the country could be steered on some sort of authoritarian course. Was this what he meant when in these days he so frantically prided himself on having steered a "straight course"?[129] But he was well aware of defeat. His health once again took a turn for the worse, the tedious negotiations for a new government having left their mark on him. In late November, when the Vaugoin cabinet finally resigned, Seipel's name faded more and more into the background.

On December 2 the ailing Prelate, in spite of the fact that his doctor had "urgently" advised a vacation, made a point of attending the first session of the newly elected Nationalrat. Entering the chamber, he shook hands with Schober and bowed in the direction of the Social Democrats before taking his seat. As it happened, the ex-Chancellor sat in the right wing of his party, and when at last the Heimatblock contingent entered, arrogantly in uniform but still uneasy in the unfamiliar parliamentary surroundings, it was Seipel who signaled them to take their seats across the aisle to his right, and then after a "hearty handshake" engaged his neighbor, Prince Starhemberg, in a lengthy discussion. He thus gave his sanction to an episode unprecedented in Austrian history. The session itself, during which the seats reserved for the cabinet were never taken, was a short one. But after it was all over and the hall had emptied, Seipel lingered, shaking hands with the Heimwehr delegates and engaging them in discussion.[130]

Thus ended Seipel's last major appearance as a public figure. Somehow his various bows, handshakes, and greetings symbolized his whole political career. The bow toward the Left most likely was a distant one; the handshake with his rival, Schober,

---

typescript with handwritten corrections, dated November 17, 1930, Seipel Archive; cf. *Das Neue Reich*, xiii, November 29, 1930, 177-178.

[129] Seipel to Mataja, Vienna, November 21, 1930; Seipel to Wimmer, Meran, December 18, 1930.

[130] *Neue Freie Presse*, December 3, 1930, morning ed.

stiff and perfunctory; while the exchanges with the uniformed novices were evidently fatherly and hearty. Seipel had long since burned his bridges to the Socialists, and he had come close to destroying Schober and his workable parliamentary government. As his own party began to have more and more doubts about his authoritarian tendencies as well as his Heimwehr course,[131] Seipel was more and more thrown upon the small group of Heimwehr delegates. Two days afterward the press announced the formation of a new government with Otto Ender as Chancellor, Schober as Foreign Minister, and Vaugoin as Army Minister, but without Seipel and the Heimwehr participating. It constituted a last attempt to make parliamentary government work in Austria. During the next session of the Nationalrat the sick and defeated ex-Chancellor was granted a four weeks' leave, and after quietly bidding farewell to "delegates of all parties," he prepared his departure for Meran, a resort in the Dolomites.

Seipel and the Customs Union

Not even during his retreat in the mountains did Seipel shed his political concerns. He kept mulling over the events of the outgoing year—not without reproaching himself for his "ambition and eagerness" and also for his "vanity"[132]—and kept in close touch through copious correspondence with the events at home,[133] par-

---

[131] Even in the Viennese party, which had all along been the center of Seipel's power, he found critics in President Miklas and the labor leader Leopold Kunschak. But the main opposition came from provincial leaders, notably Otto Ender, Karl Drexel (both Vorarlberg), Josef Schlegel (Upper Austria), Engelbert Dollfuss (Lower Austria).

[132] Seipel diary, January 1, 1931.

[133] During his three months' absence from Vienna (December 5, 1930 to March 18, 1931) he wrote 1,071 letters; cf. Seipel diary, March 18, 1931. He welcomed a scheme on the part of the Landbund leader, Franz Winkler—not a friend of his—to displace Schober from his "basic position" as Chief of Police. "With Schober," Seipel wrote his friend Schmitz, "we shall never work together again well," and he welcomed having a non-

ticularly on the question of the Concordat.[134] All the while Archbishop Piffl showered his Prelate with expressions of concern for his health. The Church, he wrote, looked upon Seipel as a "tool in the hand of providence." As such he had once before saved his country from "certain ruin," and as such he might have to be called upon in the coming struggle over the future of Austria.[135]

The Cardinal's solicitude did not really touch the Prelate. Seipel was not the best of patients and he somehow took pride in this fact. "In truth I have not given up treating the doctors instead of letting myself be treated by them."[136] Indeed, the more he was plagued by the deterioration of his body and, as he thought, of his soul, the more did politics assume for him an existential function. It was at this time that Seipel wrote in his diary: "I could not without force and dishonesty toward myself repress politics [*das Politische*]."[137] They absorbed his whole personality and in fact kept him going.

Early in February he moved from Meran up into the Engadine, where he looked for a more rapid relief from his cough, and here he resigned himself to a long absence from home. He consoled himself with the thought that, as he had "no family" waiting, "no social life, not even a *Stammtisch*,"[138] it made little difference where he lived, and he could give himself to his daily meditations and to his correspondence. When he received a telegram on March 9 from the Rector of the University of Vienna announcing his nomination for an honorary degree by the

---

Christian Socialist do the actual scheming, which, however "Mephistophelean," would be of advantage to him and his party friends; Seipel to Schmitz, Davos, March 4, 1931; "Lueger-Seipel," K.VIII, Schmitz Archive.

[134] Cf. Seipel to Piffl, Meran, December 8, 1930, Cardinal Piffl Archive, Archive of the Archdiocese, Vienna.

[135] Piffl to Seipel, Vienna, December 9, 1930, Seipel Archive; cf. also Blüml, *Prälat Dr. Ignaz Seipel*, pp. 40-42. Cf. Piffl to Seipel, Pressburg (Bratislava), December 28, 1930, Seipel Archive.

[136] Seipel to Mataja, Davos, February 19, 1931.

[137] Seipel diary, January 1, 1931.

[138] Seipel to Mataja, Davos, February 19, 1931.

Faculty of Law and Political Science, he sat down to outline his acceptance speech, which served as a grand review of his intellectual development and a tribute to his teachers, above all to Schindler.[139] Otherwise his plan was to stay away from Vienna until the vernal equinox, when the thaw was expected in the Alps.

But before the equinox came on, while the "most beautiful" weather prevailed in Davos, the restless ex-Chancellor was busily preparing to return home. Once again, he told himself, his presence was needed and indeed wanted in Vienna; his rival's foreign political course, increasingly dependent on Germany, worried him. Moreover the news of the impending Customs Union between Germany and Austria had reached him, and he received it caustically. Might Curtius, the German Foreign Minister, want to launch the project merely "in order to cook his soup over a resulting fire?" Clearly the outcome for Austria, Seipel feared, could not be a good one.[140] On March 17, the very day when the *Neue Freie Presse* leaked the news of the Customs Union—which, in fact, had been public knowledge for weeks—Seipel was on the train to Salzburg, where he celebrated mass at St. Peter's early next morning before returning to the capital.

Though Stresemann in his 1927 encounter with Seipel had urged that preliminary steps be taken toward a customs union, he had been compelled by diplomatic expedience to advocate caution in the matter of the Anschluss. He had thus played into the hands of Seipel, who had been reluctant to see Austria's hands tied by any power, even Germany.

The Stresemann-Seipel combination then, uneasy though it was, had precluded any drastic change in the German-Austrian relationship. However, when Curtius and Schober had assumed direction of the foreign offices of the two German states, things

[139] Ignaz Seipel, *Ehrendoktor der Rechte der Universität Wien* (Vienna, 1931); cf. Bernhard Birk, *Dr. Ignaz Seipel: Ein österreichisches und europäisches Schicksal* (Innsbruck, 1932), pp. 226ff.

[140] Seipel to Mataja, Davos, March 15, 1931.

had changed fundamentally. The former lacked Stresemann's skill and caution. Criticizing his predecessor for having concentrated too much on Franco-German affairs, he advocated an intensification of Germany's relations with the smaller states of eastern and southeastern Europe, especially Austria. It was the German election of September 1930 which actually persuaded Curtius to put an end to the Locarno policy and to embark on a more enterprising foreign policy designed to placate the German public.[141]

Curtius welcomed Schober as his Austrian counterpart. He deeply distrusted Prelate Seipel, whom he held responsible for the steady deterioration of German-Austrian relations since 1922.[142] Schober, by contrast, was assessed by the Germans as a safe and reliable friend. Indeed the preparations for the Customs Union go back to Schober's visit to Berlin in February 1930;[143] they had merely been placed in "cold storage"[144] during Seipel's brief term as Foreign Minister in the Vaugoin government.

After Schober's return to the Ballhausplatz, under Chancellor Ender, plans for the Customs Union took shape. It was, alas, Seipel's rival who set out to "roll up" the Central European question. Austria indeed ventured onto the "slippery floor of the

[141] According to Erich Eyck, Curtius's motives and calculations concerning the Customs Union centered on domestic affairs rather than on foreign policy and were designed to take the wind out of the Nazi sails and to prove him a worthy representative of the German "national interest"; Erich Eyck, *Geschichte der Weimarer Republik* (Zurich and Stuttgart, 1956), II, 406.

[142] Julius Curtius, *Sechs Jahre Minister der deutschen Republik* (Heidelberg, 1948), pp. 118f.

[143] Walter Goldinger, "Das Projekt einer deutsch-österreichischen Zollunion von 1931," in *Österreich und Europa, Festgabe für Hugo Hantsch zum 70. Geburtstag* (Graz, Vienna, and Cologne, 1965), p. 530. Cf. also Edward W. Bennett, *Germany and the Diplomacy of the Financial Crisis, 1931* (Cambridge, Mass., 1962), p. 44.

[144] F. G. Stambrook, "The German-Austrian Customs Union of 1931: A Study of German Methods and Motives," *Journal of Central European Affairs,* XXI (April 1961), 31.

grosse Politik"[145]—but, one might ask, under what conditions? What has been said of the Franco-Russian agreement of 1893-1894—that while Russia did not withdraw its cheek France did all the kissing—can also be said of the relations between the two parties of the Customs Union. Curtius did all the courting and kissing, if not pushing, while Schober not only withheld the cheek, but dragged his feet. In effect, then, the Austrians, in no position to enter into this courtship, allowed themselves to be drawn into it. Chancellor Ender, reporting to the meeting of the Christian Socialist party leadership on April 15, made it clearly understood that the initiative for the Customs Union came from Germany, that considering the attitude of "public opinion" in Austria "no government could simply say 'no' to the Reich," and that, when Schober reported to the steering committee of the Nationalrat on March 20, "no one party had dared to object."[146] Curtius, moreover, adding insult to injury—if the German pressure could be so interpreted—impressed upon the compliant Schober the need for Austria to take the diplomatic initiative in the matter, since Germany might be suspected of bringing up the Anschluss question.[147]

It is not surprising then that Seipel, for reasons other than those of principle and personal rivalry, should have been critical of Schober's procedure. The degree to which Schober let the primacy of domestic affairs prevail over foreign affairs must have infuriated the veteran statesman. If Schober had become "overnight the greatest man of German-Austria," as Hans Zehrer wrote in the Berlin *Vossische Zeitung*,[148] it was largely because of the shortsightedness and cowardice of all political parties, including Seipel's own. Furthermore, there was the matter of timing. Austria certainly was politically too weak and financially too vulner-

[145] Goldinger, "Das Projekt," p. 527.
[146] "Christlichsozialer Bundesparteirat," April 15, 1931, "Notizen über die Innere Politik 1931," K.XXVII, Schmitz Archive.
[147] Stambrook, "German-Austrian Customs Union," p. 32.
[148] Hans Zehrer, "Der höchste Trumph," *Vossische Zeitung*, April 24, 1931.

able to launch this bold project without paying a penalty. Had he been the "statesman in charge," Seipel later intimated, he would hardly have undertaken the action at this very time.[149] "If there is one contrast between both statesmen [Seipel and Schober]," Hans Zehrer commented, "it is best stated in terms of their different senses of time. Seipel will consider the time ripe neither today nor tomorrow. Schober however has acted. This immobilizes any opposition for the time being."[150]

While there was no doubt an influential faction among the Christian Socialists, which was the Vienna group close to Seipel who met the Customs Union with distinct reserve, it cannot be argued that they in any way torpedoed it.[151] Quite apart from the fact that after three months' absence from the capital he had lost some of his grip on political affairs, Seipel was also vulnerable on the subject of the Customs Union. It turned out that it was inextricably interwoven with his diplomacy during the summer of 1922; now, therefore, it tended to call forth a reassessment of his accomplishment. It was very likely out of mere routine that the Auswärtiges Amt searched its files for a record of the 1922 Seipel-Wirth meeting in Berlin.[152] Distinctly more relevant were his visits to Verona[153] and especially to Geneva. From the very

[149] Memorandum by Carl August Clodius (Councillor of the German Legation), "Unterhaltung mit dem Prälaten Dr. Seipel," June 18, 1931, Vienna, June 20, 1931; A.A., Abt. II-Ö.: Po.2, Bd.18.

[150] Zehrer, "Der höchste Trumph."

[151] *Arbeiter-Zeitung*, September 4, 1931. Cf. also the allusion to this effect in Oswald Hauser, "Der Plan einer deutsch-österreichischen Zollunion von 1931 und die Europäische Föderation," *Historische Zeitschrift*, CLXXIX (1955), 66f., and Adam Wandruszka, "Aus Seipels letzten Lebensjahren: Unveröffentlichte Briefe aus den Jahren 1931 und 1932," *Mitteilungen des Österreichischen Staatsarchivs*, IX (1956), 566ff. Cf. also Franz Gartner, "Der Plan einer deutsch-österreichischen Zollunion und die Wiener Presse" (diss., Vienna, 1949), pp. 93ff.

[152] Cf. above, p. 191n.

[153] The issue of Seipel's proposed Customs and Currency Union with Italy of 1922 was discussed before the International Court at The Hague in terms of its being prejudicial to the Customs Union of 1931; *Neue Freie*

388

beginning, when the news of the Customs Union broke, and specifically during the deliberations at the League's Council and before the International Court at The Hague, the Geneva Protocols were the center of attention. Even more clearly than Article 88 of St. Germain they were interpreted by Germany's and Austria's critics as a bar to a customs union like the one proposed by the two German states.[154] Seipel therefore had good reason to speak to Rieth,[155] Lerchenfeld's successor, about his "concern lest a failure of the plan, because of a legal interpolation of this Protocol [1922] should be blamed on him as its signatory."[156]

Presse, August 5, 1931, morning ed. Cf. also St.A., Fasz. 144, Deutschland I/III.

[154] Cf. M. Margaret Ball, *Post-War German-Austrian Relations* (Stanford, 1937), pp. 108ff.

[155] Kurt Rieth, Councillor to the Embassy in Prague since 1924, was appointed Minister to Vienna in April 1931. The removal of Lerchenfeld from his post in Vienna had been in the offing since late 1930. Evidently Brüning was dissatisfied with his reports, especially those on the Austrian National Socialists; Richard Schmitz to Seipel, Vienna, December 26, 1930, "Aussenpolitisches," K.XXVIII, Schmitz Archive. Seipel, from Meran, used his influence with Berlin to stave off the recall of Lerchenfeld. It was not love for the latter but a healthy realism and compulsive distrust of the Germans that made him take this step: "Absolutely speaking he is expendable, since we don't profit by him, particularly since he has no weight in the Berlin Foreign Office. But relatively speaking he is valuable because someone even worse could succeed him"; Seipel to Schmitz, Meran, January 1, 1931, ibid.

[156] Memorandum by Rieth, "Besuch beim Prälaten Dr. Seipel," Vienna, May 6, 1931, A.A., Abt, II-Ö.: Po.11, Nr.3, Bd.2. It seemed adding insult to injury when later during the Court proceedings at The Hague Schober directly turned to Seipel for clarification of one specific point. Professor Jules Basdevant, the agent for France, had made a garbled reference to the conclusion of Seipel's address of September 6, 1922, to the Council of the League (see Gessl, *Reden*, p. 32), deriving from it Austria's "clear obligation" to take no step in the direction of overcoming its isolation without approval of the League's Council. Professor Erich Kaufmann, Austria's agent, who was to Seipel's irritation a German national, could not deal with this argument and wrote for information to Schober, who in turn

Elder Statesman or Gray Eminence?

The main reasons, however, for Seipel's concurrence with the Customs Union project had to do with the overall interest of state. While in September 1930 he had irresponsibly rocked the Schober government, he now grasped that the country's vital in-

---

"informed" Seipel of it. Seipel, once again in the mountains for reasons of health, took the time to respond, but not without expressing his irritation over having been dragged into the argument. At the same time he lashed out against all three, Basdevant, Kaufmann and, alas, Schober. "Personally," Seipel wrote, he would certainly not have taken the trouble to react to Basdevant's obvious ignorance and to the "Reich-German's ineptness." But, to set the record straight, he lectured to the Vice-Chancellor as follows:

1. My address of September 6, 1922, is available in the German original and in French and English translations, both revised and cleared by me and the Secretariat of the League of Nations. None of the three versions contains in the quoted passage a phrase which could be interpreted as implying an obligation on the part of Austria. They speak of the *determination of Austria* and an *obligation of the League*. This obligation has been taken over by the League with the ensuing financial reconstruction of Austria.
2. Treaties, not speeches, are the proper instruments for imposing obligations. All obligations taken over by Austria in the year 1922 are incorporated in the three Geneva Protocols which have been signed and ratified.
3. Moreover, an address made approximately one month *before* the signing of the Protocols was not suited to be used if only for the purpose of interpreting the obligations derived from the Protocols.
4. The Austrian action of the year 1922 in its totality shows that we considered ourselves wholly entitled to conclude a customs and currency union with anyone, be it Prague, Berlin, Verona. Neither one of the powers consulted nor the League objected. On the contrary, they hastened to preclude any bilateral settlement by a successful collective settlement.

These four answers to M. Basdevant are wholly legal, not historical, in nature; this means that a skilled advocate could instantly have given them himself without further inquiry.

Italics in original. "Aufzeichnung" (Kaufmann to Schober), August 4, 1931; copy of letter Z.24504/13, Schober to Seipel, Vienna, August 12, 1931; letter Z.24547/13, Seipel to Schober, Zürs, August 15, 1931, St.A., Fasz. 144, Deutschland I/III.

terests were at stake; he understood that once the project had been launched there was no way of arresting it with impunity. He feared, should the project fail, a "deep disillusionment with inestimable consequences"[157] on the part of the population.

"Toward the outside world," he therefore admonished his party friends,[158] a strong and united front was needed. Lerchenfeld was not wrong in describing Seipel in a report to Berlin as an "adherent of the policy initiated by the Ender cabinet,"[159] nor was Wirth when he wrote with some emphasis on one of his trips to Vienna, "Herr Dr. Seipel is solidly behind the matter."[160] But it seems that the undertone of Seipel's continued reservations was lost on them. "If the stakes of a game are high, one must play it with a strong hand,"[161] Seipel pontificated, and he puzzled the German ex-Chancellor by recommending a resort to "the last means," in order to accomplish the Customs Union.[162] In fact, as the international tug-of-war dragged on over the Customs Union, Seipel was confirmed in his belief that "the Austrian," as he referred to his rival impatiently, as well as Curtius, had not "played" a sufficiently "strong" hand;[163] he himself would have played a stronger one.[164]

What Seipel meant by "strong hand" and by "last means" he did not spell out. If one assumes that Schober's retreat after the

[157] Memorandum by Kurt Rieth, "Besuch beim Prälaten Dr. Seipel," Vienna, May 6, 1931, A.A., Abt. II-Ö.: Po.11, Nr.3, Bd.2. Seipel had expressed similar fears in the party caucus of March 25, 1931 ("Klub, 25 III. 1931," "Notizen über die innere Politik 1931," K.XXVII, Schmitz Archive) and toward ex-Chancellor Wirth (Wirth to Curtius, Rome, April 9, 1931, G.F.O., 1485/3086/D615314).

[158] "Klub, 25 III. 1931," K.XXVII, Schmitz Archive.

[159] Dispatch Z.A.185, Lerchenfeld to Auswärtiges Amt Berlin, Vienna, March 30, 1931, St.A., Liasse Deutschland I/III, Geheim, K.461.

[160] Wirth to Curtius, Rome, April 9, 1931, G.F.O., 1485/3086/D615314.

[161] Dispatch Z.A.185, Lerchenfeld.

[162] Wirth to Curtius, Rome, April 9, 1931, G.F.O., 1485/3086/D615314-314315.

[163] Wandruszka, "Aus Seipels letzten Lebensjahren."

[164] Memorandum by Clodius, "Unterhaltung mit dem Prälaten Dr. Seipel."

391

disastrous Creditanstalt collapse on May 11 was all but inevitable, Seipel's position seems inherently fatuous. But, calculating politician as he was, he told his party friends that the criticism would be reserved for later[165]—that is in case the game was lost.

But as things turned out in the late summer of 1931, there was little room for recrimination. To be sure, the outcome of the Customs Union episode was shattering, and defeat was total. The economic and political impotence of Germany as well as Austria was decisive in bringing about the inglorious ending. Austria's traditional pride, its banking system, was ruined. Politically Austria emerged defeated; legally it emerged sentenced. It became evident, to use the language of the *Neue Freie Presse*, that there were only vanquished ones, no victors.[166]

But when on September 5 the International Court at The Hague handed down its eight to seven verdict against the Customs Union, it based its decision on the grounds of the incompatibility of the Customs Union with Protocol No. 1 of Geneva. If it had no other effect, it at least had the very indirect and certainly unintended one of recalling Seipel's own vulnerability in this matter.

As was to be expected, the Socialists did not pass by the opportunity of humiliating the hated Prelate. "The Hague judges Seipel" trumpeted the *Arbeiter-Zeitung*. It precisely stressed that the verdict was directed not against St. Germain but against the Geneva Protocol: "We Social Democrats foresaw this danger in the year 1922, and therefore fought the Geneva Treaty."[167] The chief culprit then in 1931 was Seipel. Suggesting that Schober, by

---

[165] "Die Kritik heben wir uns für später auf," Christian Socialist party caucus, March 25, 1931, in "Studie über Schobers Politik," K.IX, Schmitz Archive.

[166] "Nur Besiegte und kein Sieger"; the editorial with this heading was actually mainly directed at the general European situation; *Neue Freie Presse*, September 6, 1931, morning ed.

[167] *Arbeiter-Zeitung*, September 6, 1931.

capitulating before the decision of the International Court, had shielded his old rival at the instigation of "French imperialism," the paper wound up with a devastating summary indictment of Seipel, Schober, and the entire Austrian bourgeoisie:

> Seipel and Schober fight one another. Their rivalry has for years made up the secret history of bourgeois politics in Austria. But the history of the fight over the Customs Union judges both. Schober, by having taken up the fight over the German economic union at a time when it could only have ended in miserable capitulation, has done much damage to a great cause. . . . But if the Prelate and his cohorts should wish to exploit this defeat of Schober's for their own purposes, the verdict of the Court in The Hague shows that it was precisely their lord and master who put our people into chains. . . . Seipel and Schober—both representative of the Austrian bourgeoisie—emerge heavily compromised from this shameful chapter of our history. The foreign policy of our bourgeois parties is worthy of their domestic policy. The economic catastrophe at home, the defeat abroad—eleven years of bourgeois domestic and foreign policies have left behind nothing but a field of ruins![168]

The Cabinet Crisis of June 1931

It was in the depth of the Austrian crisis, after the collapse of the Creditanstalt, that the hour of the *triarius* seemed to strike. The Ender-Schober government, breaking up under the stresses of the economic and social disagreements within the bourgeois coalition, resigned on June 16. In the afternoon of June 19 the Austrians read in their newspapers that Seipel had been entrusted by the President with the formation of a new govern-

[168] Ibid.

"This must be brushed away! It obstructs the view!" With Bauer's support, Schober brushes away Seipel's cobweb spelling "Danubian confederation" and "foreign domination"; on the far right is Prince Starhemberg's cobweb spelling "Legitimism." Courtesy of Österreichische Nationalbibliothek, Vienna

ment. The President's idea was that in the midst of the general crisis Seipel, the *homo regius*,[169] should use his authority to explore the possibilities of a new coalition by negotiating with all political parties.[170] Seipel's friend Mataja lost no time in hailing his mentor as the *homo regius*, and prematurely saluted him, the former Chancellor (*Altbundeskanzler*), as the Chancellor-to-be (*Jung-Bundeskanzler*).[171] Actually, Seipel at this juncture had no intention of becoming chancellor himself.[172] But once again, as in 1922, it was the "need,"[173] the depth of the crisis in Austria, which impelled him to take over the assignment. As usual before taking an important political step, he consulted the Cardinal.[174] Once again, as in 1922 and in 1927, it was the question of a broad coalition including the Socialists that became acute. "We need the concentration," Seipel stated, "in order to accomplish a closely circumscribed program"; and he envisaged a coalition "for a specific purpose and a specific period," conceivably until the end of the year.[175]

In fact, Seipel's own thoughts on the nature of a coalition with the Left were no longer what they had been in earlier years. The 1919-1920 coalitions were between partners marked for their moderation and their mutual determination to reach compromises. Was Seipel now making a concession to changed conditions when he said, somewhat grandiloquently and cryptically, that "the conciliation of two opposing parties takes place not through compromise of two moderate positions, but through the

---

[169] The *homo regius* was a commissioner appointed by the Hungarian king and given full powers to perform specific tasks.

[170] *Neue Freie Presse*, June 19, 1931, evening ed.; Richard Schmitz, "Kabinetts-Krise Juni 1931," "Notizen über die Innere Politik," K.XXVII, Schmitz Archive.

[171] Cf. Mataja to Seipel, June 19, 1931.

[172] Seipel assured President Miklas of this fact; Schmitz, "Kabinetts-Krise."

[173] Seipel to Straffner, A.V.A., 53. Sitzung V.A. n.W., June 19, 1931.

[174] Seipel diary, June 19, 1931.

[175] Seipel to Straffner, A.V.A., 53. Sitzung V.A. n.W., June 19, 1931.

rapprochement of extremes"? A coalition ministry, he pontificated, was "not genuine" if composed only of moderate party members; a coalition with the Social Democrats in fact meant to him "cooperation with Otto Bauer."[176] This statement contained, if nothing else, a tacit admission that Seipel thought of himself as having moved toward extremism by 1931. It might have occurred to him as an accomplished Latinist that the kind of alignment which he had in mind made a mockery of the concept of "concentration."[177] It can perhaps be maintained that a cooperation between "extremists," like the one Seipel envisaged as a device to save the Republic, was an entirely different matter from the negative cooperation in the German Reichstag between National Socialists and Communists that was aimed at destroying the Republic. But it was not reasonable for Seipel to think, as apparently he did, that he could achieve something like the "national" government that Macdonald later achieved in England.[178]

Indeed the Social Democrats' answer to Seipel's overture was essentially negative. The general consensus among the Socialists was that they could ill afford to be trapped into backing unpopular measures within a coalition and to risk being voted out again

[176] Cf. "Eine Stunde mit Msgr. Seipel," *Österreich in Geschichte und Literatur*, VI (December 1962), 452f. Nevertheless his first gesture toward the Social Democrats in the crisis of June 1931 was a talk with Renner (A.V.A., 53. Sitzung V.A. n.W., June 19, 1931). The candidate for the vice-chancellorship, however, was Bauer.

[177] For Renner's charge that Seipel had been working toward a cabinet of concentration including the Heimwehr (Renner, *Österreich*, p. 108) there is no support in the documentary materials. In the meeting of the Christian Socialist leadership of June 19 at 8:00 P.M. Seipel defined "concentration" as including "at least four parties, that is, if needed [*höchstens*] excluding the Heimatblock." ("Kabinetts-Krise Juni 1931.") Seipel's diary entry for June 19, while listing meticulously the sequence of negotiations, carries no reference to the Heimatblock.

[178] "Eine Stunde mit Msgr. Seipel," p. 449. It is interesting, though, that Seipel recognized that such a government could not call itself "national," since the term was preempted by the Pan-Germans—hence the term "concentration"; Seipel to Mataja, August 16, 1931.

by Seipel after having wholly compromised themselves before the masses.[179] Bauer, a few months later, summarized his party's position by stating that participation in a coalition government would have meant, at this point at least, that it must *"participate in administering the affairs of collapsing capitalism."*[180]

Little is to be gained from arguing about who was guilty for the failure of the negotiations. Seipel was not engaged in a mere "tactical maneuver"[181] designed to trap the Socialists, nor were the latter impelled by mere deviousness and intransigence.[182] Quite correctly did the *Neue Freie Presse* point out that Seipel, considering his all too sharp profile as a fighter, was unconvincing in his new role as a peace maker.[183] Nevertheless, it is legitimate to raise the question of the wisdom of the negative decision of the Socialists. They underrated the basic shift in the political lineup in Austria as well as in Germany. The appearance of fascism as a political force made it imperative for both Christian Socialists and Social Democrats to think in terms of a coalition, however temporary, between the two of them against a common enemy. While there is no reason to assume that Seipel thought in these terms, his offer in fact left the door open for such a development. But the Socialists were on the verge of reorientation,[184] and nevertheless dismissed it. Norbert Leser's conjecture is inescapable: "Had this experiment been halfway successful, and

[179] Cf. Gulick, *Austria*, II, 940; Hannak, *Karl Renner*, p. 540.

[180] Otto Bauer, "Die wirtschaftliche und politische Lage Österreichs," *Parteitag 1931* (Vienna, 1931), p. 29; italics in original. Cf. *Neue Freie Presse*, November 15, 1931, morning ed.

[181] Hannak, *Karl Renner*, p. 541.

[182] Cf. Leopold Kunschak, *Österreich 1918-1934* (Vienna, 1934), p. 134; Franz Winkler, *Diktatur in Österreich* (Zurich and Leipzig, 1935), p. 13.

[183] *Neue Freie Presse*, June 20, 1931, morning ed.

[184] We are told that, according to Otto Leichter, a veteran Social Democrat, it would have taken but a "little push" for the party leadership to have accepted Seipel's offer; Viktor Reimann, *Zu gross für Österreich: Seipel und Bauer im Kampf um die erste Republik* (Vienna, Frankfurt, and Zurich, 1968), p. 351.

had it been possible for the Socialists to make out of this coalition by the grace of Seipel something that had not at all been intended by him, this coalition could have lasted into the time of the fascist threat of Austria from Germany and thus could have formed a solid basis for a defensive struggle against National Socialism on a broad basis."[185] As it was, at this late point in the struggle over Austrian democracy, the leading figures among the Austrian Marxists were like actors in a tragedy, playing out their assigned parts because they could not avoid them.

Seipel was no more successful, after the failure of the "concentration" scheme, about rallying the bourgeois parties to agree on a new government, which he now saw, alas, as a "fighting cabinet."[186] The Heimatblock aside, the bourgeois parties could still marshal a slim majority in Parliament, but the protracted negotiations of the night of June 19 to 20 show that these parties thought no more than the Socialists of long-range considerations. In view of the fact that the country was so close to the abyss, this failure to look ahead is particularly striking. It was the tiresome animosity between Seipel and Schober that played a major role in the failure of negotiations. Seipel's intrigue of the previous year now backfired; in his own petty way Schober took his revenge. The rivalry between the two men now told against Seipel, who was not after all to play the role of elder statesman.

The failure of Seipel's mission, it should be added, was not exclusively domestic. With the Customs Union project still unfinished in June 1931, the German Legation in Vienna took more than a usual interest in the outcome of the Austrian cabinet crisis. It was clearly in the interest of the Germans to have Schober continue as Foreign Minister, whereas in their eyes a Seipel comeback represented a distinct threat to a German-Austrian coopera-

---

[185] Norbert Leser, *Zwischen Reformismus und Bolschewismus* (Vienna, Frankfurt, and Zurich, 1968), p. 451.

[186] "Kampfkabinett"; handwritten insertion by Seipel into a draft of July 1931 by Richard Schmitz, "Christlichsoziale Partei Österreichs"; Aussenpolitisches," K.XXVIII, Schmitz Archive.

tion. The staff of the Reich Legation therefore went feverishly into action to forestall any move that might imply a change in Austria's foreign policy, even going so far as to sound out Seipel himself.[187] A communication with Berlin freely referred to the "interference" on behalf of Schober.[188]

It is immaterial whether, as Seipel claimed, Schober had *"ordered the German intervention."*[189] It is not even certain whether the German interference was decisive. It would be an exaggeration to see this whole matter, as Schmitz evidently did, as a "political scandal of international dimension."[190] However, the German diplomats could pride themselves, together with the Pan-Germans and Schober, on administering a blow to the *homo regius* and his friends.[191] Finally, it was under the impact of President Miklas's threat to solve the crisis by resorting to the appointment of a cabinet of civil servants that the parties of the former coalition rallied to join in a new government under the Christian Socialist Karl Buresch, Governor of Lower Austria, a man less marked in the public mind than Seipel. Otto Bauer expressed the satisfaction of the majority of Austrians when survey-

[187] For a garbled and exaggerated version of the affair, see *Magyar Hirlap*, June 21, 1931, and Hans Habe, *Ich stelle mich: Meine Lebensgeschichte* (New York, 1954), pp. 213f. Cf. telegram (in cipher) Clodius to Foreign Office, Vienna, June 17, 1931, G.F.O., 1485/3086/D615864-615866; telegram (in cipher) Clodius to Foreign Office, Vienna, June 19, 1931, G.F.O., 1485/3086/D615870-615871; Memorandum Clodius, Vienna, July 10, 1931, G.F.O., 2493/4938/E267330-267335. Cf. also Seipel diary, June 18, 1931.

[188] Telegram (in cipher) Clodius to Foreign Office, Vienna, June 17, 1931.

[189] Schmitz, "Kabinetts-Krise"; italicized words were underlined twice in the original.

[190] Cf. Habe, *Ich stelle mich*, p. 213. On July 28 Schmitz even remonstrated in Berlin with Chancellor Brüning over the intervention; Memorandum Dr. Hermann Pünder, Berlin, July 28, 1931, G.F.O., 4938/2493/E267338.

[191] Cf. telegram (in cipher) German Legation to Foreign Office, Vienna, June 31, 1931, G.F.O., 1485/3086/D615884, and A.V.A., 57. Sitzung V.A. n.W., June 25, 1931.

ing the past crisis in a public address: "The new government is a government first without Seipel, secondly without Kienböck, and thirdly with Schober [as Vice-Chancellor and Foreign Minister]—thus a government whose composition has been conditioned by three defeats of the Christian Socialists."[192] But he might have added that the new cabinet, which came to be called the "government of the weak hand,"[193] represented at the same time the swan song of Austrian parliamentarian democracy.

The Presidency?

Later in the same year when the highest public office in the country became open, Seipel at once let it be known that he was available for the office. The first presidential election according to the terms of the constitutional reform was scheduled for October 1931. However, as the day drew near there was increasing hesitation, in particular among the Social Democrats and the parties of the Schoberblock, about holding a popular election. Austria's economic plight did not justify the expenses involved in a process which would have to extend over two Sundays, and Austria's political tensions could only be aggravated by a lengthy campaign between Marxists and anti-Marxists. An important consideration, though, among opponents of popular elections was the personality of Seipel—who, they feared, stood a good chance of carrying the inevitable runoff. In fact the ailing ex-Chancellor, although he had once again retired to the high mountains late in July, kept in close touch with the political currents in the capital. Adhering to his earlier stand on popular elections, he reiterated their importance: "The popular election of the president is the height of democracy, all the more so since it does not recognize any obfuscation through party lists, proportional representation,

192 *Neue Freie Presse*, June 23, 1931, morning ed.
193 Goldinger in Heinrich Benedikt, ed., *Geschichte der Republik Österreich* (Vienna, 1954), p. 185.

400

and similar devices."[194] More unequivocally than ever, he attacked the parties as useless,[195] and took the side of the voters against the political "bosses."[196]

Concerning his candidacy Seipel went through an elaborate personal stock-taking and search for the "will of God." Were there not sufficient indications that Seipel had reached the "upper limit" of a range of possibilities allotted to him by God?[197] He recalled his unsatisfied ambitions toward the presidency in 1928 and the recent failure in his attempt to form a new government, and then considered his deteriorating health. However, his concept of the presidential office as calling for "the highest concentration of moral and spiritual forces"[198] coincided with his assessment of his own capabilities. "I openly admit that occasionally I tell myself that I myself would know better [than Miklas and other candidates] how to play a good president and that I wish to be able to do so."[199] Only a distinctly rightist candidate, he pointedly argued, not a moderate one of the "half Left," could force the "decision"[200] and lead the country "above and beyond the parties."[201] This was the course which he and he "alone"[202] could steer as federal president. The *Arbeiter-Zeitung*, therefore, was not unjustified in warning the public that Seipel as president would mean "disorder in permanence."[203]

In the decisive session of the Christian Socialist party leaders

[194] Seipel to Mataja, Zürs, August 11, 1931.

[195] "Mit den Parteien ist bestimmt nichts anzufangen," Seipel to Mataja, Vienna, September 4, 1931 (continuation).

[196] "Bonzen"; Seipel to Mataja, Vienna, September 4, 1931.

[197] Seipel to Dr. Erwin Waihs, Zürs, August 15, 1931, *Österreichische Monatshefte*, XIII (July–August 1957), 20.

[198] Ibid., p. 19.   [199] Ibid., p. 20.

[200] Seipel to Mataja, Zürs, August 11, 1931.

[201] "Über die Parteien hinauszugelangen," Seipel to Mataja, Vienna, September 4, 1931 (continuation).

[202] Ibid.

[203] *Arbeiter-Zeitung*, September 8, 1931.

of September 9 Seipel, who had meanwhile returned to Vienna, pleaded vigorously for a popular election, warning against "deals" and the sacrifice of "democracy in favor of an exaggerated parliamentarianism."[204] But while the party followed him on the subject of popular election, it did not settle on him as a candidate. As speaker after speaker declared himself for either Miklas or Seipel, it became clear to the grand old man of the Christian Socialists that the majority of his old party had turned against him. The final vote was 30 to 20 for Miklas, and it is of considerable historical interest that his defeat should have been brought about with the help of agricultural interests from Lower and Upper Austria under the influence of Engelbert Dollfuss, the Minister of Agriculture, who took over the leadership of political Catholicism in Austria after Seipel.[205]

While Seipel had been able to write off his failure to form the new government in June as a "formal failure," since he did not really want to become chancellor, this time he found no consolation in his defeat. The rejection by his own party was humiliating; furthermore the Christian Socialist party, once it had assured the continuation in office of its own candidate, went back on its initial decision on the issue of electoral procedure and fell in with the general agreement to elect the president once again, according to the terms of the 1920 constitution, in the combined Houses (*Bundesversammlung*). In this way Miklas was re-elected.[206] For the moment this meant that domestic peace prevailed at the expense of Seipel's vision of a trend toward authoritarian government. For the future, Seipel's warning that to relegate the election to the combined Houses would prove un-

[204] Bundesparteirat 9.IX. 1931, "Notizen über die Innere Politik," K.XXVII, Schmitz Archive.

[205] Anton Rintelen, *Erinnerung an Österreichs Weg* (Munich, 1941), p. 204; Seipel's support during the party deliberations came largely from the "Viennese wing" as well as from Styria and the Tyrol.

[206] *Neue Freie Presse*, October 9, 1931, morning ed.; Miklas was elected by 109 votes against Renner's 93.

fortunate "from the point of view of the interests of the whole state"[207] proved sound; and, as Goldinger has pointed out, it was because Miklas lacked the popular mandate and had a majority only of sixteen parliamentary votes that he later lacked the necessary authority successfully to defeat the dictatorial policies of Dollfuss.[208]

Seipel and the Specter of National Socialism

Seipel's state of health was not alone responsible for his inability to stage a real comeback in politics. He had suffered shattering defeats. By the end of 1931 he found himself rebuffed by his Social Democratic foes, rejected by his Pan-German partners, and even abandoned by his own party. The power base in his own party and its alliance with other bourgeois parties—which he had built up throughout the 1920s—was now crumbling. If Seipel during these years was in search of what he called "God's language," or "facts" and "symptoms" that might betray the "will of God," he should have had sufficient indication of their direction. Nevertheless, the "Nunc dimittis, Domine, servum tuum"[209] had not yet come. The continuing crisis somehow kept the ex-Chancellor from making a clear break with politics. It somehow rekindled in him the active interest in alternatives to parliamentary democracy and periodically revived speculation about his return to active politics in order to save the country.

But National Socialism, the one factor which made itself felt increasingly in Austrian politics during the early thirties, offered a challenging variable in Seipel's political calculations. Though Austria, strictly speaking, had been its birthplace, National Socialism had achieved its political ascendancy in Germany. The Austrian National Socialist movement as it existed in the twenties

[207] Seipel's speech in Vienna of October 9, *Salzburger Chronik*, October 12, 1931.

[208] Cf. Goldinger in Benedikt, *Geschichte*, p. 177.

[209] Cf. Seipel to Dr. Erwin Waihs, Zürs, August 15, 1931, p. 20.

was long plagued by inner strife, in which the "German" Munich-oriented faction prevailed over the indigenous ones without itself having achieved any political significance before the year 1930.

What was striking about Seipel's view of National Socialism was that he saw it as comparatively irrelevant politically, but yet as having a primarily religious relevance. "Simple and ignorant people," he argued, could not be condemned for their Nazi prejudices; they ought to be "instructed" and subjected to a mission which was essentially of a pastoral and not a political nature.[210] Moreover, National Socialism had a distinct scholarly relevance for the author of *Nation und Staat*[211] and proponent of a Christian commonwealth. The crude racism of the Nazis was wholly alien to him; race, as contrasted with nationality, he could not help but see as a "chimera."[212] While in his view the logic of nationality, in Central Europe especially, would and should have led to the coexistence of peoples, racism was aimed at an exclusiveness that was neither possible nor desirable.[213]

[210] Copy of letter from Seipel to "Herr Mertens," Davos-Platz, February 21, 1931; from autograph collection of Iring Fetscher, courtesy the late Klaus Epstein.

[211] Cf. Seipel, *Nation und Staat*, pp. 28ff.

[212] This term appears in Seipel's annotations for the second edition of *Nation und Staat*, quoted in Kurt Adamus, "Die Theorie Ignaz Seipels über Nation und Staat" (diss., Graz, 1952), p. 69.

[213] We have seen that, like Lueger, Seipel was not a racist. He took exception to the "excessively anti-Semitic" views which he detected in the Nazis (Seipel to Herr Mertens, February 21, 1931). A certain development, however, in his attitude toward race in general and the Jews in particular is suggested in the record which August Maria Knoll made of one of his conversations with Seipel less than two months before the latter's death:

> Much did the Chancellor talk about the Jewish problem and the race question, suggesting a more or less strong antipathy—very surprising to me—against the Jews. As is well known, Seipel is generally considered pro-Jewish. I myself thought so until now. But our conversation has changed my opinion.
>
> His Excellency observed an undermining of Christianity by the

But the comparative political irrelevance of National Socialism for Seipel, his cavalier treatment of this extremist movement, is inescapable. His basic confidence that National Socialism could be stopped at the Austrian borders[214] was coupled with the assumption that the indigenous Nazis, like Riehl, could be used to bolster the Unity Front, and that otherwise the torch of fascism in Austria could be carried by the somewhat less ferocious, more fumbling and more maleable Heimwehr. It was actually Seipel's broader vision of an Austrian-led Christian commonwealth in Central Europe that accounted for his tendency toward *Schadenfreude* concerning the political troubles that befell the predominantly Protestant sibling nation. After all, little Austria, he liked to think, was immune and could "keep itself free" for its future tasks. These were extravagant speculations, and they did not endear him to his fellow German statesmen. When Seipel attended the German Katholikentag in Dortmund in September 1927, he lectured to Chancellor Marx and other leaders of the Center party when they lamented the subversive activities of the Nazis. Hitler, Seipel retorted, was a "dangerous demagogue" but nothing else, and it was therefore advisable to take the Nazis into the

---

liberalism of 1848. He thus continued: "We have become soft. We have blurred the dividing lines between Christians and Jews. But thus Judaism has taken advantage of us. We are too trusting toward the Jews. . . ."

That the Jews are a nation is self-evident to Seipel. "Without doubt the Jews are clearly distinguishable. Baptized Jews remain Jews!"

While persisting in his rejection of race as a scientific concept, he added somewhat elliptically, "Today, as a matter of fact, the race problem is very much being explored" (August Maria Knoll, "16. Juni 1932," p. 9f., typescript, Knoll Archive).

[214] In 1924 Seipel blocked the attempt on the part of the Bavarian government to expel Hitler to Austria, "since the presence of Hitler in Austria would expose the . . . government to serious domestic and foreign dangers"; quoted in D. C. Watt, "Die bayerischen Bemühungen um die Ausweisung Hitlers 1924," *Vierteljahrshefte für Zeitgeschichte*, vi (July 1958), 274.

government. Once in a position of responsibility, he argued— lightheartedly and under the gentle influence of the Moselle wine which he relished—Hitler would prove incapable of living up to his promises, and thus the whole movement could be turned against itself.[215]

After the German elections of September 1930, when the Nazis had staged successes which alarmed world opinion, Seipel made a point of entering publicly into the argument over National Socialism. The "old parties," he said ominously to the Oslo representative of the Copenhagen *Aftenbladet*, should bow to the "will of the people." "It is undemocratic," he said, not to want to collaborate with a party which has won the elections, and he added with supreme naïveté that a party that had gained more than one hundred mandates could no longer be designated "antiparliamentarian."[216] No wonder that the Wilhelmstrasse was "somewhat startled" and inquired about the very authenticity of Seipel's statement.[217] But Seipel, even after he had resumed his public function as Foreign Minister in the Vaugoin cabinet, gave further unwanted advice to the Germans on National Socialism.[218]

Ironically, it was precisely the "liberal" Catholic strain in

[215] Clemens Wildner, *Von Wien nach Wien: Erinnerungen eines Diplomaten* (Vienna and Munich, 1961), pp. 152ff. The whole rather painful episode is vividly rendered by Wildner. Marx's sharp and "naughty" rejoinder to Seipel's unsolicited lecture emphasized that Seipel, while he had no experience in dealing with the National Socialists, would not be spared this experience. Seipel had the last word. In his "chancellor's voice" (*Kanzlerton*) he said: "Well, it's all right, you must know it better; we Austrians are after all little and modest politicians." And he left the table in irritation.

[216] *Neue Freie Presse*, September 27, 1930, evening ed.

[217] Wasserbäck to Seipel, Berlin, October 1, 1930, Seipel Archive.

[218] "Interview mit Seipel" (on a recent interview by Seipel to the *Prager Tagblatt*), *Neues Wiener Journal*, October 19, 1930; Franz von Papen stressed that Seipel's advice had preceded the meeting of the Center party leadership of November 23, 1930; Franz von Papen, *Vom Scheitern einer Demokratie 1930-1933* (Mainz, 1968), p. 134.

Seipel which carried over in his attitude toward National Social-ism. Distinguishing between the spiritual realm, which was de-clared essential to the interests of the Church, and the political realm, which was not, Seipel's "liberal" Catholicism had allowed him during the early years of the Republic to become a prag-matic, forward-looking statesman. But when in the course of events the threat to the core of Catholic interests came from the Social Democrats, Seipel increasingly geared his policy toward a confrontation with the Socialists. Seipel's Kulturkampf was wholly centered on the anti-Marxist position. We might recall here that in 1927 Seipel saw fit to include the National Socialists in the anti-Marxist Unity List. Their "idealistic longing and searching " suggested to him an "urge to find roots ideologically in a nonmaterialistic and non-Marxistic realm."[219] Seipel intimated that the Nazis spoke a political language similar to his; that they were after all an irresistible "evolutionary people's movement,"[220] and anti-Marxist at that. There were "two elements" of National Socialism, the one marked by vulgar agitation, but the other by the "fire of patriotism."[221] The latter was a proper object for Seipel's sympathetic concern and accommodative capacity.

In this particular instance the concerns of the churchman and scholar came into dismal conflict with the needs of political vi-sion. Seipel acted and reacted not much differently from the prel-ates who were in key positions in the German Center party, such as Prelate Ludwig Kaas.[222] The Austrian Christian Socialist party

[219] *Neues Wiener Journal*, October 19, 1930.

[220] "Volksbewegung"; he had used the same term repeatedly for the Heimwehr; Seipel at a meeting of Catholic students in Heiligenkreuz in July 1931, quoted in Franz Riedl, *Kanzler Seipel: Ein Vorkämpfer volks-deutschen Denkens* (Saarbrücken, 1935), p. 171.

[221] "Glühende Vaterlandsliebe," Seipel interview to the *Berliner Börsen-zeitung*, January 20, 1932, *Schönere Zukunft*, VI, February 7, 1932, 431; cf. also *Reichspost*, January 21, 1932.

[222] Cf. Ernst-Wolfgang Böckenförde, "Der deutsche Katholizismus im Jahre 1933: Eine kritische Betrachtung," *Hochland*, LIII (February 1961), 215-239, esp. 232ff.

was dominated by Seipel, its own prelate, who was unable to face up to National Socialism as a concrete political phenomenon.

Whether Seipel later came around to a more realistic assessment of National Socialism is doubtful.[223] While alluding to a certain disenchantment with the quality of the Nazi leadership,[224] he persisted in recognizing the positive sides of National Socialism.

Insofar as he felt the Nazi impact on the Austrian political scene, he went to work to steer the "partly well-meaning people into another direction, namely the one of the Austrian Heimwehr."[225] Indeed the more Seipel lost his footing in his party, the more he relied upon the Heimwehr. After the *Putsch* of the national-revolutionary, Nazi-oriented Styrian Heimwehr under Pfrimer's leadership in September 1931, he took it upon himself particularly to strengthen the Starhemberg-Steidle "Austrian"

[223] Barbara Ward, "Ignaz Seipel and the Anschluss," *Dublin Review*, ccIII (July–September 1938), 48f., relies for this argument on a letter from Seipel (Davos-Platz, February 23, 1931) to the publicist Raimund Poukar in which Seipel, not actually deviating from his basic position, conceded that National Socialism "as a movement and party . . . if proclaiming in a blasphemous language principles overtly grotesque and excessively aggressive and directed against the whole of Christianity" would, like Social Democracy and Communism, no longer be subject to pastoral concern (*Seelsorge*) and thus could not "in the future be treated gently"; cf. Raimund Poukar, *Dr. Ignaz Seipel, Nationalismus, Nationalsozialismus*, 2nd ed. (Vienna, 1935), p. 19.

[224] Cf. Seipel at the meeting of the Catholic students in Heiligenkreuz in July 1931 quoted in Riedl, *Kanzler Seipel*, p. 171.

[225] Seipel to Herr Mertens, February 21, 1932. It might be added here that on February 1 the Austrian bishops and archbishops issued a pastoral letter on "Outer- and Inner-Catholic Social-Radicalism" in which they indicted National Socialism along with Bolshevism and "revisionism," stating that National Socialism was not merely concerned with politics but was trespassing on religious matters; "Fasten Hirtenbrief der Erzbischöfe und Bischöfe Österreichs 1932," *Wiener Diözesanblatt*, LXX (February 1932), 1, 2, 1-7, quoted in August Maria Knoll, *Kardinal Friedrich G. Piffl und der österreichische Episkopat zur sozialen Frage, 1913-1932* (Vienna and Leipzig, 1932), pp. 201ff.

wing of the Heimwehr. While in all likelihood he was instrumental in preventing an absorption of the Heimwehr by the Nazi movement,[226] he placed his hopes in the former, which he felt confident would be able to stop National Socialism on the Austrian border.

But the developments in the early months of 1932 did not justify Seipel's expectations. The fall of the first Buresch government late in January was directly related to the inroads which the Nazis had made upon Austrian public opinion. While Schober, no longer *persona grata* with the Western Powers, had to be dropped from the government if it was to obtain new foreign credit, the Pan-Germans, being most vulnerable to Nazi agitation, could not afford to remain in a government steering a "non-German" course. Thus the coalition between Christian Socialists and Pan-Germans, which had been the foundation of Seipel's policy since 1922, formally broke down. The second Buresch cabinet was again a minority government. It included Dollfuss as Minister of Agriculture and Schuschnigg as Minister of Justice—the two dominating men within the Christian Socialist party who later were to take over the legacy of Seipel and steer the country onto an openly authoritarian course.

The provincial elections of April 1932 in Vienna, Lower Austria, Salzburg, Styria, and Carinthia finally brought the expected success to the Nazis. The latter now had a strong voice in the Vienna Gemeinderat and the diets of Lower Austria and Salzburg,[227] and thus became a distinct factor in Austrian politics. The three main camps which from now on determined Austrian politics were the Christian Socialists, Social Democrats, both "old parties" in Seipel's nomenclature, and the National Socialists. There was, understandably, much anxious speculation at the time

[226] Report Rieth to Foreign Office, Vienna, December 4, 1931, A.A., Abt. II-Ö.: Po.11, Nr.3, Bd.2. Cf. also Kerekes, *Abenddämmerung*, pp. 99ff.; Ernst Rüdiger Prince Starhemberg, *Between Hitler and Mussolini* (New York and London, 1942), p. 48; Winkler, *Diktatur*, p. 37.

[227] The elections held in Styria and Carinthia were municipal.

about the future of the country; but to any sober observer of the situation it must have been a foregone conclusion that the prospects for a revival of democracy were slim, very slim. Austria was on its "road to dictatorship," and the only question was whether it was to be of an Austro-Catholic authoritarian variety or whether it was to be of the Nazi variety.

A New World Order?

By early 1932, since the breakup of the first Buresch government, Austria had found herself in a situation analogous to that of Germany since the collapse of its "great coalition" in 1930. Since no more valid coalition could conceivably be found to support a majority government, election or no election, the public turned its attention toward substituting for parliamentary democracy what Arnold Brecht had called the "next best" form of government.[228] Alternatives to parliamentary democracy were considered as well as alternatives to the clear and present danger of National Socialism.

Seipel took a leading part in this search; and since he was no longer in office—he merely held on to his mandate in Parliament —he made himself heard in lectures and numerous interviews which, as usual, were carefully scrutinized by political observers. "It is naturally magnificent," wrote Mataja to his master, "how from your room the electric currents go through all of Austria and shape political events."[229] The room, which was, as Seipel acknowledged, an "electric center of energy," was also very much a sick room. His fever and cough did not abate,[230] and during the last month of his life his ill-health noticeably affected his whole style of thinking, which became less coherent and more frantic. He admitted to his friend Mataja that his "great state of sickness"

[228] Arnold Brecht, *Aus nächster Nähe: Lebenserinnerungen 1884-1927* (Stuttgart, 1966), pp. 309ff., and *Mit der Kraft des Geistes: Lebenserinnerungen, zweite Hälfte, 1927-1967* (Stuttgart, 1967), p. 127.

[229] Mataja to Seipel, Vienna, February 25, 1932.

[230] Seipel to Mataja, Vienna, March 6, 1932.

410

had a way of "paralyzing" his "will."[231] Perhaps this was the effect of his diabetes, as was suggested by one of Vienna's leading physicians who knew Seipel well.[232] At the same time there was "something 'mystical,'" as Seipel put it,[233] in him: a sense of crescendo and of "demonic aggressiveness," which Tandler attributed to the tuberculosis,[234] in the face of time that was running out. The active politician had now given way altogether to the oracle on things Austrian as well as German, on things political as well as historical and philosophical, an oracle veiled and often muddled, who wore the expression of a feverish person in a feverish time.

"To be able to witness the new world order (in contrast to the disorder) without perishing first,"[235] Seipel wrote of his aspirations to one of his former aides in the Foreign Office, and he added that he felt that it was "within grasp." He was aware of a distinct trend away from the party state towards the Right,[236] to which he had contributed his share. If he persisted in calling for a "higher democracy"[237] he was in effect burning his bridges to any kind of democracy. It was one thing to say that Germany and Austria in 1918 had not been ready for democracy,[238] or to assail

[231] Seipel to Mataja (continuation), Vienna, September 4, 1931.

[232] Cf. the perceptive and very moving analysis of Seipel's condition by Dr. Julius Tandler, Vienna's distinguished Social Democratic public health chief; T., "Seipel," *Wiener Politische Blätter*, I, August 27, 1933, 183f.

[233] Seipel to Mataja (continuation), Vienna, September 4, 1931.

[234] T., "Seipel."

[235] Seipel to Lothar Wimmer, Hütteldorf, June 30, 1932, courtesy the late Baron Lother Wimmer.

[236] Cf. Haimo Friedrich to Herold Verlag, May 17, 1949, summarizing the salient points of two letters (November 20, 1931, and January 30, 1932) from Seipel to his father; "Korrespondenz zu den Seipel Briefen," Schmitz Archive.

[237] Seipel interview to *Berliner Börsenzeitung*, January 20, 1932.

[238] Cf. Seipel to Lothar Wimmer, Meran, February 21, 1932, in Lothar Wimmer, *Zwischen Ballhausplatz und Downing Street* (Vienna and Munich, 1958), p. 188; the place of origin of the letter is mistakenly given in the book as Vienna.

the "professors," presumably including himself, who in making the respective constitutions had wrongly followed the example of the Western democracies;[239] but it was another thing to clamor for a new Cromwell in Austria and to predict that Italy with its "Cromwell" was perhaps "closest to democracy."[240] The vision of Cromwell as a protofascist was poor history, and the vision of fascism as the highest form of democracy was, however fascinating as political analysis, irresponsible as a prescription.

Seipel's political vocabulary abounded in such concepts as "movement," "leadership," "dictatorship," "authoritarian state," and the "corporate state."[241] However, all but the last of the com-

[239] Cf. Seipel interview to *Berliner Börsenzeitung*, January 20, 1932.

[240] "Vielleicht ist Italien der Demokratie am nächsten, denn es hat bereits seinen Cromwell," Seipel to Lothar Wimmer, Meran, February 21, 1932, courtesy the late Baron Lothar Wimmer; interestingly, the paragraph ending with this passage was omitted in the printed version of the letter.

[241] Among the main sources for the political thinking of Seipel's late period are his letters to Lothar Wimmer (cited above), the summary of his letters to Friedrich senior, and his interview with the *Berliner Börsenzeitung* of January 20, 1932 (cited above). Cf. also the following passage from a letter to Mataja, Vienna, November 4, 1931, in which the ex-Chancellor foresaw the era of "triumvirs, dictators, or temperators, passionately welcomed as liberators from the tyranny of the many." Cf. also Seipel's comments on the occasion of the formation of Buresch's second cabinet on January 29, 1932, which were given prominent coverage in the *Kölnische Zeitung* (January 30, 1932, morning ed.). Seipel, described as the man "in the background," as the *"coming man"* about to form a "sixth Seipel cabinet," was quoted as having said that "under no circumstances" would he lead or participate in a government formed by discussions among the parties; and also as having interpreted—wholly erroneously—the constitutional reform of 1929 as substituting the powers of the presidency for the powers of Parliament; cf. on this interview *Reichspost*, February 5, 1932. On Seipel's views on dictatorship, cf. also the correspondence between Seipel and "a personality" (Leopold von Popper-Podhragy), reproduced in *Wiener Politische Blätter*, I, August 27, 1933, 184-187. Seipel outlined in two letters (Vienna, May 31, 1931, and June 21, 1931) the conditions that would make him accept dictatorship, namely the "general need" in the country, and independence and "authority" on the part of the dictator or group of dictators. However, he lamented that in all of

ponents of this political creed had a contrived ring. The man who had so deeply experienced the shortcomings of democracy in Austria was after all not the man to rally the rightist forces for the general attack against democracy. Not only was he half dead but he could never quite jump over his own shadow. Even when he was most impatient, one could still see in him traces of the judicious priestly figure who drew back from fanaticism and violence. Although he was drifting into a world which was unmistakably fascist, his propositions had a half-hearted and fumbling quality that might have appealed to the Heimwehr's ill-defined appetites, but stood no chance in competition with the determination and dynamism of National Socialism.

Seipel had come to the end of the road of accommodation. Not only had the logic of accommodation now turned against itself, that is against its original purpose, but in this particular accommodation to the extreme Right Seipel stood no chance of drawing anything but the short end of the stick. "It is futile and fatuous," wrote Ernst Karl Winter harshly in a reassessment of Seipel's rightist policy, "to want to fight National Socialism by carrying it out oneself."[242]

It was all the more understandable that corporatism should have become the predominant component in Seipel's political thinking. With the proclamation by Pius XI of the great social encyclical "Quadragesimo Anno" on May 15, 1931, the Church had embraced the corporative state as a solution for the ills of modern society. Whether or not Richard Schmitz was correct in claiming that Seipel was actually one of the architects of the encyclical,[243] its realization was his chief objective during the last year of his life. He would have found himself "isolated, even in

Austria there were not enough independent men to form a "committee" of dictators; among the few he included himself and Otto Bauer.

[242] Ernst Karl Winter, "Die Staatskrise in Österreich," *Wiener Politische Blätter*, I, April 16, 1933, 25.

[243] Cf. Richard Schmitz, *Der Weg zur berufsständischen Ordnung in Österreich* (Vienna, 1934), p. 14.

his own camp," attested Knoll, had not "Quadragesimo Anno," with its demand for the corporative order, brought about the "legalization" of his social theories.[244] However, one cannot overlook the fact that this preoccupation of Seipel's with the corporative state was in the nature of a retreat, not merely from active political engagement, but from the whole effort toward accommodation that had guided his political career. It was a move "back to principles"[245] and away from the "politics of the day,"[246] a distinct turning away from the hazardous course that had distinguished his whole political career, which had been one of "liberal" Catholicism opening itself up to the problems of the world.

Pius XI's "Quadragesimo Anno," like Leo XIII's encyclical "Rerum Novarum" whose fortieth anniversary it was designed to celebrate, addressed itself to the social problem. Both encyclicals set out to expose laissez-faireism, individualism, and what Pius called the "tottering tenets of Liberalism,"[247] and discussed the fallacies of socialism as a means of overcoming these evils. Both aimed at a reconstruction of the social order through moral regeneration and Christian harmony and through a recognition of the role of smaller groups in contributing to the "hierarchical order" of society,[248] which St. Thomas, "the Angelic Doctor," defined as "unity arising from the apt arrangement of a plurality of objects."[249]

But while "Rerum Novarum" was the product of *détente*, how-

---

[244] August Maria Knoll, "Ignaz Seipel," *Neue österreichische Biographie ab 1815* (Zurich, Leipzig, and Vienna, 1956), ix, 128.

[245] Seipel to Franz Xavier Zimmermann, Munich, May 1, 1930, Schmitz Archive.

[246] "Tagespolitik," Martin Spahn on a talk with Seipel late in June 1931, *Deutscher Weg* (Köln), August 19, 1932, quoted in *Schönere Zukunft*, vii, September 4, 1932, 1156.

[247] "Quadragesimo Anno, Encyclical Letter of His Holiness Pius XI," in Gerald C. Treacy, S.J., ed., *Five Great Encyclicals* (New York, 1946), p. 131.

[248] Ibid., p. 147.   [249] Ibid., p. 148.

ever tentative, between the Church and modern society, "Quadragesimo Anno" marked a return by the Church to a defensive position. Liberalism was indeed "tottering," but in the place of a single socialist "system"[250] two opposing ones now confronted the Church, with Communism looming as the greater danger. Socialism of no kind, "Quadragesimo Anno" stated flatly, could be brought into harmony with the dogmas of the Church,[251] and it even rejected the expression "Christian Socialism" as a "contradiction in terms."[252] At the opposite extreme from Communism in the political spectrum there was Italian Fascism, to which the encyclical administered a carefully veiled rebuke.[253]

The difference in the general conditions surrounding the two encyclicals was largely responsible for differences between their positions on the corporative order. As "Rerum Novarum" was still concerned with accommodation to the modern state and capitalism, it included no provision for corporatism. "Quadragesimo Anno," by contrast, went back to ideas active in Catholicism before the formulation of "Rerum Novarum," namely to the ideas of Vogelsang, who outlined a specifically Catholic social order in contradistinction to the modern state and capitalism.[254]

This reversion of the Church to the premises of *Sozialreform*, indicated in the encyclical of 1931, wholly reflected Seipel's experiences and thinking. As one of the leading Catholic statesmen of Europe he had experienced the failure of *Sozialpolitik*. In fact he found his way back to the "point of departure" of his teacher Schindler.[255] The neutral state had not proven fertile ground for the growth of political Catholicism; the failure of Seipel's policies attested to this fact. Moreover, capitalism, instead of bring-

---

[250] Ibid., p. 155.   [251] Ibid., p. 157.   [252] Ibid., p. 158.
[253] Cf. ibid., p. 151.
[254] Cf. Gustav Gundlach, S.J., "Berufsständische Ordnung," *Staatslexikon: Recht, Wirtschaft, Gesellschaft* (Freiburg, 1957), I, 1124-1135.
[255] Cf. E. K. Winter, *Ignaz Seipel als dialektisches Problem* (Vienna, Frankfurt, and Zurich, 1966), p. 124.

ing social peace, had precipitated the "atomization of society."[256] Seipel conceded that he had been disappointed in his hope of reconstructing the political and economic affairs of Central Europe "in conjunction with international capitalism,"[257] and he recognized the failure of his attempt "to overcome Bolshevism with the help of capitalism alone." He was left with the awareness of having no alternative but "to put all . . . efforts into a fundamental renewal" of the people "in opposition to capitalism as well as to Bolshevism."[258]

The encyclical saved Seipel from going down in total defeat. Rallying the last strength left him, he traveled through the country proclaiming the new social order sanctioned by the Church. If politics had been for Seipel applied moral theology, moral theology in turn became the end of politics; in these last months of his life it virtually saved his face. Frail as he was, with his political career shattered, he once again faced his countrymen with the full authority of the churchman, transfigured and almost triumphant.[259] The agony of the struggle gave way to a vision of a world order that lay beyond the here and now.

Seipel's last effort at reopening the Central European issue was an attempt to realize part of this vision. On February 16, 1932, the Buresch government launched a formal demarche with the chief European Powers, calling to their attention the alarming effects on Austria of the world economic crisis and declaring its "desire to enter into negotiations concerning a rapprochement

[256] Ignaz Seipel, "Die neue Gesellschaftsordnung nach 'Quadragesimo Anno,'" *Das Neue Reich*, xiv, November 7, 1931, 103.

[257] "Durch eine Anlehnung an den internationalen Kapitalismus"; Martin Spahn on a talk with Seipel, op. cit., p. 1157.

[258] Ibid.

[259] Cf. Ignaz Seipel, "Die neue Gesellschaftsordnung nach 'Quadragesimo Anno,'" *Das Neue Reich*, xiv, November 7, 1931, 103ff.; cf. also Ignaz Seipel, "Kirche, Kapitalismus, Sozialismus und christliche Aufgaben," *Reichspost*, January 26, 1932, and "Die Gewerkschaften und die neue Sozialordnung," *Volkswohl*, xxiii (February 1932), 129-134.

with all neighboring states and with all interested states." A positive outcome of such negotiations, the Buresch government declared, was a "vital necessity for Austria."[260]

The Buresch demarche, we are told by Seipel, was in concept, text, and timing his own design.[261] Though he refrained publicly from making any sweeping claims that would have brought more embarrassment to the government and little glory to himself, he gave it his wholehearted endorsement. "There is no one who thinks of it more highly than myself, and wishes more fervently for its success.[262] While the very concept of the German-Austrian Customs Union had been alien to Seipel and only political circumstances had forced him to concur with it, the Seipel-Buresch demarche, as we can now call it, gave the ex-Chancellor a last opportunity to impress his basic ideas for a Central European reorganization upon his countrymen and upon the European Powers.[263] Even though it was not much more than an act born of despair, it constituted a meaningful gesture. It at least had the immediate effect of stirring the Powers into action and of precipitating a concrete French response, the so-called Tardieu Plan, which provided for a Danubian confederation based on preferential tariffs. It also led to the eventual convening in September 1932 of the Stresa Conference—aimed at the economic reconstruction of Central and Eastern Europe. But the competing interest of the Great Powers and the mutual distrust of the

[260] "Appell Bureschs vom 16. II. 1932," February 16, 1932, St.A., Liasse Mitteleuropa, Geheim, K.472; cf. also *Reichspost*, February 17, 1932.

[261] Seipel to a publicist living in Paris, Vienna, March 6, 1932, "Seipel Briefe," *Der österreichische Volkswirt*, xxiv, August 13, 1932, 1102f., and Seipel to Mataja, Vienna, March 6, 1932.

[262] Ignaz Seipel, "Der Plan eines mitteleuropäischen Wirtschaftsblocks," *Reichspost*, March 10, 1932.

[263] Cf. also his reiteration of the premises of *Nation und Staat* in a lecture given before the Foreign Students' Club in Vienna on February 8, 1932, in the presence of the assembled diplomatic corps; Ignaz Seipel, "Nation und Staat," *Reichspost*, February 12, 1932.

smaller ones actually carried the day. The "third act" of Seipel's Central European offensive, the Central European conference, turned out to be at best the final act of a tragedy. After 1933 Central Europe was left divided to face the threat of Nazi conquest.

Between Life and Death

On March 13 Seipel set out on his last trip abroad. He went first to Trieste for a few days, then embarked for a cruise of the Near East. In Greece he visited excavations,[264] in Egypt pyramids; but in the Holy Land the lonely traveler became a pilgrim. Even though he gave no thought to a return to politics—as he had on the Near Eastern journey a few years earlier—and even though his battle for health was a losing one, he clung to life, seizing upon the slightest hope for a final recovery.[265] Indeed, he kept sufficiently abreast of politics at home to plan for a return to the capital in time for the April elections. But he had to speed his return upon receiving the news that the Cardinal had suffered a stroke. Piffl's death on April 21 shook the ex-Chancellor. He was marked for death himself when he paid his last tribute to the spiritual leader of Austrian Catholicism, with whom he had worked harmoniously for more than a decade. As for the elections of April 24, which brought losses to the Social Democrats, as well as to all "bourgeois" parties, and striking gains to the National Socialists as well as to the Communists, Seipel persisted in interpreting the results with undisguised pleasure as a shift to the Right.[266] In fact the elections clearly demonstrated that the concepts "Left" and "Right" had lost their significance, and that in Austria, as in Germany, the strength and coherence of the mod-

[264] The visit to Greece made him think wistfully about Themistocles' achievement during the battle of Salamis in having obtained the backing of Athenian democracy for his daring venture; "Dr. Seipel schreibt," *Reichspost*, April 15, 1932.

[265] Cf. postcard Seipel to Mataja, Abbazia, April 18, 1932.

[266] Seipel to Mataja, Kurhaus Semmering, May 7, 1932.

418

erate "bourgeois" parties, including the Christian Socialists, was threatened by Nazi extremism.

But after his extended absence from the country, from the distance of his retreat in the mountains near Vienna and subsequently in the Hütteldorf Monastery, the Prelate increasingly lost touch with political affairs. There were hours when physical and mental exhaustion got the better of him and when, as he confided to Knoll, he was unable to take in even illustrated journals.[267] This was the time, in the middle of June, when he decided to engage the young sociologist Knoll to be his "Eckermann." Three times Knoll called on "His Excellency" in the monastery in the Thirteenth District,[268] and the conversations ranged all the way from very personal matters to ultimate issues. Seipel began by reviewing his own humble youth and the early death of his mother. He remarked in passing that he had "never known any women" and had "seen them only in the streets."[269] But the limitations of his background and his asceticism were precisely the reasons for his ambition to move upward into "great society."[270] "At thirty-two I was a university professor, at forty-two k.k. Minister; for five years I was Federal Chancellor and for a long time Federal Minister. I have a beautiful life behind me. My ambition was early satisfied." While he added that he had been "foolishly ambitious,"[271] he went on to lament that he had not become president. If God's will alone had kept him from the highest office he would have resigned himself to it with equanimity. But somehow Seipel got the disconcerting and mistaken idea that it was Schober who had blocked his way.[272]

There was the question of Cardinal Piffl's succession. Twice in his life Seipel had come within close range of a high ecclesiastical appointment—in 1918 as a candidate for the archbishopric of

[267] August Maria Knoll, "In Memoriam Ignaz Seipel," address over Radio Vienna, August 1, 1933, typescript, Knoll Archive.
[268] The meetings took place on June 16 and 18 and again on June 28.
[269] Knoll, "16. Juni 1932," p. 3, Knoll Archive.
[270] Ibid., p. 3.   [271] Ibid., p. 4.   [272] Ibid.

Salzburg, and in the mid-twenties as a candidate for the bishopric of Seckau. Though in the latter instance he had chosen the political career, he had never quite overcome a feeling of disappointment that he had never been made a bishop or, indeed, a cardinal.[273]

There was for Seipel something of a personal tragedy, then, in the fact that Piffl should have died at a time when he himself was threatened by death. There was some speculation afoot that Seipel was so well favored in Rome that, in spite of his illness, he was seriously considered as a future archbishop of Vienna and subsequently as cardinal.[274] But it is more likely that when Pius XI raised Seipel's hopes for the archbishopric through his nuncio Sibilia, he did so to cheer a very sick man.[275] In fact the Vatican avoided appointing a successor for Piffl during Seipel's lifetime.[276] Seipel himself was fully aware of this situation. "God," so Knoll recorded his master's argument, "had made him sick to eliminate him from possible election as archbishop of Vienna. The Viennese nuncio . . . to be sure had visited him and urged a pilgrimage to Lourdes so that he might recover and be in a position to become archbishop of Vienna soon. Smiling, His Excellency told me this and in turn reported to me his objection: one could not 'use' the Mother of God for such a purpose."[277] "I now have no tasks left,"[278] added the Prelate, with a resigned gesture of final leave-taking.

[273] Annotations by Alexander Burjan in folder "Korrespondenz zu den Seipel Briefen," Schmitz Archive.

[274] Cf. *Salzburger Chronik*, August 4, 1932, which derived its information from a "high-ranking ecclesiastical personality" in Vienna.

[275] Cf. Viktor Reimann, *Zu gross für Österreich. Seipel und Bauer im Kampf um die Republik* (Vienna, Frankfurt, and Zurich, 1968), p. 52.

[276] Interview with Prelate Karl Rudolf, April 29, 1958. Prelate Rudolf stressed, however, that a five months' vacancy of a high ecclesiastical office was nothing unusual.

[277] Knoll, "16. Juni 1932," pp. 4f.; cf. also Seipel diary, June 2, 1932.

[278] Knoll, "16. Juni 1932," p. 5.

420

But when Seipel's young and eager Eckermann shifted the conversation to substantial issues he again struck sparks from his priestly interlocutor. There was again much talk about *Nation und Staat*, Seipel's first major contribution to scholarship and politics which had never ceased to be the chief directive for his statesmanship. Not only did he now push for the preparation of a second edition, but, rallying his strength, he confided to Knoll: "A beautiful task, which I would still like to accomplish, is to work out the theory of understanding without which peace is inconceivable on the basis of *Nation und Staat*."[279] For the rest, Seipel's random comments on the world around him were as discursive as they were elliptical, and reflected a feverish intensity. He held forth on the South Tyroleans[280] and the Jews,[281] Brüning and Hindenburg,[282] General von Schleicher and National Socialism.[283] On the one hand he was searching for a "theory of under-

[279] Knoll, "Aufzeichnungen von Unterredungen mit Seipel (16.6.32)," manuscript, Knoll Archive.

[280] "Not honest without irredentism. Away from the state"; ibid. But also: "In reality the Brenner is the Northern frontier of Italy"; Knoll, "16. Juni 1932," p. 9.

[281] Cf. above, pp. 255ff.

[282] "Chancellor Brüning—from the national point of view—has been 'mistaken' in his East Prussian colonization project. East Prussia would be abandoned to Poland if the city population were settled there. The German does not assimilate others well, particularly in a city setting. And there were also 'the Polish women . . . !' They would strongly attract those German settlers and Polonize them.

"But this mistake does not justify the departure of Brüning. 'What fuss,' so Seipel criticized the Center, 'has been made with Hindenburg.'

"To make understandable Hindenburg's behavior toward Brüning, Seipel explained: 'Hindenburg is a good Protestant. He does not want to have to face his God empty-handed, weighed down by the feeling to have merely supported and furthered the Catholic Center.' " (Knoll, "16. Juni 1932," pp. 12f.)

[283] "Let the young people drill in the S.A. Schleicher is pacifistic!— Very brave front-line soldier"; Knoll, "Aufzeichnungen von Unterredungen mit Seipel (16.6.32)." Also: "National Socialism! 'Man ought not to inter-

standing," while on the other he was justifying war between nations in contrast to war between classes.[284] Finally he observed a "receding" of parliamentarianism everywhere. While he stated that he himself had "never blindly pursued a great deed," he also conceded that only dictators could accomplish "great deeds."[285]

Even in his feverish confusion Seipel could not hide the fact that he saw himself as a transitional figure—which indeed he was—on the Central European scene, standing between parliamentary democracy and dictatorial rule. At least his political experiences of the last decade and a half had suggested to him the limits of moderation and of conciliation. He had learned the hard way that priestly mildness does not carry over into politics, and his parting words to his assistant expressed this bitter lesson. Having said that it was the state's duty to take action against an opposition "hostile to the state," the Prelate with his failing strength sat up in his bed and murmured *sotto voce,* "One must shoot, shoot, shoot," waving off any objection with a professorial gesture.[286]

Starting in May, Seipel's diary entries had become increasingly short. The patient generally said his mass at home, too weak even to stand up. Early in July he was finally moved to a sanatorium

---

marry promiscuously,' said the Chancellor while discussing the race question, and in this respect he lauded National Socialism, which represented a similar position." But in the same vein he condemned the Nazi racial view of marriage as "stupid"; Knoll, "16. Juni 1932," p. 13.

[284] "One must first stand up for one's nation. There is a *bellum justum.* Class warfare? *No!!* War is the prerogative of the highest *societas!* It can be waged only between states and for national reasons"; italics in original; Knoll, "Aufzeichnungen von Unterredungen mit Seipel (16.6.32)."

[285] Ibid.

[286] Ernst Karl Winter, *Christentum und Zivilisation* (Vienna, 1956), pp. 409f.; Winter, *Seipel,* pp. 159, 192. This episode, though not recorded by Knoll himself, has been verified by him; interview with August Maria Knoll, April 8, 1958.

in the Vienna Woods under the care of two Sisters of the Sacred Heart. Away from the capital he received few visitors, and these were chiefly state dignitaries.

One of these visits had a dramatic note. In the afternoon of July 10 Engelbert Dollfuss, who had taken over the Austrian government on May 20, came to pay his last respects to the ex-Chancellor.[287] What happened was a last-minute changing of the guard within Austrian political Catholicism. The relations between the two men had never been close. Dollfuss, Seipel's junior by sixteen years, belonged to the so-called front generation,[288] which had fought shoulder by shoulder with the Germans in the war. Seipel's old-Austrian horizon had become increasingly meaningless to a generation whose central experience had been the collapse of the Empire. Dollfuss after 1918 had gone the way of most of his fellow students, looking across the border to Germany. In fact, after the war he had obtained his doctorate in Berlin and subsequently returned to Vienna with a German wife. Within the fold of Catholic academicians he had come to identify himself with the distinctly "national"—that is German-oriented— forces. In the Christian Socialist movement he had been one of those who felt oppressed by the titanic stature of the party leader; as a matter of fact, Dollfuss's association with the Lower Austrian Peasants' Union (*Niederösterreichischer Bauernbund*) had made him one of the chief agents of opposition to the Seipel- controlled "Viennese wing" of the party.

At best, then, the relation between the two men had been an ambiguous one. Seipel, the long uncontested leader, was deeply distrusted. Their first public encounter, on the occasion of Seipel's New Year's Eve address of 1929 in Vienna,[289] had

[287] Dollfuss had come once before on June 9 when Seipel was still in Vienna.

[288] Cf. Wandruszka in Benedikt, *Geschichte*, pp. 336ff.

[289] Cf. Kurt Schuschnigg, *My Austria* (New York, 1938), p. 81, cf. above, p. 359.

brought into the open a disagreement over the issue of self-government[290] which had remained one of Seipel's most painful experiences.[291] Indeed Dollfuss had not only actively helped prevent Seipel from reaching his cherished goal of the Austrian presidency in 1931, but again in January 1932, together with the Minister of the Interior Winkler, he had kept the German Legation "continuously" informed about the plans for reshuffling Buresch's first cabinet which, in part, were aimed at preventing Seipel's comeback.[292] When Dollfuss had assumed the chancellorship on May 20, Seipel's congratulatory note had been curt. It had not even contained the "Du" with which political associates customarily addressed each other.[293]

During this last meeting between the new Chancellor and his predecessor, by all accounts past animosities gave way to mutual esteem. In the neighborhood of death the two men discovered their common concerns, and it must have been at this moment that the priest shed his unfulfilled secular ambitions, transferring them upon his successor. Of all those who had tried since April 1929 to fill the void left by Seipel, the small and sturdy man of peasant stock was clearly the first who showed any signs of distinction or promise of leadership. He now stood by Seipel's sick-

[290] Seipel questioned its advisability.

[291] Burjan in folder "Korrespondenz zu den Seipel Briefen," Schmitz Archive. Soon after this episode Seipel remarked on Dollfuss as follows: "Now, Dollfuss has an admirable energy; he also *knows* much about agrarian matters, but I am afraid that he *understands* nothing. Indeed all his constructs up to now have remained but constructs. He should not become minister at times of economic crisis, in which one must have ideas which also could be realized"; italics in original; Seipel to Mataja, Vienna, March 30, 1930.

[292] Memorandum by Rieth (German Minister to Vienna), "Vorgeschichte und Verlauf des Regierungswechsels . . . ," Vienna, January 31, 1932; A.A., Abt. II-Ö.: Po.2, Bd.22.

[293] Handwritten copy of telegram from Seipel to Dollfuss, n.d., Seipel Archive.

424

bed, taking in the ex-Chancellor's advice and indeed directives.[294] It can be assumed that Seipel, like Dollfuss once an advocate of a reconciliation with the Left,[295] now presented his junior colleague with the net result of the failure of his policy, and that during that afternoon the outlines of Dollfuss's authoritarian regime were drawn. It can also be assumed that Dollfuss was ready to report on the success of the negotiations in Lausanne over the twenty-year 300-million-schilling international loan, in which the loan negotiated by Seipel ten years before had been renewed,[296] and also on the guarantee of Austria's independence. Dollfuss, in a domestic situation far more complex and explosive than that of 1922, saw himself cast in the role of a man responsible for the future of his little country, of the captain who must steer the course of Austrian independence.[297] While the Lausanne Protocol hardly denoted "Seipel's victory,"[298] as had been maintained, it brought together the two men who, once removed from the arena of aroused passions, shared the experience of political decision-making in the face of hard and irreducible alternatives.

It was at the very time of Dollfuss's last visit to Seipel that the contours of Dollfuss's domestic and foreign policies emerged, making the young Chancellor appear as the "real executor of Seipel's will."[299] We have no way of confirming the assumption that the dying ex-Chancellor, performing his "last significant political action," persuaded Prince Starhemberg to cast the decisive

[294] Eduard Ludwig, "Seipel, ein katholischer Staatsmann," *Wiener Wirtschafts-Woche*, vii, January 12, 1938, 10.

[295] Winter, *Christentum und Zivilisation*, p. 380.

[296] Cf. *Reichspost*, July 11, 1932. The Lausanne Protocol was signed on July 15; cf. *Reichspost*, July 16, 1932.

[297] Cf. *Reichspost*, July 22 and 24, 1932.

[298] Franz Klein, "Ignaz Seipel," *Der österreichische Volkswirt*, xxiv, August 6, 1932, 1086.

[299] "Die Staatskrise in Österreich," *Wiener Politische Blätter*, i, April 16, 1933, 24.

Heimatblock votes in support of Dollfuss's policies.[300] In any case the agreement between the two men on Austria's future course was significant enough. "Sister," Seipel called out to his nurse after the encounter, "the world is getting healthy again."[301] And Dollfuss left the sanatorium with the blessings of the master.[302]

Seipel's last diary entry, on July 23, included the facts that he had been unable to celebrate mass that day, and had received the visits of a physician and "one visitor." Still, on July 25 he sent out a telegram to his ailing rival Schober: "From sickbed to sickbed I extend my hand to you." Schober was to survive Seipel by little more than a fortnight.

In the morning hours of August 2, 1932, Ignaz Seipel died. In Prague on the same day and almost at the same hour, died the Suffragan Bishop Wenzel Frind, the man who had been Seipel's long-time companion in the struggle for equity among the nationalities of Central Europe. But of the two men Seipel was the one who had chosen to implement his vision by turning toward politics. This decision had left him struggling in the services of both God and Caesar. The conflicts inherent in this dual role were resolved only by his death.

[300] Cf. Kerekes, *Abenddämmerung*, p. 111.

[301] Gordon Brook-Shepherd, *Dollfuss* (London, 1961), p. 85. Cf. also Seipel to Kurt Schuschnigg on July 17: "Thank God Austria is on the right road"; Schuschnigg, *My Austria*, p. 82.

[302] Cf. Brook-Shepherd, *Dollfuss*, p. 85.

'TWAS A TERRIBLE TIME. SO DISTURBED. PEOPLE
WERE ANGRY. STIRRED UP. FANATICS. . . .[1]

---

[1] Munich, 1962, p. 11.

Conclusion

THE MAN to whom on that rainy August 5 a quarter of a million Viennese paid their last respects had been one of their own, a man of the people. Even though his career had carried him far and high, he had lived a life of simplicity. His asceticism had confined him to rigorously modest habits. Both in and out of office, he had lived in a quiet two-room apartment in a monastery. His days had been regular, meticulously regular ones, given to the service of God and of men; and he had kept an almost pedantic account of his doings, for the purpose of "self-control," as he put it. Of his income he had spent only a fraction for his own needs— the rest had gone to the needy; and he had kept an almost pedantic account of both his expenses and of his charity. Seipel had been a plain man in every respect. He had been no genius and no demon. His mind had been sharp, but not brilliant and barely even subtle. The many tributes that poured in after his death agreed in praising his exemplary modesty, discipline, and devotion; and as they referred to his gentle humor and his pleasure in laughter and the quick repartee they sketched the portrait of a man who had always remained honest to his background: down-to-earth and unaffected.

But when Seipel's funeral cortege wound its way from the Schwarzenbergplatz to St. Stephen's Cathedral, and from there to the Ballhausplatz and on to Parliament, bearing him past the scenes of his public life before laying him to rest in Vienna's Zentralfriedhof,[2] it was quite evident that this plain and exemplary

Carl Merz and Helmut Qualtinger, *Der Herr Karl*[1]

[2] In September 1934 the remains of Seipel, along with those of Dollfuss, were transferred to the Seipel-Dollfuss Memorial Church, to be removed once again by the Nazis to the Zentralfriedhof, where they now rest.

man had long since become legend. There was after all something "supradimensional" about him.[3] In this hour of leave-taking both his friends and his foes came together to celebrate the statesman who had carried over into the terrible times after the war, times of degradation and suffering, a sense of imperial splendor and of greatness. Many of those lining the streets at the same time may well have felt that they were the ones who had to pay the price for this imperial extravagance.

At the time of Seipel's death there prevailed, however, an almost unanimous appreciation of his stature, at home as well as abroad. Even those dissenters whose hatred of Seipel did not abate with his death paid tribute to his significance. Seipel, wrote the *Rote Fahne* in the name of the small Communist party of Austria, had been one of the outstanding representatives of "bourgeois class consciousness" and of the "old powers" of clericalism and monarchism. "Therefore the curse of hundreds of thousands of workers and working people, who rightly have always seen in him their greatest enemy, resounds over the grave";[4] and the Berlin *Vorwärts*, mouthpiece of the German Social Democrats, echoed the slogan of the "Chancellor without mercy," adding without much fanfare, "Only fascism will mourn his death."[5] Otherwise, in this hour of funereal armistice, there was general agreement that a great man had died. "He was carved out of the kind of wood from which cardinals are shaped," wrote the *Neue Freie Presse*, and, changing metaphors, it reminisced about Seipel's "Caesarian profile."[6] Perhaps unwittingly the paper thus touched the very roots of a major problem of Seipel's life, namely the double role that he had played in serving both Church and state. But at this solemn moment, at least, the *Neue Freie Presse* was unwilling to expose an issue which was, or at

[3] Cf. *Wiener Politische Blätter*, I, December 3, 1933, 199.

[4] *Die Rote Fahne*, August 3, 1932.

[5] *Vorwärts*, August 3, 1932.

[6] *Neue Freie Presse*, August 3, 1932, morning ed., and August 2, 1932, evening ed.

430

least should have been, central to its liberal position; instead it eulogized Seipel's "courage in the face of unpopularity," his "inner consistency," his "gift of authority," and, last but not the least, the "greatness of concept."[7]

One of the most moving tributes to the eminence of the dead statesman came from his chief rival among the Austrian Social Democrats, Otto Bauer. Although it has been often quoted in the past, it deserves to be quoted again here, not only as a notable, almost classical, example of political chivalry, but also as a shrewd and perceptive Marxist critique of Seipel's life and work.[8]

"By far the most significant man of the Austrian bourgeoisie, the only statesman of European stature whom the bourgeois parties of the Republic have brought forth, Dr. Ignaz Seipel, died yesterday." As a churchman, Bauer continued, Seipel had taken up the struggle against socialism, beginning with his early attempt to *embourgeoiser* the Church fathers. "As he saw in the Church above all the great conservative power that would stem the onslaught of revolution, he considered it to be the function of the Church to defend the bourgeois social order against the onslaught of socialism." Giving Seipel due credit for his connections with the group of "patriotic pacifists" during the war, he made the following distinctions: "If Lammasch became a speaker for this group out of a pure humanity which abhorred war, and Josef Redlich out of his close ties with the culture of the Anglo-Saxon countries, Seipel joined both out of concern over the fate of the great Catholic Monarchy, which needed to be saved in the interest of the Church." It was this struggle against socialism that Seipel had carried on during the Republic as uncontested leader of the Christian Socialist party. "Of the old tradition of the Christian Socialist party . . . there was nothing in him." He had used his foreign political success in 1922 to fan the flames of "bourgeois class warfare at home," and he had followed up his failure in the 1927 elections with his alliance with "Heimwehr fascism,"

[7] *Neue Freie Presse*, August 2, 1932, evening ed.
[8] *Arbeiter-Zeitung*, August 3, 1932.

which was further cemented by the bloody events of July of the same year. And Bauer concluded thus:

> The substance of his life was his fight against us. But he con-
> ducted this fight without doubt from an honest inner convic-
> tion—he was as convinced of the justice of his cause as we
> are of the justice of ours. He was a personally clean human
> being; hard though he could be as a fighter in public life, he
> could be kindly in his private relations. . . . In his official
> capacity he was serious, hard, impenetrable; in private he
> was cheerful, full of pleasure over every successful joke, not
> without an appreciation of the small pleasures of life. He
> fought us, as we fought him, with all means and weapons. It
> may often, particularly in the years since 1927, have been a
> source of misfortune for the country that he was not a man
> of compromise, but one who only felt well in a ruthless fight.
> But whoever is himself a fighter would not withhold human
> esteem from the genuine fighter in the camp of the enemy.
> Now he is dead; the bourgeois parties of Austria no longer
> have a leader who exceeds mediocrity. By the side of his bier
> even we can say of him: this was a man. The soldier does not
> deny to the fallen enemy the last military honors. We thus
> fire three salvos over the bier of our great foe.

There was no doubt that Seipel had become the great man, with "Faustian," and indeed "demonic," traits after all.[9] If he had been the "field marshal" for the Christian Socialists,[10] Otto Bauer's last tribute made it clear that he had also been great and respected as the adversary of the Social Democrats.[11] What has been said

[9] *Neue Freie Presse*, August 3, 1932, morning ed.

[10] Vaugoin once publicly addressed Seipel in this way; *Neue Freie Presse*, January 2, 1930, morning ed.

[11] Cf. also Renner who, in this capacity as President of the Nationalrat, praised Seipel as "the exemplary statesman, the exemplary party leader, admired by friend and foe"; Rudolf Blüml, *Prälat Dr. Ignaz Seipel* (Klagen-

432

of old Austria, that only the fallen oak can be measured,[12] was also applicable to the death of one of its last servants.[13]

Seen in historical perspective, however, the greatness of Seipel must be somewhat qualified. He was not endowed at birth with charisma; God's angels did not hover over him protectively, as a contemporary devotional print had it;[14] nor was he a "master of lethal poisons."[15] He was, as he himself sensed, no Cromwell, and certainly no Mussolini. If he was at all destined for any career, it was for the ecclesiastical one, and no doubt he would have risen to be a prince of the Church. His life would have been an infinitely happier, though perhaps a less distinguished, one. In that case, we can also conjecture, the history of the Austrian Republic might have been a less rocky though certainly less interesting one. In this light, how poignant the dying statesman must have found the prospect, however faint and unreal, of presiding over the archbishopric of Vienna. This would have meant a coming home to himself before the great homecoming to his God.

Seipel has been compared to Austria's Francis Ferdinand.[16] Though he was a much gentler person, more akin temperamentally to the young Emperor whom he served than to the rough

---

furt, 1933), p. 175. It is precisely Otto Bauer's chivalry that has recently been attacked as a "tragic error"; Jacques Hannak, "Die Seipel-Legende," *Die Zukunft* (July 1950), p. 181; cf. also Jacques Hannak *Karl Renner und seine Zeit* (Vienna, 1965), p. 430. Bauer, it has been charged, underestimated Seipel's wickedness in paying tribute to him, and thus himself contributed to the building up of the "Seipel legend."

[12] Heinrich Benedikt, *Die Monarchie der Gegensätze* (Vienna, 1947), p. 8.

[13] Incidentally, it did not escape notice that Empress Zita had no wreath sent to the grave of Seipel; Dispatch Prince Erbach-Schönberg (Councillor of Legation) to German Foreign Office, Vienna, August 31, 1932, A.A., Abt. II-Ö.: Po.11, Nr.3, Bd.2.

[14] Blüml, *Prälat Dr. Ignaz Seipel*, p. 57.

[15] Jacques Hannak, "Die Seipel-Legende," *Die Zukunft* (July 1950), p. 182.

[16] *Neue Freie Presse*, August 2, 1932, evening ed.; the author of this interesting essay was Dr. Ernst Benedikt.

and tempestuous Archduke, the comparison is apt up to a point. "As in the case of the heir presumptive, his character and will were greater than his sensitivity [*das Gemüt*], and like Francis Ferdinand he sought to seize upon an idea and to realize a plan with a determination which exceeded his own strength and over whose difficulties he finally had to break physically." Just as Francis Ferdinand, when appalled by the deadlock over the nationality struggle, had planned to break it with the help of every means available to him, Seipel in the face of the "need" of the people drove himself, by the mere power of his will, to become a leader of men. In Seipel's case, though, political concerns came into conflict with pastoral ones, the statesman with the churchman. Moreover, while Francis Ferdinand had never been burdened with actual political responsibility, Seipel had been. He had in fact seized the "state coach," and steered it into the treacherous paths and detours of politics. While he appeared to be serene and controlled, he was, in effect, torn and tormented. He never again found the inner harmony which, it has been said, generally characterizes the truly great.[17]

Otto Bauer hardly knew how right he was when he wrote that Seipel had died "as a man vanquished."[18] While the years between 1922 and 1927 had seen Seipel at the height of his political power, he had, thereafter, suffered setbacks in his conduct of domestic as well as foreign affairs. He had lost the firmness of his control even over his own party, and he died "isolated, a politically dead man."[19] However, Seipel was a failure in far deeper ways than those intended by Bauer. He failed himself. The one-time Christian pacifist died murmuring "One must shoot, shoot, shoot"; the saintly priest became—and not only in the eyes of his foes—the "prelate without mercy"; the open-minded Catholic ended up defensive and embittered against modernity. He left the world as a "dying lion."[20]

[17] Cf. ibid.   [18] *Arbeiter-Zeitung*, August 3, 1932.
[19] Ernst Karl Winter in *Wiener Politische Blätter*, I (April 16, 1933), 23.
[20] Ibid.

With the privilege of hindsight, the historian can point to Seipel's numerous mistakes. Might he not, in 1922, have allayed the fears of the opposition by drawing it into the negotiations in Geneva? Did he not, by intriguing behind the scenes against Schober, destroy the very foundations of parliamentary government which he had taken pains to lay in the early years of the Republic? Was he not wholly wrong in expecting to gain control over the Heimwehr, and, alas, in giving unsolicited and thoughtless advice to his German colleagues on how to deal with the threat of National Socialism? But all these mistakes must be seen in the context of the incredibly complex domestic problems which a truncated Austria faced after 1918, and which hardly even a Metternich or Schwarzenberg could have mastered. Judgment in history is inadequate if unaccompanied by understanding, and misleading if biased by the all too convenient plot theory. We would actually give too much credit to Seipel's greatness if we considered him the demon of the first Austrian Republic, the "devil in the robe." As we have seen, the mistakes committed by the Social Democrats—their intransigence, obstructionism, and sterile dogmatism—were no less detrimental to the survival of the Republic. In Austria the danger came from the Left as well as from the Right. And the historian of this time of crisis might be well advised to accept the wise words from none less than Karl Renner: "We all have failed, all without exception. By the force of things, by the dialectics of the civil war psychosis were we driven, all of us, to commit follies."[21]

The story of Seipel's statesmanship also demonstrates the strength and the weaknesses of "liberal" Catholicism. Seipel's accommodative position was in keeping with that of Leo XIII, who had aimed at disengaging the Church from the shackles of political and social reaction. Within the confines of Austria Seipel's accommodative position helped his fellow Catholics toward a rethinking of their views on culture, politics, and society. His "leftist" course during the first two years of the Republic was neither

[21] *Sten. Prot.*, 56. *Sitzung, III, G.P.*, October 3, 1928, p. 1624.

Conclusion

disloyal, as was often charged by his Catholic critics, nor opportunistic, as was often charged by his Socialist critics. It had its origins in Seipel's prepolitical period: it was prompted by his scholarly examination of the economic thinking of the Church fathers and by his conscience as a young moral theologian. The very concept of legitimacy gained a new meaning in being related to the basic values of the Christian tradition rather than to a specific form of state or economic order. Similarly, revolution could appear in a new light, as something that did not necessarily violate the moral order. Thus Seipel's democratic orientation was essentially Leonine in character. His accommodative policy between 1918 and 1920, his identification with the Republic, democracy, social policy, and the coalition with the Social Democrats, had a liberating effect in the spirit of Leo XIII.

But accommodation became a problem for Seipel because of the intensified civil war situation and the Kulturkampf of the twenties. It was not the logic of Leo's and Seipel's scholasticism, but rather the general crisis, and in particular the crisis of parliamentarism, that impelled Seipel to steer the "state coach" to the Right in search of alternatives to parliamentary rule. But the son of the Viennese *Fiaker* did not manage to get his coach off this dangerous course. He was altogether irresponsible and, in the last analysis, dishonest in his position toward the radicalism from the Right. It is a plain, though painful, historical fact that in Seipel's Austria, as in Brüning's Germany, the Leonine accommodative position could not stand the test of political and social crisis. Seipel then translated the generosity of Leonine Catholicism into terms of a complete relativism of the Church toward the secular world. Thus the moral theologian Seipel created, in the terms of Ernst Karl Winter, a "ferment of decomposition."[22]

In his conduct of foreign affairs Seipel proved himself a statesman of major stature, the peer of leaders like Stresemann and Beneš. In his encounters with them he appeared, as the German

[22] E. K. Winter, *Ignaz Seipel als dialektisches Problem* (Vienna, Frankfurt, and Zurich, 1966), p. 54.

436

Chancellor Wirth attested, as the "master of the European overview."[23] Though he was the leader of a country vanquished in the war and truncated by the Treaties, he had a distinct and impressive concept of a Central European order worthy of a Metternich and Schwarzenberg, a concept which was by no means oriented toward the past. His main concern was neither the restoration of the Habsburgs nor the reestablishment of Austria's position as a great power, but the creation of a political order that would be appropriate to the ethnic and economic structure of Central Europe. A direct line leads from the young theologian of *Nation und Staat* to the mastermind of the Ballhausplatz charting out exchanges with his colleagues in the neighboring states and appearing at the League. Seipel himself had become the Christian statesman, the Central European statesman par excellence in the 1920s, and also one of the most effective protectors of the many and neglected minorities. Indeed Seipel's lasting significance in the field of European diplomacy lies in his insistent advocacy of minority rights, which to this date have not found proper recognition, within the framework of institutional organization.

Seipel's ingenuity in the game of diplomacy was commensurate with his vision. There is little point in using his policies to compare the importance of foreign and domestic affairs; the fact is that in Seipel's case the two were encompassed by one and the same idea. However unfortunate and disastrous the breakdown of the Red-Black coalition in October 1920, it did free Seipel to establish the domestic foundations, within his party and in Parliament, for making the Central European question a major concern of the Powers. The Geneva accords represented a major triumph in the coordination of domestic and foreign affairs. And if Seipel's gradual shift from a prosocialist to a procapitalist domestic policy was in part dictated by the nature of the international settlement of 1922, it speaks for his impressive flexibility in politics. The man with the great concept could justly pride himself on conducting *Realpolitik*.

[23] Joseph Wirth, "Ein Logiker der Politik," *Reichspost*, August 7, 1932.

Conclusion

If Seipel exploited to the fullest the possibilities of small-power diplomacy, he did not always see its distinct limitations. If anything, he often overplayed his hand in international negotiations. Was the German Minister to Vienna not justified, then, in ridiculing what he called the "great-power policy" of Austria?[24] There was after all something outright quixotic in Seipel's conduct of foreign affairs, particularly in his dealings with Stresemann and Mussolini. His tactical victories were generally but temporary palliatives for inevitable strategic defeats. But it was due to Seipel's skill, as well as to his cherished illusions of grandeur, that the Central European problem was as much as brought before the powers of Europe, and that Seipel's Central European offensive went at least through its first and second "acts." And if the third "act" did not come off, it was not his fault but rather that of the divided and undecided major European Powers.

All in all, Seipel was a transitional figure. He straddled the big divide represented by the first war. He had fully experienced the certainties provided by his Church and the sense of repose that emanated from the Monarchy, and in particular from its long-lived ruler, Francis Joseph. While he saw the Church challenged and the Monarchy toppled, he never understood the uncertainties of the doubters or the agonies of the disinherited, and he turned toward democracy and the Republic with his reason but not with his heart. The shape of the world to come was as yet tentative in the twenties and in the thirties its clarity was deceptive. It became definite only after the second war.

Seipel was not the kind of man to take hold of this transitional world and shape it according to a vision of his own. He was too deeply rooted in the old order, too much a guest in the world of democracy, too humane and rational and not sufficiently ruthless after all to find his home among the fascists who seemed to be

[24] Strictly Confidential Report, Pfeiffer, "Das österreichische Problem und die Anschlussfrage," Vienna, April 15-18, 1925, p. 16; A.A., Geheimakten II-Ö.: Po.2, Bd.1.

438

riding the "wave of the future" in the late twenties and early thirties. When he became disillusioned with parliamentary democracy he was left fumbling in a search for alternatives. The solutions with which he toyed were all more or less of a restorative kind, and even corporatism meant essentially a return to a past position, to the position of his teachers Vogelsang and Schindler, once the experiment in Leonine optimism in politics seemed to have proven wrong after all. Even though it must be said that Seipel toyed with fascism, that he approached it in his despair, he was not ready to abandon himself to it. "Partly against his own volition,"[25] pushed by the events of the fatal July 15, 1927, he moved in its direction. Moreover, he never fully understood it in all its comprehensive wickedness. This is why he underrated it so lamentably. But to portray Seipel as a fascist, or "clerico-fascist," as is generally done by his various Marxist critics, detracts from a right understanding of his place in history. The Christian statesman, which Seipel was, did not see himself called upon to sway the masses with a new revolutionary secular ideology. Might it then be suggested that Seipel, who as a churchman certainly went far out to meet fascism, was nevertheless a living proof of the absurdity of the very concept of "clerico-fascism"? The clerical commitment to the Christian faith, however superficial an accommodation it allowed to democracy and however ready an accommodation it invited to fascism, did in the last analysis defy a commitment to and an identificaton with a new secular counterfaith.

In the end, then, Seipel was not a villainous but a tragic figure in history, and the tragedy of his statesmanship is accentuated by the fact that, transitional as it was in character, it was conditioned by the increasingly ideological mood of the last decade of Seipel's life. Like Don Quixote, he fought windmills. He spent himself during that time fighting and inflicting wounds where as

[25] Karl Renner, "Die Wendung in Österreich," *Sozialistische Monatshefte,* LXVIII (May 21, 1929), 375.

a churchman he should have been healing. This is why the early years of his statesmanship were so impressive, in retrospect, and the later ones so disappointing.

When early in December 1933 the Austrian episcopate decided to withdraw its clergy from active politics, no direct reference was made to the great leader of Austrian political Catholicism[26] who had been dead for more than a year. But insofar as the Church was concerned, the decree put an end to the Seipel era. There was no fanfare, no invective in the Socialists' reaction to the new ruling. The "depolitization" of the Church was assessed merely as a "blow for the Christian Socialist party" and as "useful" for the Church.[27] This was the time when the threat of National Socialism caused a rethinking of political positions in Austria. Dollfuss, Seipel's disciple, set out valiantly to stem it, but the attempt to drive out fascism by imitating it proved fatal. Dollfuss's sharp anti-Socialist course was in many ways the ugly fruit of Count Bethlen's "Austrian Action" and was forced upon him by Mussolini. Meanwhile, it ought to be recorded in the honor of a great Austrian Catholic, Ernst Karl Winter, a long-time critic of Seipel's militancy,[28] that as Dollfuss's deputy mayor of Vienna he made desperate efforts to bring Austrian Catholicism and the Social Democrats together again.[29] These efforts, however, were in vain. Late in 1933, moreover, Otto Bauer made a number of overtures to the Catholic camp in the *Arbeiter-Zeitung*, suggesting that the workers could, after all, reconcile themselves to a non-fascist corporative order that would complement political democracy instead of replacing it.[30] On this level Bauer and Seipel might well have agreed before it was too late, if only Bauer had performed his mental acrobatics in this direction earlier. But

[26] Information by courtesy of Professor Erika Weinzierl.

[27] *Arbeiter-Zeitung*, December 6, 1933.

[28] Cf. Klemens von Klemperer, "Seipel und Winter—Gegner und Brüder," *Neues Forum*, XIII (October 1966), 658-660.

[29] Cf. "Briefe an den Bundespräsidenten," *Wiener Politische Blätter*, I, April 16, 1933, 39-49.

[30] *Arbeiter-Zeitung*, November 24, December 9 and 27, 1933.

440

when he finally did so, his counterpart, who had certainly respected him immensely, was dead, and the switches had long been set for the fratricidal clash on February 12, 1934, which in fact prepared the ground for Hitler's return to Austria.

After Seipel, Dollfuss, Hitler, a sequence for which Seipel had not exactly worked but which he had somehow helped bring about, Austria miraculously revived. Today neutrality seems acceptable to the one-time "conquerors of the Turks," as does a political climate which is more pragmatic than it had been. After thirty years of transition and indecision, some of which have been the subject of this book, Austria has entered, for once without reservations and regrets, into its postimperial and also postheroic era. Aspirations and pretensions have given way to an honest and successful search for an active role in international affairs as a small power.[31] The civil-war situation of the twenties and thirties has given way to a new consensus, deeper and more positive than the all too fragile one established during 1918 and 1919. By turning its back on political illusions and social utopias Austria has at long last committed itself to facing up to the strains and hazards inherent in an open and free society. In these circumstances the figure of Seipel—like that of Otto Bauer—has receded into the background. To the present-day Catholic Church, more at ease than before in a pluralistic world, the towering figure of the political Prelate seems as inconceivable[32] as the cantankerous figure of Otto Bauer does to the younger generation of Socialists.[33]

---

[31] Cf. the excellent article by Hanni Konitzer, "Der Ballhausplatz versteht sich auf Aussenpolitik," *Frankfurter Allgemeine Zeitung*, May 2, 1969.

[32] Cf. Cardinal Franz König of Vienna commenting on the "now unimaginable" fierceness of the ideological fights during the Seipel era; Franz Kardinal König, "Mosaik der Geschichte: Nach einem halben Jahrtausend," *Die Furche*, xxv, May 3, 1969, 18; cf. also the sharp rejection of Seipel's policy along with the one of Pope Pius XII by a contemporary left-wing Catholic writer, Friedrich Heer, *Der Glaube des Adolf Hitler* (Munich, 1968), p. 330.

[33] Cf. Norbert Leser, *Zwischen Reformismus und Bolschewismus: Austromarxismus als Theorie und Praxis* (Vienna, Frankfurt, and Zurich, 1968).

Conclusion

" 'Twas a terrible time," reminisced "Herr Karl," the figure which dominated Vienna's political cabaret, the reborn *Volkstheater*, during the 1960s. However cruel a caricature of Vienna's "little man," he came closer in his disposition to old Ignaz Karl Seipel, the "Deutschmeister Karl," than to his priestly son. "Herr Karl," cunning, tough, treacherous, and not without a veneer of joviality, somehow muddled through the catastrophic decades from the twenties through the forties. Philistine and unheroic, indeed antiheroic, he could claim the one distinction of having suffered and of somehow having overcome suffering. To him "The Seip . . ." was part of a remote world of big politics that by the mid-forties had become a mirage of the past. Shrill, overdrawn, and offensive as "Herr Karl" is as an image of the average Austrian, as he is for the historian a type contrapuntal to the statesman Seipel. Both types have their place on the stage of Austrian tragedy: father Seipel, as cartooned in "Herr Karl," pathetic, ever suffering, but surviving, and son Seipel, the statesman-priest, ever struggling in the service of a higher cause, but failing. Both types, it might be recalled at this point, are chief actors also on the stage of the Great World Theater.

442

Bibliography

I. Archives and Document Collections

1. HAUS-, HOF-, UND STAATSARCHIV, NEUES POLITISCHES ARCHIV, 1918-1938 (St.A.), VIENNA

Politische Berichte, Berlin: Fasz. 10, 1921; Fasz. 11, 1922; Fasz. 12, 1923; Fasz. 13, 1924-1927; Fasz. 14, 1928-1932.

Politische Berichte, Prag: Fasz. 81, 1921-1922; Fasz. 82, 1923-1924; Fasz. 83, 1925-1926; Fasz. 84, 1927-1928.

Politische Berichte, Rom, Quirinal; Fasz. 107, 1927-1928; Fasz. 108, 1928-1929; Fasz. 109, 1929-1930; Fasz. 110, 1930-1931.

Politische Berichte, Rom, Vatikan: Fasz. 116, 1920-1923; Fasz. 117, 1924-1928.

Deutschland: I/III, Fasz. 144, 1922-1931.

Deutschland: I/1, Fasz. 147, 1921-1925.

Deutschland: I/1, Anschlussfrage: Fasz. 148, 1926-1933.

Präsidialakten des Staatssekretärs Dr. Otto Bauer: Fasz. 262, 1918-1919 (1, 2).

Liasse Österreich: 2/3, Innere Lage, 1922-1928, K.275.

Liasse Schweden: I/1, K.749.

Liasse Südslawien: I/III, K.771; 9/1, K.803.

Liasse Tschechoslowakei: I/III, Geheim, K.479; I/III, 1920-27, K.822.

Liasse Ungarn: I/III, K.879; I/1, K.880; K.884; 2/12, K.892; 7/III, K.898.

Liasse Mitteleuropa: Geheim, K.472, K.473.

Liasse Völkerbund: Innere Organisation, K.162.

Liasse Minderheiten (Allgemeines): K. 138, K.140.

Bibliography

Liasse Minderheitenschutz (Deutschland): K.142.
Liasse Minderheitenschutz (Österreich): K.143.
Liasse Personalia: K.481.
Liasse Präsidialakten: 1, 28.
Liasse Privatkorrespondenz Dr. Seipel: K.257, K.260.
Liasse Seipel: K.508.
Schüller, Richard. "Das Erbe Österreichs" (in English); typescript deposited with St.A.
Liasse Österreich: 2/3, Innere Lage, 1929-1930, K.276; 7/1, K.342; 8/IV, K.345; 8/IV, K.346; 8/IV, K.347; 19/48, K.402; 7/1, Geheim, K.470; 8/IV, K.471.
Liasse Deutschland: I/III, Geheim, K.460, K.461, K.462, K.464, I/1, Geheim, K.465.
Liasse Frankreich: I/1, K.615.
Liasse Italien: Geheim, K.476; I/II, K.654, K.658; 2/8, K.664, K.665, K.667, K.668, K.678, K.680.
Liasse Norwegen I/1, K.703.
Liasse Päpstlicher Stuhl, K.710.
Liasse Polen I/III, K.716.
Liasse Rumänien I/III, K.729.

2. ALLGEMEINES VERWALTUNGSARCHIV (A.V.A.), VIENNA

Ministerrats-Protokolle (M.R.), Nr.64 (October 28, 1918) to Nr.656 (October 29, 1930).
Verhandlungsschriften über die Sitzungen des Verbandes der Abgeordneten der Grossdeutschen Volkspartei (V.A.G.V.), January 14, 1922 to July 16, 1930.
Verhandlungsschriften über die Sitzungen des Verbandes der Abgeordneten des nationalen Wirtschaftsblocks (V.A.n.W.), November 18, 1930 to June 20, 1931.
Bundeskanzleramt Inneres: Korrespondenz Schober, K.66, K.67a; Korrespondenz Seipel, K.79, K.80, K.81, K.82; Korrespondenz Seipel Div. K.83a; Korrespondenz Seipel (Sekr.); Korrespondenz Starhemberg, 1930, K.86.

444

3. Bundespolizeiarchiv, Schobersammlung, Vienna

Folders: 1922.
   Internationale Wirtschaftskonferenz in Genua, April
      1922.
   Prälat Dr. Ignaz Seipel, Politische Korrespondenz 1921-
      28.
   Staatspolizeiliche Information (sehr wichtig) 1930.

4. German Foreign Office (G.F.O.) microfilm records of
   the Auswärtiges Amt (Politisches Archiv) in the National Archives, Washington, D.C.

(Cf. *A Catalogue of Files of the German Foreign Ministry
Archives 1867-1920*, Oxford, 1959; *Index of Microfilmed Records of the German Foreign Ministry and the Reich's Chancellery Covering the Weimar Period*, Washington, 1958; George
O. Kent, ed., *A Catalog of Files and Microfilms of the German
Foreign Ministry Archives 1920-1945*, 3 vols., Stanford, 1962-
1966.)
Microcopy T-120 (the citations include in each case provenance,
container number, and serial number):
   Büro des Reichsministers (B.d.R.), 1483, 3086; B.d.R., 1484,
   3086; B.d.R., 1485, 3086; B.d.R., 1584-88, 3242; Alte Reichskanzlei, 1680-81, 3617; B.d.R., 1736, 3398; Büro des Staatssekretärs,
   2344-47, 4567; Geheimakten der deutschen Gesandtschaft
   Wien 1928, 2491, 4938; Presseakten der deutschen Gesandtschaft Wien, 2492-93, 4938; Handakten der Direktoren (Köpke),
   2543, 5138; Abt.IA, Österreich, 3270, 7479; Nachlass des
   Reichsministers Dr. Gustav Stresemann (N.R.G.S.) (cf. Gustav
   Stresemann, *Vermächtnis: Der Nachlass in drei Bänden*, ed.
   Henry Bernhard, Berlin, 1932-1933; Hans W. Gatzke, "The
   Stresemann Papers," *Journal of Modern History*, xxvi [March
   1954], 49-59), 3112, 7126-28; N.R.G.S., 3113, 7129-31; N.R.G.S.,
   3114, 7132-36; N.R.G.S., 3120, 7178-80; N.R.G.S., 3143, 7313-
   15; N.R.G.S., 3144, 7323-25; N.R.G.S., 3160, 7197-99; N.R.G.S.,
   3168, 7316-18; N.R.G.S., 3169, 7319-22.

Bibliography

Microcopy T-136 (the citations include in each case provenance
and container number):

Österreich 70, SA 24; Österreich 95, SA 25; Abt.IA, Österreich,
SA 76.

5. AUSWÄRTIGES AMT, POLITISCHES ARCHIV (A.A.), BONN

Büro RM Nr.16, Österreich, Bd.1-4.

St.S. (alt) "SO," Anschlussfrage, Bd.1-10.

Abt.II-Generalia: Po.4, Südtirol, Bd.1.

Abt.II-Österreich: Po.1, Allgemeine Politik Österreichs, Bd.1-2.

Abt.II-Österreich: Po.2, Politische Beziehungen Österreichs zu
Deutschland und die Anschlussfrage, Bd.4-22.

Abt.II-Österreich, Po.2-A, Gegenseitige Besuche führender Staatsmänner, Bd.1.-5.

Abt.II-Österreich: Po.2-1, Anschluss Tirols an Österreich. Bd.7-
11.

Abt.II-Österreich: Po.11-Nr.3, Staatsmänner in Österreich, Bd.1-
2.

Geheimakten II-Österreich: Po.2, Politische Beziehungen Österreichs zu Deutschland, Bd.1-2.

6. HERMANN BAHR ARCHIVE, NATIONALBIBLIOTHEK, VIENNA

Seipel's letters to Hermann Bahr.

7. ERZBISCHÖFLICHES ARCHIV (ARCHIVE OF THE ARCHDIOCESE),
VIENNA, CARDINAL PIFFL ARCHIVE (SEE ALSO SEIPEL ARCHIVE)

Seipel letters to Cardinal Piffl.

Protocols of the Austrian Bishops' Conferences of 1920 and 1921,
including Seipel's reports on the political situation.

Seipel's commentary on the draft for the Pastoral Letter of the
Austrian Bishops on the Social Question of Advent 1925,
November 8, 1925.

8. ERZBISCHÖFLICHES KONSISTORIALARCHIV (ARCHIVE OF THE
ARCHDIOCESE), SALZBURG

Papers relating to the Katholischer Universitätsverein and to

446

Seipel's activities on behalf of the establishment of a "compromise university" in Salzburg, 1913-1917.

Copy of Seipel's Memorandum to Emperor Charles on the Conference of the International Catholic Union in Zurich, January 29-31, 1918.

9. KNOLL ARCHIVE

Seipel Papers, including personal papers mainly of the Salzburg years, notes for the second edition of *Nation und Staat*, Seipel correspondence.

Aufzeichnung, Donnerstag, 11. August 1932, erfahren von Herrn Kettenburg.

Aufzeichnungen von Unterredungen mit Seipel (16.6.32).

16. Juni 1932 (typescript).

Aufzeichnungen von Unterredungen mit Seipel, 18. Juni 1932, PM.

10. MANUSCRIPT COLLECTION, NATIONALBIBLIOTHEK, VIENNA

Seipel letters.

11. SCHMITZ ARCHIVE (HEROLD VERLAG)

(A collection of personal papers of Richard Schmitz and documents pertaining to the Christian Socialist party and to Seipel.)

Boxes: Seipel Briefe; Korrespondenz zu den Seipel Briefen; Seipel-Lueger, K.VIII (party documents of May and November 1922); Studie über Schobers Politik, K.IX (Customs Union); Notizen über die Innere Politik, K.XXVII (party documents 1930, 1931); Aussenpolitisches, K.XXVIII (1930, 1931); Copies of letters from Seipel to Heinrich Lammasch, 1917-1919 (also copy of letter from Seipel to Marga Lammasch, July 17, 1927); Copies of correspondence Seipel–Heinrich Mataja, 1925-1932. The collection has been moved recently to the Haus-, Hof-, und Staatsarchiv.

12. SEIPEL ARCHIVE

(The documents and books left by Seipel to the Order of the

Bibliography

Servants of the Sacred Heart of Jesus in the Monastery, Vienna III, Keinergasse 37. The collection has been moved in recent years to the Archive of the Archdiocese, Vienna.)

Seipel library (unfortunately many books have been removed).

Seipel papers (family papers, personal papers, memoranda, drafts, etc.).

Seipel diaries, February 1916–July 1932 (for a detailed listing of the diaries see Rudolf Blüml, *Ignaz Seipel, Mensch, Christ, Priester in seinem Tagebuch*, Vienna, 1934, p. 27).

13. MANUSCRIPT COLLECTION, STADTBIBLIOTHEK, VIENNA

Seipel letters, including letters from Seipel to Kralik, 1913, 1914.

14. FROM THE PAPERS OF JOSEF REDLICH

"Politische Tagebuchnotizen, 1920-1936," unpublished continuation of Josef Redlich, *Schicksalsjahre Österreichs 1908-1919: Das Politische Tagebuch*, ed. Fritz Fellner, 2 vols., Graz and Cologne, 1953-1954.

15. FROM THE PAPERS OF DR. ANTON JULIUS WALTER

"Gedächtnisprotokoll über die Unterredung mit Exzellenz Dr. Seipel am 4. Dezember 1929."

16. FROM THE PAPERS OF LOTHAR WIMMER

Seipel letters, 1930-1932.

II. Interviews

Professor Heinrich Benedikt
Dr. William F. Czerny
Dr. Friedrich Funder
Professor Walter Goldinger
Professor August Maria Knoll
Miss Marga Lammasch

Professor Reinhold Lorenz
Dr. Ernst Mosing
Dr. Alma Motzko
Prelate Dr. Karl Rudolf
Dr. Friedrich Schreyvogel
Dr. Raphael Spann

448

Dr. Anton Julius Walter   Professor Adam Wandruszka
Dr. Ernst Karl Winter   Ambassador Lothar Wimmer

III. Published Documentary Materials

League of Nations. *Official Journal*, III-V (1922-1924).
———. *Monthly Summary*, II (1922).
———. *The Restoration of Austria*. Geneva, October 19, 1922.
Papers Relating to the Foreign Relations of the United States 1919: The Paris Peace Conference, II, Washington, 1942.
Stenographische Protokolle [*Sten. Prot.*] *über die Sitzungen der Provisorischen Nationalversammlung für Deutschösterreich* (1918-1919).
Stenographische Protokolle über die Sitzungen der konstituirenden Nationalversammlung der Republik Österreich (1919).
Stenographische Protokolle über die Sitzungen der Nationalversammlung (1920).
Stenographische Protokolle über die Sitzungen des Nationalrates der Republik Österreich (1920-1932).

IV. Chronicles

The Annual Register. New Series, 1919-1932. London.
Alfred Kasamas, *Österreichische Chronik*. Vienna, 1948.
Schulthess' *Europäischer Geschichtskalender*. Munich, 1918-1932.
Arnold J. Toynbee, *Survey of International Affairs*, 1920-1932. London.

V. Newspapers and Journals

Allgemeines Literaturblatt (Vienna)
Arbeiter-Zeitung
Daily Telegraph
Der Anschluss

449

Bibliography

Hochland
Journal de Genève
Katholische Kirchenzeitung (Salzburg)
Kultur (Vienna)
Der Kampf
Neue Freie Presse
Das Neue Reich
Neues Wiener Journal
New York Times
Der österreichische Volkswirt
Reichspost
Schönere Zukunft
Sozialistische Monatshefte
Le Temps
Über den Wassern (Salzburg)
Volkswohl
Wiener Diözesanblatt
Wiener Politische Blätter
Wiener Zeitung

Central European History
Historische Zeitschrift
Journal of Central European Affairs
Journal of Contemporary History
Journal of Modern History
Mitteilungen des Österreichischen Staatsarchivs
Österreich in Geschichte und Literatur

VI. Works by Seipel

For a grouping and selective listing of Seipel's writings, see Rudolf Blüml, *Prälat Dr. Ignaz Seipel: Ein grosses Leben in kleinen Bildern* (Klagenfurt, 1933), pp. 159ff. Cf. also Franz Zehentbauer, "Seipel als Gelehrter und Professor," *Reichspost*, August 3, 1932. Among the many writings by Seipel the following are of particular importance for this book.

Theological Writings

"Novissimae quae circumferentur sententiae de divinis proces-
sionibus inquiruntur et discutuntur"; Seipel's unpublished dissertation for the theological faculty at the University of Vienna,
1903.
Die wirtschaftsethischen Lehren der Kirchenväter, Vienna, 1907.
*Im Dienste des Wortes: Der Kaplan, Katechet, Kanzler in seinen
Predigten, Exhorten und Ansprachen*, ed. Rudolf Blüml, Vienna and Munich, 1955.
Neue Ziele und Aufgaben der katholischen Moraltheologie, Vienna, 1926.

Political Theory and Practice

A. Books

Weltmission und Weltfriede, Salzburg, 1917.

Nation und Staat, Vienna, 1916.

Seipels Reden in Österreich und anderwärts, ed. Josef Gessl,
Vienna, 1926; an important collection of speeches.

Der Kampf um die österreichische Verfassung, Vienna and Leipzig, 1930; an important collection of memoranda, articles, and
speeches on constitutional issues between 1917 and 1929.

*Wesen und Aufgaben der Politik: Der gegenwärtige Stand der
Weltpolitik*, Innsbruck, 1930.

Ehrendoktor der Rechte der Universität Wien, Vienna, 1931.

Der christliche Staatsmann, Augsburg, 1931.

Der Friede: Ein sittliches und gesellschaftliches Problem, Innsbruck, 1937; Seipel's lectures at the University of Vienna,
winter semester 1929-30.

"Die neue Gesellschaftsordnung nach der Enzyklika 'Quadragesimo anno,'" in *Die soziale Botschaft des Papstes: Vorträge
über "Quadragesimo anno,"* Vienna, 1931.

B. Articles and speeches (in addition to those contained in
Seipel, Kampf, and Gessl, Reden)

"Sylvesterbetrachtungen," *Katholische Kirchenzeitung*, December 28, 1911.

451

Bibliography

"Der heilige Ambrosius von Mailand: Ein literarisches Charakterbild," *Über den Wassern,* vi (August 1913), 436-51.

"Wege und Irrwege in der Weltfriedensfrage," *Reichspost,* May 25, 1917.

"Das Problem der Revolution," *Hochland,* xv (February 1918), 543-52.

"Weltkirche und Weltfriede," *Abendland,* October 1, 1925, pp. 8-10.

"Die Aufgabe der österreichischen Deutschen," *Volk und Reich,* ii (January 1926), 4-9.

"La discussion générale," *Journal de Genève,* September 19, 1928.

"Die österreichische Idee," *Schönere Zukunft,* iv (July 21, 1929), 884-86.

"Österreichische Tradition," *Winkelried* (Egern-Cheb, Czechoslovakia), viii (December 1929).

"Der Kampf um die Demokratie," *Neue Freie Presse,* April 24, 1930 (morning ed.).

Seipel's address to the League of Nations Assembly, September 8, 1928, *Neue Freie Presse,* September 8, 1928 (evening ed.).

"Grundsätzliches zur Reform des Wahlgesetzes," *Das Neue Reich,* xiii (November 29, 1930), 177-78.

"Die neue Gesellschaftsordnung nach 'Quadragesimo Anno,'" *Das Neue Reich,* xiv (November 7, 1931), 103-105.

"Kirche, Kapitalismus, Sozialismus und christliche Aufgaben," *Reichspost,* January 26, 1932.

"Die Gewerkschaften und die neue Gesellschaftsordnung," *Volkswohl,* xxiii (February 1932), 129-34.

C. Interviews

"Dr. Seipel über die Anschlussfrage," *Neue Freie Presse,* September 5, 1926 (morning ed.).

"'Immer daran denken; nie davon sprechen. . . .' Exzellenz Seipel: 'Keine Anschlussdemonstration!' Ein Gespräch mit dem ehemaligen Bundeskanzler in Berlin," *8-Uhr-Abendblatt*, February 4, 1926.

Ignaz Seipel, "Österreich und Deutschland," *Neue Freie Presse*, June 9, 1928 (evening ed.).

W.M., "L'Anschluss," *Journal de Genève*, September 18, 1928.

"Heimwehr Hopes and Fears; Interview with Dr. Seipel," *Daily Telegraph*, September 3, 1929.

Magyar Hirlap, May 20, 1930, quoted in *Neue Freie Presse*, May 21, 1930 (morning ed.). On internal disarmament.

Aftenbladet (Copenhagen), quoted in *Neue Freie Presse*, September 27, 1930 (evening ed.); on National Socialism.

Prager Tagblatt, quoted in *Neue Freie Presse*, September 29, 1930 (evening ed.); on the fall of the Schober government.

"Interview mit Seipel," *Neues Wiener Journal*, October 19, 1930; on National Socialism.

Berliner Börsenzeitung, January 20, 1932; on National Socialism.

"Das zweite Kabinett Buresch," *Kölnische Zeitung*, January 30, 1932 (morning ed.); cf. *Reichspost*, February 5, 1932.

Schönere Zukunft, VII (September 4, 1932), 1156-57; Martin Spahn on two meetings with Seipel in June 1923 and June 1931; on Seipel's relations to Germany and his thoughts on the Heimwehr and National Socialism, socialism and capitalism.

Victor Dillard, "Eine Stunde mit Msgr. Seipel" (September 16, 1931), *Österreich in Geschichte und Literatur*, VI (December 1962), 447-54.

D. Letters

Seipel to a German colleague, Vienna, December 17, 1918; Viktor Reimann, *Zu gross für Österreich: Seipel und Bauer im Kampf um die Erste Republik*, Vienna, Frankfurt, and Zurich, 1968, 177ff.; cf. Z.703-Präs. St.A., Präsidialakten Otto Bauer, K.262; on the Anschluss or Danubian confederation.

Seipel to Josef Zuck, Vienna, July 2, 1919; Alexander Novotny,

Bibliography

"Ignaz Seipel im Spannungsfeld zwischen den Zielen des Anschlusses und der Selbständigkeit Österreichs," *Österreich in Geschichte und Literatur*, VII (June 1963), 265f; on the Anschluss.

Seipel to Princess Fanny Starhemberg, 1923-1932; Erwin Rieger, *Fürstin Fanny Starhemberg: Ein Lebensbild einer österreichischen Frau*, Vienna, 1935; cf. Nationalbibliothek, Vienna; on personal and domestic matters.

Seipel to Dr. W. Bauer, Hütteldorf, July 30, 1928; Paul R. Sweet, "Seipel's Views on Anschluss in 1928: An unpublished Exchange of Letters," *Journal of Modern History*, XIX (December 1947), 320-23; cf. ad Z.23808/13, St.A., Liasse Deutschland I/1, Geheim, K.465; on the Anschluss.

Seipel to Bishop W. Frind, Vienna, August 16, 1928; Franz Lorenz, "Weihbischof Dr. W. Frind und Prälat Dr. I. Seipel," *Schönere Zukunft*, VIII (January 29, 1933), 399-400; on the Austrian mission and the Anschluss.

Seipel to Prof. Blümelhuber, Vienna, May 1929; Reimann, *Zu gross für Österreich*, 190ff.; cf. Z.21953/13, St.A., Liasse Deutschland I/1, Geheim, K.465; on the neutralization of Austria.

Seipel to Dr. Friedrich Funder, Vienna, October 3, 1929; Freidrich Funder, *Als Österreich den Sturm bestand*, Vienna and Munich, 1957, 29ff.; on his political plans.

Seipel to *Der österreichische Volkswirt*, Vienna, February 16, 1930; *Der österreichische Volkswirt*, XXII (February 22, 1930), 557f.; on the overthrow of Schober in 1922.

Seipel to Lothar Wimmer, Vienna, June 7, 1930, Meran, February 21, 1932, Hütteldorf, June 30, 1932; Lothar Wimmer, *Experiences et tribulations d'un diplomate autrichien*, Neuchâtel, 1946, 32ff.; on the Austrian bureaucracy, the crisis of democracy, and fascism.

Seipel to Herr Mertens, Davos-Platz, February 21, 1931; Reimann, *Zu gross für Österreich*, 237f.; on National Socialism.

Seipel to Lothar Wimmer, Meran, February 2, 1932; Lothar

Wimmer, *Zwischen Ballhausplatz und Downing Street,* Vienna and Munich, 1958; cf. "From the Papers of Lothar Wimmer"; the book erroneously cites Vienna as the place of origin, and omits a crucial passage comparing Mussolini's Italy with Cromwell's England, on democracy and dictatorship.

Seipel to an "important personality," Vienna, November 2, 1930; *Neues Wiener Journal* (September 4, 1932); on monarchy.

Seipel to Raimund Poukar, Davos-Platz, February 23, 1931; Raimund Poukar, *Ignaz Seipel: Nationalismus, Nationalsozialismus,* 2nd ed., Vienna, 1935, p. 19; on National Socialism.

Seipel to "a personality" (Leopold von Popper-Podhragy), Vienna, May 31, June 21, 1931; *Wiener Politische Blätter,* ɪ (August 27, 1933), 186f.; on democracy and dictatorship.

Seipel to Dr. Erwin Waihs, Zürs, August 15, 1931; *Österreichische Monatshefte,* xɪɪɪ (July-August 1957), 19ff.; on Seipel's aspirations to the presidency.

Seipel to Dr. Friedrich Nelböck, Meran, Vienna, 1931-1932; Adam Wandruszka, "Aus Seipels letzten Lebensjahren," *Mitteilungen des Österreichischen Staatsarchivs,* ɪx (1956), 565-69; Seipel's views on the Customs Union.

Seipel to a publicist living in Paris, Vienna, March 6, 1932; "Seipel Briefe," *Der österreichische Volkswirt,* xxɪv (August 13, 1932), 1102f.; on the Buresch demarche.

VII. Works on Seipel

The general comments (below, Section VIII) about partisanship in the literature on twentieth-century Austria apply particularly to the literature on Seipel: much is either hagiography or demonology.

BOOKS

Birk, Bernhard, *Dr. Ignaz Seipel: Ein österreichisches und europäisches Schicksal,* Innsbruck, 1932; the best among the hagiographies for interpretative depth and information.

Bibliography

Blüml, Rudolf, *Ignaz Seipel: Mensch, Christ, Priester in seinem Tagebuch*, Vienna, 1934; hagiography (written by a close ecclesiastical associate), but contains important data on Seipel's religious life and excerpts from his diaries.

————, *Prälat Dr. Ignaz Seipel: Ein grosses Leben in kleinen Bildern*, Klagenfurt, 1933; hagiography, some editions contain an important appendix with excerpts from Seipel's diaries covering political affairs.

Ludwig, Eduard, *Dr. Ignaz Seipel: Der Wegbereiter einer neuen Zeit*, Vienna, 1936; hagiography by Seipel's press chief.

Poukar, Raimund, *Ignaz Seipel: Nationalismus, Nationalsozialismus*, 2nd ed., Vienna, 1935; hagiography.

Riedl, Franz, *Kanzler Seipel: Ein Vorkämpfer volksdeutschen Denkens*, Saarbrücken, 1935; written by a nationalist Catholic journalist, who makes Seipel out to be a *völkisch* statesman.

Schmitz, Richard, *Ignaz Seipel*, Vienna, 1946; hagiography by one of Seipel's closest political associates.

Thormann, Werner, *Dr. Ignaz Seipel: Der europäische Staatsmann*, Frankfurt/M., 1932; one of the most interesting and useful treatises on Seipel, dealing primarily with his attitudes toward the secular state.

Winter, Ernst Karl, *Ignaz Seipel als dialektisches Problem: Ein Beitrag zur Scholastikforschung*, Vienna, Frankfurt, and Zurich, 1966; a brilliant inner-Catholic critique, written in 1933, of Seipel's Thomistic position.

For demonology, see the works by Gulick, Braunthal, Hannak mentioned below (Section VIII).

ARTICLES

Hannak, Jacques, "Die Seipel-Legende," *Die Zukunft* (July 1950), 179-85; demonology.

"Ignaz Seipel," *Encyclopaedia Britannica*; based on "Lebenslauf," handwritten draft by Seipel himself; Seipel Archive.

von Klemperer, Klemens "Chancellor Seipel and the Crisis of

Democracy in Austria," *Journal of Central European Affairs*, xxii (January 1963), 468-78.

————, "Seipel und Winter-Gegner und Brüder," *Neues Forum*, xiii (October 1966), 658-60.

Knoll, August Maria, "Ignaz Seipel," *Neue österreichische Biographie ab 1815*, ix (Zurich, Leipzig, and Vienna, 1956), 113-29; a critical disciple's view.

————, "Ignaz Seipel," *Schweizerische Rundschau*, xxxiii (March 1933), 1065-77.

————, "Ignaz Seipel und die österreichische Leo-Gesellschaft," ed. Oskar Katann, *Jahrbuch der österreichischen Leo-Gesellschaft* (Vienna, 1933), 183-204.

————, "Ignaz Seipel über seine Bücher und literarische Pläne," *Volkswohl* xxiv (October 1932), 10-12.

Ludwig, Eduard, "Seipel, ein katholischer Staatsmann," *Wiener Wirtschafts-Woche*, vii (January 12, 1938), 8-10; interesting account of Seipel's conduct of foreign affairs.

Melville, C. F., "Dr. Dollfuss and Mgr. Seipel," *Dublin Review*, cxiv-v (October 1934), 169-79; on Dollfuss's inheriting the courage but not the finesse of his master.

Merkl, Adolf, "Seipel und die Demokratie," *Der österreichische Volkswirt*, xxv (August 12, 1933), 1005-1008; on Seipel's positive attitude toward democracy.

Olden, Rudolf, "Österreichische Köpfe; Ignaz Seipel," *Die Weltbühne*, xxi (February 3, 1925), 162-65; a masterful, though hostile, character sketch.

Räuscher, Josef, "Ignaz Seipel und sein Werk," *Hochland*, xxii (January 1925), 376-88.

Redler, Richard, "Nachdenkliche Bemerkungen zu einem Tagebuch," *Hochland*, xxxii (July 1935), 322-34.

Reisenberger, Johann, S.J., "Prälat Dr. Ignaz Seipel: Versuch einer Charakterzeichnung," *Wiener Kirchenblatt*, xiv (August 14, 1932), 6-8; about the "Ignatian virtues" of Seipel.

Riedl, Franz, "Seipel und Südtirol," *Der Donauraum*, i (1956), 174-78.

Bibliography

Tandler, Julius, "Seipel," *Wiener Politische Blätter*, I (August 27, 1933), 183f.; a brilliant analysis of Seipel's medical problems by the Social Democratic health expert.

Tzöbl, Josef A., "Ignaz Seipel," in Hugo Hantsch ed., *Gestalter der Geschicke Österreichs*, Innsbruck, Vienna, and Munich, 1962, 579-609; a positive assessment of Seipel by one of his former political associates.

Verax, "Monseigneur Seipel," *Revue des Deux Mondes*, XCIX (March 1929), 54-87; a subtle, though from the French position excessively defensive, analysis of Seipel's foreign policy.

Wandruszka, Adam, on Seipel, see Benedikt, *Geschichte*, 322ff.; an excellent scholarly assessment of Seipel by a professional historian.

Ward, Barbara, "Ignaz Seipel and the Anschluss," *Dublin Review*, CCIII (July-September 1938), 33-50; a first-rate analysis of Seipel's foreign policy, based on secondary materials. Unfortunately Barbara Ward gives too much credulity to Riedl, *Kanzler Seipel*, and therefore overestimates Seipel's readiness to accept the Anschluss.

Weinzierl-Fischer, Erika, "Seipel und die Konkordatsfrage," *Mitteilungen des Österreichischen Staatsarchivs*, XII (1959), 437-45.

Cf. also conclusion, and the many articles in the Austrian and international press after Seipel's death.

VIII. General Comments on the Historiography of the First Austrian Republic

Stirring times generally yield vivid materials for the historian, but they tend to make for distorted history. Austria went through such times after the First World War, experiencing latent civil war followed by invasion, war, and occupation. As the Reds gave way to the Blacks and the Blacks to the Browns, there were charges and countercharges, but little readiness to explain and understand; there was much pamphleteering and little history.

When the nightmare, the shouting, and the shooting were all over there was silence. Historians understandably hesitated to deal with the period between the world wars: the passions still spilled over; the wounds had cut too deep.

Even more than the study of Weimar Germany, the study of the first Austrian Republic was marked at first by political passions and thereafter muffled by scholarly tact and caution. All too many works on Austria after 1918 carry the stamp of partisanship, and scholars have kept off this admittedly treacherous terrain too long. But the time has now come for an intensive historical appraisal of the first Austrian Republic, and there are distinct indications that, with the growing distance in time, historians are increasingly willing and able to deal with this field of study and to incorporate it into the by now wholly accepted discipline of contemporary history.

The basic scholarly introduction to the history of the first Austrian Republic is *Geschichte der Republik Österreich*, edited by Heinrich Benedikt (Vienna, 1954). This work constitutes the first, and on the whole successful, attempt after the second war to deal with the "stirring times" between the wars in a detached manner. Particularly important is the chapter by Walter Goldinger, "Der geschichtliche Ablauf der Ereignisse in Österreich von 1918 bis 1945" (cf. also Walter Goldinger, *Geschichte der Republik Österreich*, Vienna, 1962), a highly informed narrative by one of Austria's leading archivists, and the one by Adam Wandruszka, "Österreichs politische Struktur," an exemplary analysis of political parties and movements. Two excellent earlier works by outsiders deal with the first Republic: Brita Skottsberg, *Der österreichische Parlamentarismus* (Göteborg, 1940), and Mary Macdonald, *The Republic of Austria 1918-1934* (London, Toronto and New York, 1946); the latter appeared under the auspices of the Royal Institute of International Affairs, and focused on constitutional developments. C. A. Macartney's *The Social Revolution in Austria* (Cambridge, 1926) offers a perceptive topical approach to Austria in the early twenties.

Bibliography

More or less rampant partisanship is apparent in the following works: Leopold Kunschak, *Österreich 1918-1934* (Vienna, 1934) (Christian Socialist); Gordon Shepherd, *The Austrian Odyssey* (London and New York, 1957) (generally conservative); Reinhold Lorenz, *Der Staat wider Willen* (Berlin, 1940) (fiercely Nazi). A formidable accomplishment in terms of research and scope is Charles A. Gulick's *Austria from Habsburg to Hitler*, 2 vols. (Berkeley and Los Angeles, 1948); but its commitment to the plot theory of history, with Seipel playing the villain, is hardly defensible. Gulick's strongly pro-Socialist bias has set the tone for much of the historiography on Austria. Other Socialist approaches to the subject are to be found in Julius Braunthal, *The Tragedy of Austria* (London, 1948); Jacques Hannak, *Im Sturm eines Jahrhunderts* (Vienna, 1952), a very readable and useful history of the Socialist party; and Jacques Hannak, *Karl Renner und seine Zeit* (Vienna, 1965). As for the pertinent biographical sketches in the series *Grosse Österreicher, Neue Österreichische Biographie ab 1815*, they were generally written by political associates of the people involved who were too close to them to be objective (Julius Deutsch on Otto Bauer in Volume x, August Maria Knoll on Seipel in Volume ix, Adolf Schärf on Karl Renner in Volume ix). The biographies of Johannes Schober are also marred by excessive subjectivism; of the two, Jacques Hannak, *Johannes Schober—Mittelweg in die Katastrophe* (Vienna, 1966), with all its criticism, is distinctly preferable to the admiring work by Oskar Kleinschmied, *Schober* (Vienna, 1930).

I have refrained from adding to this bibliography a detailed listing of the secondary sources pertaining to the first Austrian Republic, since my indebtedness to the various authors and works has been elaborately acknowledged in the footnotes of this book.

460

Index

Acton, Lord, 56-60
Adenauer, Konrad, 307n
Adler, Max, 253
Adler, Viktor, 22, 63, 98, 99, 100, 135, 228, 231
Ahrer, Jakob, 249-50
Allied Powers, 127, 185
Anglobank, 184
Anschluss, Allies and, 127, 128; Christian Socialists and, 78, 103n, 113-14, 163, 175; Czechs and, 325, 326, 328, 329; election of 1919 and, 110, 112-17; foreign and domestic policy and, 159, 160, 162-63, 165-68; Germany and, 182-84, 192n, 193; Pan-Germans and, 102, 113, 175, 192, 203; Seipel and, 114-17, 189, 192-94, 196, 215, 301-306, 309, 312-19, 322, 327-28, 339, 340, 343, 344n; Social Democrats and, 113, 114, 312-13; universities and, 22; Yugoslavia and, 338
anti-Semitism, 23, 180, 255-58, 260, 262, 276, 404, 422n
Augustinian tradition, 38-39, 55, 291
Auriti, Giacinto, 332, 335
Ausgleich, 19-20
Austerlitz, Friedrich, 263
Austria-Hungary, 4-5, 6-7, 11, 81, 82, 95-98, 222-24; Seipel and, 12, 19-20, 50-51, 53-58, 60-63, 66-67, 72-73, 77-78, 85, 95, 105

Austromarxism, 22, 63, 64, 65, 227, 398
Austro-Scholasticism, 227, 228

Bahr, Hermann, director of Burg-theater, 83-84; on Austrian Monarchy, 20; on Austrian Germans, 43, 44; on bureaucracy, 105; on the Emperor, 21; on nationalism, 50-51; on politicians, 223; on postwar Austria, 128; on revolution of 1918, 97; Seipel and, 52, 55, 71-72, 92, 111, 267
Balfour, Arthur James, 1st Earl of, 201, 205-206
Banhans, Karl von, Baron, 87, 90n, 93
Bauer, Otto, Anschluss and, 312-13; compromise and, 120, 131, 133-36, 228, 231-32, 253, 254, 396, 397, 440; constitution and, 139, 140; economic policy, 182; Foreign Secretary, 98, 115n, 163; on Pan-Germans, 226; on referendum, 285n; on revolution of 1918, 96, 100, 101, 263-64; on social legislation, 122, 123, 124; on Treaty of Lana, 170; proletariat and, 62, 63, 226; reform of Monarchy, 12; Renner and, 164; Seipel and, 153, 155, 203, 204, 210, 212, 233-38, 254, 264-65, 267, 338, 346, 347, 372-73, 431-32, 433n, 434

461

Index

Index

464

Index

Paulucci, de Calboli, Marquis, 321, 322

personality principle, 61-62, 78

Peter, Franz, 306n

Pfeiffer, Maximilian, 249n

Pfrimer, Walter, 278, 356, 357n

Piffl, Friedrich, Cardinal, 24, 102, 103, 257, 333-35, 384, 418, 419-20

Pius X, Pope, 36

Pius XI, Pope, 214, 413-16, 420

Platonic tradition, 38, 290

Poincaré, Raymond, 88, 145

political parties, *see* Christian Socialists, Heimatblock, National Socialists, Pan-Germans, Social Democrats

Preuss, Hugo, 94

Quakers, 68, 69

Ramek, Rudolf, 249-51, 310

Redlich, Josef, 67-68, 70, 72, 82, 159, 223, 257n; Bauer on, 431; Minister of Finance, 83, 84, 85, 87, 96; on Austrian Monarchy, 75, 90n, 91, 92, 93, 95; on Social Democrats, 123; Seipel and, 182, 291-92

Reformkatholizismus, 36

Renan, Ernest, 59

Renner, Karl, 11, 12, 72; Anschluss and, 113, 304; Bauer and, 136, 154; Chancellor, 96, 97, 99, 100, 120, 130, 131, 139; coalition policy, 99, 100, 134, 135n, 228, 243, 271, 272-73; foreign policy, 163-64, 170, 190; on constitution, 253; on Empire, 87, 89, 95; on failure of Austria, 435; on nationality, 62, 63, 64; on new era, 352; on socialization, 124; on

Republic's symbol, 365n; on Treaty of St. Germain, 127, 128, 129; Seipel and, 154, 198, 203, 208-209, 217, 237, 347, 432n

rent control, 241-42, 350-51

revolution, Austrian, 94, 97, 98, 99, 100-101, 102-109, 436, 439

Rieder, Ignatius, Archbishop, 80

Riedl, Franz, 302n

Riehl, Walter, 260

Rieth, Kurt, 389

Rintelen, Anton, 356

Roman Catholic Church, accommodates to Republic, 102-109; bishops' conferences, 152, 156; Church versus state, 12, 14, 35-36, 39-40, 138, 142, 275-76, 286, 435-36, 439, 440, 441; modern world and, 4, 48-49; National Socialism and, 260-61, 408n; nationalism and, 53-58, 60, 63; peace and, 68-69, 247; political parties and, 228-31, 232-36, 269, 280, 406-407. *See also* Leo XIII, Pius XI

Rousseau, Jean Jacques, 140-41

St. Ambrose, 72, 73

Salter, Sir Arthur, 213n, 216, 219

Schanzer, Carlo, 186, 194, 195

Schattendorf, 258-59, 262-63

Scheidemann, Philipp, 87

Schindler, Franz Martin, 23, 32-33, 34, 66, 67, 77, 385, 415

Schlegel, Josef, 383n

Schleicher, Kurt von, General, 421n

Schmitt, Carl, 291n

Schmitz, Richard, 258, 413

Schober, Johann, 11; and 1931 crisis, 398, 399, 400; Chancellor, 168-74, 178, 210n, 357-63, 365, 367-70, 372-77; Foreign Minister,

467

Index